Contemporary American Fiction

Contemporary American Fiction

Kenneth Millard

OXFORD
UNIVERSITY PRESS

OXFORD

UNIVERSITY PRESS

Great Clarendon Street, Oxford OX2 6DP

Oxford University Press is a department of the University of Oxford.
It furthers the University's objective of excellence in research, scholarship,
and education by publishing worldwide in

Oxford New York

Athens Auckland Bangkok Bogotá Buenos Aires Calcutta
Cape Town Chennai Dar es Salaam Delhi Florence Hong Kong Istanbul
Karachi Kuala Lumpur Madrid Melbourne Mexico City Mumbai
Nairobi Paris São Paulo Shanghai Singapore Taipei Tokyo Toronto Warsaw

with associated companies in Berlin Ibadan

Oxford is a registered trade mark of Oxford University Press
in the UK and in certain other countries

Published in the United States
by Oxford University Press Inc., New York

British Library Cataloguing in Publication Data
Data available

Library of Congress Cataloging in Publication Data
Data available

ISBN 019–871178–6

10 9 8 7 6 5 4 3 2 1

Typeset in ITC Stone Serif
by RefineCatch Limited, Bungay, Suffolk
Printed in Great Britain
on acid-free paper by
Biddles Ltd., Guildford and King's Lynn

Acknowledgements

I would like to thank Audrey for providing and explaining the full lyrics of Johnny Mercer's song 'Dream', and Jim for his knowledge of syncopation and the useful discussions about his favourite book; Simon for his professional advice ('The large print giveth, and the small print taketh away'), and Caroline, for teaching me how to talk to a hunter.

K.M.

Edinburgh and Arizona
1999

Contents

Introduction

This book is intended as a guide to late twentieth-century American fiction for the undergraduate student and the general reader. The principal objective has been to offer substantial and detailed interpretations of the primary texts, and to suggest contexts in which those novels might usefully be considered. The discussions of the novels attempt to achieve a balance between interpretation and sometimes necessary expository comments, although even exposition is interpretative in the way that it prioritizes certain aspects of narrative above others. The chapters take certain subject areas in American life and investigate their representation in fiction. This is necessarily a two-way process in which the reading of fiction conditions what the reader deems to be important in the American social text, and this relationship is one of the most difficult issues that this book seeks to tacitly manage: how does a critic move with confidence between the literary text and the social text? Clearly, it is no simple correspondence. The texts that a culture produces must in some way be a measure of its social reality because the authors of those texts are themselves products of their culture. An equally difficult issue is the one of selection; it is not claimed that the novels of this study are 'representative' of the United States, rather that they are detailed fictional enquiries into the particular subject areas. There is an important formal aspect here too: none of these novels can be limited ultimately to considerations under one subject heading only, and the chapters of this book are not discrete and exclusive categories. *The Bluest Eye* is considered here under 'family', but it also addresses issues of racial politics, of culture and nature, of gender and history, of economics and the power of the media to propagate particular ideas about aesthetic value. It is the novel's powerful synthesis of these themes that makes *The Bluest Eye* worth studying. *White Noise* is not simply about technology, but equally about the family, and *High Lonesome* is a collection of stories not just about the power of language but which also offers an analysis of male desire. All of these works might be configured in terms of different cultural and critical rubrics to give different readings: *In Country* can be interpreted as a novel about gender and history, but equally about the power of consumerism. One thing remains constant, given that *Contemporary American Fiction* does not pretend to be value-free: all of these novels have a high degree of artistic merit; they are not simply indicative of a cultural category or social trend but stand as significant achievements as novels. In 1971 Tony Tanner wrote that *City of Words* was 'motivated mainly by a sense of admiration for the wide range of individual talent' in American fiction of the 1950s, 1960s, and 1970s. That view is strongly endorsed here. American fiction of the late twentieth century is characterized by an extraordinary proliferation of excellent primary texts, both from established writers who are still producing remarkable works (John Updike, Philip Roth) and from younger writers whose first novels are worthy of inclusion alongside the best of their elders (Gish Jen, Chang-rae Lee). This book then is a synthesis of a number of different and competing critical agendas.

To represent late twentieth-century fiction of the United States in a single critical survey is a difficult proposition involving issues of selection which only beg more difficult questions about cultural value and ideological choices. These are matters of politics because ultimately all aesthetic issues are political issues. Students of the politics of the canon might reasonably ask, why these authors and texts, and on what ideological bases are critical decisions made about cultural value; what world-view is implicitly invoked in the selection of these texts, and what subject positions are denied or refuted when other authors and texts are silently passed over? Students should always ask what is valorized as culturally significant and why, because that question is always part of any cultural enquiry or education, and asking it of this book can only be beneficial. This book might betray its author's European origins and prejudices about what is interesting and significant in American fiction, and, of necessity, it involves anthological compromise, but the writer is confident that its authors will still be studied seriously into the twenty-first century. *Contemporary American Fiction* concentrates on the younger writers who bear the marks of their elders, for example the influence of Thomas Pynchon on Don DeLillo. Pynchon's best and most influential work, like that of Norman Mailer, belongs to an earlier period. So does that of many of Tony Tanner's authors in *City of Words: American Fiction 1950–70* (1971): Malamud, Bellow, Barth, Hawkes, Vonnegut, Burroughs, Heller. Only two of Tanner's authors survive in this work: Updike (1992) and Roth (1997), both recently prolific.

In *The Pleasures of Babel* (1993) Jay Clayton argued that 'we certainly do not live today in a country with a single, shared culture', and he acknowledged that 'such a comforting illusion of consensus' probably never existed in the first place (9). The emergence in the late twentieth century of a post-industrial and a multicultural society has made available to American culture a wider diversity of narrative voices than ever before. Concurrently, the rapidly expanding concept of 'culture' has made serious attention to those voices more prevalent. The fiction of the United States is too multiple and diverse for any single theoretical, hermeneutic or interpretative paradigm to accommodate all of it with any degree of fidelity to the individual texts, and it is just such a fidelity to the individual texts that this book strives most to maintain. Students should be alert to the dangers of what one critic has called 'attractive but frequently reductive totalisations', especially in the context of postmodernity.[1] In fact, there is a heterogeneity of creative languages and of subject matter in American fiction at the end of the twentieth century which is itself worth emphasizing as a fundamental critical value of a book such as this. Jay McInerney might concur: in his 1994 *Penguin Book of New American Voices*, McInerney argued that 'much recent fiction tends to deconstruct the idea of a single national literature. Identity is more narrowly parsed by those who may not feel "the American tradition" is exactly coextensive with their own' (p. xviii). One of the questions that every interpretation of each individual novel included here tries to address is what does it mean to be American now? How might it be possible to extrapolate characteristics that could be identified as recognizably American, or is such an enterprise always doomed to superficial generalizations and

---

[1] Brian Jarvis, *Postmodern Cartographies: The Geographical Imagination in Contemporary American Culture* (London: Pluto Press, 1998), 80.

stereotypes? Gore Vidal once argued that all Americans have in common with each other is a belief in 'something called "the American way of life", an economic system involving the constant purchase of consumer goods on credit to maintain a high standard of living'.[2] But is economics the only constituent of 'the American way of life'?

William Blake once wrote that, 'To generalise is to be an idiot', and this is a useful warning for Europeans who are tempted to regard the United States as having a single and universally accepted culture. The heterogeneity of the culture of the United States and of its contemporary literature is one of its most remarkable features, and now more than ever it is characterized by copiousness and diversity. This book can only hope to represent a small part of that range and variety, and give a sense of the extraordinary vitality and inventiveness of American fiction at the end of the century. As long ago as 1961 Philip Roth argued that 'the American writer in the middle of the twentieth century has his hands full in trying to understand, describe and then make credible much of American reality. It stupefies, it sickens, it infuriates, and finally it is even a kind of embarrassment to one's meager imagination. The actuality is continually outdoing our talents'.[3] In an interview in 1990 Don DeLillo said that 'what's been missing over these past twenty-five years is a sense of a manageable reality'.[4] The United States contains enough 'manageable reality' to permit imaginative narratives about almost anything. This limitlessness is one of its great assets and surely enhances its literature immeasurably. Both Roth's and DeLillo's arguments crucially implicate various forms of media in the proliferation of America's 'manageable reality', and their fiction investigates the relationship between history, media, and myths of national identity. To quote another contemporary New Yorker who has pursued his own fictional enquiry into this territory: 'History is the present. That's why every generation writes it anew. But what most people think of as history is

[2] G. Vidal, 'Paranoid Politics', in *United States: Essays 1952–1992* (London: Abacus, 1993), 769–70. The article was originally published in 1967.

[3] P. Roth, 'Writing American Fiction', in *Reading Myself and Others* (London: Jonathan Cape, 1975), 120.

[4] F. Lentricchia (ed.), *Introducing Don DeLillo* (Durham, NC: Duke University Press, 1991), 48.

its end product, myth.'[5] The United States has a history in which myth and mediation were crucially involved right from the beginning, so that writing has a special place in the formation of a national identity that became 'American'.

To give them a context in earlier American writing, attempts have been made to relate this book's late twentieth-century fictions to an idea of 'America' partly by reference to earlier writers to whom they seem indebted and that students might be familiar with from the nineteenth century and earlier twentieth century. This too is fraught with difficulty involving matters of value as they concern the canon. Students should always be reminded that writing is often a response to earlier writing as much as it is to social reality, and as McInerney warns, 'Europeans are a little too eager to value American fiction for what they imagine to be its childlike freedom, as if we were all cowboys scratching our names on the tabula rasa of the great American landscape' (p. xi). American fiction of the late twentieth century has a heritage stretching back two hundred years, and this book draws on that heritage at appropriate moments.

Bradbury and Ro in their *Contemporary American Fiction* published in 1987 argued that the contemporary period 'is that since 1945'. The present book understands 'contemporary' to mean since 1970, and more especially the last twenty years of the twentieth century. Alison Lurie's *The War between the Tates* marks a watershed; published in 1974, it is set in 1969–70 and dramatizes domestic and political upheaval at the end of the 1960s. Erica Tate has a nostalgia for a pre-1970s America: '1969—it doesn't sound right, it's a year I don't belong in. It doesn't even feel real. Reality is when the children were small, and before the housing development. . . . Everything's changed, and I'm too tired to learn the new rules. I don't care about 1969 at all. I don't care about rock festivals or black power or student revolutions or going to the moon.' (200). Lurie's novel concerns conflict and antagonism on many levels as some sort of cultural 'consensus' begins to break and the Tates are seriously discomfited by social changes that disrupt their privileged WASP position; the novel ends with the question ' "Mommy, will the war end now?" ' (314) and

---

[5] E. L. Doctorow, in G. Plimpton (ed.), *Writers at Work: The Paris Review Interviews*, Eighth Series (London: Penguin, 1988), 308.

the answer is surely 'no'. American culture is as diverse and contested now as it was in 1969, only in different ways. In 1985 the history teacher of Mason's *In Country* defines a watershed in similar terms: '"the biggies in your lifetime were the moon landing, the assassinations, Watergate and Vietnam". Mr Harris said everything was downhill after Kennedy was killed' (66–7). In 1988 DeLillo's *Libra* defined the assassination of Kennedy as 'the seven seconds that broke the back of the American century' (181). The years of the Nixon administration, 1969–74, was perhaps the crucial period in recent American history, years that saw the culmination of an extraordinary period of social upheaval which had included the assassinations of John F. Kennedy in 1963, Malcolm X in 1965, Martin Luther King in 1968, and Robert Kennedy in 1968, and which also saw the Apollo moon landing of 1969, the Kent State University shootings in 1970, and the unique disgrace of the resignation of President Nixon in 1974. The war in Vietnam (1965–75) especially marked what has been characterized as 'the massive transformation in the nation's self-understanding which took place during those same years'.[6] Paul Kennedy expresses it succinctly:

In so many ways, symbolic as well as practical, it would be difficult to exaggerate the impact of the lengthy campaign in Vietnam upon the national psyche of the American people . . . [it] helped to cause the fissuring of consensus in American society about the nation's goals and priorities, was attended by inflation, unprecedented student protests and inner city disturbances, and was followed in turn by the Watergate crisis, which discredited the presidency itself for a time . . . [the effects] were interpreted as a crisis in American civilisation.[7]

Most of the novels of this book are products of that post-Vietnam civilization, and each of them is used to try to define the distinctive qualities of the contemporary.

Finally a word for the 'general reader': in 1992 Elizabeth Young and Graham Caveney in their *Shopping in Space: Essays on America's Blank Generation Fiction* wrote that 'No one should feel excluded from a passionate engagement with modern fiction; it does not belong to

---

6 D. Pease and C. Kaplan (eds.), *Cultures of United States Imperialism* (Durham, NC: Duke University Press, 1993), 3.

7 Paul Kennedy, *The Rise and Fall of the Great Powers* (London: Unwin Hyman, 1988), 404–5.

academia'. The interpretations of this book are not dependent upon a prior knowledge of American history or cultural theory, and the introductions of its individual chapters are provided to help histori-cize contemporary fiction in terms of both the culture of the United States and its representations in earlier modern fiction. It is the primary texts that are important here, and *Contemporary American Fiction* is a work of advocacy that hopes to stimulate a passionate engagement with them.

1

Family Values

Often with unadulterated joy
Mother, we bent by the fire
rehashing Father's character—
when he thought we were asleep.

Robert Lowell, 'During Fever'

In the United States the family is the principal means by which the individual is socialized. The family is the agency through which children are brought up in the knowledge of the values of their parents and of American society. The nuclear family is widely regarded as the sacred cornerstone of the American social project and it is perceived as fundamental to the happiness and success of the individual, the nation, and corporate life. An American myth of the family is still generally subscribed to and commonly recognized as a natural ambition and primary means of personal fulfilment. Furthermore, the nation family of the United States is a governing narrative for those who purport to speak on behalf of society and is integral to their ideas of American citizenship. Both conservative and liberal politicians strive to portray themselves as the guardians of family values because they understand that it is important to align themselves with something of broad public appeal, like the flag, which signifies a wide but wholesome and homogeneous social agenda. Such values are epitomized by the family ethos of the Disney films, for example, which have remarkable and worldwide appeal, and which emphasize strongly the security and nurture that families can provide. Although it has been argued that 'Divorce is America's great contribution to marriage',[1] it is

---

[1] E. Fawcett and T. Thomas, *The American Condition* (New York: Harper & Row, 1982), 127.

also true that Americans marry and remarry with an unfailing optimism in the future, in the hope of fresh opportunities to find personal fulfilment, and the institution of marriage is still a central part of that quest. At the end of the twentieth century rhetorical obeisance to family values was as fervent as ever, and abortion and the social welfare of single parents were still explosive issues in American politics.

The late twentieth century was also a time of great pressure on the conventional family unit that was common in the 1950s and 1960s. The success of the feminist movement enabled more women to pursue career paths and to postpone having children, women's conceptions of themselves were less likely to be determined by models of domesticity, and financial pressures have made large families less common as children are increasingly regarded in terms of economic commitment. Even more recently the legal rights of children not to be subordinate to their parents in the ways that were traditionally acceptable have been widely culturally endorsed and the abuse and neglect of children has become a subject of great public concern. Much social study has sought to uncover the inhibiting and even debilitating pressures of the family, and the authority of the father especially has come under close scrutiny. It seems less likely now that the family can be relied on unequivocally as a *Haven in a Heartless World*.[2] In 1981 Sar A. Levitan and Richard S. Belous asked *What's Happening to the American Family?* and part of the answer was fundamental social change.

Since Nathaniel Hawthorne's *The Scarlet Letter* (1850) the family unit has been used to examine the particular conditions of the wider culture to which it belongs. More precisely, American novelists have often used the histories of children and adolescents as a means to offer social criticism of American life, and the American *Bildungsroman* has an illustrious pedigree since Huckleberry Finn ran away from his drunken father in 1884. This tradition continues into the twentieth century with Holden Caulfield, for example, in *The Catcher in the Rye* (1951) and his ironic and perfunctory acknowledgement of family heritage: 'If you really want to hear about it, the first thing you'll probably want to know is where I was born, and what my lousy

---

[2] C. Lasch, *Haven in a Heartless World: The Family Besieged* (New York: Basic Books, 1975).

childhood was like, and how my parents were occupied and all before they had me, and all that David Copperfield kind of crap.' It is a striking feature of this chapter's novels that they are partly characterized by acts of emotional or physical violence towards children, and by the abuse or collapse of the authority of the father. In some ways these novels are close to Lowell's *Life Studies* in revealing the debilitating effects of family inheritance, and especially in the ways that they investigate ideas about culture and authority by 'rehashing Father's character'.

Toni Morrison **The Bluest Eye**

One of the many remarkable aspects of Toni Morrison's first novel *The Bluest Eye* (1970) is that, while it centres on the harrowing and traumatic narrative of an individual, the novel contextualizes her life and the lives of those similarly brutalized around her in a way which shows that nothing happens in isolation.[3] One way in which *The Bluest Eye* does this is through the use of the family. Pecola is shown to be the victim of, even the product of, violent tensions within her family, the Breedloves, who perceive themselves to be ugly beyond redemption: 'They took the ugliness in their hands, threw it as a mantle over them, and went about the world with it' (28). Pecola inherits this profoundly negative self-image from her parents and it is reinforced by the absence of positive representations of black Americans in her culture. Pecola's sense of diminishment is so complete and fundamental that she becomes invisible to the white store owner, in whom she registers 'The total absence of human recognition' (36), and which she interprets as a white distaste for her blackness. These are the cultural conditions that pertain for working-class black families in Lorain, Ohio, in 1941.

Pecola's relationship with her mother Pauline is not one which fosters her self-esteem. In one of the many scenes of violence and pain in the novel Pecola accidentally spills a blueberry cobbler on the kitchen floor of the house where her mother works as a maid. Pecola receives a beating from her mother, whose love and affection are reserved for

---

[3] Page references are to the Picador edition.

the white girl she is paid to wait on. The contrast is not confined to the different physical treatment that the two girls receive from Pecola's mother: the daughter of the white family calls her 'Polly' with easy familiarity: 'Her calling Mrs Breedlove Polly when even Pecola called her mother Mrs Breedlove seemed reason enough to scratch her' (84). This alienation of the black family from one another is partly a consequence of their poverty in a steel town on Lake Erie (where they are 'Festering together in the debris of a realtor's whim', (25)), such that the best they can do is try 'to make do with the way they found each other' (25). Economic and social pressures put unbearable strains on the Breedlove family, and Sammy Breedlove has run away from home twenty-seven times by the time he is 14 (32), but Pecola is younger and a girl and must stay to endure the terrible inheritance of her parents' violent marriage: 'Cholly and Mrs Breedlove fought each other with a darkly brutal formalism that was paralleled only by their lovemaking' (32). Pecola is trapped in a turbulent and loveless family and bears the brunt of the novel's ugly denouement.

The Bluest Eye is careful however not to make Pecola's fate seem extraordinary or inexplicable, and this tact is a central part of the novel's political agenda. The anguish of Pecola's parents is fully contextualized by accounts of their childhoods, and their respective family histories. Pecola's parents pass on their self-loathing to their daughter, but are themselves revealed as the products of difficult childhoods. Pecola's mother Pauline Williams is a deracinated southerner who came to Ohio from Alabama via Kentucky and who, despite reminiscing about 'down home', was an outsider in her own family who 'never felt at home anywhere, or that she belonged anyplace' (86). This cultural and familial displacement contributes strongly to her susceptibility to northern urban cultural pressures that are in fact inimical to her ethnic identity. Pauline's family background also contributes to her acceptance of her role as a servant in the Fisher household. It is notable that the Fishers give Pauline the nickname, and misnomer, 'Polly', where in her childhood home in Alabama 'she alone of all the children had no nickname' (86). Pecola's father was abandoned by his mother: 'When Cholly was four days old his mother wrapped him in two blankets and one newspaper and placed him on a junkheap by the railroad' (103). Cholly goes in search of his father in Macon, Georgia, when he is 14, finds him playing craps, and is aggressively rejected by him with the expression 'Now, get the fuck outta my face' (123), and so Cholly becomes free of all familial bonds and dangerously bereft of social responsibility: 'Abandoned in a junk heap by his mother, rejected for a crap game by his father, there was nothing more to lose' (126). In this condition of despair he meets Pauline and they become bound together in a marriage of mutual antagonism, Cholly projecting his anger on to his wife as a desperate means of self-preservation: 'He poured out on her the sum of all his inarticulate fury and aborted desires. Hating her he could leave himself intact' (31). The violence of Cholly's marital relations and his attitude to women is also derived from a formative event in his adolescence when he was surprised by two white men while having sex with a young black girl. Unable to confront the white men in his racist culture, Cholly directed his anger towards the girl 'with a violence born of total helplessness' (116). Cholly's sexual relationships are crucially informed by such scenes of painful humiliation, and his marriage was unlikely to be a happy one: 'But the aspect of married life that dumbfounded him and rendered him totally dysfunctional was the appearance of children. Having no idea of how to raise children; and having never watched any parent raise himself, he could not even comprehend what such a relationship should be' (126). This observation returns the narrative to Pecola; the important point about the compressed account of Cholly's childhood is that it immediately precedes his rape of his daughter and is therefore strategically placed to help account for his behaviour. In this way *The Bluest Eye* shows how oppression is passed on from one black family to another. Cholly Breedlove's abuse of his daughter is dramatized in part as a displaced desire for his wife, in which 'The confused mixture of his memories of Pauline and the doing of a wild and forbidden thing excited him' (128). The novel here is uncompromisingly explicit and depicts the taboo of incest in direct language, but the scene is structured to occur as an almost inevitable consequence of Cholly's brutalized life: this perspective of family history serves not to ameliorate Cholly's actions but to give a material account of how he comes to abuse his own daughter.

This strategy is repeated elsewhere in *The Bluest Eye*, where family history is shown to be a consistently determining factor in the novel's action. The best example of this is the final section of 'winter' which culminates with the black woman Geraldine returning home to discover her son terrorizing Pecola; Geraldine casts the innocent Pecola out of the house with the words 'Get out . . . you nasty little black bitch' (72). This section of the novel begins with an account of the migration of black people from the rural south to the industrial north in the 1940s. Geraldine's assimilation into the new middle-class black urban culture is accompanied by the erasure of a vital part of her Afro-American identity: 'In short, how to get rid of the funkiness. The dreadful funkiness of passion, the funkiness of nature, the funkiness of the wide range of human emotions. Wherever it erupts, this funk, they wipe it away; where it crusts, they dissolve it; wherever it drips, flowers, or clings, they find it and fight it until it dies' (64). Geraldine's identity, and that of thousands of other black Americans like her, is compromised to an idea of American aspiration which is white and middle-class and which will not tolerate the fact that she is black. Geraldine learns to eradicate all signs of her ethnic cultural identity in order to conform to white social standards and white cultural values. This prohibition against black 'funkiness' invades even the most intimate areas of her sexual life. Geraldine's self-denial is passed on to her son, Junior, who becomes a torturer of cats at an early age. His mother explains to him, 'the difference between colored people and niggers' (67) and Junior, the direct product of his mother's enforced self-hatred, becomes a bully and a sadist and a loner; he bullies girls especially, including, eventually, Pecola. The moment at which Geraldine calls Pecola 'nasty little black bitch' includes an instantaneous recognition that the little girl is everything that Geraldine has worked so hard to distance herself from: 'They slept six to a bed, all their pee mixing together in the night as they wet their beds each in his own candy-and-potato-chip dream' (72). Here then the cycle of black oppression is complete, Geraldine passes on her self-loathing to her son Junior, who internalizes it as an essential condition of his identity. This is part of the novel's criticism of white ideas of social aspiration, and it mirrors Pauline's neglect of her daughter Pecola in dramatizing the corrosive effects of parental relationships that are not loving. Geraldine's history is used to show how the low-esteem of black people is transmitted through the agency of their families. It is this family-history perspective that prevents the fate of individuals from being interpreted as isolated events, and enables *The Bluest Eye* to offer an analysis of a whole cultural history and not simply the story of one tragic individual.

Morrison's interest in the family is shown strongly in her use of the Dick and Jane primer at the beginning of *The Bluest Eye*: 'Here is the house. It is green and white. It has a red door. It is very pretty. Here is the family. Mother, Father, Dick and Jane live in the green-and-white house. They are very happy' (1). This text is an idyllic representation of the white nuclear family from which the Breedloves depart dramatically, and this departure is a fundamental aspect of the novel's ideological freight. The primer text is put to two other important uses in the novel: first, sentences from it are used as section headings in order to comment ironically on the action of the novel (so that the section which ends with Cholly's rape of Pecola begins with the words 'see father he is big and strong father will you play with Jane', (103)), and second, the primer is the text by which children learn to read, so that their very knowledge of language is bound up with the ideological values that the Dick and Jane primer carries. It might even be argued that the corruption of the primer into a solid block of text without space between the words is a representation of the lack of space that black people have in the culture that produces such a text and promotes its values. This latter point is very important, because the novel is full of references to the ascendancy of white aesthetic values (such as blue eyes) and offers a cultural analysis of the way that those values are promulgated to black people to whom they are inimical. This is especially true of the twin ideas of romantic love and physical beauty, which *The Bluest Eye* describes as 'Probably the most destructive ideas in the history of human thought' (95). Very little escapes the debilitating and corrosive presence of a white aesthetic in *The Bluest Eye*; even Claudia MacTeer, the narrator who attacks 'those round moronic eyes' of Shirley Temple, eventually succumbs: 'I learned much later to worship her, just as I learned to delight in cleanliness' (16), and Claudia also learns to erase her anger and rebelliousness. Furthermore, it is not only Cholly who abuses his own daughter: both Mr Henry and Soaphead Church are guilty of child abuse and therefore of contravening one of the most fundamental sanctities of the family, the trust of children in fathers. This corruption of the father's integrity has one notable exception in *The Bluest Eye*, the father of Claudia, Mr MacTeer, who shoots a gun at Mr Henry when he finds out about the interference with his daughter Frieda (77). The MacTeers are very important to the novel's concern with the role of family as a kind of microcosm of the ethnic family of Afro-Americans that must be nurtured and sustained if individual black Americans are to survive the pressures of white America. As one critic has pointed out, 'The MacTeers retain a commitment to the idea of the black community as their extended family',[4] and this enlargement of the concept of family is consistently fundamental to Morrison's vision of a better future for Afro-Americans.

There is a black style of aesthetic value which appears occasionally in *The Bluest Eye*, in the form of song, or the blues, which functions as an affirmative alternative to white America's value system. Claudia loves to hear her mother singing:

She would sing about hard times, bad times, somebody-done-gone-and-left-me times. But her voice was so sweet and her singing-eyes so melty I found myself longing for those hard times, yearning to be grown without 'a thin di-i-ime to my name'. I looked forward to the delicious time when 'my man' would leave me, when I would 'hate to see that evening sun go down . . . cause then I would know my man has left this town'. Misery colored by the greens and blues in my mother's voice took all of the grief out of the words and left me with a conviction that pain was not only endurable, it was sweet. (17–18).

The 'blues' of Claudia's mother is an authentic black art form that both resists and is resistant to the incursions of white America's dominant aesthetic values, and is one that has its origin 'working behind a mule way back in slavery time'.[5] Poland too sings about 'blues in my mealbarrel / Blues up on the shelf' (38). When Cholly's aunt falls ill her sisters comfort her with 'a threnody of nostalgia about pain, rising and falling, complex in harmony, uncertain in pitch, but constant in the recitative of pain' (107), and Cholly's broken personal history is such that 'The pieces of Cholly's life could only become coherent in the head of a musician. Only those who talk their talk through the gold of curved metal, or in the touch of black-and-white rectangles and taut strings and skins echoing from wooden corridors, could give

---

[4] Denise Heinze, *The Dilemma of 'Double Consciousness': Toni Morrison's Novels* (Athens, Ga.: Georgia University Press, 1993), 74.

[5] Houston Baker, Jr, *Blues, Ideology and Afro-American Literature* (Chicago: University of Chicago Press, 1984), 8.

true form to his life' (125). These references to the blues and to jazz (and of course another connotation of the word 'funk') represent a black art form which emerges from suffering, which is distinctively black, which tells the story of family histories, and which is passed down as a black aesthetic through families, like the oral histories of earlier Afro-American artists. In this sense, the family might still be the repository of positive values that are both deeply personal and culturally significant. Morrison's art as a novelist also aspires to be part of a quintessentially black creative tradition; it might be argued that the novel's title *The Bluest Eye* puns on the word 'eye' to refer to the first person singular 'I' which thus designates Pecola's desperate emotional impoverishment. Pecola is 'the bluest I'. In this way the novel becomes Pecola's blues, a musical precursor to Morrison's 1992 novel *Jazz* which also appropriates black musical structures for literary purposes. This too is an important point about family, Morrison's first novel positioning itself as part of an Afro-American artistic tradition from which it draws a sustaining sense of family continuity. One critic has argued that Claudia functions in *The Bluest Eye* as a 'griot' who addresses 'a communal imperative to know what has happened to the town and to its people, thus exemplifying the storyteller's role in providing perspective on difficult periods in communal history',[6] and this too connects the function of the artist with their community or family.

Russell Banks **Affliction**

Russell Banks's *Affliction* (1989) is also a novel that uses the family as a means of cultural analysis, and like *The Bluest Eye* it examines how individual family members are informed by economic conditions, by the deterioration of a particular community, and by the corruption and collapse of the role of the father, culminating in domestic violence and childhood trauma.[7] *Affliction* is the story of two brothers, Rolfe and Wade Whitehouse, one of whom narrates the tale of the other's psychological collapse. Rolfe is a high school history teacher

---

6 Trudier Harris, *Fiction and Folklore: The Novels of Toni Morrison* (Knoxville, Tenn.: University of Tennessee Press, 1991), 16.

7 Page references are to the Harper Perennial edition.

who escaped Lawford, New Hampshire, by going to college, and who now tells Wade's story from a dispassionate distance. The role of the brother as narrator is a crucial one and a significant contribution to the novel's investigation of family inheritance. Rolfe, who is 31, unmarried, childless and teetotal and suffers from 'periodic headaches' (5), recognizes that Wade's story is the flip-side of his own in some crucial way: 'His story is my ghost life, and I want to exorcise it' (2), and it is not until he has told his brother's story that he could imagine beginning a family of his own and ending his life of meticulous routine: 'Will I marry then? Will I make a family of my own? Will I become a member of a tribe? Oh lord, I pray that I will do those things and that I will be that man' (49). Rolfe's obsession with telling Wade's story is a cathartic and potentially redemptive one which mirrors the 'isolated explosion of homicidal rage' (354) which comprises the novel's dramatic denouement. In *Affliction*, one brother needs to tell the other's story so that he might rid himself of the same trauma, the trauma of domestic violence handed to both Whitehouse brothers by their father. In this respect Banks's novel uses the family to offer a criticism of a certain type of masculinity. Rolfe recognizes that he is 'a little weird' (137) and that in his logical and dispassionate nature he might conform to the characteristically male Whitehouse traits which he hoped to leave behind when he left New Hampshire: 'The woman had feelings. But Rolfe did not. Or at least he did not seem to have any feeling. He was the strange one, not Wade' (233). This is the anxiety that pervades Rolfe's text, the fear that although he fled the family at an early age, he might still carry its legacy with him.

Rolfe tells the story of his brother Wade's psychological and social disintegration. Wade's marriage has already collapsed, but he is desperate to maintain a good relationship with his 10-year-old daughter Jill, because fatherhood is integral to Wade's ideas of proper manhood. Wade also thinks that he can banish the legacy of his father by being a better father himself. Fatherhood has an important redemptive potential for Wade; he recognizes that 'When you take a man's child from him, you take much more than the child' (162). Jill's reluctance to spend weekends with her bad-tempered father causes Wade acute pain, and his breakdown is framed by two meetings with her which go badly wrong, partly because she no longer needs him as much as he needs her to support his sense of identity. Wade's vain fantasy of winning custody of Jill from his ex-wife is a desperate attempt to reconstitute a lost sense of family and a failing sense of masculinity. The psychological and social functions of fatherhood are closely connected for Wade: 'That was all he really wanted. He wanted to be a good father; and he wanted everyone to know it' (158). Wade's frustration at having this aspiration blocked is a major contributing factor to his breakdown; at the end of the novel when Jill reprimands her father for drinking while driving she tells him 'You're a policeman', and he replies abjectly 'I'm not nothing anymore' (326). Wade's lover Margie, with whom he hopes to shape a new family, is already familiar with this male desire for fatherhood; her ex-husband left her when he discovered that she could not conceive, because he wanted ' "a real family" ', and therefore felt 'as if she were depriving him of an essential right' (205). Despite the terrible legacy of his own family, Wade is incapable of thinking of himself without a family and he married immediately upon graduating from high school. Like much in Wade's life, his ideals have a fairy-tale quality: 'He would be the good father; she would be the good mother; they would have a beloved child' (279). This is a social need as much as an emotional one, and to be robbed of it is as calamitous to Wade as losing his job as the town policeman because it is integral to his ideas of manhood and social responsibility.

The narrative of Rolfe Whitehouse is not entirely dispassionate and detached; an important part of the novel's dramatic action takes place in chapter 19 when Wade tells him that he too was beaten by his father, and beaten so badly that he was hospitalized with broken ribs. There is an interesting analogy here with Jane Smiley's *A Thousand Acres* because Rolfe has no memory of the attack, having apparently been traumatized by it as a 6-year-old. Rolfe insists that the story (a Freudian primal scene in which the father is displeased by the son who watches his mother bathing) was told to him by his brother as a cautionary tale. Rolfe believes that the story has made him especially wary, but safe: 'at least I managed to avoid being afflicted by that man's violence'. Wade replies pointedly, 'That's what you think' (277). The implication here is either that Rolfe can never recognize himself as the subject of his father's violence and therefore the cathartic potential of his storytelling has failed, or that his caution helped him to escape: 'I was a careful child . . . now I am a careful adult' (277).

Either way the implication is clear, that Rolfe did not escape his father's legacy any more than his brother did, and that even from his position as narrator that legacy is his affliction too. Rolfe has internalized his father's violence in a way which is as self-damaging as his brother's response to it.[8]

Like the other novels of this chapter, *Affliction* places its family history in the broader context of an account of a culture and a community. While Rolfe has avoided the Whitehouse family inheritance only 'with excruciating difficulty' (95), his brother Wade is gradually stripped of each of his roles as a husband, a father, a lover, a policeman. Striving to attain a conception of manhood that his environment will not permit, Wade feels outmoded and redundant and has a dream in which he senses that men are peripheral because 'Men do not have babies, women do'. Wade wakes up screaming, 'What do men do?' (137). Wade's authority, position, and status as a man are each taken from him, and his sense of identity disintegrates into obsession, psychosis, and paranoia. Much of this is a consequence of ideas of manhood which no longer serve him well, by which he is trapped, and that are closely associated with being a member of a family.

Wade's custody suit never gets started because his attorney knows he has a history of violence towards his wife; this is the terrible legacy that he has learned from his father and which his brother has left New Hampshire to escape. Wade and Rolfe's father, Glen Whitehouse, is a bitter and violent man who shows no love for any of his five children because his 'impoverished family only served to remind him of his own failings' (97). The father becomes an alcoholic, threatens his wife into submission, and can only relate to his sons in terms of challenges to his authority. Glen beats the two elder boys routinely; they leave home by joining the army and are killed in Vietnam, and the father turns his attention to Wade. The scenes in the novel in which Glen thrashes Wade inexplicably are at the centre of the text's consideration of family because all the violence of the narrative originates

---

[8] This is an important point that one contemporary reviewer misunderstood when he wrote that 'Banks allows certain suspicions to arise concerning Rolfe's reliability as a narrator and commentator . . . he can be annoyingly obtrusive in his lengthy explanations of his own part in the story' (Robert Towers, 'You Can Go Home Now', *New York Review of Books*, 7 Dec. 1989, 46).

with them. The violence of Glen Whitehouse, 'a failure of individual character' (255) is socially and culturally informed; two of the most harrowing attacks take place against a backdrop of wrestling on the television, and the television series 'Gun Smoke'. This is not to say that Banks glibly accuses the media, but that Glen Whitehouse is the product of an older New Hampshire culture which measures masculinity in terms of physical strength. This is the significance of the arm-wrestling scene where the father's authority is threatened by his growing sons, so he moves to dominate and subdue them by force. The tough New Hampshire landscape produces men who aspire to a model of masculinity predicated on violence, and here it is concurrent with an American history which goes back to 'Gun Smoke'.

Wade feels the humiliation of his attacks acutely, but as a child he has no option but to accept it 'as just one more of the many brutalities of our life so far, as one small corner of the rough terrain of childhood' (182). It is worth noting though that, in sharing his family secret with his wife Lillian, Wade is conscious that 'he had left out of his account something that was crucial and filled him with shame' (109). In beginning to imagine his own future family, many key things are brought together: 'his pain and shame, his secret exhilaration and the heat and drama of it, his pathetic fear of his father and incomprehensible anger at his mother' (279). Perhaps it is this 'secret exhilaration' at his father's demonstrations of power which enables Wade to carry it forward into his own domestic life, especially in the context of the narrative when he is, like his father, most powerless.

The myth of masculinity which traps Wade has a broad cultural currency. When the brothers meet, they keep a space between them: 'That is the way we men are, we New England men, we Whitehouse men' (224). This is seen especially in sports: the novel takes place during one November hunting season, the shooting of deer characterized as 'an ancient male rite'. Wade's friend Jack Hewitt derives his sense of identity from his sporting ability: 'when he found out that he couldn't play baseball anymore, he changed' (171), and Margie points out that 'women can see the little boy in the man pretty easily. . . . It happens when he's paying attention to something else. Like watching sports on tv' (173). The outmoded idea of manhood that New Hampshire men subscribe to in *Affliction* is sharply exposed by Wade's astonishment when he discovers that his attorney is in a wheelchair;

it is a myth of masculinity learned from his family and his culture which, he knows, has always been precarious: 'this particular kind of fragility' (108).

The disintegration of Wade's family life takes place against the disintegration of the community he was raised in. Ambitious people move away from Lawford, leaving only the failures behind. This is part of the American dream of social aspiration and personal fulfilment, as Rolfe comments, 'From log cabin to President: it is our dominant myth' (202). But even Rolfe has only contempt for the people who have 'gone to Florida, Arizona and California, bought a trailer or a condo, turned their skin to leather playing shuffleboard all day and waited to die' (82–3). Ironically, Wade does escape to a new life at the end of the novel, but only as a fugitive across the border north to Toronto, and on the run for a double murder. Rolfe speculates that Wade has become 'one of those faceless fellows we see working behind the counter at our local video rental store' (354), and his narrative turns its attention to the replacement of the Lawford community by a ski resort, a story of property development, commercial enterprise, and social alienation. Just as Wade disappears from the text, so too does Lawford: 'The community, as such, no longer exists' (353). The breakdown of the family precedes the collapse of the community, and Lawford disappears as the Whitehouse family disintegrates. This is a theme that Banks pursues closely in *Rule of the Bone* (1995) a contemporary *Adventures of Huckleberry Finn* in which a 14-year-old boy escapes the sexual abuse of his stepfather and goes in search of a new life of self-esteem and surrogate families, 'a homeless kid pretending not to give a shit that no one wanted him' (130). This novel, like *The Bluest Eye* and *Affliction* explores the relationship between family dysfunction and social violence through the use of an outcast or victim, and Bone's tone of voice is sometimes reminiscent of Holden Caulfield. At one point Banks's protagonist imagines walking into a Pizza Hut and indiscriminately shooting dead everyone there, 'That's how far gone I was on account of my stepfather and the collapsed situation at our house and family' (199).

E. A. Proulx The Shipping News

Annie Proulx's *The Shipping News* (1993) is also a novel which asks what it means to belong to a family, and investigates how the individual is informed by family relationships; the novel has a positive view of family heritage as a repository of value amid the chaos of modern society, but this is not a sentimentalized ideological perspective.[9] The novel is very much concerned with domestic violence and its traumatic consequences both for the individual and the community. *The Shipping News* does not necessarily idealize family, but it does suggest that coming to know one's family, even distant family, is a way to know oneself. For this novel however, family is something radically different, and the politics of family is where this novel's real cutting edge lies. The novel's protagonist, Quoyle, the offspring of loveless parents who, like Glen Whitehouse, see their own failures reflected in him, feels at an early age that 'he had been given to the wrong family, that somewhere his real people . . . longed for him' (2). Quoyle senses that 'some anomalous gene' has cast him as a gargantuan misfit and absurd outsider to his own family and it is this alienation that hurries him into a calamitous marriage with Petal Bear, characterized as 'a month of fiery happiness. Then six kinked years of suffering' (13). Quoyle does find briefly a surrogate family in Partridge, and he momentarily glimpses the nurturing potential of being among people who accept him and care for him without prejudice. But Quoyle's wife fails to provide the stable domestic life he longs for; she rejects the role of motherhood, pretends not to recognize their daughter, and when she finds herself pregnant a second time 'fumed until the alien left her body' (14). Petal too is an alienated product of contemporary American culture, 'In another time, another sex, she would have been a Genghis Khan [but] she had only petty triumphs of sexual encounter' (13). Petal perceives her only mode of conquest to be sexual, but she resents her own promiscuity, with its repeated failure to provide fulfilment; to Quoyle she was 'starved for love' (23), but for Agnis she is merely 'a bitch in high heels' (24). Quoyle's family disintegrates entirely when his wife deserts him, sells their two

---

[9] All page references are to the Fourth Estate edition.

children to paedophiles, and then dies in a road crash. Simultaneously, Quoyle's parents commit suicide leaving only a message for him to contact his aunt Agnis, his father concluding enigmatically, 'I don't know where the rest of them are' (19). The modern ills of contemporary society are again satirized here, Quoyle's parents contracting cancer because they live beside a power station, and Quoyle's father's final message left on an answerphone that cuts off abruptly because the tape runs out.[10] It is worth noting too that Quoyle's children are only narrowly saved from featuring in a paedophile video (26), and this is important because it connects the sexual abuse of children in contemporary urban America with that which the novel portrays as endemic in Newfoundland. Violent and abusive sex (sex as a weapon) is a significant theme in *The Shipping News*, and is closely associated with the novel's satirical depiction of what some American politicians like to refer to dotingly as 'family values'.

It is specifically through the agency of his aunt Agnis Hamm that Quoyle embarks upon that most American of journeys, a new life; ushered in by a reference to Horace Greely (21) Quoyle heads off not west but north for Newfoundland, 'the rock that had generated his ancestors' (1) as part of what Agnis calls 'some atavistic drive to finish up where you started' (29).[11] It is Agnis who tells Quoyle, 'What place would be more natural than where your family came from?' (29), and it is Agnis who takes Quoyle and his two young daughters to begin again in Newfoundland and so rescues him from the wreckage of his modern urban life: 'Quoyle hated the thought of an incestuous, fit-prone, seal-killing child for a grandfather, but there was no choice. The mysteries of unknown family' (25). Agnis provides Quoyle with a history lesson in family lineage, and they travel together to Newfoundland already constituting a new kind of family unit: the aunt, the nephew, and the two motherless daughters. This is just the beginning of the novel's exposition of ideas about family connections.

---

[10] It is worth noting that this last message is one in which Guy Quoyle offers his own narrative of a uniquely American self-determination, one in which 'I had to make my own way in a tough world ever since I came to this country. Nobody ever gave me nothing' (19). This narrative bears interesting relation to the one on which Quoyle is about to embark.

[11] Atavistic: 'The reappearance of a characteristic after several generations of absence, caused by a recessive gene'. This word is perhaps more pertinent to Bunny than it is to Quoyle himself.

Quoyle is compelled to Newfoundland by his aunt, who has her own reasons for wanting to return to their family origins (unknown to him) and she also has her own family demons to come to terms with. Agnis Hamm provides a further example of an individual without immediate family, and so the novel begins by positing alternative models of what a family can be, and how individuals can establish loving relationships in the absence of traditional or conventional family forms. Crucially, Quoyle's disabling passivity is broken by the emergence of family ties, the responsibilities of paternity, on one hand, and the appearance of Agnis, on the other, who tells him immediately of his likeness to his grandfather (25) and so arouses his curiosity in family antecedents.

The Newfoundland that the Quoyles discover is no pastoral retreat or rural idyll but a place of desperate hardship and historic struggles to survive, of 'the father who shot his oldest children and himself that the rest might live on flour scrapings ... trousers made of worn upholstery fabric' (33). The poverty and suffering of Newfoundland is a function of its isolation, the barren landscape and the remorselessly severe weather, and Proulx's evocation of these aspects of northern life is as significant a part of her novel as the evocation of a New Hampshire winter is to Banks's. Moreover, the novel is littered with references to violence within local families: 'sexual abuse of children is an old Newf tradition' (218). Quoyle's job on the newspaper gives him access to this first hand and enables him to judge how wide-spread it is: '"This week I've the most sexual abuse stories I've ever had", said Nutbeem. ". . . The usual yaffle of disgusting old dads having it on with their kiddies, one more priest feeling up the choirboys, . . . ripped his trousers stem to stern and sexually assaulted him with a tomcod" (155). This paragraph, and the many other graphic references to sexual violence in the novel (217, 218, 221), are there to remind the reader that depravity is not simply some degenerate aberration of contemporary urban lifestyles. In this way the novel subtly and consistently avoids any simple opposition between the rural and the urban, the old and the modern.

Two of these quotations in particular are worth paying close atten-tion. The most detailed and graphic catalogue of sexual violence in the whole novel occurs on pages 217–18: 'And here in Killick-Claw a loving dad is charged with sexually assaulting two of his sons and his teenage daughter in innumerable incidents between 1962 and the present. Buggery, indecent assault and sexual intercourse. Here's another family lover, big strapping thirty-five-year-old fisherman spends his hours ashore teaching his little four-year-old-daughter to perform oral sex and masturbate him'. Note the language here, 'a loving dad', and 'a family lover', says Nutbeem, punning on 'family lover' to mean both a lover *of* the family and a lover *in* the family. 'It's not necessarily worse here', he adds, 'just more openly publicized' (218). But is this really true? How are we to take the dark humour of Proulx's presentation of this especially ugly aspect of Newfoundland life in the context of the novel's political agenda about family values? Surely it does seem worse, much worse, and suggests that Newfoundland is a backward and brutally violent place for many of its inhabitants. The second quotation is equally important: it is revealed that Jack gives his writers assignments that force them to confront their personal traumas from the past. Nutbeem has to cover 'the wretched sexual assaults. And with each one I relive my own childhood' (221). This is true for each of the writers. Nutbeem philosophically concludes that these kinds of confrontation with the pain of the past are therapeutic: 'it dulls it because you see your condition is not unique, that other people suffer as you suffer' (221). This is important to the theme of renewal and redemption, of overcoming the traumas of the past, and it is vital to the relationship of Quoyle and Wavey which brings the novel to a conclusion.

If the catalogue of sexual violence in Newfoundland families is disconcerting to Quoyle, then so is the family heritage that he uncovers there; it is no cosy album of illustrious forebears, but something of a curse. The Quoyles were in fact 'a savage pack' who once '"Nailed a man to a tree by 'is ears, cut off 'is nose for the scent of blood to draw the nippers and flies that devoured him alive"' (139). More than any other fabled family, the Quoyles, 'wild and inbred, half-wits and murderers' (162) represent the mythic ethos of the country. The only surviving Quoyle is old cousin Nolan: '"They say there's a smell that comes off him like rot and cold clay. They say he slept with his wife when she was dead and you smell the desecration coming off him"' (162). This is the family heritage that Quoyle has to come to terms with in Newfoundland, 'Ancestors whose filthy blood ran in his veins, who murdered the shipwrecked, drowned their unwanted brats' (174) and whose legendary ugliness is such that local people still say, 'Nothing good ever happened with a Quoyle' (182). As with *The Bluest Eye* and *Affliction*, family is something to be suffered and overcome, a form of socialization that is violent and painful, that configures children as victims, and that takes mature adults years of struggle to come to terms with.

The narrative of *The Shipping News* unfolds for Quoyle in terms of revelations about family relationships, with his daughters, his aunt, and his cousin Nolan. Nolan, an illiterate fisherman but 'some kind of fork kin from the old days' (161) resents the incursion of Quoyle and family and haunts them (literally) by placing witch-knots at the threshold of each room of their house. Eventually Quoyle is forced to confront the wretched and starving old man who lives alone in abject squalor: 'He called, Mr Quoyle, Mr Quoyle, felt he was calling himself' (264). Here Quoyle is painfully reminded of the family history that his father fled, and he discovers a mysterious affinity between Nolan and his daughter Bunny whose imagination has been terrorized by the fear of a dog that has been planted there by Nolan's witchcraft. Nolan, on the verge of death from malnutrition, is institutionalized in an asylum and Quoyle visits him to try to lay to rest Nolan's lunatic animosity: ' "Cousin Nolan". How strange the words sounded. But by uttering them bound himself in some way to this shrivelled husk. "Cousin Nolan Quoyle. It's all in the past" ' (296). Quoyle tries to put Nolan's hostility at a distance, but the novel insists repeatedly upon the continuity of the Quoyle family blood. Quoyle's own talent for seeing the commonplaces of life in terms of newspaper headlines ('Dog Farts Fell Family of Four', (54) 'Phone Rings in Empty Room', (8)) is an attenuated remnant of the Quoyle magical genius; it is an imaginative ability which his daughter Bunny has inherited, unable to eat apricots because they look like 'little fairies bottoms' (139) or lobsters because they remind her of red spiders. In this way the quintessential Quoyle gene is passed on through generations, expressed as the father's anxiety that 'his daughter might glimpse things beyond static reality' (134). Bunny, more than her sister, carries the unique Quoyle characteristic, and her refusal to believe in death is an important part of the novel's theme of resurrection. After all, is it not Bunny who brings Jack Buggit back to life, standing transfixed at the side of his coffin and gazing at Jack's corpse? Jack coughs, and Bunny shouts '"He woke up!"' (333). Bunny is part of the mystic belief in miracles associated with going native and being attuned to the continuity of one's ancestral heritage. As early as chapter 5 when Quoyle is trying to explain to Bunny the death of her mother, she says simply '"If I was asleep I would wake up"' (46).

The Shipping News is a novel which uses the investigation of family as a vehicle for ideas about history and redemption. For Quoyle, coming to the place of his ancestors 'was as though he'd found a polarised lens that deepened and intensified all seen through it' (241), and Quoyle comes to realize that he could never return to New York. For Quoyle, Newfoundland has a special redemptive power which is derived from his family's historical identification with it, and he has moments of epiphany: 'The sharpness of his gaze pierced the past. He saw generations like migrating birds, the bay flecked with ghost sails, the deserted settlements vigorous again, and in the abyss nets spangled with scales. Saw the Quoyles rinsed of evil by the passage of time. . . . A sense of purity renewed, a sense of events in trembling balance flooded him' (196). Quoyle realizes that he has the potential to prove history wrong, to redeem the family name by writing his own future with it. But what of Agnis? The novel ends with a heterosexual partnership and Agnis disappears. Why does the novel refrain from giving details of her future?

Newfoundland is by no means an innocent place to recover Quoyle's family lineage. Nutbeem comments that, '"I'm going to remember this place for many things"', and he adds '"Most of all for the inventive violence"' (247). But there is a contrast between the violence of Newfoundland and the violence of the Los Angeles riots in chapter 36, in which 'the whole country got infected with some rage virus' (290). This violent outbreak in L.A., described as 'a fucking miserable crazy place' by Partridge, is the consequence merely of a newspaper's decision not to print a letter in its letters page, and involves the death of six people with a machine gun. The violence of Newfoundland is particularly amenable to Proulx's macabre sense of humour, 'Filthy Old Dad Rapes Children's Horse' (270), and there seems to be something redemptive about even that, which is a function of her macabre wit. This kind of violence facilitates creative writing, and therefore renewal. This view of social violence is associated with Jack's belief in the two alternative ways of living in Newfoundland:

There's the old way, look out for your family, die where you was born, fish, cut your wood, keep a garden, make do with what you got. Then there's the new way. Work out, have a job, somebody tell you what to do, commute, your brother's in South Africa, your mother's in Regina, buy every goddamn cockadoodle piece of Japanese crap you can. Leave home. (285–6)

This is the social agenda of *The Shipping News*, not a nostalgia for an idyllic past that was in fact brutal and impoverished, but a desire for organic connectedness with family and place. This is how Billy expresses it: 'it was a satisfying life in a way people today do not understand. There was a joinery of lives all worked together, smooth in places, or lumpy, but joined. The work and the living you did was the same things, not separated out like today' (169).

Another aspect of the novel's exploration of family is provided by aunt Agnis, who, in her relationship with Irene Warren, posits an unconventional alternative 'family' lifestyle which she repeats at the end of the novel with Mavis Bangs. Agnis has returned to Newfoundland in memory of Irene, her 'significant other' (123), and her talent for sewing is analogous to the knots of the novel's chapter headings which bind people together. This analogy makes Agnis the author of the novel, with its reliance for authoritative epigraphs on *The Ashley Book of Knots*. Like Quoyle, Agnis has a dark family legacy to come to terms with: she was routinely abused by her brother when she was a child. Agnis remembers her brother's violent attacks (135, 225–6) and has kept them a secret from everyone. Some readers might argue that the novel encourages the view that lesbianism is a function of childhood sexual abuse. Furthermore, the abbreviated ways in which the attacks on her are dramatized suggest that Agnis has merely repressed the pain of the past and, unlike Quoyle, not come to terms with it. Agnis returns to the scene of the crime too late, having already internalized (perhaps as her generation did) the guilt and pain of suffering, and having become a hardened (in some ways stereotypically male) character. In this reading, Agnis is distinguished from Quoyle because she could 'get over the loss of a cheating mate' (92), and she has survived in a different way: 'Well, that life had hardened her, she had made her own way along the rough coasts, had patched and mended her sails, replaced chafed gear with strong, fit stuff. She had worked her way off the rocks and shoals. Had managed. Still managed' (226). The language of repair, of 'management', and of servicing the craft that bears one along, might suggest that Agnis's role is merely to facilitate Quoyle's path to self-assurance, and that she passes out of the novel at the point where Quoyle begins to discover the mastery of his own vessel. But there is another way to read Agnis. Agnis and Quoyle have both been profoundly damaged by the same person: her brother, his father. But by saving Quoyle, Agnis saves herself; Agnis deals with the pain associated with her brother by showing compassion and enabling a better life for Guy Quoyle's son. In this way Agnis's relationship with Quoyle junior is the redemptive element of her narrative, conquering the demons of her past while facilitating a better future for that demon's son. In this reading, Agnis's narrative is not about repression or internalization, but about creating something positive from her own mode of coming to terms with childhood sexual abuse.

Quoyle however, finds out about Agnis's history from cousin Nolan in a lucid moment; Nolan remembers the child which Agnis came to his wife to abort: ' "It was 'er brother done it y'see, that clumsy big Guy Quoyle. Was at 'er from when she was a little maid" ' (297). Guy Quoyle is, of course, Quoyle's father; the knots of family rope from which he is constituted draw in around him such that 'He seemed to be treading a spiral, circling in tighter and tighter' (232). It is precisely such a coil of rope, the slingstone line of a lobster trap (329), which drowns Jack Buggit in the novel's final chapter, because 'it was tangled kind of crazy'. But Jack is miraculously resurrected at his wake, and so is Quoyle by his marriage to Wavey Prowse. Here again a new model of family life is put forward by the novel, Quoyle and Wavey taking on each other's children by previous marriages and the novel ending in a moment of epiphany expressive of the resuscitation of Jack Buggit and the revival of love for Quoyle. The row of shining hubcaps surrounding the Quoyles' new home reminds the reader that his first wife died in a car crash; yet in this context the hubcaps are transformed into something beautiful, miraculous and celebratory. The novel's final chapter is called 'Shining Hubcaps' and it exemplifies succinctly Proulx's dark comedy of redemption by appearing to make a joke of the motor car's significance to Quoyle's married life. The chapter's epigraph is particularly significant too: ' "There are still old knots that are unrecorded, and so long as there are new purposes for rope, there will always be new knots to discover" ' (324). Such new knots are a metaphor for the new family ties of Quoyle and Wavey and their newly-constituted family.

It is not just renewal for Quoyle, but crucially, for Wavey too, and the convergence of their histories is vital to their relationship. Like Quoyle, Wavey suffered the torments of an unfaithful partner. Her husband Herold, Quoyle is told, 'sprinkled his bastards up and down the coast' (304), and in a scene which is vital to the understanding of their relationship, Quoyle and Wavey share the secrets of their painful histories: Quoyle tells Wavey that Petal 'liked other men . . . A lot' (307), and Wavey confesses to the anguish of her marriage too, telling Quoyle that Herold was a womanizer: ' "He treated me body like a trough. Come and swill and slobber in me after them. I felt like he was casting vomit in me when he come to his climax. And I never told that but to you" ' (307–8). It is in sharing this history that they begin to conquer it, and it is by including the specific and ugly details of their painful marriages that the novel sidesteps sentimentality and mawkishness in its happy and cathartic conclusion. The precision of the details of their relationship make it convincingly emotional rather than sentimental (this is true of the whole novel), and their night together in St John is a good example of this, Wavey remembering suddenly and unexpectedly that the hotel where she sleeps with Quoyle is the same place she came with Herold on their honeymoon (298). In this way they overcome the trauma of the past by sharing it, and by telling it.

Jay McInerney **Bright Lights, Big City**

Childhood trauma and adult recovery are also central to Jay McInerney's *Bright Lights, Big City* (1984), a work of social satire which depicts the hedonistic pursuit of pleasure among the yuppie denizens of the club scene whose mission in life is 'to have more fun than anyone else in New York City' (2).[12] The central protagonist's participation in a

---

12 All page references are to the Vintage Contemporaries edition.

party life of excess and indulgence in a social milieu full of glamour and excitement where people 'thought an invitation to X's birthday bash at Magique was an accomplishment equal to swimming the English channel' (74) is brilliantly deflated by McInerney's sharp satirical eye. The recreational utility of drink, drugs, and casual sex is employed to maximum effect in the quest for mindless enjoyment in the hope that 'with practice you will eventually get the knack of enjoying superficial encounters' (52). It is a world of Bolivian Marching Powder, models with cheekbones 'to die for', Wall Street high rollers, friends of the New York literati, and 'Latin types with long knives and short tempers' (117). The style of the novel is pointed and acerbic, its irony used to expose the banality of a profoundly alienated lifestyle where despite the intensity of social activity 'you feel like the only man in the city without group affiliation' (57). Why is the novel's narrator here, and why does he commit himself to this lifestyle despite his apparent distance from it?

Bright Lights, Big City is structured upon a careful strategy of revealing the depth of the protagonist's despair and its origins in family disorder; his wife has left him, 'shed me with a collect call from Paris' (140), and his mind is gripped by fantasies of 'tender reconciliation' (82) which stem from a desperate need for sincere emotional contact with the woman who deserted him. His need for Amanda takes increasingly desperate forms of expression, and too embarrassed to admit to his brother or father that his wife has abandoned him, he finds himself lonely and anguished: 'The stereo is a special model that plays only music fraught with poignant association' (37). The protagonist's marriage was partly an attempt to rescue Amanda from 'a childhood grimmer than most' (71) in which her father left home when she was 6, her mother remarried, and her stepfather 'was either abusive or amorous to both mother and daughter' (71). She left home at 16, 'There was no bride's side at the church' when she married, and the protagonist's mother 'greeted Amanda as if she were a refugee' (72). This fractured and disorientating childhood is one which Amanda shares with the protagonist, who moved around often as a child while his father was 'in between corporate postings' (151) and who lacked a stable childhood because 'Your father's annual job transfers made you the perennial new kid' (47). In Amanda's childhood deracination the novel's protagonist recognizes something of the

displacement of his own: 'The primal scene is not the encounter of
parents in coitus: it takes the shape of a ring of schoolchildren, like
Indians surrounding a wagon train, laughing with malice, pointing
their vicious little fingers to insist upon your otherness' (47). This
painful sense of otherness is something the protagonist seeks to overcome with frenetic social activity and which he had hoped to alleviate
entirely by marrying, especially because he recognized an important
affinity with his wife, 'Amanda's need to belong was part of her attraction' (72). But there is also a crucial social dimension to their relationship, because while he believes that Amanda as a midwesterner holds
the key to some idea of the wholesomeness of 'American virtue', she
regards him as the embodiment of New England tradition and status
and uses him as 'her ticket out of Trailer Park Land' (116). In fact, the
protagonist's family is moribund and redundant and provides no sustaining culture for him to draw on in a time of crisis such as domestic
separation; his colleagues at work are characterized as being 'like a
cold impenetrable New England family which keeps even the black
sheep suffocating within the fold' (15). The most revealing observation about the protagonist's family lineage is succinctly provided by
the drug-dealer Bernie: ' "You got Ivy League written all over you. But I
could buy you and your old man and his country club. I use guys
like you in your button-down shirts to fetch my coffee" ' (116–17). The
family's heritage is worthless in the face of competition from modern
American commercial enterprise such as Bernie's.

The social satire of *Bright Lights, Big City* is more than skin deep, and
it places the disintegration of the family in a broader context, one of
cultural degeneracy and decline. The protagonist, for example, has a
voracious addiction to the *New York Post:* 'Killer Bees, Hero Cops, Sex
Fiends, Lottery Winners, Teenage Terrorists, Liz Taylor, Tough Tots,
Sicko Creeps, Living Nightmares, Life on Other Planets, Spontaneous
Human Combustion, Miracle Diets and Coma Babies' (11). This
voyeuristic delight at the lurid aberrations of late twentieth-century
urban society is symptomatic of the emotional emptiness of the protagonist's life. Here there is a strongly moral agenda to McInerney's
satire which suggests a connection between the disordered individual
and his degenerate society. The archivist at the magazine for which
the novel's protagonist works as 'a willing emissary from the land of
pedantry' (23) is able to locate for him the very first appearance, in

1976, of a four-letter word; she laments falling standards and warns that ' "The dam is crumbling" ' (81). The touching innocence of the archivist (with her enthusiasm for the Hollywood comedies of the 1930s and 1940s) is not treated with irony; she cannot repeat the obscenity that a child used to her on her way to work that morning because it was 'unbelievable', but the protagonist's jaded palate is immune to shock: 'You know all about unbelievable; you don't even think about it' (82). Here as elsewhere in the novel, women stand at the floodgates of moral collapse, and family is the touchstone by which redemption might be possible.

Two women exemplify this potential: Vicky who enjoyed a 'child-hood Arcadia' (94) until her parents divorced, but who still hopes to live in 'the kind of house someday where a carousel horse wouldn't be out of place in the living room' (94), and Megan whose 13-year-old son lives with his father and 'a wonderful stepmother' in northern Michi-gan, 'a good place for a boy to grow up' (138). It is Megan who rescues the protagonist in a practical sense, and Vicky who rescues him emotionally by hearing the confession of the secret of his mother's death. While he is discarded by his wife, the protagonist is redeemed by the agency of two sincere and authentic good women who see beyond the empty surfaces of his social behaviour and offer the possibility of genuine emotional contact and generosity. As the novel characteristically expresses it, 'Coma Baby Lives'.

Bright Lights, Big City capitalizes on the reader's early laughter by revealing at the end that the source of the protagonist's neurosis is the circumstances of his mother's death from cancer. Here again the young man's relationship with a woman is crucial, determining his attitude to all of the women in his life and encouraging him to regard them as agents of redemption. The protagonist was profoundly trau-matized by the special moments of emotional intimacy and honesty that he shared with his mother at the point of her death, and the compulsive nature of his shallow hedonism is revealed in the pen-ultimate chapter as a form of grief. This revelation of the son's response to the loss of his mother is made to the protagonist's brother, following a cathartic punch-up, and here some remnant of family unity is restored: ' "You should have told us," Michael says, sprawled out on the couch in your apartment. "I mean, what's a family for?" He bangs his head on the coffee table for emphasis. "What's family for?"

"I don't know" ' (163). The meeting of the brothers and the sharing of the grief for their mother again affirms the importance of family in assuaging emotional pain. The revelation of the trauma of his mother's loss is also the origin of the novel's unique stylistic device of using 'you' as the appellation of its unnamed narrator: 'The candour was infectious. It spread back to the beginning of your life. You tried to tell her, as well as you could, what it was like being you. You described the feeling you'd always had of being misplaced, of always standing to one side of yourself, of watching yourself in the world even as you were being in the world, and wondering if this was how everyone felt' (166-7). The central formal device of the novel goes back to this special shared moment with the narrator's mother, and beyond that 'to the beginning of your life' where the absence of a father and the loss of the mother forces a rupture in the protagonist's consciousness that fundamentally shapes his subjectivity. *Bright Lights, Big City* is a novel with a strong moral agenda about the need for stable parental relationships.

The rebirth of the protagonist at the end of the novel is a witty psychological parallel to the story of the coma baby that he has been following in the *Post*. In the final chapter there are two other important textual allusions, to *The Great Gatsby* ('the wooden shoes of the first Dutch settlers on these same stones') and to Raymond Carver, whose story 'A Small, Good Thing' is invoked when McInerney's protagonist breaks the freshly baked bread at dawn and recognizes he will 'have to learn everything all over again' (182). There is one other important textual allusion in *Bright Lights, Big City*, that of the novel's epigraph from Hemingway's *The Sun Also Rises* in which Mike, asked how he went bankrupt replies ' "Gradually and then suddenly" '. Hemingway's novel is also one in which drunken oblivion is a male response to that which cannot be broached emotionally, and the word 'bankrupt' is appropriate to characterize McInerney's protagonist's emotional and financial status. It is perhaps surprising that McInerney consistently traces this corruption back to family relationships, especially using the clinically dispassionate 'you' instead of a name for his protagonist; this is suggestive of a social or psychological type rather than an individual, perhaps the yuppies of mid-1980s America with whom the novel was so popular. Where Hemingway's lost generation suffered the aftermath of war, McInerney's protagonist is emotionally bereft amid an alienating modern American culture in which superficial appearances have replaced sound family bonds: 'Where skin deep is the mode, your traditional domestic values are not going to take root and flourish' (116). By the end of *Bright Lights, Big City* humour turns to pathos (narrowly avoiding sentimentality) and the novel's adroit social satire gives way to a longing for secure family relationships and emotional honesty. A minor character from McInerney's novel uses the expression 'story of my life' (154) and in the 1988 novel which is called *Story of My Life* this young woman acquires a name, Alison Poole, and recounts her own tale of night-club decadence and family dysfunction far worse than that of McInerney's male protagonist. *Playboy* called *Bright Lights, Big City* 'a *Catcher in the Rye* for the M.B.A. set', and this nicely catches both its adolescent milieu and its concern for individuals who are at odds with their families. One critic has pursued the correspondence closely: 'both titles come from songs—*Catcher in the Rye* from the children's nursery rhyme and *Bright Lights* from a Jimmy Reed blues ballad; both plots involve the narrator's inability to grieve for the death of a family member; and both novels owe their commercial success to popular misreadings'.[13] That *Catcher in the Rye* was the literary forebear to *Bright Lights, Big City* was clearly not lost on McInerney, who once said in an interview that a consequence of naming his protagonist 'you' was that 'he'll never become a household word like Salinger's Holden Caulfield'.[14]

Barbara Kingsolver **The Bean Trees**

Barbara Kingsolver's *The Bean Trees* (1988) is a novel which challenges traditional ideas of family based on blood relationships and suggests alternative kinds of affinity between apparently disparate individuals.[15] This novel is a journey narrative in which a young woman

---

[13] Stephanie Girard, 'Standing at the Corner of Walk and Don't Walk: Vintage Contemporaries, *Bright Lights, Big City*, and the Problems of Betweenness', *American Literature*, 68: 1 (Mar. 1996), 172.

[14] S. Pinsker, 'Soft Lights, Academic Talk: A Conversation with Jay McInerney', *Literary Review*, 30 (Fall 1986), 112.

[15] Page references are to the Harper Perennial edition.

from Kentucky leaves home to drive west to Arizona and is presented on the way with an Indian baby girl who has been abused on a reservation in Oklahoma. At the same time the novel presents the story of another Kentucky woman Lu Ann arriving in Arizona with her Hispanic husband, who has recently abandoned her for the rodeo circuit in Montana, and their son Dwayne Ray. In chapter 5 Taylor's car breaks down in Tucson and the two women meet and immediately take to each other as fellow southerners. This then is the novel's first reconstituted family, the two single women with their Hispanic and native American children living together as a family unit of displaced Kentucky folk in Arizona. But while Taylor and Lu Ann are bonded as single mothers and as southerners, this version of family is also challenged: 'We were like some family on a tv commercial, with names like Myrtle and Fred. I could just hear us striking up a conversation about air freshners' (85). The stereotype that Taylor is anxious to avoid ('We're acting like Blondie and Dagwood here') is one which comes from their respective functions of breadwinner and homemaker and is therefore no improvement on the traditional family structure which has ill-served them both: 'It's not like we're a *family*, for Christ's sake. . . . I never even *had* an old man, why would I want to end up acting like one?' (85). The two women find themselves falling into the cultural cliche of a family where in fact new ideas of what constitutes family in the first place need to be formulated and experimented with. *The Bean Trees* is dedicated to imagining these new structures and testing their value for the individuals involved in them.

One such structure, involving the Hispanic couple Estevan and Esperanza, goes right to the heart of the social and political constitution of the United States and draws upon America's history of accepting immigrant peoples to posit an alternative vision of family. Estevan and Esperanza have fled Guatemala following political persecution in which their daughter was taken as a hostage in exchange for the lives of seventeen colleagues. Esperanza, whose memories of the torture she suffered occasion several suicide attempts, recognizes in Taylor's adopted Indian baby the image of her lost daughter. The central narrative of *The Bean Trees* therefore involves many different ideas of family at once: Estevan and Esperanza escape the authorities in Arizona when Taylor drives them to Oklahoma where they impersonate the Indian baby's parents in order that Taylor might legally adopt her. This is made possible largely because the child is a Cherokee and Esperanza is a South American Indian, so the family resemblance between ethnic peoples is exploited to remedy the motherlessness of the little girl. During the road trip to Oklahoma (symbolically finding the right route by a sign to 'The Pioneer Woman Museum') Estevan explains that deracination and displacement from home is a more complex affair than Taylor's move from Kentucky to Arizona: ' "I don't even know anymore which home I miss. . . . In Guatemala City I missed the mountains. My own language is not Spanish. . . . We are Mayan people; we speak twenty-two different Mayan languages. Esperanza and I speak to each other in Spanish because we come from different parts of the highlands. . . . Mayans lived here in the so-called New World before the Europeans dis- covered it. . . . Our true first names are Indian names. . . . We chose Spanish names when we moved to the city" ' (193). Estevan's multi- cultural historical perspective aligns him with the native American Indians of the United States who were killed by colonizing Europeans, and many of whom died coming to Oklahoma on the Trail of Tears when they were forcibly removed from Florida. One such Cherokee was Taylor's grandfather. The similarity in their family heritage is emphasized here in their respective name changes; Taylor's real name is Marietta, after the town in Georgia where her parents' car broke down and she was conceived: 'I was a mistake'. Taylor marvels at the cultural changes Estevan has had to accommodate, and at 'how lan- guages could accumulate in a family' (194). It is appropriate that their journey ends on the land of the Cherokee nation in Oklahoma where Estevan and Esperanza 'were transformed in an inexplicable way' (204).

Transformations in family structures are central to *The Bean Trees*, because it is a narrative which insists that culture and community are more important in shaping the individual than immediate family. Taylor's mother puts this explicitly: ' "I don't think blood's the only way kids come by things honest. Not even the main way" ' (223). Although much of the novel is devoted to the pressures of maternal responsibility (in an environment where most men are shown to be inadequate to the task) it also argues that people have a responsibility to each other, and in the United States it is one which extends beyond national borders. Taylor argues that it is nonsense to designate someone as 'illegal' because it is anti-humanitarian and in a sense un-American. All people need a community which accepts and values them, but she argues, especially persecuted people, and America was founded on the welcome it extended to families who wanted to begin life again as part of a new multicultural nation. At the end of *The Bean Trees* Taylor finds herself remembering 'the poem on the Statue of Liberty that started out, "Give me your tired, your poor"' (224) and she laments the degree to which recent American history has fallen away from this ideal. Estevan tells her the story of the choice his wife was forced to make in Guatemala between the life of her daughter and the lives of seventeen friends, and although it seems shocking and distant, he quietly informs her: 'You live in that world' (137). The traditional ideas of blood family that Taylor brought from her southern background are inadequate to meet the demands of modern American culture and contemporary political pressures.

John Dufresne **Louisiana Power & Light**

John Dufresne's *Louisiana Power & Light* (1994) is also a distinctively southern depiction of the trials and tribulations of family heritage, but one which (significantly) never leaves the strict parameters of its location in Monroe, Louisiana.[16] The South in this novel is immediately recognizable as a world of mint green leisure suits, moccasin snakes, barbecued pork sandwiches, tractor pulls and carp-fishing tournaments, Tony Lama snakeskin cowboy boots, 'heat so intense it was like being hit on the head with a shovel' (29), redheaded vultures, spaceship abductions and cockroach infestations, biscuits and gravy, canebrakes and 'Bubba', crawfish, 'a rendezvous in the dirt lot of a windowless juke joint' (175), and chapter titles such as 'I Have Begotten a Strange Son, Diverse from and Unlike Man'. These stereotypically southern characteristics are extraordinarily exaggerated in Dufresne's novel, such that there is a knowing appeal to the reader's familiarity with the ludicrous hyperbole of southern fictions. This heightened fictional quality extends to the depiction of family in the novel because into this culture is born Billy Wayne Fontana, one of a

---

16 Page references are to the Plume/Penguin edition.

long line of Louisiana Fontanas, 'the most executed white family in the history of Louisiana' (12), who must come to terms with his family lineage and struggle to find independence from its terrible legacy: 'The fact is that the Fontana family has a celebrated history of catastrophe' (10). Billy Wayne's antecedents include Peregrine Fontana, who 'sloshed his way out of the spongy gumbo of the Delta . . . who stunk like marsh gas, had webbed fingers, and caused a panic among the women and children of Talla Bena when he appeared on Main Street in nothing but alligator-hide drawers' (10). Other forebears include Tennis Fontana who claimed to be Emma Bovary and received messages from God through his teeth; Mendel Fontana who won the Miss Monroe Beauty Pageant, even though he was a man; Aubrey Fontana, who died when he 'got stabbed up the nostril with the aerial off a taxi cab' (211); Aeneas Fontana, 'a boy so dumb he wouldn't know enough to pour piss out of his boot with directions on the heel' (212–13) and whose breath was so bad it 'could knock a buzzard off a shit wagon' (213). Billy Wayne is the last surviving Fontana and it is his fate to wrestle with the legacy of this family history and to wonder if he can ever be free of his 'familial penchant for ruination' (210). Such is the history of the Fontanas that for generations all of the offspring have been male: 'God's only way of keeping the Fontana family from committing the abominable sin of incest' (11). The style of the novel begs the question, to what extent is this account of family history the demented and brilliant product of an imagination that is full of the mythology of southern family to the point of glutinous saturation?

In *Louisiana Power & Light* all of the characters are defined by their family lineage. Billy Wayne's first wife Earlene has a cousin who robbed a gas station in Ozona, Texas, and set the attendant on fire after soaking him in petrol. She believes that Billy Wayne has rescued her 'from a life of squalor and grime, from a future as bleak as her past' (38). Billy Wayne's second wife Tami Lynne, from Oklahoma, has a father who is welding pipes somewhere in Alaska and a mother in a sanatorium in Georgia who 'makes her living faking injuries and illnesses and collecting disability checks' (143). Even George Binwaddie from Pakistan has come to America to 'restore the family to the prominence it had enjoyed under the viceroys' (31) and he suffers in the knowledge that he has disgraced most grievously his ancestors, 'the progenitors of the magnificent family' (32). It is George who informs

Billy Wayne prophetically ' "A family can be a terrible thing" ' (33), and George ultimately commits suicide rather than live with the disgrace and failure that he has brought to his family's name: ' "My family must know by now that I've failed them" ' (95). The southern culture of *Louisiana Power & Light* exerts a particular pressure on its characters to conform to the legacy of their family, and in this novel it is impossible to escape the family narrative, even if that narrative is apocryphal, mythological, or more likely an outrageous fiction. The historical precedent of family is deterministic, and the historical veracity of the family narrative is not as important as Billy Wayne's oppressive sense of that narrative's pervasive acceptance in the Monroe community where he lives and the oppressive feeling of inevitability that Fontana stories burden him with. Like a grotesque southern Quoyle, Billy is constantly reminded by his southern environment that 'some sorry waters have washed over your kin' (84). Billy Wayne is thus defined by his relationship with the past, and like all good southerners he unwittingly affirms its legacy even while striving to repudiate it.

Billy Wayne's narrative dramatizes his struggle for self-determination in a southern culture that would determine his fate in terms of his family, irrespective of his free will, and the prevalence of superstitions and portents becomes an integral part of his uniquely southern predicament, especially in the context of his Catholic upbringing. It is not the purpose of *Louisiana Power & Light* to resolve these questions, but to combine them in a fresh narrative which can take its place in the tradition that it affectionately parodies. The 'Prologue' establishes the novel as an oral account from a front porch, 'you hear these voices', and it places itself within a southern tradition of vernacular storytelling. The fertility of southern families ('like frogs in a slough', (20)) is analogous to the fertility of stories about them, and the fecundity of the southern imagination that creates remarkable and inventive mythologies of family history is a central subject of the text. The elaboration of these apocryphal family narratives is part of Billy Wayne's problem, a southern storytelling habit which is shown to inhibit and oppress southerners with a fated sense of their inevitable failure and defeat. The proliferation of narratives of family decline thus becomes part of the special character of the South, and this culture reflects back on the novel's characters in a way which serves only to debilitate them further and so perpetuate a southern mythology of defeat. The narrative which is *Louisiana Power & Light* is of course a significant contribution to precisely such a tradition, and the novel self-consciously acknowledges this at many points and jokes self-reflexively about its own rhetorical strategies. The idea of family in Dufresne's novel extends to the family of stories and mythologies from which the novel is generated, and the textual progenitors of narrative from which *Louisiana Power & Light* is derived are as much the parents of Billy Wayne as the infamous line of Fontanas who precede him. The 'father' that Dufresne's novel chooses to 'rehash' is thus the spectre of its textual authorities.

2

Gender and History

I have done this thing,
I and the other women this exceptional
act with the exceptional heroic body,
this giving birth, this glistening verb,
and I am putting my proud American boast
right here with the others.

Sharon Olds, 'The Language of the Brag'

Hayden White's *Metahistory* (1973) was an important work of historiography, a book that revealed the ways in which any understanding of history is powerfully conditioned (even determined) by the linguistic form that it takes. This occurs because historical narratives are structured in terms of the devices of language, tropes or 'protocols', that are anterior to historical consciousness. For White, the historian's methodology is always crucially anticipated by the structures of language in ways that strongly influence the perspective on any history that claims to have been arrived at independently, naturally or dispassionately. The shapes of historical narrative cannot be innocent, but work in the service of power, and that power exists prior to historical consciousness. The ideas of *Metahistory* have been taken up by works such as Dominick La Capra's *Rethinking Intellectual History* (1983) and Hans Kellner's *Language and Historical Representation* (1989) and the value of these ideas to feminism has also been recognized: history has traditionally been written by men and about men. If the representation of history privileges certain kinds of experience and is predicated on a particular language, then is that not a male experience and a male language? Feminist historiography might be said to have two intellectual projects. The first of these is to recover the occluded narratives of women, perspectives that have been ignored, neglected, or suppressed. This aspect of women's history is dedicated to the retrieval of the lost or unarticulated stories of women in specific social and cultural contexts, studies that reveal the contribution of women in areas of social life that were traditionally thought of as the exclusive province of men. In an article called 'Placing Women in History', for example, Gerder Lerner argued that women's 'culturally determined and psychologically internalized marginality seems to be what makes their historical experience essentially different from that of men. But men have defined their experience as history and left women out'.[1] Beyond this thesis, it has also been argued that women conceive of history in a fundamentally different way from men. Clearly history does not exist in some ontological sense but is discursively constituted from a particular position or viewpoint. Is it the case then that women think of history intellectually and experience it materially in ways that are fundamentally different from men, and is such a difference exclusively a function of gender difference? In other words, what part does gender play in the very conception of historical consciousness that society endorses, or, how is gender central to the formation of discursive historical paradigms? In 'Resisting Amnesia' Adrienne Rich argued that 'Feminist history is not history about women only; it looks afresh at what men have done and how they have behaved, not only toward women but toward each other and the natural world. But the central perspective and preoccupation *is female*, and this implies a vast shift in values and priorities'.[2]

American women's fiction has its own history of investigating these issues, a history that includes Harriet Beecher Stowe's *Uncle Tom's Cabin* (1850), Charlotte Perkins Gilman's *The Yellow Wallpaper* (1892), Kate Chopin's *The Awakening* (1899), and Zora Neale Hurston's *Their Eyes Were Watching God* (1937). Jane Tompkins has argued that the exclusion of *Uncle Tom's Cabin* from Sacvan Bercovitch's scholarly study *The American Jeremiad* 'is a striking instance of how totally academic criticism has foreclosed on sentimental fiction; for, because

---

[1] G. Lerner, *The Majority Finds its Past: Placing Women in History* (Oxford: Oxford University Press, 1979), 158.

[2] A. Rich, *Blood, Bread and Poetry: Selected Prose 1979–85* (London: Virago, 1986), 146–7. 'Resisting Amnesia' was originally published in 1983.

Uncle Tom's Cabin is absent from the canon, it isn't "there" to be referred to even when it fulfils a man's theory to perfection. Hence its exclusion from critical discourse is perpetuated automatically, and absence begets itself in a self-confirming cycle of neglect'.[3] It is significant that this debate about the canon should focus on a novel about slavery because the concept of women's history in the United States is crucially affected by the issue of race. Afro-American history was originally conceived of as male (Richard Wright, James Baldwin, Ralph Ellison) and so the perspectives of black women were doubly occluded. The publishing history of Hurston's novel is itself an important part of this story. *Their Eyes Were Watching God* was strongly criticized in 1937 for its racial politics, especially by Alain Locke and Richard Wright, and it was not therefore widely known until the 1970s when Robert Hemenway's biography of Hurston was published (1977), the novel was reprinted (1978), and Alice Walker produced a Hurston 'Reader' (1979). These events have established Hurston's novel as a canonical text, and they coincided with the remarkable burgeoning of black women's fiction that took place in the 1970s in the novels of Morrison, Walker, Toni Cade Bambara, and Audre Lorde. Janie Crawford's oral narrative of a struggle towards self-fulfilment in a society that is both sexist and racist is told in a black vernacular to a female auditor, Phoebe, who learns that 'De nigger woman is de mule uh de world', and who discovers through Janie's example the possibility of a different future for herself and for other black women. It is that idea of an alternative history and a different future that the novels of this chapter investigate.

Bobbie Ann Mason **In Country**

Bobbie Ann Mason's *In Country* (1985) is a novel about a 17-year-old called Samantha Hughes who lives in western Kentucky.[4] Sam's father died in Vietnam and she now lives with her uncle Emmett, since Sam's mother has remarried and moved away to Lexington. The novel

---

3 J. Tompkins, 'Sentimental Power: *Uncle Tom's Cabin* and the Politics of Literary History', in H. A. Veeser (ed.), *The New Historicism: A Reader* (New York: Routledge, 1994), 219.

4 All page references are to the Flamingo edition.

is both journey narrative and *Bildungsroman*, about Sam growing up and learning what happened to her father; it is a novel about recovering the past, and understanding the nature of what history is by assessing the status of a variety of discourses which compete for textual authority. Sam's journey towards maturity is one in which a meaningful future is recuperated from a lost past, and it is also a journey from the margins of American culture to the centre of national public life as represented by the Vietnam War Memorial in Washington, DC. The education of Sam principally involves her interpretation of texts about history and her understanding of a relationship between historical knowledge and empowerment. *In Country* is an investigation of the status of history as a kind of fiction, a story about the past in which Sam is trying to recover the lost narrative of her father through the agency of various and multiple mediating texts; the novel is packed full of references to the possible duplicity of textuality and forms of textual representation, and yet Sam must come to terms with the vicissitudes of interpretation if she is to recover something of value to herself. Part I of the novel includes references to a Chevy Chase movie about a family on vacation, George Orwell's *Nineteen Eighty Four*, Bruce Springsteen's 'Born in the U.S.A.', the story about the boy who died, of which Sam's grandmother says 'That was such a sweet story I couldn't get it out of my mind' (14), and the Johnny Carson show in which Joan Rivers is standing in for Carson, much to Sam's dismay; she has seen this show before, so it is doubly bogus, and Emmett comments significantly of this mode of duplication, 'it's a re-run. Nothing's authentic anymore' (19). This is a crucial observation about the simulations of American culture, and it is one which Sam's search for historical truth must challenge if she is not to be overwhelmed by the swamp of texts that contemporary American culture purveys to her. *In Country* is aetiological in its attempt to retrieve Sam's father from the swamp of textual representation. In a comment on Andrew Cawood during her simulation of being 'in country', Sam thinks, 'Her father was dead, and no one cared. That outlaw was dissolved in the swamp' (216). This comment synthesizes Andrew Cawood and Sam's father both in terms of their bodies and the bodies of historical and mythological knowledge about them. In this respect (and others) *In Country* owes a debt to Margaret Atwood's novel *Surfacing* (1972) in which a young woman goes in search of the body of her lost father and finds it in a swamp.

There are several important history texts which inform Sam's education. The Springsteen song 'Born in the U.S.A.' provides the novel with its epigraph:

> I'm ten years burning down the road
> Nowhere to run ain't got nowhere to go.

This is a song about a Vietnam veteran which has some relevance to Emmett's predicament, as Sam seems partially aware: 'In the song his brother gets killed over there, and then the guy gets in a lot of trouble when he gets back home' (42). The significance of history here is multiple, partly due to the continuing legacy of Vietnam in contemporary (popular) culture, and partly in the importance of 'ten years', because as Emmett observes of Hopewell, Kentucky, 'Everything is always ten years behind here' (59), but also because Sam finds herself, in 1984, ten years beyond the end of the war, and her consciousness of coming 'after history' is part of her contemporary condition: 'I was born too late', she says, lamenting the passing of the 1960s (234–5). It is worth noting too that Sam takes the Springsteen album with her to the Vietnam Memorial in Washington, a further reminder of its importance, and that when she buys it she finds that 'On the cover Bruce Springsteen is facing the flag, as though studying it, trying to figure out its meaning' (236). There is also an association between Sam and Springsteen in their androgyny: Sam's jogging gives her the body of a young man (as well as the name of one), and it has been argued that Springsteen's stage persona too relies on an androgynous malleability.[5] In terms of musical culture, The Beatles are also important to Sam's hermeneutic skill, and she describes one of their songs as 'a fresh message from the past, something to go on' (125). Popular music culture then is an important text in Sam's attempts to read history, but it is a text that can prove duplicitous and difficult to read.

Sam's high school history teacher Mr Harris succinctly defines the parameters of Sam's historical moment: ' "The biggies in your lifetime were the moon landing, the assassinations, Vietnam and Watergate".

---

[5] A. DeCurtis (ed.), *Present Tense: Rock & Roll and Culture* (Durham, NC: Duke University Press, 1992).

Mr Harris said everything was downhill after Kennedy was killed' (66–7). Mr Harris identifies the postmodern generation for whom critical interpretation of history or definitive historical knowledge is especially problematical. It is notable that reading real history texts is for Sam completely fruitless; she undertakes some serious historical research 'about how the United States got involved. All the names ran together. Ngo Dinh Diem. Bao Dai. Dien Bien Phu. Ho Chi Minh. She got bogged down in manifestos and State Department documents' (55). The language here, 'bogged down', recalls the swamp of textual history which has claimed both Andrew Cawood and her father. This particular kind of historical account remains for Sam indecipherable and opaque. Tom asks her what she has learned from history books and Sam replies, 'Nothing. . . . The books didn't say what it was like to be at war over there. The books didn't even have pictures' (48).

Another important text for Mason's novel is the television show 'M*A*S*H' which Sam and Emmett watch together obsessively, sometimes twice a day, even though Sam knows that it is actually about the war in Korea, and even though she understands its status as fiction: 'On tv people always had the words to express their feelings [because] on tv, they had script writers' (45). Sam also recognizes the television show's tendency to reduce the complexities of history ('On M*A*S*H sometimes, things were too simple', (83)), but nevertheless it is necessarily a constitutive part of Sam's knowledge even while she attempts to maintain a critical distance from its fictionality, and this point is made clearly in the novel. It is worth noting too that the television show was made in the 1970s following the success of the original film by Robert Altman, a film which was also set in Korea but which was understood by contemporary audiences to be about the war in Vietnam. This is also true of the television show, which late twentieth-century audiences still often assume to be about Vietnam. This is a good example of the ways in which the interpretation of texts involves a knowledge of their history, and of how investigations of that history give rise to epistemological questions in which the history of knowledge is inseparable from the history of its representation. In this case too, issues of power, politics, and censorship are implicated in the novel's depiction of an American discourse of colonial enterprise, and its impact on a contemporary audience who do not know that history is shown to be confusing and duplicitous.

Sam's knowledge of texts is not restricted to historical records but also concerns her knowledge of herself, and this is especially true of her name: 'Sam used to think Irene named her after an actress named Samantha something. . . . If she couldn't know a simple fact like the source of her name, what could she know for sure?' (53). The knowledge of Sam's name is bound up with an apocryphal story about bullfighting in chapter 5 of Part II, and her name is also a matter of textual transmutation: 'If you married Lonnie, your name would be Sam Malone, like that guy on *Cheers*'. This is characteristic of how Sam's identity is subject to media invasion and of how texts are an integral part of her life. Most importantly, Sam's name (like her author's, Bobbie) is androgynous, as she says to Dawn, ' "Sam's an all-purpose name. It fits boys and girls both" ' (82). It is this androgyny which permits Sam to read her name on the panel of the Memorial and which also facilitates a reference to Uncle Sam, a common personification of the US government and a derogatory nickname for federal authority. This national father figure is a parallel to her father Dwayne, as if in seeking him she is also seeking something valuable about America. Here, as elsewhere, Sam's predicament is strongly reminiscent of the position of Oedipa Maas, transposed into the 1980s from the 1960s, from Pynchon's *The Crying of Lot 49* (1966), and struggling to establish a sense of identity in the face of the mass media that threatens to reduce her to a mere function of its information. Like Sam, Oedipa is a woman committed to a quest by the death of a father figure (Pierce Inverarity) whose legacy is something important about the whole of America: 'She had dedicated herself, weeks ago, to making sense of what Inverarity had left behind, never suspecting that the legacy was America' (123). The use of the name 'Sam' neatly facilitates an understanding of her predicament that has, simultaneously, gender and nationhood implications.

There are other references to the authority of texts that have an important bearing on the novel's enquiry into the power of representations, and they are connected with ideas of isolation:

She had to write a theme once on what book she'd want to have with her if she were stranded on a desert island. It was a dumb question. . . . Miss Castle had wanted them to choose a Shakespeare play or the Bible, but Sam had perversely chosen the dictionary. Sam thought that going around with your favorite book in case you got stranded on a desert island sounded paranoid. . . . With a dictionary, she could make up any book she wanted to. (143)

The important distinction here is between a single authoritative text which is already written, and a book of words which permits any narrative to be written, a distinction between deference to a canonized work and freedom to create one's own imaginative work. The multiplicity of discourses which the dictionary allows is favoured over the single sacred discourse of the Bible or Shakespeare. The other key word in the quotation is 'paranoid', and it is a word that occurs again in an important scene when Sam goes 'in country' after reading her father's diary: 'It wasn't as though she were running away to New York to be a prostitute in a dope ring. Her English teacher who thought Thoreau's retreat to Walden Pond was such a hot idea would probably approve. If it was in a book, there was something to it. But in Sam's opinion Thoreau was paranoid' (210). Both quotations here are concerned with cultural isolation and make an explicit connection between being outside society and the importance of reading and interpretation. Paranoia, an abnormal tendency to suspect and mistrust others, is a function of western Kentucky's distance from centres of power. The reference to Henry David Thoreau's *Walden* (1854) proposes this tendency as an integral part of an American ideological condition, part of the cultural politics of every American citizen's relationship with national affairs. This is one of a number of textual allusions which, paradoxically, give the authority of literary history to Sam's historical investigations. The novel proposes that it has always been the case that Americans have been encouraged to examine the nature of their relationship to national identity, and that this type of enquiry is characteristically American. Here it is significant that the young girl is seeking to come to terms with a history that is presented as the exclusive province of men, and that her literary education is a male one too; Sam's English teacher does not encourage her to read *The Crying of Lot 49*.

Another kind of historical account from which Sam might have been expected to benefit is the oral testimony of the veterans who have returned to Hopewell: Pete, Tom, and Emmett. But these men are characterized by their unwillingness or inability to discuss their experiences in Vietnam and by their tacit agreement that ' "nobody else could ever know what you went through except guys who have been there"' (78). There is more to this than simply the unwillingness to discuss harrowing experiences; *In Country* presents history as being as much about gender as it is about other forms of power relationship. This is seen most dramatically in Sam's life with Emmett and in Emmett's problems with women: '"It seems to me like some vets I could name are afraid of women." "Women weren't over there", Emmett snapped, "So they can't really understand"' (107). This exclusion of women from the history of war is something that Sam's investigations seek to challenge; there is in the novel a characteristically male tendency to interpose themselves between women and matters of public or national life, and this is not confined to the war: 'When Lorenzo Jones started coming over a couple of years ago he'd talk when we tried to watch television together. He'd talk during the news too and tell us his opinion on world affairs so you couldn't hear the news' (42). When Sam tells this story, Dawn replies pointedly, '"I've got a brother like that".' Part of this is a patronizing attempt to protect women from what men perceive as the ugliness of world affairs, and Tom tells Sam '"You shouldn't think about this stuff too much. . . . You don't want to know how real it was"' (95), and to some extent Sam's mother Irene ('"It had nothing to do with you"', (57), and Anita ('"It *was* the Dark Ages"', (64)) are complicit in this view of history as an exclusively male arena. Emmett used to tell Sam stories about Vietnam when she was a little girl, but Irene 'stopped the stories' (51). Sam discovers however that women were not excluded from the war zone, and she tells Emmett, '"There were women in Vietnam too"' (107). The gender politics of *In Country* is dedicated to finding a way for women to make a valuable intervention in historical discourse, one by which they can find personal fulfilment but also one which is culturally underwritten and historically sanctioned. Like the other novels of this chapter, *In Country* seeks to discover the discourse by which women can write themselves into the dominant male culture.

The gender politics of *In Country* is an especially valuable aspect of its characteristically postmodern interrogation of history and textuality. For part of the novel Emmett is depicted wearing a skirt, perhaps in imitation of the character Klinger in M*A*S*H who hopes to escape the war by 'bucking for a section 8' (27). Emmett confirms the value of dressing as a woman when he argues seriously that 'It's healthier for a man to wear a skirt' (30) and that 'All them Greeks and Romans wore dresses' (31). The suggestion is that to impersonate a woman is safe and beneficial and Emmett's imitation of Klinger is a replication of the desire to escape war. Emmett only abandons the skirt when Anita is invited to dinner (99–100). In a separate but related scene, Dawn fantasizes about acting in a video and suggests to Sam that they pretend to be a band from California: '"We'll call ourselves the Gay Deceivers"' (105). 'Gay Deceivers', Dawn tells Sam, are false breasts, '"It's a real old term. I came across it in an old book of my mother's"' (105). In both of these examples, ideas of cross-dressing or sexual disguise are routes to freedom, and in both cases the authority for such a transformation comes from another text, Klinger and 'an old book'. In this, as in much else in the novel's analysis of textuality, the deferral of authority from one text to another affords the possibility of escape, and modes of personal metamorphosis are textually sanctioned. Textual deferral also, of course, establishes a labyrinth of representations from which the material world seems remote or even excluded; here again Sam's condition recalls that of Oedipa Maas: is their scepticism about all that is representational the sign of a critical and enquiring intelligence, or is it simply paranoia? Can either of them discover a 'reality' or 'truth' that is anterior to its textual mediation?

Gender politics is important in one further respect in the relationship between Sam and Emmett. Although Emmett is Sam's uncle, she adopts the role of surrogate mother towards him (especially in his furtive courtship of Anita) and he often adopts the behaviour of an awkward teenager. This is appropriate because he was a teenager when he was sent to the war and he has hardly developed since; there is a suggestion that his post-war virus might only be acne, and Irene correctly diagnoses Emmett's problem as '"A case of arrested development"' (234). Emmett's particular view of history is relevant here: '"You can't learn from the past. The main thing that you learn from history is that you can't learn from history. That's what history is. . . . There are some things you can never figure out"' (226). This intransigent male perspective is the real cause of Emmett's problems, and Sam's enquiry into history serves to prove him wrong and ultimately to redeem him from his historical aneurism so that he may live again in the present and the future. Sam's female historical curiosity liberates Emmett from historical paralysis and releases him into a new life. Emmett's unwillingness to investigate his medical symptoms is characteristic of his attitude to the past. It might be argued that the uncertainty about his medical condition is an analogue to Sam's uncertainty about the past, and that his malady is a physical manifestation of the continuing relevance of the past and the importance of coming to terms with it.

Part of the journey narrative of *In Country* is to bring the margins of culture to the nation's capital as a way of showing that small-town life is of national significance. Western Kentucky (significantly a southern state) seems so remote to Sam that 'It was like being stranded on an island, far away from civilization' (143), but her pilgrimage to Washington brings three generations of the Hughes family to the centre of public life: Dwayne's mother, his brother, and his daughter. The last chapter of the novel accomplishes many different things simultaneously by virtue of its economical narrative language, and again much of it is to do with reading and writing. The Washington Monument is 'a gleaming pencil' (238) and the Vietnam Memorial is a wall with 58,000 names written on it. Unable to touch her son's body, Mamaw touches his name affectionately, and then Sam touches it too: 'She feels funny touching it. A scratching on a rock. Writing. Something for future archaeologists to puzzle over, clues to a language' (244). The archaeology of knowledge almost complete, Mamaw sees herself symbolically reflected in the wall, and then suddenly Sam discovers her own name on the wall: 'She touches her own name. How odd it feels, as though all the names in America have been used to decorate this wall' (245). Many different things take place at once here: Sam recognizes herself as part of American history, and as a casualty of that particular American history that took her father from her; she also achieves a kind of community with America and a tacit recognition too, as the language puns on the word 'decorate', that the dead have been honoured even while the memorial to them is merely decorative. Furthermore, Sam's narrative resolution is still bound up with ideas about texts; what Sam finds is not her father but her father's name, another piece of writing. Having touched the name of her father, a sacred text, she can find herself and be released from Oedipal deference to her absent parent.

But the crucial point in this final scene is how we respond to Sam touching 'her own name' at the Memorial, because it is a point which has a fundamental bearing on the rest of the text. One critic has argued that when Sam touches her name 'Sam's discovery here releases her from the depthless present into an engagement with history: a process of recording, and accounting that both assumes the presentness of the past and accepts the long reach of time. Everything becomes history: that is what Sam has learned. Sam has come into reality, out of hyperreality, by meeting her own name inscribed in history'.[6] But, of course, Sam does not touch her own name, only the name of a dead man who shares her name, and this is a fundamental difference because it involves an act of (almost) wilful misreading and Sam is therefore in danger of misunderstanding and seriously misappropriating a historical narrative which is not hers and which cannot represent the material circumstances of her life. It is an extraordinary moment of epiphany for Sam, but one which is predicated specifically on an act of misreading; readers should be especially alert to this point because it is a habit that characterizes Sam's entire narrative, from 'The Ancient Mariner' to 'Apocalypse Now' (215). But to what extent does this undermine the novel's apparent resolution?

That the answer might lie in the novel's interest in gender politics is signalled by the fact that the novel's final image is not of Sam but of Emmett, and the language of his final moment is similarly enigmatic; as Mamaw recalls the language of Vietnam when she asks ' "Did we lose Emmett?" ', Sam points to him, 'studying the names low on a panel. He is sitting there cross-legged in front of the wall, and slowly his face bursts into a smile like flames' (245). The imagery is suggestive of the self-immolation of the monk who famously protested about the war in Vietnam, and also of a purging of Emmett's facial acne. Most of all, Emmett is the phoenix reborn from the ashes of his former self, released into the future by Sam's efforts to come to terms with her own broken past. It is significant that the young woman facilitates this phoenix image for the Vietnam veteran, because it is the woman's historical perspective which proves salvation for the man. There can be no 'authentic' place for the 17-year-old girl in a

---

[6] R. Gray, 'Afterword', in R. H. King and H. Taylor (eds.), *Dixie Debates* (London: Pluto Press, 1996), 223–4.

piece of writing that is principally a list of fifty-eight thousand dead men's names. It must finally be allowed however, that *In Country* interrogates the very idea of 'authenticity' with such forensic energy that it almost disappears.

Jayne Anne Phillips **Machine Dreams**

Jayne Anne Phillips's *Machine Dreams* (1984) is also a novel that attempts to recover something from Vietnam, to retrieve from the swamp of history something meaningful for the survivors. In this novel the sister of a lost pilot wants to send someone 'to sink into the morass of Vietnam and find out what happened to Billy, actually bring him back' (324).[7] It is the author herself who fulfils this role, imagining herself as 'some weird mercenary' (324) attempting to understand Vietnam in its context, but also trying to elucidate a relationship between the ordinary individual American and American history, and beyond that, between human consciousness and time. It is a complex and elusive theme in which Pegasus, the winged horse of Greek mythology who caused the fountain of the Muses to flow, is here the agent of flight, a representative of the heroic dead, an archetypal image of man's aspirations for aerial mastery, and a unifying image of the creative consciousness which facilitates the novel's imaginative flights. The magic horse is the prototype for the flying machines of Vietnam; the aerial freedom that flight offers is an ancient dream of mankind. Simultaneously, dreaming offers an alternative perspective, a different consciousness of time which contains glimpses of the future as well as revisionary narratives of the past. This much alone is compressed into the novel's enigmatic title *Machine Dreams*. The novel strives to understand the consciousness of history through a perspective which goes back to the Depression and forward to Danner's association with Vietnam veterans (like Sam's), but also forward to the future through dreaming and imagining. The novel is also like *In Country* in giving its attempts at historical recovery important and central consequences which are closely associated with gender. Note the contrast between the first two chapters for

---

[7] All page references are to the Faber and Faber edition.

example: chapter 1 is a shared history between women, a 'Reminiscence to a Daughter', in which Jean tells Danner about her grandmother and family stories are passed down among women from mothers to daughters. This communal activity of sharing tales facilitates a more informed historical perspective: 'Later you look back and see one thing foretold by another' (4). This idea is of central importance to the narrative's themes of history and prophecy; it is a kind of recovery for which a woman's consciousness has a special capacity. Chapter 1 ends with Jean's reminiscence about the moment of Danner's birth: 'when I knew I had a daughter, I was so thankful—like my own mother had come back to me' (22). By contrast, chapter 2 is the narrative of Jean's husband Mitch, whose male view of history recalls Emmett's in the novel *In Country*; Mitch comments: 'All this was before I was born and no one ever talked about it. Why would they? What's the difference? It don't matter' (28). Mitch's chapter, 'The Secret Country', is a private history shared only with the reader, and it is one in which he identifies closely with ideas of extreme existential isolation dramatized by the Chinese leper. It is a male legacy passed on to his son Billy, who, many years later in Vietnam suddenly realizes, 'I never asked you about the war you went to' (292). Thus, the novel establishes a contrast between women's understanding of history as shared, communal, and vital, and a male view of history as broken, separate, and discontinuous. This gendered opposition informs the novel's conduct at many points, and is sometimes very similar to the kind of historical enquiry that is dramatized by *In Country*.

Machine Dreams is substantially devoted to the detailed and vivid evocation of small-town life in West Virginia in the mid-twentieth century as it follows three generations of the Hampson family through domestic struggles, marriage problems, and the trials of growing up; all this takes place against the backdrop of historical events such as the Watts riots, the Cuban missile crisis, and the moon landing of Apollo 11 in 1969. All of the family are touched by history, and their lives are shaped by the pressure of the past and their consciousness of the present historical moment and how to act upon it. *Machine Dreams* is remarkable for the way in which it combines the domestic lives of the Hampsons with the major events of twentieth-century American history to show that the very fabric of their lives is in itself historically significant; it is a novel which undermines any simple distinction between the public and private lives of American citizens. Both *In Country* and *Machine Dreams* accomplish this as part of their agenda about historical narratives.

A good example of how the prose of *Machine Dreams* brings together many of its key images is given in the chapter 'Moonship, Danner 1969' in which Mitch gives his daughter the newspaper to preserve for history which has an account of the moon landing: 'Two Steps on Moon, Armstrong Pilots Beyond Boulders' (240). The newspaper, from 20 July 1969, is preserved for posterity by Danner as her parents' divorce becomes final and her father clears out the family home now that the two children are at college. This historical moment for the family is coincident with America's historical achievement in space. The landing however is given in terms of the everyday; Danner remembers that moon dust 'was heavy and fine like black flour', and that the dust smelled like gunpowder, or, 'Danner remembered the exact phrase—"spent cap-pistol caps"' (241). Danner's consciousness of history is finely interwoven into the texture of her life. She has another key memory of the moon landing: 'Neil Armstrong's mother had said he'd had a recurrent childhood dream of hovering above the ground' (241). The act of dreaming is often associated with premonitions in the novel, momentary glimpses of the future; they are also combined with the clarity of perspective given by flight or aerial elevation, of being raised above the ground. At the same time, this is associated with the flight of Pegasus and the flying horse's representation of the heroic dead (cited in the novel's epigraph). This idea is pressed further in the next lines: 'Danner had repeated that story to a boy she was dating. He'd smirked. "I wonder if all the guys flying Hueys in Nam had the same dream"' (241). Although he has not been drafted yet, Danner's brother Billy will be killed two chapters later when his helicopter is shot down in Vietnam in 1970, and in this way the connection is made between man's conquest of the moon and his political involvement in south-east Asia, suggesting that both territorial struggles are a function of the same male aspiration towards technological superiority and American colonial expansion.

Again at the same time these ideas about history are given a gendered dimension by Danner's observation that the moon landing 'was just machines' (241) and by Billy's faith in the American army's desire 'to protect the machine' (286). Here then in two short paragraphs about the moon landing are many of the central elements of *Machine Dreams* brought together in such a way as to create a unique creative language: the history of an ordinary American family and American history; consciousness of the past and premonitions of the future; the intimate and exotic made intimate and personal; the significance of dreaming; of Pegasus in all its various aspects, and the association of men with technology. All of these elements combine in the moment when Danner sits at her parents' kitchen table and reads the newspaper in 1969. It is testimony to Phillips's talent that the narrative can carry so many connotations at once in vivid and economical language. During the later scene in which Billy's mother is told that he is missing in action and that there is no knowledge of his whereabouts, she comments: 'He might as well be on the moon' (312).

There are parallels between the depiction of Billy's experience of Vietnam and his father's experience of war in New Guinea. Both historical incidents are recorded and preserved in their letters, so that war (for men) becomes a matter of language and textual representation. For both men, the experience of fighting for America in a distant and exotic country is preceded by disorientating changes of location within America: Mitch is sent to Wyoming and California, Billy to Kentucky and New Jersey. For both men the war is their first time abroad. Both men express a strong desire to keep the worst of the combat a secret from their families. Mitch writes, 'Of course you will not say anything about this to the family' (53), and Billy writes 'I only tell you this because I know you will keep it to yourself' (286). Both men have some self-sustaining belief in what they are fighting for, Mitch 'a Main Street where people exchange talk is one reason the war was fought' (67), and for Billy for his fellow soldiers rather than something at home, ' "These guys are the only country I know of, they're what I'm defending" ' (324). Both narratives are preceded by quotations from official publications, as if to parody the authority of the discourse which precipitates and perpetuates war (as if it is a mode of discourse itself, and a male one at that), and both men are traumatized by their exposure to technological weaponry. Note also that the names of the two major male characters Billy and Mitch, are derived from one historical man's name: Billy Mitchell (1879–1936). Mitchell was an officer in the US Army who became an outspoken champion of a strong air force independent of the army or navy. Mitchell advocated the creation of a separate air arm to the American forces even to the point of being critical of his superiors, and in 1925 he was court-martialled and suspended from duty. There is a great deal of continuity between the historical experiences of Billy and Mitch which is a function of their gender, and which distinguishes them from the novel's women characters.

The vulnerability that men become prone to when they invest a sense of identity in machinery is dramatized everywhere in *Machine Dreams*. Mitch thought he would be killed in the war, and that 'it would be an accident with machinery' (68), and he senses that his feeling of security is an illusion: 'he'd thought his apparent safety somehow made his odds worse' (68). Similarly, Billy is doomed in Vietnam because of his close association with the M-60 because '"they always go for the gunners"' (286). This wartime fear is learned at home in man's association with his vehicle, Clayton's Studebaker, Reb's Pierce Arrow coupe 'high off the ground, with windows all around like you were in a cockpit' (37). Mitch lovingly itemizes the features of his new car: 'absolutely clean, shining and private and quiet like the interior of a big jewel' (68). Later, while waxing 'the broad snout of the machine' he sees 'His own reflection distorted on the cloudy surface' (70). The closed interior world of Mitch's mind resembles too closely the hushed privacy of his new Pontiac; beyond it he feels anxiety and fear. The motor cars are also vehicles for ideas about male control; the incident in which Reb deliberately drives his Pierce Arrow into the river nearly killing himself and Marthella (41–2) is contrasted with the scene where Mary drives Mitch's Pontiac into a barn and pulls up sharply so that he bangs his head on the dashboard: 'he thought they were still moving and he looked out into the blackness and didn't know where he was. Didn't know' (66). There is a kind of existential panic which is associated with this loss of male control and this continuity of male experience is bound up with their identification with machines, motor cars, spaceships, helicopters, and cement trucks. The faith of men in technology is perilous because by investing their identity in something outside themselves they lose a measure of control over their lives. The men are isolated in their consciousness by their close identification with machines. Man's vulnerability in this respect is succinctly dramatized in the scene when Sargeant Dixon brings the news that Billy is missing in action and Danner takes him to her father's house to deliver the telegram: 'The car was spotless, a machine that belonged to no one, and it smelled new. Sargeant Dixon was beside me; he turned the key in the ignition and adjusted the blower of the air conditioner. Both hands on the wheel, he sat erect and looked at me with care. "Would you please direct me, ma'am?"' (313–14). The man, suitably positioned in the driving seat, still needs to be guided by the woman if he is to take them in the right direction. This is as true of American history as it is of driving a rental car around the block. The domestic sphere of the family vehicle acts as an analogue to the public sphere of the space-craft and the military technology of American history. When Billy picks Danner up from college in 1969 in his Camero, he insists that she locks the doors: '"Why? Are you going to fly all the way to Bellington?"', asks Danner; in language prophetic of his death in an American helicopter Billy replies, '"I don't like to lose passengers"' (237). Three years later in 1972, traumatized by the loss of her brother, Danner (like Sam) sleeps with Vietnam vets and is rescued by Riley in a car journey which symbolically changes the direction of her life: 'After that I stopped sleeping with anyone' (321). The direction of the lives of the Hampsons, of American history, of the multiple car journeys of the text, all become synonymous: 'What journey was this, and where were we all going?' (307).

The jewel-like secrecy and interiority of man's consciousness cuts him off from valuable social exchange and isolates and starves him. When Mitch waxes his car he thinks of 'unconnected things, no stories' (70) and this is indicative of man's isolation in history and his isolating historical perspective. The existential despair that lies beyond this male consciousness is dramatized by the story of the leper in chapter 2. The Chinese man suffering from leprosy is quarantined in a tent by the river on the edge of town. No one knows anything of his history, or can communicate with him, and when he dies all trace of him is incinerated and he is not spoken about. This figure haunts Mitch's imagination, especially during the war:

No country, no family, no job. No one. Maybe he wasn't sure anymore who he was. He was a secret. I was the only one ever saw him. He could have stopped talking because I didn't seem real either, only another sound he heard in the woods. A sound in his head. During the war I used to dream of him, walking toward me on one of the tarmac landing strips we laid in New Guinea. I'd wake up in a sweat. I was a secret myself. . . . I'd fall asleep and hear a voice I'd never heard. I was called Mitch, or nicknames like Cowboy. But this voice said 'Mitchell . . . Mitchell . . . Mitchell' with no question, till the sound didn't seem like a name or a word. (45)

The leper lived a secret interior life which could only be glimpsed in retrospect, the 'secret country' of his mind is a territory that Mitch inhabits too, a private place which is inviolable but dangerously solipsistic: 'The man could go crazy if he never spoke with anyone' (34). Mitch faces the same kind of annihilation, of his name, his history, and his identity. In this, *Machine Dreams* offers an analysis of a kind of male consciousness which is synonymous with death. Danner encounters it in 1972, fifty years beyond her father's childhood memory of the Chinese leper, in the shape of the character Junior, a 5-year-old who cannot speak except to make one-syllable noises; he is also like the leper in being asocial, and in having 'no name at all' (308). Danner achieves a breakthrough when Junior says to her the word 'honeysuckle' and attains a rare moment of communication which shows that even the most disablingly solipsistic (male) mind can make itself understood.

Billy is drafted to Vietnam by the lottery, a fateful historical circumstance that he is resigned to accepting. Rather than flee to Canada he tells his sister '"I decided I'd go with the numbers"' (266). He has a dream about the lottery in which the balls become the arbiters of history which goes back to the beginning of time:

Sometimes Billy dreamed about the lottery, a close-up interior view: hundreds of days of white balls tumbling in a black sphere, silent and very slow, moving as though in accordance with physical laws. A galaxy of identical white planets. No sun. Cold, charged planets, simple, symmetrical, named with months and numbers. Nov. 1, no. 305 of 365. Universe stops. Hand reaches in. Suddenly everything in color, and the black sphere turns midnight blue. Crazy dream. (248)

The idea of the constellations suggests a historical inevitability which is so ancient as to be pre-temporal, and it is this history which Billy submits to. At the same time though, the lottery is a mechanical device ('numbers were pure') and therefore the historical process demands human intervention; as Billy asks, 'Exactly whose hand would touch the machine?' (248). The lottery machine is the human agent of death, prefiguring the death machines of Vietnam and taking man's history out of his hands. The numerals of the novel's numerous clocks (306, 154) press this analogy further between history and the measuring process. Mitch experiences a similarly disorientating twist of historical fate in the same terms: 'somehow after he'd got back from the war, all the numbers changed around' (89).

Most important for *Machine Dreams* is the impact that the experiences of both men have on the women, Jean and Danner, whose perspective in history is necessarily different from that of husbands and brothers. This is succinctly dramatized in chapter 9 where Jean returns to college and the intransigent and resentful Mitch 'grew more silent' (160). It is characteristic of the novel's representation of history that the scene which precipitates the Hampsons' divorce takes place very closely in the context of the political turmoil caused by the Cuban missile crisis in October 1962. Mitch is preoccupied with the design and construction of a fallout shelter and working for the Civil Defence League and studying government manuals and official publications (the discourse of male authority). Jean's energy is consumed by domestic struggles closer to home which are, on the surface at least, of less obviously significant historical importance: 'No questions about the meaning of things; you don't think that way if you have children. The meaning is right in front of you and you live by keeping up with it.' As a consequence of different values, priorities, and social roles, Jean has a fundamentally different perspective from behind her ironing board, 'as though I were standing behind the scenes of some production' (162), and the cathartic argument takes place as Mitch dumps his official publications on the ironing board which is already heaped with children's clothes: 'I shoved the ironing board against him to get out from behind it' (164). Mitch's desire to build a (significantly) defensive shelter (like the capsules of spacecraft, airplanes, and motor cars), is contrasted with Jean's more social suggestion that they take their place in the town shelter. The relationship collapses because Jean cannot continue 'struggling on his ground', and this chapter, again a 'shared reminiscence to a daughter' demonstrates the ways in which women are not circumscribed by those male structures of knowledge which inhibit Mitch and Billy. As one critic has argued, 'Jean and Danner are at the center of their culture'.[8] Those structures are not simply to do with different domestic functions. From the attic, Jean sees Mitch: 'Looking at him from above, I felt so distant I could have been watching him from another planet' (162). This aerial elevation is experienced by Danner too: 'a sudden wintry vision of the house from above' (221). The perspective that they share is not gained from one of the flying machines of M. B. Zisfein's *Flight: A Panorama of Aviation* quoted in the novel's epigraph.

The mother and sister of Billy come to accommodate his loss by sharing stories about him, but as with all historical narratives in *Machine Dreams* this retrospective reconstruction is a process integral to Danner's contemporary life, and it is one which harbours prophetic intimations: 'Her stories about the past seem to comfort her, but they sadden me. After all, I'm in the stories. I'm here, relating the stories to the present and to the future, and I'm always looking for hints' (306). American involvement in Vietnam has alienated Danner profoundly from her sense of 'America', but she will not leave the country although she does leave the south for California, which she describes as 'the far frontiers' (324) having learned from one of Billy's letters that just as his fellow soldiers were 'the only country I know of' (324) so Danner's parents 'are my country, my divided country' (324). Like the androgynously named Sam of *In Country*, Danner learns to go 'in country' not in Vietnam but in terms of a critical enquiry into a narrative of American history which threatens to overcome her. The expression 'in country' was a slang term for the battle areas of Vietnam, but both of these novels' female protagonists remain within the United States to investigate the version of American history that has confined and excluded them there.

Jane Smiley A Thousand Acres

In Country and *Machine Dreams* are novels that attribute a gendered quality to various forms of technology, and this is characteristic too of

---

[8] O. W. Gilman, *Vietnam and the Southern Imagination* (Jackson: University Press of Mississippi, 1992), 68.

Jane Smiley's Pulitzer prize-winning novel *A Thousand Acres* (1991), a novel about a family in rural Iowa during Jimmy Carter's presidency, the father Larry Cook and three daughters whose mother died many years ago.[9] The father is in his dotage, and the daughters, Ginny, Rose, and Caroline, are married. The novel is narrated by Ginny, who still lives in close proximity to her father and who sometimes cares for her sister Rose's two children, having no family of her own. The narrative begins with Larry, 'Daddy', planning to divide up his land among his three daughters, and here, as elsewhere, the novel bears a passing resemblance to Shakespeare's *King Lear*. Daddy's pride is injured when his youngest daughter Caroline says simply 'I don't know' to his plan for the new corporation. As Ginny correctly interprets this mistake, 'She had simply spoken as a woman rather than as a daughter' (21). Book I closes with Caroline refusing to apologize to her father ('"I hate that little girl stuff"', (34)), and Daddy unequivocally and whimsically cuts her out of his plans. Daddy, a wilful and obdurate patriarch, appears to be losing his mind, and the novel's analogy with *King Lear* includes a night of a ferocious midwestern storm in which he becomes completely irrational and loses all self-control; he calls his daughter Ginny 'a dried up whore bitch' and adds resentfully: '"It's you girls that make me crazy, I gave you everything and I get nothing in return"' (182). Daddy's eccentricity intensifies, causing family tensions between the three daughters in their responses to his aberrant behaviour, testing their loyalty to one another and straining their respective marriage relationships too, because their husbands' futures are closely bound up with Daddy's decisions about the land. Such is Daddy's power in this isolated rural community that his eccentric foibles have serious and permanent consequences for everyone. But an interpretation of the novel that is devoted to spotting correspondences with *King Lear* must be inattentive to the cultural specificity of the Iowa landscape, to the crisis in agriculture during Carter's presidency, and to the history of the frontier which has no antecedent in Shakespeare's play. Worse, such a reading would encourage a far more sympathetic reading of Larry Cook than his behaviour will allow. A more sophisticated reading of the novel might propose that it offers tentative parallels with Shakespeare's play only to expose their

---

[9] All page references are to the Flamingo edition.

limitations in ways that encourage a creative rereading of *King Lear*. If this is possible, then Smiley's novel can be used to interpret Shakespeare more than Shakespeare can be used as a paradigm by which to understand *A Thousand Acres*.

Despite the expansiveness of the frontier-like Iowa landscape, there is a claustrophobic intensity to family relations in the novel which is predicated on a sensitivity to Daddy's authority. But his power is not simply based on his ownership of land; the narrative reveals that since the death of their mother, Ginny and Rose have been systematically abused by their father, and this is the legacy of his rule that they struggle to come to terms with. It is not until after the night of the storm that the text of the novel alludes to this abuse, Rose sharing the family secret for the first time with her sister: ' "He didn't rape me, Ginny. He seduced me. He said that it was okay, that it was good to please him, that he needed it, that I was special. . . . We were just his, to do with as he pleased, like the pond or the houses or the hogs or the crops" ' (190–1). At this point in the novel Ginny has no memory of having been the victim of her father's abuse, but the memory returns violently and explicitly when she returns to the room in the old house and lies on the bed where it took place: 'Lying there, I knew that he had been in there to me, that my father had lain with me in that bed, that I had looked at the top of his head, at his balding spot in the brown grizzled hair, while feeling him suck my breasts. That was the only memory I could endure before I jumped out of the bed with a cry' (228–9). Daddy's standing in society, his success and power and influence, disguises his sexual exploitation of Rose and Ginny, while Rose is complicit in keeping it a family secret and Ginny has been so traumatized as to have forgotten it. What Ginny discovers in the course of narrating the novel is a different family history from the received one, a secret family history which, when it is exposed, tears the family apart and causes a transformation in Ginny's sense of identity that is fundamental and permanent.

Like *In Country* and *Machine Dreams* Smiley's novel uses the family to dramatize ideas about history, culture, and power, and is vitally concerned with the ways in which gender is the determining factor in the historical narratives of America. The recovery of Ginny's memory for example is immediately preceded by the momentary appearance of her mother in the text: 'She had a history . . . and for us this history was to be found in her closet. . . . The clothes in the closet . . . intoxi-cated us with a sense of possibility, not for us, but for our mother, lost possibilities to be sure, but somehow still present when we entered the closet. . . . Now, when I seek to love my mother, I remember her closet' (224). These clothes represent an alternative life which Ginny's mother relinquished when she moved to Iowa to become a farmer's wife; indeed, Rose once preferred to think that their mother had not died at all but 'had escaped and taken an assumed name' (187), which is precisely Ginny's course when she uncovers her own history and takes possession of the lost mother's narrative towards the end of the novel. Daddy derives some of his power from the absence of the mother, permitting him to become more tyrannical and sadistic. As the sole male parent he becomes omnipotent to his young daughters: 'My mother died before she could present him to us as only a man, with habits and quirks and preferences, before she could diminish him in our eyes enough for us to understand him' (20). This idea of the alternative life that her mother's clothes represent, and the different life that Ginny might have had if her mother had lived, is paralleled closely by Ginny's own baulked history. Ginny's five miscarriages represent a future of which she is violently deprived: 'I just wadded the nightgown and the sheets and the bed pad into a paper bag and took them out and buried them under the dirt floor of the old dairy barn' (26). This potential family of her own is withheld from Ginny, either as a consequence of her father's abuse, or of his exploitation of the land with nitrate fertilizers which poison the water system. It is of central importance to the novel that even this personal history of Ginny's pregnancies is a secret one: her husband Ty does not know that there have been as many as five because Ginny believes that 'If I kept the secret I thought I could sustain the pregnancy' (25). This history, the real history, is known only to the women, but is sup-pressed by them in a patriarchal culture where their desires are sub-servient to the expectations and demands of men. This occluded women's history goes back at least to Ginny's grandmother Edith, 'a silent woman' (132), and is a consequence of male authority; Ginny wonders if Edith's 'reputed silence wasn't due to temperament at all, but due to fear' (132–3).

The crucial difference here, and one which informs everything in the novel, is the divergence in the historical perspectives of the men and women in this particular culture. Ginny believes that men lack the ability to regard the events of their lives in a historical context which helps to explain them: 'there seemed to be a dumb, unknowing quality to the way the men had suffered, as if, like animals, it was not possible for them to gain perspective on their suffering' (113). In fact, this is not an absence of historical perspective at all, but a very particular kind of male perspective which enables Ty and Daddy to interpret events in a manner which suits their respective positions of authority. This is part of the discourse by which they legitimize their power; it takes Rose to point out to Ginny that, 'Daddy thinks history starts fresh every day, every minute, that time itself begins with the feelings he's having right now. That's how he keeps betraying us, why he roars at us with such conviction' (216). This is a male discourse of power, one in which gender and knowledge are intimately associated, and Daddy uses it to fuel his resentment at what he feels to be his daughters' insubordinate behaviour. Again it is Rose who, fully cognizant of her family narrative, explains this to Ginny: 'People pat him on the head and sympathise with him and say what bitches we are, and he believes them and that's that, the end of history' (303). The patriarch has an institutionally sanctioned discourse of power by which the autonomy of his daughters is annihilated, and Ginny in particular is a victim of the ways in which in this culture its overwhelming authority has been entirely naturalized: 'Of course it was silly to talk about my point of view. When my father asserted his point of view, mine vanished. Not even I could remember it' (176). The erasure of Ginny's subjectivity includes, she discovers, the history of her father's sexual abuse of her, and her husband too is characterized by his adherence to this form of male power: 'He had counted on each pregnancy as if there were no history' (114).

The discovery of the ways in which the discourse of history is bound up with forms of power and the subsequent struggle to establish an alternative liberating discourse for Ginny is at the heart of *A Thousand Acres*. Ginny's self-awareness involves a rejection of male forms of discursive exposition, and in her language this is represented by particular forms of record; it is significant that Ginny's new life in Minnesota includes a rejection of authorized accounts: 'News was what I didn't want. I didn't own a television or a radio. It didn't occur to me to buy a newspaper' (334). Ginny's tentative attempts to

articulate a female discourse and to recover her own occluded narrative are centred on the history of her body and on the land, 'a kind of
ongoing narrative and commentary about what was happening that
grew out of our conversations' (113). Towards the end of the novel
Ginny writes: 'Lodged in my every cell, along with the DNA, are
molecules of topsoil and atrazine and paraquat and anhydrous
ammonia and diesel fuel and plant dust. . . . All of it is present now,
here; each particle weighs some fraction of the hundred and thirty-
six pounds that attaches me to the earth, perhaps as much as the
print weighs in other sorts of histories' (369). Ginny proposes here
that her body is constituted of the elements of farming, some of them
natural, some of them not, and it is an important recognition of the
legacy of her body and the irrevocable damage done to it by men. The
abuse of her father and his abuse of the land become synonymous as
they are dramatized by Ginny's five miscarriages. Rose's mastectomy
parallels Ginny's lost children in making manifest in violent forms
the physical cost to the women of their place in this culture, the
breast and the womb epitomizing a female reproductive capacity
which might have been a site of resistance to the men's rapacious
desire for control and commodification. The male world of farming is
built on the efforts of their supporting wives and the novel elucidates
this by revealing the cost to the woman's body. Ginny's alienation
from her body constitutes another narrative within the text, one
which began when she was a child, and she remembers it as 'the
familiar strangeness of one's parts' (277) and that it was coincident
with her ' "getting out of hand" ' (278) when Daddy first taught her to
internalize his authority: 'As far as I knew then, my hands and my
body had never met without an intermediary washcloth' (278). Ginny
has been brought up to be profoundly embarrassed by her body
which she describes as 'ridiculous in its very femininity' (114) and
which she has always regarded at a distance: 'Shame is a distinct
feeling. I couldn't look at my hands around the coffee cup or hear my
own laments without feeling appalled, wanting desperately to fall
silent, grow smaller. More than that, I was uncomfortably conscious
of my whole body, from the awkward way that the shafts of my hair
were thrusting out of my scalp to my feet, which felt dirty as well as
cold. Everywhere I seemed to feel my skin from the inside, as if it now
stood away from my flesh, separated by a millimeter of mortified

space' (195). This phrase 'a millimeter of mortified space' characterizes adroitly the difference in gendered forms of history in the novel, the space in which Ginny feels alienated from her body is a tiny but crucial measure of distance thrust upon her by her father's abuse; simultaneously it reminds the reader of the wide open spaces of Iowa and her father's kingdom of a thousand acres. Both spaces are mortified, dead, abject. Where the men see expanding horizons, the women see 'my pound of flesh' (303).

As this interpretation of the novel suggests, the space for Ginny to reconstitute her history lies in taking possession of her body, while for the men space signifies a kingdom of ownership and the heritage of a male history of the frontier. Ginny's relationship with Ty reveals succinctly his continued allegiance to this form of historical discourse; he exclaims, ' "There was real history there! And of course not everybody got what they wanted, and not everybody acted right all the time, but that's just the way it is. Life is. You got to accept that" '. Ty subscribes blindly to the ideology of the frontier, and because the men are the embodiment of that history they are unable to see outside it or beyond it. This is something that Ginny learns to understand: ' "You see this grand history, but I see blows" ' (342). This frontier thesis (some sense of which is alluded to in the novel's echo of John Schlesinger's account of the Kennedy administration *A Thousand Days*), is important to the gender politics of the novel. While the names of Larry's daughters recall the daughters of Lear (Ginny, Rose, Caroline: Goneril, Regan, Cordelia), many of the other proper names of the text are those of male explorers and colonizers: Cabot, Cook, Amundsen, Livingstone, Ericson, Clark, Hudson, Drake, Columbus. The land is a male province to be managed, cultivated, and exploited. Ginny's family lineage begins with the great-grandparents who drained the land to plant flax, and the text is careful to point out that the entire landscape is in fact man-made, a product of the subjection of its natural state: 'However much these acres looked like a gift of nature, or of God, they were not' (15). It could be argued that *A Thousand Acres* shows the legacy of the frontier spirit for contemporary America. Every aspect of the Cook family's life is consumed by struggles over the land, such as who will take possession of a neighbour's acres if mortgage payments are not met, and this is typical of every family's connection with the land as commodity: 'We've always known families for whom . . . a historic dispute over land or money burns so hot that it engulfs every other subject' (8). The desire for ownership, possession, and expansion is a form of lust. Even in their free time, the Cook family play 'Monopoly' and Ginny comments that 'it was hard for me to keep track of who owed me what' (82). In this respect the novel is like Tim O'Brien's *Northern Lights* (1975) in giving an account of the end of the frontier spirit and especially in dramatizing the emotional cost of its heritage to contemporary Americans. Both texts feature a young man returning from Vietnam who is presented in a clear contrast to the elder generation and who is dismayed and inhibited by the elders' ideological baggage. Both novels include crucial historical accounts of European immigrants' settlement of the frontier, accounts which are at the centre of both novels because they represent the legacy that the younger generation must break free from. Although O'Brien's novel offers a critique of a certain type of masculinity, *A Thousand Acres* is crucially different from *Northern Lights* in the way that it exposes the frontier mentality as a specifically male enterprise with serious and debilitating consequences for women. Smiley's novel is also a product of its own historical moment in late twentieth-century America when there was an extraordinary cultural concern with incest, as evidenced by the outpouring of 1990s investigations of the issue of what became known as False Memory Syndrome or Recovered Memory Syndrome, for example: Elizabeth Loftus and Katherine Ketcham, *The Myth of Repressed Memory: False Memories and Allegations of Sexual Abuse* (1994); M. Yapko, *Suggestions of Abuse: True and False Memories of Childhood Sexual Trauma* (1994); M. Prendergrast, *Victims of Memory: Incest Allegations and Shattered Lives* (1995); Louise Armstrong's *Rocking the Cradle of Sexual Politics* (1996), and, of course, Roseanne Arnold's much publicized *My Lives* (1994). Elaine Showalter is sufficiently persuaded by the pressure of this cultural paradigm at this particular 1990s historical moment that she asks if it might be possible to regard Ginny as an unreliable narrator, one whose memories of abuse are suggested to her by Rose: 'Is this memory or the aftereffect of powerful suggestion? . . . none of the critics who so much admired Smiley's impressive novel questioned the reliability of Ginny's narrative, asked about the circumstances in which the partial memories were recovered, or pointed to the devastating effects on

Ginny and her family'.[10] But if the central dramatic event is a false memory of abuse, then most of what is valuable about the novel disappears, and especially its indictment of a frontier mentality as industrialized farming and the recovery of a valuable and important women's history. Ginny's attitude to her body, that 'millimeter of mortified space' (195), only makes sense in the context of the novel's themes if it is recognized as a consequence of her father's sexual violence.

While the men of *A Thousand Acres* strive to subdue the land for profit, Ginny discovers, with Jess Clark, a private space where she can have a different life. The dump at the back of the farm, 'the most interesting spot on the farm' (122) is a female space, organic, fertile, marginal, and outwith the colonizing interests of the men. The existence of the dump enables Ginny to experience a moment of 'daring privacy' (124) with Jess, just as it allows wild flowers and snakes and butterflies to prosper: 'the secluded nature of the spot where we were standing allowed it but did not create it' (124). This freedom to be involved in the natural environment is controlled strongly by her father's attitude to land as a commodity: ' "Daddy's not much for untamed nature. You know, he's deathly afraid of wasps and hornets. It's a real phobia with him" ' (123). Daddy's desire to subdue and control governs his attitude to his daughters' bodies as much as to the land, and his anxiety about 'untamed nature' is a fear about the nature of women.

Alice Walker **The Color Purple**

The forms of historical discourse that women interrogate through the narratives of *In Country*, *Machine Dreams*, and *A Thousand Acres* have a strongly gendered aspect. Alice Walker's *The Color Purple* (1982) has both a gendered and a racialized perspective on history, one in which the idea of history is exposed as having been conceived as 'white' to the profound disadvantage of black Americans.[11] *The Color Purple* is not only about the brutalization of one black 14-year-old, but con-

---

[10] Elaine Showalter, *Hystories: Hysterical Epidemics and Modern Culture* (London: Picador, 1997), 158.

[11] All page references are to the Pocket Book edition.

cerns a historical discourse of international politics which makes Celie's suffering possible; the novel shows how the structures of power which oppress her are institutionalized and historicized as 'natural'. Nettie's educative journey to Africa examines the racist and sexist ideology which underwrites Celie's oppression in Milledgeville, Georgia. One of the remarkable aspects of Walker's novel is the way it contextualizes Celie's suffering in terms of the entire history of black Americans. Nettie too discovers a history different from the received one, one which fundamentally reshapes the image of Afro-Americans. Nettie also recuperates and reintegrates something valuable and important by bringing Celie's two children back from Africa to live as Americans with significantly informative African childhoods.

Celie has a childhood full of violence, poverty, and brutalization; she writes letters to God which begin with her own self-erasure, crossing out the words 'I am' as she recounts how she was raped by her stepfather at the age of 14. Celie's suffering is a consequence not of her behaviour but of her subject position, unequivocally stated by Mr: 'You black, you pore, you ugly, you a woman. Goddam, he say, you nothing at all' (213). These categories of race, class, and gender condemn Celie to a life of deprivation and exclusion; it is the purpose of *The Color Purple* to dramatize strategies of survival and self-fulfilment which find value and affirmation in Celie's subject position.

Celie is first raped while she is cutting hair, and when she recounts the story to Shug Avery she explains her pleasure in the creativity that it was an expression of, saying, 'I did love to cut hair' (117). This creative impulse finds a different outlet following the domestic disputes between Harpo and Sofia in which Celie is complicit in encouraging Harpo's violence towards his wife: ' "Beat her", I say' (38). Confronted by Sofia, Celie begins quilting, a new creative enterprise which takes place as a social activity between women and which here is a response to the violence of men. This creative activity will eventually lead to 'Folkspants' the redemptive imaginative and financially successful venture which finally accommodates even misogynists like Mr.

The role model for the women in their creative endeavour is Shug Avery, the blues singer whose power and independence is also derived from her creative talent. Shug Avery's singing gives her the authority and self-esteem that the other women lack, but it is a form of singing, the blues, which has its origins in suffering. Significantly, when Shug sings the song about Celie it is 'all about some no count man doing her wrong' (77),[12] and it is a song inspired by Celie which was written while Celie was attending to Shug's hair, hence the multiple references of Shug's phrase, 'Something I made up. Something you help scratch out my head' (55). Shug Avery embodies the classic blues aesthetic which black women are uniquely positioned to articulate. Harpo's mistress, his 'little yellowish girlfriend' (86) called Squeak, also appropriates the genre as part of her progress towards self-realization when, following the fight with Amazonian Sofia ('"I used to hunt game with a bow and arrow"', (42)) she first takes possession of her name, Mary Agnes, and, after her rape by her uncle, she sings the enigmatic song about her own racial identity: '"They calls me yellow / Like yellow be my name"' (104). This song, inspired by racial sectarianism, puns on the word 'yellow' and so defiantly creates a blues lyric from pain which involves the history of Mary Agnes, her race, and their suffering. It is in this creative synthesis that Mary Agnes attains fulfilment and a sustaining sense of identity; it is a specifically racialized one, one which is dependent on her racial identity and history. The creative acts of a woman, and especially the woman's voice, are the means to her salvation. Celie's liberation is dramatized partly through her finding her voice when she says to Harpo, '"your daddy here ain't dead horse's shit"' (207), and when she curses Mr, saying '"Until you do right by me, everything you touch will crumble"' (213), a declaration which closely recalls Janie Crawford's condemnation of Joe Starks in Hurston's *Their Eyes Were Watching God* (1937), a novel to which *The Color Purple* is indebted.

The acts of creative discovery and self-affirmation by which the women of *The Color Purple* liberate themselves from oppression are closely associated with their sexual identities as well as their racial identity. Shug teaches Celie self-confidence partly by example but primarily by telling her about the clitoris or 'little button' (81) which Celie was unaware of even though she has had children; this is why in Shug's estimation Celie is 'still a virgin' (81). Celie's discovery about her own body and the pleasures of masturbation (83) is a crucial stage in her learning her own value as a person, and her sexual relationship with Shug is a liberating and an empowering one. Similarly, when

---

12 Note the allusion to Bessie Smith here.

Mary Agnes begins singing Shug tells her, 'listening to you sing, folks git to thinking bout a good screw', and when Mary Agnes blushes Shug asks her rhetorically 'What, too shamefaced to put singing and dancing and fucking together?' (120). Creativity and sexuality are intimately connected because they are both deeply personal and self-affirmative. When Celie begins making Folkspants she writes that 'Every stitch I sew will be a kiss' (221).

The character Doris Baines is a significant counterpoint here, the white missionary from an aristocratic English family who writes hugely successful novels under the pen-name 'Jared Hunt'. Doris has no interest at all in the Africans' soul, but uses the money of her family to build hospitals and schools in her African village, for which the local chief presents her with two wives in the mistaken belief that Doris is a man. Returning to England because of the imminent war, Doris is determined to continue her philanthropy; her mission is stated punningly in her desire to 'put a stop to their bloody encroachments' (237). This statement combines references to the ritual of female circumcision ('a bit of bloody cutting around puberty') to colonialism (in the allusion to road building), and is made possible by Walker's pun on 'bloody' as a common British expletive. In this way, the minor character synthesizes and articulates three crucial elements which are of central importance to the major themes of the novel: androgyny, creativity, and economic power.

The Color Purple is not only about women; the narrative shows how men are capable of redemption from ethical positions apparently beyond the pale, such as rapists and women-beaters. 'Folkspants', like 'Sam' and 'Danner', is a significantly androgynous name, and it is an enterprise which can accommodate even Mr, who learns that African men wear robes, like dresses, not pants, and that they sew. In this, he has something in common with the cross-dressing of Emmett in Mason's *In Country*. Mr confesses to a childhood enjoyment in sewing (279) that he was discouraged from indulging because he was a boy. His participation in Celie's sewing and his contribution to Folkspants shows him overcoming the strict gender roles of his upbringing. Harpo also learns not to live according to gender stereotypes by which he oppresses both Sofia and himself. The juke joint that he builds attracts no customers because no one wants to hear the man Swain 'pick his box' (75) and the venture is only successful once it is graced by the presence of Shug Avery. Nevertheless, the juke joint is a symbolic space that he has created and which becomes a showcase for the narrative talents of women such as Shug and Mary Agnes. The success of the venture is a mutual and reciprocal one for men and women. Even more dramatically, in the domestic struggle with his wife Harpo's traditional role is usurped by Sofia who wears 'an old pair of Harpo's pants' (64) and Harpo eats compulsively while he does the housework partly so that he can be stronger than Sofia, but also because he experiences something of a phantom pregnancy: 'His belly grow and grow, but the rest of him don't. He begin to look like he big. "When it due?" us ast' (64). This ability to take on the attributes of the other gender is a mode of survival for the characters of *The Color Purple*, not just for the women in their struggle for self-determination, but for the men too who are inhibited by outmoded gender roles which are restrictive and debilitating. It is an important point that *In Country*, *Machine Dreams*, and *A Thousand Acres* also have valuable lessons for their male characters, and that issues of gender are not restricted to women.

The discourse of gender, like the discourse of race, is subverted and undermined by the narrative of *The Color Purple* which has a radical feminist agenda yet is capable of including evil men in its liberal vision of humanity. The novel extends the parameters of racial oppression by including two references to native American Indians, once when Shug visits her son on a reservation near Tucson, Arizona, where he is called 'the black white man' (275) and again in Nettie's letters from Africa when she writes about the Trail of Tears of 1838 in which the Cherokee people in Georgia 'were forced to leave their homes and walk, through the snow, to resettlement camps in Oklahoma' (241). Through these allusions, the novel shows an awareness that Afro-Americans do not have a monopoly on oppression at the hands of the dominant white culture in the USA. The international political perspective of the novel also includes a reference to Cuba: ' "Lots of gambling there and good times. A lot of colored folks look like Mary Agnes. Some real black, like us. All in the same family though. Try to pass for white, somebody mention your grandma" ' (257). This wider cultural and historical perspective is important to Walker's novel because the form of knowledge that it offers is vitally liberating and empowering.

The first thing Nettie discovers on her journey is that there is a black community in America which is organized quite differently from the southern culture she knows. Nettie visits Harlem in New York City and discovers black Americans 'living in houses that are finer than any white person's house down home' (141), and that these black people are knowledgeable about, and proud of, their African descent. She also learns, before she arrives in Africa, that Jesus was not a European white, that white people in America come from Europe, that the Egyptians who built the pyramids were coloured people, and that black Americans were sold into slavery and came to America in ships. Nettie's first real history lesson is learned from a book written by J. A. Rogers which argues that 'Africans once had a better civilization than the European', and her political consciousness is awakened when she recognizes that Africans' hard times were made harder by English colonial expansion and involvement in the slave trade, which includes ' "you and me Celie" ' (145). Nettie's first port of call in Africa is Monrovia the capital of Liberia, an independent republic founded by American philanthropists who in 1822 organized the first settlement of freed black American slaves on Africa's west coast. In Monrovia (named after American President James Monroe) Nettie meets the Liberian President William Tubman (President 1944–1971) and is immediately sensitive to social and political tensions between the country's indigenous Africans and the Americo-Liberians or 'white looking colored men' in Tubman's cabinet (148). Although in coming to Africa Nettie feels as though she has come home to 'the land for which our mothers and fathers cried' (149) and despite finding that Africa is not 'a place overrun with savages who didn't wear clothes' (137) as she was taught in school, Nettie does not find Africa to be any kind of utopia for black people. In fact, there are many disturbing parallels between culture and society in Africa and the southern American states, and the exposition of these parallels is an important part of both the novel's structure and its ideological freight.

The struggles of race, gender, and economics are present in Africa as they are in the United States. Nettie's letters tell us that 'The Olinka do not believe girls should be educated . . . like white people at home who don't want colored people to learn' (162) and she discovers that the Olinka husband 'has life and death power over the wife' (172) and that they brutalize women with circumcision: 'the one ritual they do have to celebrate women is so bloody and painful' (195). The Olinka reject Christianity and do not recognize Afro-Americans as part of the same racial family. Samuel realizes this when he says that the Africans '"don't even *see* us"' (243) and certainly do not recognize them as '"the brothers and sisters they sold"' (243). Slavery is a function of economics, and the violence of colonialism is still strong in the part of Africa that Nettie visits. The whole territory of the Olinka 'belongs to a rubber manufacturer in England' (175) and eventually the Olinka start to die from a blood disease because of the loss of yams to the rubber plantations (263–4). Tashi and her mother join the Mbele bush people who plan the destruction of whites in Africa and the self-mutilation or scarification that Tashi and Adam submit to can be interpreted as a desperate internalization of the violence brought by colonial expansion in Africa; the Olinka begin 'Carving their identification as a people into their children's faces' (248).

It is important to recognize that Nettie's educative journey is not an abstract historical lesson but has a direct bearing on many key aspects of Celie's life. It is specifically in Africa, for example, that Celie's family history is uncovered, when Samuel explains how he came to adopt Celie's children. This story occasions a fundamental revision of Celie's sense of identity: 'My daddy lynch. My mama crazy. All my little half-brothers and sisters no kin to me. My children not my sister and brother. Pa not Pa' (183). History learned in Africa undoes the taboo of incest that Celie has lived with, and it offers her a different family lineage in which her real father was a prosperous and successful entrepreneur and her mother was a woman who had aspirations which her black neighbours found 'grander than anything they could even conceive of for colored people' (181). This affirmative family inheritance is complemented by the positive images of black people and the alternative history of her race that Nettie discovers.

The invidious and hostile effects of Christianity are perceived both in Africa where the missionaries' Western metaphysic of God is completely alien to the native culture, and in Georgia too where Celie has been brought up to think of the deity as a white man; in fact she thinks that God looks 'like some stout white man work at the bank' (96), an image which neatly combines both racial and economic power. The novel is also devoted to defining a kind of alternative spiritualism, represented by the novel's title, which stands in opposition to the discourse of Christianity which in its very whiteness is inimical to black people. Shug Avery, acting as liberation theologian, explains to Celie that God too is androgynous and sexualized: 'it pisses God off if you walk by the color purple in a field somewhere and don't notice it' (203). The colour purple is a pantheistic rather than Christian spirituality, it is immanent and natural and mystical. The colour purple combines many central themes of the novel—it is associated with pain, as in the colour of bruises, it is linked to the African race who are so black that they shine as if they were purple, it is a regal colour suggesting authority, respect and status, and it is also a sexual colour, the colour of sex. Nettie learns this lesson about Christianity too: 'God is different to us now, after all those years in Africa. More spirit than ever before, and more internal. . . . And not being tied to what God looks like, frees us' (264). The use of the word 'free' here reminds the reader that one of the history lessons of the novel is the rejection of a particular form of Western Christianity and the forms of enslavement that go with it.

Each of these novels examines history closely and dramatizes the position of women in relation to it, especially by uncovering the personal history of women and its radical difference from that which the novels' male characters subordinate them to. The new women's history of these texts challenges the discourse of knowledge and control which men have used to guard positions of authority and structures of power in their own interests. These novels' revelations about epistemology and historiography are liberating for women, and also have the potential to release men from conceptions of themselves which are debilitating and outmoded.

3

The West

I am the horizon
you ride towards, the thing you can never lasso.

Margaret Atwood,
'Backdrop Addresses Cowboy'

The West is more than simply a geographical region of the United
States, it is the cardinal direction that has come to represent, with all
its frontier associations, something uniquely American. As Wallace
Stegner put it, 'America is the West'. Expressing a sense of the vast
open spaces west of the Mississippi, Gertrude Stein wrote that 'In the
United States there is more space where nobody is than where anybody is. That is what makes America what it is'. Frederick Jackson
Turner famously argued in 1893 that 'American social development
has been continually beginning over again on the frontier. This
perennial rebirth, this fluidity of American life, this expansion westward with its new opportunities, its continuous touch with the simplicity of primitive society, furnish the forces dominating American
character'.[1] Turner believed that the history of European colonization
of the West, the experience of the frontier, represented the first truly
American experience, and argued that it was in the West that the
United States really distinguished itself from Europe. This influential
thesis has given way to more recent political debates such as those of
P. L. Limerick's *The Legacy of Conquest* (1987) and Richard Slotkin's
Gunfighter Nation (1992) which take issue with the historiography of
the West and how it should be understood as part of the history of

---

[1] F. J. Turner, 'The Significance of the Frontier in American History', in *The Frontier in American History* (New York: Holt Rinehart Winston, 1962), 2–3.

the United States. Slotkin argues for example that 'The Myth of the Frontier is our oldest and most characteristic myth'.[2] These writers emphasize the importance of an understanding of the frontier to the historical development of the United States as a nation, and show that the debate over its historical significance is one that has a strong contemporary resonance. The emergence of New Western History and the fierce debates over the novelty of its parameters is evidence of the continuing relevance of the frontier West to contemporary America.

The West is not only the birthplace of a sense of American cultural identity, but also the origin of a uniquely American language and literature, and there is a substantial body of writing that articulates the particular ethos of the West in the language of American colloquial speech patterns and American idiom. Novels such as Fenimore Cooper's *The Prairie* (1827), Mark Twain's *Roughing It* (1872), O'Henry's *Heart of the West* (1907), and Willa Cather's *O Pioneers!* (1913) are just a few of hundreds of texts that gave expression to western American experience and helped to shape a distinctively American literature in the process. Hemingway, for example, claimed, in *The Green Hills of Africa*, that 'All modern American literature comes from one book by Mark Twain', and it is remarkable how many twentieth-century writers continue to show a fascination with the West: Edgar Laurence Doctorow, *Welcome to Hard Times* (1960); Richard Brautigan, *The Hawkline Monster: A Gothic Western* (1975); Wallace Stegner, *Angle of Repose* (1971); Thomas Berger, *Little Big Man* (1965); Larry McMurtry, *Lonesome Dove* (1986); Ishmael Reed, *Yellow Back Radio Broke-Down* (1969); James Welsh, *The Indian Lawyer* (1990), Ivan Doig, *Ride with Me Mariah Montana* (1990); Barry Hannah, *Never Die* (1981); and Pam Houston's *Cowboys are my Weakness* (1992). In 1999 T. C. Boyle and Tim O'Brien both published western short fiction in *The New Yorker* in stories called 'Captured by the Indians' and 'Nogales: Seductions of the Desert', respectively. Writers are attracted to the West as a subject for a variety of reasons, but especially because it goes to the heart of American ideas of freedom of identity, or as one critic expressed it: 'We still read Cooper today because he was the first of our authors to seize upon the dramatic possibilities of that unfallen

[2] Richard Slotkin, *Gunfighter Nation: The Myth of the Frontier in Twentieth-Century America* (New York: Atheneum, 1992), 10.

western world that stands at the beginning of our national life'.[3] The texts of this chapter engage with that history in terms of themes such as innocence, the land, opportunity, violence, and masculinity, and each of them makes some attempt to historicize contemporary struggles by reference to a narrative of the past. Writing about three of the most prominent advocates of western life, Owen Wister, Frederick Remington, and Theodore Roosevelt, one critic commented that 'Playing out their personal and class fantasies, these genteel Easterners mythicized the era the more urgently because it was clearly vanishing',[4] and it is worth considering whether the survival of western writing, even beyond the genre fiction of Louis L'Amour, is itself a form of nostalgia (fuelled by cinema) and a way to address origins and formative moments through the agency of literary legend.

Cormac McCarthy **Blood Meridian**

In the popular imagination the colonization of the West is often associated with ideas of adventure and heroism, and these terms are seriously challenged by Cormac McCarthy's *Blood Meridian* (1985). This novel is, in its simplest form, a journey narrative from east to west, Tennessee to California, and from youth to age, kid to man, a *Bildungsroman* of the unnamed protagonist and of the United States in its infancy. It is a journey of violent confrontations in which metaphysical questions about human existence are situated in the context of brutal life-and-death encounters. It is a journey in which characters are frequently referred to as 'pilgrims', and they toil across an extraordinarily hostile landscape, a 'terra damnata' (61)[5] full of invitations to immediate death, where moral law is suspended and human actions are regarded with extreme dispassion and placed in temporal and spatial perspectives so vast as to render the novel's protagonists puny and diminutive. This journey has its antecedents in Conrad's *Heart of Darkness* and Browning's 'Childe Roland to the Dark Tower

---

[3] Donald Pease, quoted in Gerald Graff, *Beyond the Culture Wars* (New York: Norton, 1992), 155.

[4] C. Bold, 'Regions and Regionalism', in M. Gidley (ed.), *Modern American Culture: An Introduction* (London: Longman, 1993), 112.

[5] All page references are to the Picador edition.

Came'. Judge Holden, 'like an icon', tells stories to the assembled company in an attitude like Conrad's Marlowe, 'set before the fire naked save for his breeches and his hands rested palm down upon his knees' (147). The gang of scalphunters ride across the desert like the knights-errant of antique fable, but committed to random violence appropriate to their western genre. Nevertheless, the association with medieval quest is a strong one and the words 'They rode on' become a telling refrain. At one point Toadvine is questioned by a Mexican in a cantina: 'He looked like some loutish knight beriddled by a troll' (102). The men of Glanton's gang are 'condemned to ride out some ancient curse' (151) and they prosecute their journey 'like men invested with a purpose whose origins were antecedent to them, like blood legatees of an order both imperative and remote' (152). This journey is littered with prophetic warnings of doom, from the hermit, fortune teller, and the Mennonite who tells them ' "Do ye cross that river with yon filibuster armed ye'll not cross it back" ' (40), and these portentous adumbrations contribute to a fated quality as the characters are seen 'pursuing as all travellers must inversions without end upon other men's journeys' (121).

To describe *Blood Meridian* as a narrative of violent confrontation is of course a dramatic understatement; the novel is a catalogue of unmitigated carnage in which some of McCarthy's most inventive imaginative and linguistic skills are dedicated to vivid descriptions of slaughter. The novel's depiction of violence raises important moral and historical issues that are central to this text and to McCarthy's oeuvre. Most of all, the language of McCarthy's violence transforms it into something that holds the reader's attention; people here are not simply killed but tortured, butchered, dismembered methodically, reduced to anatomical components (to mere physical matter) in ways that are sumptuous with lyrical intensity. Pain is never referred to. Consider the bush that is decorated with the bodies of dead babies, 'hung so from their throats from the broken stobs of a mesquite' (57), or a Mexican who is shot, 'A fistsized hole erupted out of the far side of the woman's head in a great vomit of gore and she pitched over and lay slain in her own blood without remedy' (98). McCarthy is especially fond of this kind of violence and this kind of writing. When Jackson is challenged by a bar owner, he shoots him 'and a double handful of Owens's brains went out the back of his skull and plopped on the floor behind him' (236), and when Glanton's gang attack a tribe of Gilenos one of them seizes two infants by the heels 'and bashed their heads against the stones so that the brains burst forth through the fontanel in a bloody spew' (156). McCarthy writes about violent death in a way that is especially attentive to its physical actions, for example, when Jackson is decapitated 'Two thick ropes of dark blood and two slender rose like snakes from the stump of his neck and arched hissing into the fire' (107), and the text uses words such as 'aghast' and 'swapt' to contribute to the barbaric vigour of the action. When Glanton is killed, an axe is used to split his head 'to the thrapple', an old Scots word for the windpipe. *Blood Meridian*, as befits its title, is full of a special creative language of violence which strives to do justice to the inventiveness of its historical period's styles of violent death. When Brown torches the young soldier, he runs out into the street 'like a man beset with bees or madness and then he fell over in the road and burned up. By the time they got to him with a bucket of water he had blackened and shrivelled in the mud like an enormous spider' (268). Elsewhere the dead are often reduced to inanimate matter 'like the victims of surgical experimentation' (184) or they are scattered about in grotesque attitudes like the men who 'wore strange menstrual wounds between their legs and no man's parts for those had been cut away and hung dark and strange from out their grinning mouths' (153). Not even the mortally wounded are permitted dignity in death; in the battle with the Comanches some of the combatants 'fell upon the dying and sodomised them with loud cries to their fellows' (54). For one critic, the stories of Glanton's brutality 'appeases a deep-down blood lust',[6] but the motivations to violence in McCarthy's West are more complex than this allows.

In this maelstrom of violent death it is not only Glanton's scalphunting that is murderous and barbaric; in one story the Comanche make a white man walk across the west Texas desert to Fredericksburg having 'Cut the bottoms of his feet off' (77). In another scene Glanton's gang come across two of their missing scouts hanging upside down from a paloverde tree: 'They were skewered through the cords of their heels with sharpened shuttles of green wood and they

---

[6] E. Miles, 'John Glanton, Scalphunter', in *Tales of the Big Bend* (College Station, Tex: A & M University Press, 1976), 131.

hung gray and naked above the dead ashes of the coals where they'd been roasted until their heads had charred and the brains bubbled in the skulls and steam sang from their noseholes' (226–7). The violence of *Blood Meridian* is uncompromising, historically accurate, and indiscriminate in being committed in equal measure by Anglo, Mexican, and Indian alike. The violence has its origin in the novel in the scalp-hunting of Glanton's gang which reduces the Indians, and then Mexicans, to the commodity-value of their body parts; this violence is precipitated by the contracts of the Mexican Governor of Chihuahua, Angel Trias, who was desperate to protect his citizens from the attacks of the Comanche. But McCarthy's novel is not even remotely interested in the cultural politics of this. The bulk of *Blood Meridian* is given over to the episodic murderous exploits of Glanton's gang; in this there is no development in the conventional narrative sense, the carnage is merely cumulative and there is no moral comfort to be derived from it. The violence is committed by Glanton's gang for money, and then purely for the joyless availability of it, such as when they drive the Mexican quicksilver caravan from the mesa. It is true that the Anglo kid comes to the south-west with 'a taste for mindless violence' (3), but the novel constantly moves beyond human agency to larger perspectives which govern its design, and it is in this crucible of multicultural slaughter and violent encounter that American identity is shaped. When Jackson is killed by the Yuma Indians 'a long cane arrow passed through his upper abdomen. . .and began to drift downstream' (273). The man is incidental to the trajectory and action of the arrow which passes through him as if he was an incidental feature of the landscape. Nor is the arrow and the others that follow it connected to any human agency because the attention of the language is to material actions, so that even the spurtings of Jackson's 'dark arterial blood' render the human presence almost inconsequential to the larger scheme of destruction and annihilation. This is partly a function of the south-western desert landscape which can be equally terrifying in its murderous extremes; when the kid and Toadvine are pursued across the Yuma Desert for example 'the periodic arrows sprang aslant from the sands about them like the tufted stalks of mutant desert growths propagating angrily into the dry desert air' (279). There is also a dark southern humour in some of the violence of *Blood Meridian*, the legacy of Flannery O'Connor, such as when

Sproule, his arm gangrenous and maggot-ridden and his chest full of consumption, says to the kid: 'I come out here for my health' (58).

The dramatic narrative of *Blood Meridian* lies in the relationship between the kid and judge Holden. The kid is characterized by his proclivity to violence but his father was a schoolmaster who 'quotes from poets' (3) as the judge does, and the text of the novel here itself quotes Wordsworth: 'the child the father of the man'. It would be wrong to claim that, like Stephen Daedalus, the kid is in search of a father, but his relationship with judge Holden is a very important one. The judge tells the kid 'I'd have loved you like a son' (306) and he argues that 'it is the death of the father to which the son is entitled and to which he is heir' (145). The kid and judge Holden are ultimately the only survivors of Glanton's gang, and that survival and their shared experience gives them a special relationship, one which the judge invokes: 'The last of the true. The last of the true. I'd say they're all gone under now saving me and thee' (327). The drama of the novel emerges suddenly and unexpectedly in the last three chapters of the novel when the kid becomes a man and has the opportunity to challenge the judge. Chapter 20 especially is a crucial turning point in the antagonism of the judge for the kid, and it coincides with the end of the primary historical source from which McCarthy is working, the recollections of Chamberlain's autobiography. As one scholar tells us: '*My Confession* concludes as Chamberlain exits the desert west of the Yuma Crossing within days after the massacre'.[7]

Following the massacre of Glanton and most of his gang by Yuma Indians, the kid escapes with Toadvine, to be pursued by a group of Yumas across the desert. At Alamo Mucho they meet another survivor, the ex-priest Tobin, and under siege at the well the scalphunters begin to cooperate for survival; the kid is now an excellent gunshot, ' "He's a deadeye aint he?'. Tobin nodded' (281). These are rare signs of a camaraderie not previously noted among Glanton's company as the novel briefly flirts with a more conventional western scenario of the kind typical of the novels of Louis L'Amour or Thomas Eidson. The survivors are joined by the judge, but the kid is the only one with a weapon, and he refuses to sell it to the judge. It is important to note

---

[7] J. E. Sepich, ' "What Kind of Indians was them?" ', in E. T. Arnold and D. Luce (eds.), *Perspectives on Cormac McCarthy* (Jackson: University Press of Mississippi, 1999), 140

that it is here that the kid and the judge become adversaries. The kid emerges as the only one with an opportunity to kill the judge, and he refrains from murder despite Tobin's whispered entreaties, '"Do it or I swear your life is forfeit"' (285). The judge understands the kid's position, and here they become mortal enemies until the novel ends.

The sudden dramatic emergence of a deadly antagonism with the judge at chapter 20 is coincident with the kid's emergence as a man. Born in 1833, the chronology of *Blood Meridian* has moved forward to 1878 and the kid is now 45. This shift is dramatized in several import-ant ways. The kid's adroit one-liner to Toadvine, for example, is evi-dence of his acquired western wisdom: '"It ain't country you've run out of"' (285). Having escaped the judge's first attempt to murder him, the kid becomes uncharacteristically loquacious, and in a prison cell in San Diego 'he began to speak with a strange urgency of things few men have seen in a lifetime' (305). The function of the kid's encounter with Elrod is to dramatize again the Oedipal nature of the novel's conflict (Elrod is a version of the kid as he once was himself) and, silently absent for two hundred pages, the kid can now emerge as a veteran of atrocious proportions. Elrod has no chance:

I was fifteen year old when I was first shot.
I aint never been shot.
You aint sixteen yet neither. (321)

Elrod also makes the mistake of challenging the historical veracity of the kid's scapular of Apache ears, and so moves swiftly from satirizing the authority of the kid's history, to death. The lesson here is not to doubt the violent record of the past. As the kid vanquishes Elrod, the judge takes the life of the younger generation's sole survivor in a moment of deathly paternal embrace because his ability to do so is a testament to his own history. The judge's adoption of the imbecile is evidence of his desire for an infant, acolyte or son, but the kid defies the judge's will, '"you turned a deaf ear to me"' (307), and the judge identifies in the kid a point of weakness, '"a flawed place in the fabric of your heart"' (299) which gives him the opportunity to appropriate and subsume the kid to his own domineering will. The judge is a multilingual intellectual, a well-read and well-travelled man, a proto-Darwinian and a quasi-Nietzschean. He is also a murderous paedo-phile. The judge's Nietzschean discourse acts as a commentary on the novel, but he too is subordinate to the larger forces of the text, forces to which he is alert and which he alone seeks to understand himself in the context of: '"Our animosities were formed and waiting before ever we two met"' (307). The judge understands the larger parameters of the violent struggles of *Blood Meridian* and his project of putting everything in his book is part of his will to power which necessitates the subordination of the kid. This is all part of the ritual of the dance that the judge expounds as he laments the passing of the old West and the 'sanctity of blood' that it consisted of (331).

Blood Meridian is a text that dramatizes everywhere perspectives of time and space so enormously beyond human lifespans that the histories of the novel's characters are profoundly diminished by the natural history of the desert landscape they occupy. This geological history is combined with imagery of the shifting of the planets and adumbrations of future epochs so completely beyond the ken of the novel's participants that their actions are diminished to microscopic significance in the larger drama of the matter of the physical universe. It is significant that *Blood Meridian* has no single central character in the conventional western sense, and in this the novel is 'a critique of our culture's anthropocentrism'.[8] It is also notable that the birth and death of the kid are accompanied by astronomical portents and movements: 'Night of your birth . . . God how the stars did fall' (3). The moment prior to the kid's death is also one of cosmic annihilation: 'Stars were falling across the sky myriad and random, speeding along brief vectors from their origins in night to their destinies in dust and nothingness' (333). It is a stereotype of western genre fiction that its heroes are phlegmatic, laconic, taciturn, and in its last three chapters especially *Blood Meridian* indulges the expectations of the western, but the novel's most taciturn moment is in its depiction of the death of the kid, extinguished in the 'immense and terrible flesh' of the judge (333). The kid simply disappears, a characteristic fate of the figures of McCarthy's West, where Anglo scalphunters, Mexicans, and Indian nations alike are annihilated in the violent crucible of the vast desert spaces at the birth of the North American empire. Captain White acts as a mouthpiece for the ideology of Manifest Destiny

---

8 V. Bell, *The Achievement of Cormac McCarthy* (Baton Rouge: Louisiana State University Press, 1988), 124.

which helped to sustain rapacious western expansion, but his head ends up in a glass bottle at a Mexican travelling circus (70). McCarthy's West is a purgatorial waste entirely indifferent to the human dramas played out on it, it is the high point (meridian) of the United States' bloody history, and the physical space where the empire's violent origin is historically situated. McCarthy's West is a spectacle of 'Itinerant degenerates bleeding westward like some heliotropic plague' (78) and a spectacle observed with such extreme dispassion that when Glanton shoots a bear, his gunshot is depicted as speeding towards the stars to join the realm of material things that over-shadows everything in this western landscape: 'The shot rose and rose, a small core of metal scurrying toward the distant beltways of matter grinding mutely to the west above them all' (137).

What remains is style, the aesthetics of McCarthy's language, its Faulknerian fifteen-line sentences (52, 195, 276), remarkable recondite diction, arresting reversals of syntax, plangent epic declamations, austerity of tone, and attention to visual detail that is simultaneously intense and clinical. Denis Donoghue argues that *Blood Meridian* endorses Nietzsche's claim that 'art rather than ethics constitutes the essential metaphysical activity of man', and he cites the dance of the judge as McCarthy's dramatization of this.[9] The judge, like McCarthy, seeks to put everything in his book. But this is not to say that the judge is a metaphor for McCarthy as artist; the judge's performance is not McCarthy's, it is simply accommodated by *Blood Meridian* as a spectacle of one man's attempt to become 'suzerain' (198). Another way of thinking about the artistry of *Blood Meridian* is in terms of the freedoms of imagination that McCarthy's creative choices seem to permit. The nineteenth-century setting gives the novelist licence to select and adapt historical materials (especially judge Holden) and to abandon them when they have served their purpose, as with the dramatic shift that occurs towards the end of the novel when the usefulness of Chamberlain's *My Confession* is exhausted. The setting in this particular topographical space gives the narrative freedom of movement in the vast territory of the American south-west and northern Mexico. Although it is still possible to plot the gang's movements on a map, their exploits seem to take place in an uncharted

[9] D. Donoghue, 'Reading Blood Meridian', *Sewanee Review*, 105: 3 (1997), 418.

region characterized principally by the absence of order, control, or social sanction. It might be proposed that there is a topographical expansiveness and liberty that has an analogue in the imaginative and creative freedom with which the novel is artistically composed. As one critic commented of *Blood Meridian*, 'fittingly for a work set in a borderland, it seems curiously suspended, not just between regions and geographies, but within literary history'.[10] McCarthy's novel appropriates recognizably southern and western elements according to the exigencies of the moment, and this is characteristic of the eclectic formal synthesis that marks *Blood Meridian* as a text.

E. A. Proulx **Close Range**

Two of western fiction's most famous texts are set in Wyoming, Owen Wister's *The Virginian* (1902) and Jack Schaefer's *Shane* (1949), and although Annie Proulx's *Close Range* (1999) includes the standard disclaimer that 'Any resemblance to actual events or locales or persons, living or dead, is entirely coincidental', her text is subtitled 'Wyoming Stories' and it uses real Wyoming towns such as Tie Siding, Ten Sleep, and Thermopolis, and real Wyoming landscapes such as the Tetons, Yellowstone National Park, and the Shoshone Indian Reservation. One of the ways that the West is often valorized, even today, is in terms of a certain honesty, integrity, and trustworthiness that is allegedly found there, a particular western probity that is refreshingly free of the corruption of the cities of the East. The narrator of *The Virginian* is quickly sensitive to this western quality when he arrives in Wyoming and he criticizes 'the celluloid good-fellowship that passes for ivory with nine in ten of the city crowd. But not so with the sons of the sagebrush. They live nearer nature, and they know better.' The narrator of *Shane* is brought up on the Wyoming high plains where 'The silence was clean and wholesome', and he idolizes Shane because he is 'as self-reliant as the mountains', and because he exemplifies a direct moral clarity that is archetypally western: 'Straight and superb, not a tremor in him, he came to us and you knew that the spirit in

---

10 D. Phillips, 'History and the Ugly Facts of Cormac McCarthy's *Blood Meridian*', *American Literature*, 68: 2 (June 1996), 452–3.

him would sustain him thus alone and for the farthest distance and forever.' This kind of mythologizing has long been integral to the appeal of the West, where dreams of freedom and rebirth and personal fulfilment have a special currency; such dreams thrive and flourish to sustain a particularly American sense of identity. In Edith Wharton's *Ethan Frome* the eponymous protagonist longs to escape the paralysing claustrophobia of Massachusetts: 'He knew a case of a man over the mountain, a young fellow of about his own age, who had escaped from just such a life of misery by going West with the girl he cared for'. Wilson, the garage mechanic of *The Great Gatsby*, tells Buchanan, 'I've been here too long—I want to get away. My wife and I want to go West.' Paul Auster concludes his novella 'Ghosts' (1986) by packing off his protagonist like a latter-day Ethan Frome: 'I myself prefer to think that he went far away, boarding a train that morning and going out West to start a new life',[11] and this phrase 'a new life' is of crucial importance to the culture of the United States and of fundamental importance to the West. Auster's words recall the title of Bernard Malamud's novel *A New Life* (1961) in which Sy Levin, who has never been west of Jersey City, moves to Oregon and finds himself welcoming students to college there: 'They represented the America he had so often heard of, the fabulous friendly west.' These characters all subscribe to the myth of the West which has engaged the imagination since the birth of the nation. The young protagonist of Tobias Wolff's *This Boy's Life* (1989) expresses it most succinctly when he leaves Florida for Salt Lake City: 'I didn't come to Utah to be the same boy I'd been before. I had my own dreams of transformation, western dreams, dreams of freedom and dominion and taciturn self-sufficiency.' These twentieth-century characters all answer Horace Greeley's nineteenth-century imperative: 'Go West'.

Annie Proulx's writing has always shown an interest in the frontier, the wilderness, and in the forms of American identity and American dreaming that are found there. The title story of *Heart Songs* (1994) ends with the character Snipe fantasizing about escape from the East:

There were other things they could do, maybe go out west, New Mexico or Arizona. . . . He thought how it would be out west with the flat, sepia-tinted

[11] Paul Auster, 'Ghosts', in *The New York Trilogy* (London: Faber and Faber, 1988), 195.

earth and the immense sky of a hard, lonely blue. Out there the roads stretched forever to the horizon. Snipe saw himself alone, driving a battered old truck through the shimmering heat, the wind booming through the open windows. The windshield was starred with a bullet hole. He wore scuffed cowboy boots, faded jeans, and a torn black shirt with a cactus embroidered on the back, and the heel of his hand beat out a Tex-Mex rhythm on the cracked steering wheel.' (86)

Where Snipe longs to escape to the West, many of the characters of *Close Range* (1999) are desperate to escape from it. Some of them get away successfully, to Austin, San Diego, and Tucson, but most are trapped forever by the unforgiving landscape and dedicate their lives to survival rather than flight. There is little evidence of dreaming in *Close Range*, there simply is not time for the luxury of imagination, and if dreaming is indulged, the results are despair, madness, and murder.

'The Half-Skinned Steer', for example, tells the story of the return to Wyoming of Mero, for the funeral of his brother. Mero embarks on the four-day drive from Massachusetts to Cheyenne as if to emulate the trailblazers of the frontier, here given as an arduous and hazardous journey west in which the Cadillac replaces the horse and proves far less reliable. Mero's long drive west at the age of 83 dramatizes the pull of history, as he is drawn back to Wyoming in a way that shows that the 'sons of the sagebrush' can never entirely escape its legacy. Mero has ample time to contemplate that legacy as he drives across Iowa and Nebraska and remembers why he left 'to find his own territory' away from the inheritance of his father, and especially his father's girlfriend who seems also to have a relationship with Mero's brother. In Mero's long absence the economic circumstances of Wyoming have changed and the ranch is now a tourist enterprise called 'Down Under Wyoming'. New commercial ventures also have their hazards; one of the ranch's emus attacked Mero's brother and 'laid him open from belly to breakfast', a fatal accident that is regarded with a typically phlegmatic western resignation: 'Emus is bad for claws' (21).[12] Mero left because he was never suited to ranch work and even now cannot eat steak, 'a cattleman gone wrong' (28), but he still wants to discover whether his brother took their father's

---

12 All page references are to the Scribner edition.

girlfriend and has 'thrown a saddle on her and ridden off into the sunset' (23).

The most important aspect of the story is its parallel narrative in which the unnamed girlfriend tells the story of the half-skinned steer. This story is clearly in the tradition of the western tall tale in which frontier humorists were noted for spinning yarns of comic exaggeration about adventures and outrageous turns of fortune, often with a special interest in grotesque and macabre subjects, and in a language that was exuberant and racy and full of the colloquial idiom. These tall tales were an oral genre that preserved the character of a distinctly American western experience in a regional vernacular that matched the unsophisticated physical action that they described. The girlfriend's tale subscribes to this tradition; its protagonist is a lazy rancher who has a metal plate in his head that is eating away at his brain, and its central incident is an ugly scene in which a half-skinned steer gets up and walks away, 'the raw meat of the head and the shoulder muscles and the empty mouth with no tongue open wide' (35). The girlfriend who tells this tale is twice described as a 'liar' (24, 30) and this too associates her with the western tradition in which storytellers were often raconteurs and braggarts. The girlfriend is a particularly skilled exponent of the tall tale, 'She could make you smell the smoke from an unlit fire' (33).

The girlfriend's tale is interpolated into the account of Mero's return to Wyoming and the last lines of the story suddenly conflate the two narratives. Mero is brought to his death as 'the violent country showed itself' and his age and his foolishness are exposed by the severity of the western weather. Mero is tracked by a single animal, 'the half-skinned steer's red eye had been watching for him all this time' (38). The sudden conflation of the parallel narratives proves the veracity and continuity of a western narrative tradition, one which the stories of *Close Range* seek to emulate and develop in a contemporary context. Furthermore, the story also emphasizes Mero's fear of women because he believes that the girlfriend's tale is a curse of death on him that has come true, and that her story has foretold of his demise. This fear is a part of Mero's western legacy that began in the cave where he was introduced to the Indian drawings of the bodies of women, as a result of which 'no fleshy examples ever conquered his belief in the subterranean stony structure of female genitalia' (26). His father's girlfriend's tale has an authenticity which his death proves true, and even though this occurs principally in his imagination, his belief that she has taken her revenge on his family is evidence only of his fear of women, and this particular woman storyteller especially. Mero's belief in the final value of her narrative confirms the efficacy of the imagination's importance in the West, and this is an importance that the stories of *Close Range* consistently affirm.

'The Half-Skinned Steer' tests the credulity of the reader, and this too is a common strategy in *Close Range*. 'The Bunchgrass Edge of the World' tells the story of a lonely girl who is courted by a tractor; in 'The Blood Bay' a horse eats a cowboy while he sleeps and leaves only his boots; in '55 Miles to the Gas Pump' the desperate isolation of the plains drives a man to serial murder and he fills his attic with corpses; in 'People in Hell just want a Drink of Water' the narrator informs us that such desperate things no longer happen, and then adds 'If you believe that you'll believe anything' (115). In each case Wyoming is presented as a place where the fantastic and grisly often occurs, or where narrative contrivance and exaggeration is part of the genius of the West. The issue of credulity is picked out by the collection's epigraph: 'Reality's never been of much use out here', which suggests that the West is a place of fable and romance, an open space where the proliferation of western fictions is given free range to continue to condition the lives of contemporary westerners. These fictions of the fabled West, however, are almost always debilitating in *Close Range*.

'The Mud Below', for example, is also a story that addresses the relationship between the old West and the new West, and especially the inheritance of western paternity and ideas of western 'cowboy' masculinity. Here the legacy of the old West survives in the rodeo circuit, and the contemporary inflexion of the new West is represented by the chain of stores selling western 'antiques' to eastern tourists. Diamond Felts has not left the West but has embraced its nineteenth-century history by becoming a bull rider on the rodeo circuit in Colorado, Oklahoma, and Wyoming. Diamond discovers 'a feeling of power' (47) at the rodeo because he derives a sense of identity from the image of masculinity that it promotes. Diamond, a diminutive five feet three, finds at the rodeo 'the bull in himself' (62). Diamond's mother has worked hard to keep her son away from this western lifestyle and she is utterly contemptuous of cowboys (57) because she knows them from her father's ranch to be little more than poorly paid hired hands. Diamond is not the tall slim model of cowboy good looks, even his mother calls him 'Shorty', but the rodeo is an opportunity for him to subscribe to a cowboy manliness and glamour that he finds seductive. The rodeo then is a fabled fiction of western American manhood. However, 'The Mud Below' reveals this to be the consequence of a failed paternity. It is significant that Diamond's desire for the rodeo is a childhood memory of a merry-go-round that his father took him to at the age of 5 (48). Bull riding is for Diamond an expression of a desire for his lost father and a memory of the pain of his father's absence. The violence of this inheritance is dramatized by Diamond's rape of Londa in Cheyenne (63) and by his memory of his father's brutal rejoinder 'Not your father and never was' (65). Similarly, Diamond's mother's angry accusation 'You're just like him' (50) is testimony to the trauma of their broken family, the real subject of this story. The rodeo cowboys' drunken paeans to 'family values' are simply the sentimental nostalgia of adolescent men who are away from their families so often that the western rodeo circuit has become their family. Diamond has the honesty to recognize this and not be fooled by a western travesty of 'family values' rhetoric which is very sharply satirized here (Musgrove splits his winnings 'between his grandmother and a home for blind orphans', (71)). The rodeo cannot be used in the service of family values, the cowboys are surrounded by groupies or 'buckle bunnies', and they sentimentalize the family they abandoned for their peripatetic lifestyle on the road. The cowboy, like Shane, is an utterly solitary figure, and, as Pake Bitts tells Diamond, ' "You can't have a fence with only one post" ' (69). Here then, the legendary self-sufficiency of the cowboy is revealed to be a function of his broken past, and Diamond's isolation is a consequence of his failure to form a relationship that lasts for more than 'two hours' (53).

The tension of the old and the new is brought together, as in the previous story, by the final incident, in which Diamond asks his mother who his father was. Her enigmatic answer, ' "Nobody" ', deprives Diamond entirely of paternity and the story ends with a symbolic memory of castration, 'slitting the scrotal sac' (78), which signifies the impotence of contemporary western stereotypes of manhood and the ersatz glamour of the kind of manhood purveyed by rodeo. The story ends on an elegiac note with Diamond's final accident; like Mero, he discovers that the physical demands of the West are too much. This too is a story about failure in which the influence of paternity is malign and contemporary westerners are fated to suffer the debilitating pressures of a history which defeats them in the end. Both stories include references to prostate cancer. The narrative of Diamond's life is like a bull ride, and the only skill consists of hanging on as long as possible before being forced to confront 'The Mud Below'. That the story's title is a quotation from a country song is further evidence of Proulx's interest in the conflict between the material conditions of the contemporary West and the continued pressure of fictions about its fabled past.

The first two stories establish the agenda for Proulx's vision of the West: entrapment and escape, history and survival, economics and landscape, masculinity and violence. Each of these subjects is treated with an awareness of its nineteenth-century history and in the full knowledge of that history's survival in fictions and myths about the West that continue to exert an influence on the lives of contemporary westerners. 'The Governors of Wyoming' dramatizes the struggle between opposing ideas of what the West means, and how those ideas are sustained by competing fictions, myths, and images. In the changing political economy of Wyoming, Hulse represents the old way of life where survival is paramount and calls on all his rancher's resources of resilience and stoicism: 'Hulse stood as thousands of men in the west, braced against the forces bending him' (233). The qualities that Hulse exemplifies are those of the frontier, 'the territory' (229) and his philosophy of ' "last as long as you can" ' (235) is characteristic of the legacy of the nineteenth century, a legacy captured by the collection of photographs of the Governors of Wyoming. The photographs are a reminder that ' "important things happened in this place" ' (227). But can this lifestyle continue in the 'New West' of corporations, suitcase ranchers and telecommuters ' "Drinkin cappuccino while they watch the elk" ' (234)? The new West is represented in this story by Wade Walls, the vegetarian environmentalist who opposes ranching for the damage that it does to the land and who argues that ranchers like Hulse are ' "destroying the west" ' (222). Walls's political rhetoric is satirized as romantic nostalgia (' "I want it to be like it was" ', (218)) and it is important to note that he is a disciple of Edward Abbey and that his environmentalist activism is motivated by reading Abbey's texts, especially *The Monkey Wrench Gang* (1975), rather than any close personal experience of the West. Walls 'seemed to come from nowhere and belonged to no one' (215). Another version of the new West, but significantly one that does not challenge the lifestyle of the ranchers, is seen in the tourist trade, represented by the very successful business enterprise of Renti who sells 'potions and pony-skin vests' in Taos, New Mexico (225). Again Proulx suggests that economic survival of the West lies in merchandising phoney images of its fabled past and exploiting its Indian culture ('Cheyenne', (219)) to tourists whose understanding of the West is derived from baneful movie images and risible songs such as 'I Shot the Sheriff' (228). Between the old West and the new West stands Shy, the reluctant eco-warrior 'champion of nothing, a kind of tame cowboy without the horse sweat and grit' (219) who is hopelessly emasculated by economic hardship and cruises for sex with a Shoshone girl from the reservation despite his 'classic western good looks' (236).

The particular ingenuity of 'The Governors of Wyoming' is the way that it brings together in a dramatic form the political ideologies and texts of the old and new West without making a simple moral choice between them. Most of all, it frames Shy as a victim of those opposing forces, abandoned by Walls and suddenly confronted by the image of Governor Emerson. Walls is a charlatan and a coward who disappears as surreptitiously as he arrived and whose true identity is revealed as he flees, 'avenging son of an assembly line butcher' (243), leaving Shy to face the music. But the final image is reserved for Shy and the bathos of his predicament. It is an elegiac and enigmatic finale in which the satire of Abbey's western environmentalist politics is slightly offset by the reference to pollution from refineries in Utah (242) and the violence of Abbey's manifesto ('Keep America Beautiful . . . Burn a Billboard') is placed alongside the violence of the old West's 'Ricochet' and bobwire neckties (245). Hulse's bullet skips the story's intended satirical target and catches Shy, but he is equally struck by the image of the past, captured momentarily (and like Mero, principally in his imagination) as part of Wyoming's political history. Shy 'might have ridden through this country a long time ago' (244) but now finds himself framed by the conflicting mythologies of the old and the new West, captured forever at a particular moment as an image of what the West means now. With the reference to the photograph, Shy becomes an image for posterity of the debilitated predicament of the contemporary West, stranded by the conflict between its nineteenth-century past and its twenty-first-century future, 'past his apogee and falling, sidewise and awkward' (245).

Sherman Alexie The Lone-Ranger and Tonto Fistfight in Heaven

The western Chicano writer Rudolfo Anaya once wrote that 'To read a story from New Mexico and one from Iowa and feel that either story could have taken place in either locale defeats the story',[13] and this idea of the importance of landscape is certainly central to *Close Range*, the stories of which are firmly grounded in a sense of Wyoming's topographical particularity and the politics of identity that are associated with it. The West has often been written about as if it were an Edenic open space for Europeans to colonize, a space for them to occupy because it was essentially an open space. This, of course, is not true. The West was inhabited by an indigenous native American population that had to be forcibly removed so that frontiersmen of various kinds could exploit its rich natural resources. The West was only a virgin land from a Eurocentric perspective, and it is this apparent ignorance of native populations that prompted Elizabeth Cook-Lynn to argue that there is a pervasive tendency in western writing to render the American Indian as invisible, non-existent: 'It serves to make the claim of the nativeness of all European immigrants to this land more valid because such indigenous populations as are described here will not last long, and if they do somehow survive their own ridiculousness, they will do so as degenerates of history, defeated and outrageous'.[14] Attacking the cultural promotion of Wallace Stegner in particular, Cook-Lynn argues that 'There is perhaps no American fiction writer who has been more successful in serving the interests of a nation's fantasy about itself', and she calls for 'a shift in attitude

---

13 R. Anaya, in D. K. Dunaway (ed.), *Writing the Southwest* (Harmondsworth: Penguin, 1995), x.
14 Elizabeth Cook-Lynn, *Why I Can't Read Wallace Stegner and Other Essays* (Madison: University of Wisconsin Press, 1996), 34–5.

concerning the history and literature of the region called the West'
(29, 30). A necessary corollary of the westward expansion of the frontier was the western containment of its indigenous population. The
story 'Imagining the Reservation' from Sherman Alexie's collection
The Lone-Ranger and Tonto Fistfight in Heaven (1993) is acutely attentive to the politics of identity in the West, to the freedoms and
opportunities of 'a new life' (152) as they are dramatized by 'the story
of the hobo who hopped a train heading west' (150).[15] The hobo died
on the journey, locked in a refrigerator car, not because of the temperature but as a consequence of the simple act of entrapment and
confinement, as if the curtailing of his liberty had robbed him of the
will to live: 'It happens that way: the body forgets the rhythm of
survival' (150). This story acts as an analogue to the history of Indian
experience in Alexie's West, one of relocation, imprisonment, and a
desperate struggle for survival in the enclosed space of the reservation
where Eurocentric ideas of western opportunity are replaced by a
profound sense of physical and cultural limitation. 'Imagining the
Reservation' combats this history of confinement with its imperative
call-to-arms 'Imagine', and it utilizes the convenience store, the 7-11,
as the impoverished space where dreams might begin that could
change the course of history and offer Indians a different future:
'Imagination is the only weapon on the reservation' (150). The particular subtlety of the story is the way that it accommodates in an
extraordinarily compressed form a history of the significance of
Indian imaginative endeavour and its close association with the
material circumstances of reservation life. The story is comprised of
affirmations of the power of imagination and the ways that it can be
both circumscribed by poverty and inspired by poverty; the narrator's
sisters used food colouring to brighten their diet of potatoes (151). It is
a story that is composed of stories (the hobo, the Indian visionary, the
address to Adrian, the alternative histories) which challenges the
reader to understand these narratives' multiple significance and to
recognize how the story addresses the history and function of
imagination in Indian culture. The word 'Imagine' begins with the
visionary Indian child, the legatee of 'some medicine man come back
to change our lives' who demonstrates the power of imagination to

---

[15] All page references are to the Vintage edition.

transform the prosaic into something miraculous. The story of the child is enacted in the material life of the narrator whose behaviour is transformed 'reflecting every last word of the story' (151). Subsequently, the story 'Imagining the Reservation' takes its place in this tradition by beginning with the word 'Imagine'. In this way life on the reservation can be changed, just like the narrator's shared stories with his father had the power 'to change the world' (151).

'Imagining the Reservation' contains many further contemplations of the history of representations, because the reservation is a place that is latent with creative potential, 'The reservation doesn't sing anymore but the songs still hang in the air', and it is a place that has the power to change the lives of the people who live there. There is an urgency and an important oral quality given by the use of the imperatives 'Imagine' and 'Listen' and in the repeated address to 'Adrian' the poet who is quoted as sharing the narrator's creative frustration at the prosaic limitations of domestic survival: *'I want to rasp into sober cryptology and say something dynamic but tonight is my laundry night'* (152). By this quotation Adrian's lyric is enlisted to the narrator's Independence Day plea for the revitalization of an authentic Indian narrative, which, of course, 'Imagining the Reservation' becomes part of. The narrative of Indian defeat is merely 'the same old story' and it is the purpose of Alexie's story to imagine the means by which new narratives of Indian life might be fashioned: 'How can we imagine a new language when the language of the enemy keeps our dismembered tongues tied to his belt? How can we imagine a new alphabet when the old jumps off billboards down into our stomachs?' (152). The rhetorical questions combine a nineteenth-century history of violent suppression with a twentieth-century history of economic servitude, one form of enslavement succeeded by another. The enclosed space of the convenience store aisles and the paucity of the 'pocketful of quarters' that the narrator has for purchasing power, offers a metaphor for the freedoms of American consumer society that the narrator uses to imagine a different Indian history. This is 'the 7-11 of my dreams' where Indians can choose by agency of the imagination a different history and a different future 'on the cover of a rock-and-roll magazine' (152). A further subtlety of the story is its awareness of the duplicity of this metaphor: no 'new alphabet' can come from a store full of 'convenient lies' where the image of diminution and confinement is found again in the cashiers who 'insist on small bills' (150). This is a criticism that has wider cultural currency in the story's question 'Does every Indian depend on Hollywood for a twentieth-century vision?' (151), which, in context, acts as a three-way pun associating the real visions of the Indian child, the perception of Indians by non-Indians in terms of patronizing stereotypes, and the understanding of Indians themselves in terms of the images peddled 'in the cable television reservation' (149). The baneful stereotypes of Hollywood contribute to the limiting pressures on contemporary Indian identity. The story asks: who has the power to imagine, what really useful forms can imagination take, and which are the duplicitous imaginative forms that should be resisted or challenged?

'Imagining the Reservation' utilizes a combative politicized conception of imagination to break out of enclosures and fight back. The story's epigraph emphasizes the value of imagination in the antagonistic struggle for survival, 'ours is stronger than theirs', and the story's plea is for Adrian to 'save us . . . save us' (152) with a new mythology of contemporary Indian life. This mythology will give Indians new stories to live by and so help face down the threat of cultural and ethnic disappearance. The often intense self-consciousness of Alexie's stories is always politicized in this way, their self-reflexivity dedicated to the material ways that storytelling can be a method of cultural salvation with practical consequences beyond the realm of the purely textual: 'Imagine a story that puts wood in the fireplace' (153).

The very title 'Imagining the Reservation' conflates topographical and imaginative space so that the reservation is configured as a sacred place that is characterized by the proliferation of myths and stories. 'The Only Traffic Signal on the Reservation Doesn't Flash Red Anymore' also establishes the reservation in terms of a community of shared hardship where stories of survival help to protect Indians from erosion and disappearance. This story dramatizes the history of expectation and defeat in the shape of the career of the young basketball player Julius Windmaker. In the alcoholism and boredom of the reservation, basketball is a way to achieve respect, status, and self-esteem, both within the tribal community and beyond that in the white world of Spokane. The boy Windmaker looks like a promising player but by the end of the story his promise is exhausted. The community needs great players, as heroes and role models, and they look out for the prospects of each new talent in great anticipation of a saviour. Such failures as Windmaker's are mythologized, their memory kept alive by communal reports that become more exaggerated as time goes by. There is an immortality in the shared stories of every player's career, and this is characteristic of how the community sustains a belief in itself: 'A reservation hero is a hero forever' (48). The protagonists Victor and Adrian are passive, feminized in shawls (51) they sit on the porch and can only watch. Their Russian roulette is a desperate adult parallel to the petty crime of Windmaker 'looking for honor in some twentieth century vandalism' (44). Victor and Adrian are already defeated, but they function as mythologizers and this is a crucial role in the maintenance of a sustaining sense of Indian identity. Their storytelling is a powerful affirmation of the value of the individual's importance to the tribe; at the same time their stories dramatize the sustaining sense of oral history that the tribe can offer the individual.

The passing of one year in the story dramatizes the decline of Windmaker's promising future, the defeat of Victor's expectations of him, and the rise of another potential hero, Lucy. One year on, and the traffic signal is still broken. This is typical of how Alexie can take something prosaic and use it to creative effect: 'only one car an hour passed by' (48). The signal is an image of futility, irrelevance, 'what's the point of fixing it in a place where the stop signs are just suggestions?' (52). The story's title turns another image of defeat into something of creative significance to reservation life. One year later and the strengths of the communal life of the reservation are affirmed: Adrian's return, his camaraderie with Victor, their shared battle against alcoholism, the shared mythology of the reservation and how it succeeds in taking in everyone somehow, even those who only played for five minutes and only made one shot, their stories survive in this space. Above all the story emphasizes the necessity of storytelling to tribal survival in the face of white culture's denigration of Indians. The story ends with a remarkable moment. Adrian, never having played basketball, throws his coffee cup, in despair and frustration, but there is something magical about the moment of its trajectory, its falling, like Windmaker's, is special, even miraculous: 'And we both watched it with all of our eyes, while the sun rose straight up above us and settled down behind the house, watched that cup revolve,

revolve, until it came down whole to the ground' (53). Unlike the traffic signal, the cup is not broken. Adrian's desperate and pointless shot is a moment of ludic magic, and it will in turn become the material for future stories in which a kind of artistic victory is snatched from gestures of anger and despair.

Like many of the stories of the collection, 'The Only Traffic Signal on the Reservation Doesn't Flash Red Anymore' posits an opposition between 'the outside world' which is 'the white world' and the ethnic space of the reservation. Contact with the white world at the state basketball championships is death; in the all-Indian competition, Victor scores baskets even when he is drunk. Contact with the white world is usually to the detriment of Indians in Alexie's stories: 'Still, Indians have a way of surviving. But it's almost like Indians can easily survive the big stuff. Mass murder, loss of language and land rights. It's the small things that hurt the most. The white waitress who wouldn't take an order, Tonto, the Washington Redskins' (49). The deathliness of encounters between reservation Indians and western urban society is dramatized everywhere in the collection, and its five-hundred-year history of Indian loss is often accommodated within the parameters of Alexie's twentieth-century encounters.

The title story for example begins again in a 7-11, this time in Seattle, where at 3 a.m. the cashier's suspicion of Victor as a potential armed robber is played off against his innocence as he lets the cream-sicle melt on his hand like a child. This meeting, full of wariness and distrust, gives way to memories of his white girlfriend and that relationship's failure because of ethnic difference. Both relationships are made difficult by a shared awareness of a history of mutual antagon-ism between ethnic groups. The cashier is nervous of 'this dark skin and long, black hair' (183). His girlfriend concedes that for their romance to prosper it would be necessary for them 'to change the world' (190). Away from the reservation Victor is entirely out of place, the police stop him and ask ' "Where are you supposed to be?" ' (182) and his return 'back home' is expected and inevitable because it is part of Indian lore that 'Indians can reside in the city, but they can never live there' (187). The 7-11 is used to introduce the duplicity of com-mercial transactions and its history for Indians in which they were cheated of vast areas of land in the West and confined to the enclosed spaces of the reservations: 'We'll take Washington and Oregon and you get six pine trees and a brand new Chrysler Cordoba' (183–4). This is typical of how Alexie's stories make the connection between the physical space of the West and the drastic foreshortening of Indian horizons. The violence of Indian enclosure is another example of 'that kind of evil in the old West' (186). Indian perspectives are diminished on all fronts in the West: the newspaper is full of reports of momentous and socially significant upheavals, but meanwhile 'A kid from Spokane won the local spelling bee by spelling the word rhinoceros' (187). White incursion into Indian life has only served to destroy it. The final straw in the title story comes for Victor when the son of the head of the Bureau of Indian Affairs comes to the reservation to play basketball: 'that white kid took over the game' (189). In any form of cultural engagement with whites, Indians cannot win, and their two modes of cultural lifestyle are 'mutually exclusive'.

The open space which in other western texts is a metaphor for opportunity and freedom is diminished in Alexie's work to a shifting tension between the physical limits of the reservation and difficult negotiations with white urban culture, 'the world of cable tv and delivered pizza'. On the other hand, the imaginative space of the reservation, its fecund, open potential for mythologizing, is something of a sanctuary in contrast with urban America. Confinement of topographical space encourages an embattled creative ability and the magical expansiveness of imagination on the reservation is everywhere affirmed as the mode of survival. In 'A Good Story' the community remembers Moses's house and this is 'just enough to ensure survival' (141). Moses's identity is maintained in the communal memory of the place where he belonged and remembering the past in this way opens up the possibility of a different narrative of the future. Moses's house is 'held up by the tribal imagination' (141). The story of Moses is itself framed as 'The story' within 'A Good Story' and its affirmative potential is dramatized by the narrator's mother singing an 'it is a good day song' (144) in emulation of Moses at the end of the story. A good story in the context of Alexie's collection must be one that is both aesthetically and politically valuable; only good political art is really worthwhile.

The threat of disappearance is a constant source of anxiety in Alexie's stories, such that 'sometimes it seems that all Indians can do is talk about the disappeared' (222). This is not only a cultural memory of Indian history in 'the old West' but of modern attempts to move them to urban America: ' "All those relocation programs sent reservation Indians to the cities, and sometimes they just got swallowed up" ' (212). One of Victor's friends tells him, ' "Every one of our elders who dies takes a piece of our past away and that hurts more because I don't know how much of a future we have" ' (167). The past is disappearing and with it goes the possibility of a tribal future, 'swallowed up' in the new urban West of Seattle, Phoenix, Los Angeles. It is this history that gives Victor a fear of modern technology; in 'Crazy Horse Dreams' Victor is asked ' "What are you scared of?" ', and he replies, ' "Elevators, escalators, revolving doors. Any kind of forced movement" ' (40). These features of urban life occur again in 'Somebody Kept Saying Powwow' where fear of entrapment and confinement is represented by the technology of movement which recalls the death of the hobo in 'Imagining the Reservation' (207). This anxiety about 'forced movement' is given a historical origin in 'Jesus Christ's Half-Brother is Alive and Well on the Spokane Indian Reservation' in terms of the story of the Anasazi, the Indian tribe that completely disappeared: 'I know somebody must be thinking about us because if they weren't we'd just disappear just like those Indians who used to climb the Pueblos. Those Indians disappeared with food still cooking in the pot and air waiting to be breathed and they turned into birds or dust or the blue of the sky or the yellow of the sun' (119). This allusion accomplishes several things at once, it gives a historical precedent to the fear of annihilation (one which precedes the old West), it expresses the survival of the Anasazi in terms of their transformation into the elements, and it also articulates a faith in the power of narrative to ensure survival in myth, story, and shared concern—'somebody must be thinking about us'. This helps to explain the recurrence of saviour-figures in Alexie's stories, magical individuals who will help to guarantee the future of Indian nations and who promise to redeem the tribes from disintegration and diaspora; Alexie's saviours will 'come again' as the Anasazi do, to redeem the suffering of contemporary Indians and help save them from disappearance.

Tim O'Brien **Northern Lights**

The idea of the depletion or declension of the myths of the West is given a different narrative by Tim O'Brien's first novel *Northern Lights* (1975), which is set in 1970 when Harvey Perry returns from Vietnam to northern Minnesota to live with his brother Paul in their father's house.[16] Although Harvey's agitation and desire for adventure might be interpreted as a response to his experiences in south-east Asia, the novel contextualizes his restlessness in terms of two other specific moments in American history, the Cuban missile crisis of 1962–3, and the frontier expansion of the nineteenth century. Both Harvey and Paul live in the shadow of their forefathers' pioneering achievements, which they are unable to emulate and which cause Paul especially to feel debilitated and impotent (both figuratively and literally). The bomb shelter which Harvey built for his father in October 1962 is a constant reminder of that moment of crisis in American history when nuclear attack seemed inevitable to many Americans: 'Jets scrambling over Miami Beach, trawlers in the Caribbean, an address by the President that began: *Good evening my fellow citizens. . . . This government, as promised, has maintained the closest surveillance of the Soviet military buildup on the island of Cuba*' (208). The nuclear shelter also reminds Paul of his father because the old man died just as its construction was completed, and because the language of contemporary nuclear apocalypse reminds him of the language of his father's Lutheranism: '*On the contrary, the Soviets are rapidly continuing their construction of missile support and launch facilities* . . . the language of the old man's religion' (210). The young brothers were brought up to contemplate the end of things, and a sense of atrophy and defeat pervades the whole novel; the psychological malaise of Paul in particular is an emotional analogue to the decline of America's status as a world power at this particular historical moment. The novel's publication in 1975 comes immediately after the unique disgrace of President Nixon's resignation, and it is possible to interpret *Northern Lights* partly as a response to the traumatic social and political upheaval that took place in the late 1960s and early 1970s, and especially to the military defeat of the

---

[16] All page references are to the Delacorte edition.

United States in Vietnam. In other words, O'Brien uses the myths of the frontier West to dramatize the collapse of America's self-image that had taken place in a much larger arena. It is worth noting briefly that *Northern Lights* was published in the same year as Doctorow's *Ragtime*, and the difference between them is instructive. Doctorow's novel embraces change and treats with energetic delight the opportunities for women and ethnic groups that the modern period opened up. *Northern Lights* looks back from 1975 not to the early modern period but to the mid-nineteenth century, and can see only a desperate and irrevocable falling away in the comparison.

It was Harvey who built the nuclear shelter while his father lay watching from his deathbed, and it is Harvey who strives hardest to live up to his father's expectations to fulfil the role of an American hero in the frontier spirit, 'like Davy Crockett and Daniel Boone' (312). Harvey still tries hard to have faith in what he jokingly refers to as ' "all the outdoor crap" ' (337), and as the elder son, Harvey carries the burden of family history; he is characterized primarily as taciturn: 'He did not talk about the long days of being lost. The same way he never talked about the war, or how he lost his eye, or other bad things' (312). This laconic and stoical pose prefigures Emmett in *In Country*, but in O'Brien's novel it is as much an echo of the western macho stereotype as it is an inability to come to terms with history. It is Harvey who initiates the ill-conceived hike across the snowy winter landscape of northern Minnesota in which both brothers nearly die, but rather than interpreting this as simply adolescent and reckless, it is important to recognize Harvey as aspiring to be a particular kind of man in an environment which no longer has a place for him. Harvey is engaged in a form of role-play which is redundant and which is analogous to the loss of the United States' position as the world's military policeman. Harvey is still captivated by ideas of the frontier even though his experience in Vietnam has taught him a lesson about the end of American cultural myths: ' "Wilderness. The old man says you can catch fish with your bloody *hands* there's so many of them" ' (355). For Harvey, the frontier is still a relevant myth and one which his time in Vietnam has only served to fuel; he wants to escape, to Boston, to Key West or Seattle (all points at the margin of the North American continent) and to start his life over again in a new context: ' "The idea is to go and *not* come back. Just go" ' (313). But Harvey might have learned from Hemingway's Jake Barnes that 'going to another country doesn't make any difference. . . . You can't get away from yourself by moving from one place to another. There's nothing to that' (*The Sun Also Rises*, (13)).

Harvey's younger brother Paul is melancholy and self-absorbed in the classic adolescent style, an office worker with spectacles who looks too much like a professor for frontier life. But it is Paul who makes it clear to Harvey that there is no need to escape Minnesota in search of challenges: ' "I have an adventure", Perry said "I am a pioneer in this town. Scratching for a living, married, trying to help a bunch of crazy farmers grow corn in the woods, living in my father's house. That's an adventure" ' (36). Paul cannot aspire to his forefathers' achievements; even his office job is discontinued because the farmers whose loan applications he processes are going out of business, and his office's administration is being centralized in Duluth. Nevertheless, it is Paul who makes the decision to sell their father's house and move away, a cowardly admission of defeat which he feels sure would have shamed his father. The sale of the house and what it represents is the real heart of the novel, because it is an admission by Paul that the ethos which sustained the lives of his forefathers is now redundant; he is not only selling his father's house, but 'selling out of the great histories' (343) and he recognizes that his father would have regarded a move south to Iowa as a 'cop-out and sellout' (350). But since the Cuban missile crisis and Vietnam, American culture has changed: the Perrys move away and are replaced by an investment banker from an Italian family (not northern Europeans like the Finns and the Dutch) who is an abstract painter and who will use the nuclear shelter as an artist's studio. This is the new social reality of post-1970 America.

The history of the Perry family is of crucial significance to understanding the brothers' aimlessness and debility. Their grandfather Pehr Peri came from a village around Helsinki, landed near Baltimore, worked his way west to St Louis and then north up the Mississippi to Minnesota. This is the classic narrative of the struggle for self-determination in the new land of opportunity: 'immigrants homesick for the Old World, hard winters, danger, relentless work, fist fights, mosquitoes and loneliness and barracks yarns, campfires and boredom, northern hardships, frontier trials' (68). The brothers cannot come to terms with this heritage, and their ill-fated hike across

Minnesota is futile and fruitless—it does not cure Paul of his melancholy or make a man of him in the conventional sense, it merely serves as a reminder that they are the epigoni of the true woodsmen Peris and that their outdoor interlude is more of an irresponsible escapade than an adventure, and one that nearly kills them.

Northern Lights is very much indebted to Hemingway, and especially to *The Sun Also Rises* in several important respects; at one point Harvey suggests they move to Italy (in language reminiscent of Jake Barnes) where 'we could probably be kings and queens and all that rot' (318), and O'Brien's novel's last line, ' "Doesn't it sound great?" ' (356), recalls the emptiness of Jake's final rejoinder to Brett: ' "Isn't it pretty to think so?" '.[17] A more contemporary literary antecedent for *Northern Lights* is perhaps James Dickey's southern novel *Deliverance*, published five years earlier in 1970, another novel in which an adventure in the great American outdoors goes badly wrong, and where male characters are merely acting out empty roles:

I was light green, a tall forest man, an explorer, guerrilla, hunter. I liked the idea and the image, I must say. Even if this was just a game, a charade, I had let myself in for it, and I was here in the woods, where such people as I had got myself up and were supposed to be. Something or other was being made good. I touched the knife hilt at my side, and remembered that all men were once boys, and that boys are always looking for ways to become men. (69)

For the twentieth-century protagonists of *Close Range* and *Northern Lights*, the experience of 'the frontier' (the inverted commas signal its attenuated status) can only be 'a game, a charade' because the real frontier is now only a remnant and historical memory. The exception, of course, is Vietnam and it is worth noting here that O'Brien's interest in the frontier in his first novel anticipates closely his texts about the United States' frontier in south-east Asia, *Going After Cacciato* (1979), *If I Die in a Combat Zone* (1973), and *The Things They Carried* (1990). Several critics have even argued that *Blood Meridian* can be interpreted as a novel about Vietnam: J. E. Sepich wrote that 'The literature of atrocities in Vietnam seems consistent, in its language,

---

[17] One contemporary reviewer asked facetiously 'Is it possible to read *The Sun Also Rises* too often?'. R. Sale, 'Fathers & Fathers & Sons', *New York Review of Books*, 13 Nov. 1975, 31.

with that of Glanton's atrocities',[18] and J. G. Cawelti believes that 'It's pretty clear that *Blood Meridian* is also, like such sunnier post-Westerns as Thomas Berger's *Little Big Man*, a tacit commentary on the American invasion of Vietnam'.[19] But one of McCarthy's epigraphs, from the newspaper *The Yuma Daily Sun* of June 1982, in which it is reported that 'a re-examination of a 300,000-year-old fossil skull found in the same region earlier shows evidence of having been scalped' suggests that the perspectives of *Blood Meridian* are much wider.

Donald Antrim Elect Mr Robinson for a Better World

One characteristic of the West is its history of different forms of violent confrontation and its belief in the sanctity of the individual's right to protect himself. In words that might easily serve as a slogan for the contemporary politics of the National Rifle Association, Jack Schaefer's *Shane* tells us that 'a gun is as good—and as bad—as the man who carries it'. In Donald Antrim's *Elect Mr Robinson for a Better World* (1993) the desire to be separate from one's neighbours, to have a space of one's own, and to be able to protect that freedom to the point of death, has become suburbanized. The violence of Antrim's novel is a function of its characters' determination to have their own piece of land and to be able to live independently of the pressures of social responsibility or commitment. This is a classic American tension, one which is seen in the history of the West and in the Puritans' colonization of what became New England. *Elect Mr Robinson for a Better World* neatly pulls these histories of violent struggle together in its dramatization of the desperate search for value in a rapidly disintegrating suburban culture. In the novel's beach-side (Californian?) paradise of luxury condos, the neighbours are at war and are forced by the conflict to protect their homes with anti-personnel mines, automatic rifles, and tarp-covered pits full of poisonous snakes: 'a network of electronically triggered fragmentation bombs armed and ready in

---

[18] J. E. Sepich, ' "What Kind of Indians was Them?" ', in E. T. Arnold and D. Luce (eds.), *Perspectives on Cormac McCarthy* (Jackson: University Press of Mississippi, 1999), 140.

[19] J. G. Cawelti, 'Cormac McCarthy, Restless Seekers', in J. J. Folks and J. A. Perkins (eds.), *Southern Writers at Century's End* (Lexington: University Press of Kentucky, 1999), 176.

the nasturtiums' (86).[20] This is a community of desperadoes who devote their money and ingenuity to the design of home defence systems, and especially to the installation of unique pits on their well-trimmed lawns:

Their pit was designed by Betsy Isaac, a local earthwork installation conceptualist interested in our culture's debasement of sex. Her non-linear pit wound serpentine from side to front yards, and was chock-full of anatomically semicorrect Barbie and Ken dolls, shredded and pulped men's magazines, several cases of hideous punch-out dime store valentines, and about two tons of dead mackerel. All in all, a provocative work, functional yet challenging. (14)

The high-tech conveniences of suburban affluence have been adapted to protect the neighbours from each other now that hostilities have reached murderous proportions and there has been a complete breakdown of civic order. It is a neighbourhood 'overrun by kin groups brandishing private arsenals' (49). Bill Nixon, 'out sitting on the porch with my family, taking pleasure in the twilight sounds of birdsong' is interrupted by gunfire; his 6-year-old son asks authoritatively, ' "Daddy, are those AK-47s or M16s?" ' (85). In an early comic scene, the ex-mayor is ritually quartered, his neighbours using their Toyotas and Subarus in the absence of horses to tie him down with heavy nylon rope which 'radiated from Jim's wrists and ankles, ran across the grass and Jim's beautiful Japanese rock garden to the back bumpers of cars poised to travel different directions' (8). The origin of the violent conflict between these neighbours is lost in history, 'someone does something and someone else does something back. After that things have a life of their own. Who can say what it's about anymore?' (60–1). *Elect Mr Robinson* is a novel witnessing the total collapse of civic law and the degeneration of affluent suburban lifestyles into a battle-hardened war zone where Americans murder each other simply because they always have.

At the centre of the novel is the narrator Pete Robinson, a megalomaniacal unemployed kindergarten teacher who recounts the disintegration of civic life from a vantage point in his attic. Robinson's speciality as a teacher is military history, and especially physical torture; he believes that 'teaching the history and theory of warfare is

---

[20] All page references are to the Minerva edition.

a perfectly legitimate method of demonstrating patterns of social reformation in the modern era' (25). Robinson's interest in historical conflict, and especially in the struggle of culture to socialize individuals within structures of conformity, is clearly a comment on his own violent society. He gives a talk to the Rotary Club: 'My intention was to draw parallels between ancient and modern concepts of punishment and guilt, and to demonstrate a few of the ways contemporary society has internalized, even subtly institutionalized "the barbarity of the past", which was the title of my talk' (5). *Elect Mr Robinson for a Better World* is a fable which dramatizes the historical inevitability of its violent conflict as a product of American history. The narrator's interest in the Inquisition is a dark comic suburban symptom of America's intolerance of heretics, 'a template for institutionalized cruelties that have abided throughout modern history' (51). Robinson's prurient and voyeuristic obsession with forms of torture (as a hobby he models a 'balsa-and-styrofoam cutaway reproduction of a Portuguese interrogation chamber', (31)) is not an aberration but a sign of his ideological concurrence with historical struggles. Robinson is entirely in accord with his culture. The American neighbourhood of the novel is characterized by violent conflict and as Robinson reminds us, Americans 'are all heirs to a legacy of blood and grief' (141). What makes this novel remarkable is that the black comedy of its violence is situated adroitly in the context of American history so that social comedy becomes cultural analysis. Ideologically the macabre humour of Robinson's narrative has its origins in Puritanism and especially in the uniquely American inflection of the struggle between the individual and society, between personal freedom and social responsibility. This is why the narrator is transformed into a special kind of writer, 'it's my duty as town scrivener to record and type such official civic business of the body politic' (79). Pete Robinson is a contemporary American Robinson Crusoe, locked in his attic hideaway, reconstructing a narrative of the society from which he is exiled, drawing on a belief in the sacred authority of texts to record the pressures of the individual to conform to social imperatives. Here at least the frontier is not 'a game, a charade' but a legacy of violence which is uniquely American and, in the context of the gunbattles at Waco, Texas (1993), and Columbine High School, Colorado (1999), compellingly contemporary.

4

Consumerism, Media, Technology

Down Wall, from girder into street noon leaks
A rip-tooth of the sky's acetylene

Hart Crane, 'To Brooklyn Bridge'

The United States is overwhelmingly a free-enterprise culture, a market economy in which commercial and industrial progress is fundamental to the structure and fabric of society, and in the twentieth century America has been in the vanguard of technological and business innovation associated especially with mass production and investment capital. In American capitalism the forces of the marketplace are paramount and concepts of private ownership, property, and the drive towards profit are integral to social organization. As Henry Ford once said, 'There is something sacred about big business. Anything which is economically right is morally right.' Moreover, there is often a close association between the idea of freedom and economic prosperity; American freedom and opportunity are often conceptualized in commercial terms and the language of trade has a long history of association with American emotional life. In 1922 Sinclair Lewis's *Babbit* challenged the superficial values of business culture and their corrosive effects on the individual. In 1925 *The Great Gatsby* registered the overlapping of personal wealth and emotional values ('Her voice is full of money'), and following the Wall Street Crash of 1929 the fiction of John Dos Passos, John Steinbeck, and Nathanael West dramatized the profoundly debilitating impact of commodification on American consciousness and the attenuated limits of commercial enterprise culture: 'Men have always fought their misery with dreams. Although dreams were once powerful, they have been made puerile by the movies, radio and newspapers. Among many betrayals, this was the worst'('The Day of the Locust'). Arthur Miller famously dramatized the *Death of a Salesman* in 1949, and Flannery O'Connor showed the spiritual dereliction of America in *Wise Blood* (1952) where religious and moral values are superseded by commercial imperatives, preachers are replaced by potato-peeler salesmen, and the characters' perspectives are desperately inhibited by the seductions of consumer culture: 'No one was paying any attention to the sky. The stores in Taulkingham stayed open on Thursday nights so that people could have an extra opportunity to see what was for sale.' The limits of American aspiration are sometimes simply reduced to matters of purchasing power, and this uncritical materialism has often been the target for American novelists.

In the late twentieth century there has been a second technological revolution, one where the production and manufacture of goods has been superseded by the dissemination of signs in a new 'information age' as part of what Daniel Bell termed *The Coming of Post-Industrial Society* (1974). This is a late twentieth-century world in which, as Marshall McLuhan famously wrote, 'The medium is the message'. In this society the omnipotence of business corporations and of the media become powerful regulators of the kinds of freedoms that Americans are permitted, and the pressures of commercial interest are felt at pervasive and subliminal levels. The texts of this period are concerned with issues of the manipulation and control of individuals in the service of business profits. The novelists investigate the powerful capacity of the media images of the entertainment and advertising industries to generate desire for products and to determine the forms of American aspiration in the interests of profit. Pynchon's *The Crying of Lot 49* (1965) dramatized in part the powerlessness of individuals to function outwith the seductive and omnipotent influence of one person's commercial empire (the title itself refers to a form of commercial transaction), and for writers like Thomas Pynchon, William Gaddis, and Gore Vidal, the pervasive force of commercial and media pressures threatens the very idea of individuality. As McLuhan wrote with great prescience 'the ad agencies and Hollywood are always trying to get inside the public mind in order to impose their collective dreams on that inner stage'. McLuhan's ideas have been taken up by

Stewart Ewan's *Channels of Desire: Mass Images and the Shaping of American Consciousness* (1982) and also given fresh theoretical impetus by the French writer Jean Baudrillard, especially in *For a Critique of a Political Economy of the Sign* and *Simulations* (and less so in his *America*, 1984). The novels of this chapter scrutinize the extent to which American forms of business and media influence have come to represent a kind of tyranny which is antithetical to American freedom and the forms of corporate and state power they serve. Again McLuhan's *Understanding Media* (1964) provides a valuable rubric for the texts of this chapter: 'Technology may become the great connector of men, or it may become the ultimate means of their subjection and control'.

E. L. Doctorow **Ragtime**

E. L. Doctorow's *Ragtime* (1975) is set in the early twentieth century when the industrialization of American society was booming and technological advances were having a dramatic impact on the lives of millions of Americans.[1] Much of the novel is devoted to an evocation of the energy and vitality of American commercial expansion at this historical moment (1902–15) and to a dramatization of the consequences of that remarkable industrial shift for American citizens: 'America was in the dawn of the Twentieth Century, a nation of steam shovels, locomotives, airships, combustion engines, telephones and twenty-five-story buildings' (150–1). This new American modernity is indiscriminate in its energies and it forges great social changes which determine the fates of the novel's characters. *Ragtime* examines the social and political consequences of changes in the forms of capitalism for the lives of ordinary Americans, and shows how exploitation of 'the storehouse of technology' (151) was responsible for the material conditions of Americans' lives at that historical moment throughout the presidencies of Theodore Roosevelt and Woodrow Wilson.[2] *Ragtime* is structured around the narratives of three American families who represent American identity in its European, Jewish, and African aspects. The family of European descent, the WASP family, consists of

---

[1] All page references are to the Picador edition.
[2] Roosevelt, Sept. 1901–Mar. 1909; Wilson, Mar. 1913–Mar. 1921.

Mother, Father, Mother's Younger Brother, and the Little Boy. The Jewish family is similarly designated in terms of family roles as Mameh, Tateh, and Little Girl. The Afro-American family is the only one given proper names: Coalhouse Walker and Sarah. *Ragtime* tells the story of these three families, of their respective fates in modern industrial America, of how their paths cross one another, and of how they cope with the challenges that the burgeoning capitalist economy presents them with. The narrative, which races towards a vision of modern American multiculturalism, is one of national identity, of the nation family, at a crucial historical moment in its transformation, a national *Bildungsroman* that dramatizes the social consequences of technological advances and industrial developments in a rapidly expanding free-market economy.

Ragtime takes as its leading metaphor the idea of syncopation on which ragtime music is founded. Syncopation finds expression in the novel in the creative synthesis not only of Doctorow's three families but also of these fictional characters with many historical figures of the early twentieth century such as Harry Houdini, Emma Goldman, Henry Ford, Sigmund Freud, and Emiliano Zapata. *Ragtime* syncopates the narratives of the fictional and the historical in a way which privileges neither and raises political questions about historiography, or, to put it another way, makes a 'rag' of time, or simply 'rags' time. This interpretation is not facetious; the novel utilizes the image of rags at several important points. At one point the novel refers directly to ragtime music; Mother's Younger Brother stands between the carriages on a train and momentarily considers killing himself: 'He considered throwing himself under the wheels. He listened to their rhythm, their steady clacking, like the left hand of a rag. The screeching and pounding of metal on metal where the two cars joined was the syncopating right hand. It was a suicide rag' (131). There are many important points here: the correspondence with the train journey of Tateh and his daughter in which they flee New York City by rail, oblivious to their destination and allowing the network of tracks to determine their route (73–7); the idea of the train symbolizing the new technological future, 'the future lay at the end of parallel rails' (77), and most importantly the association between the new technologies and the guiding musical metaphor of the narrative. This final association, which is simultaneously one of death, is given an important reprise on the novel's final page as the text comes to an end: 'And by that time the era of Ragtime had run out, with the heavy breath of the machine, as if history were no more than a tune on a player piano' (236). The suggestion here is that history is determined by the shapes and patterns of its particular machine technologies (here the player piano) and further, that the historical consciousness of the novel's narrator is also a function of a mechanistic determinism which dictates the narrative's every note. Is ragtime music merely another fashionable consumer product of the new machine age? Are the characters of Doctorow's novel simply the function of a new industrial modernity which is completely beyond their control, and what consequences does this have for the novel's politics?

The word 'ragtime' has other interpretations in this novel; rags are referred to directly on many occasions: the most affluent members of American society have charity balls at which 'Guests came dressed in rags' (37); the peasant army of Zapata are characterized by their poverty: 'They wore rags' (225); the novel ends with the idea for a film about America as 'a society of ragamuffins' (236), and most importantly, when Father leaves New York on Peary's polar expedition he passes 'an incoming transatlantic vessel packed to the railings with immigrants. . . . It was a rag ship with a million dark eyes staring at him' (18). This momentary glimpse of the rapidly expanding immigrant culture of the United States occasions an extraordinary crisis in Father's consciousness 'and the great ocean began to tumble and break upon itself as if made of slabs of granite and sliding terraces of slate' (19). This language suggests simultaneously the tenement blocks of New York City and also the shifting tectonic plates as the earth's crust undergoes a structural upheaval. This rag ship of immigrants represents the future American population, people who for various social and political reasons 'set great store by the American flag' (18) and who, as the 'scraps' of other nations, 'stitched themselves to the flag' (20). Rags then are a crucial element of the novel's vision of early twentieth-century America because rags are remnants or fragments and *Ragtime* has a serious interest in doing justice to the marginal or neglected as constituting elements of modern America. In this respect it is also important to note that ragtime was originally a black musical form of expression, here appropriated by a white artist (novel's narrator; Doctorow), and so the very form of the novel is indebted to

Afro-American culture, a different kind of immigrant contribution to something now considered quintessentially American. This is important to the novel partly because of its depiction of racial politics (Coalhouse Walker, Booker T. Washington, Mathew Henson) which might owe more to the later 1960s than to the 1910s. This question returns us to the problem of the novel's narrator.

Ragtime is composed of some extraordinary coincidences in which the paths of its characters cross in a way that dramatizes the connectedness of the fabric of American society at this historical moment. These meetings are numerous, and very artfully designed: the Franklin Novelty Company to which Tateh sells his first movie book (102) is the same company that Henry Ford is indebted to for his views on reincarnation (116); Carl Jung sees Tateh's daughter 'and experienced what he realized was a shock of recognition' (35); the New York Giants are watched by Little Boy at the Polo Grounds (169) and then turn up as tourists in Egypt to the annoyance of J. P. Morgan (230), and the Giants' manager J. J. McGraw is prominent on both occasions. Towards the end of the novel Tateh and Mother are both on vacation in Atlantic City, 'And so the two families met' (192), but twenty-two chapters earlier the paths of Little Boy and Little Girl had already crossed, in the street in New Rochelle where 'the boy's eyes looked into hers' (75). These are only a few of the syncopated sleights-of-hand that the novel's narrator engineers. Coincident with this formal composition is the historical consciousness of the novel's anonymous narrator. At several points the narrator interjects with omniscient knowledge of historical information which he alone has privileged access to. The narrator tells us that J. P. Morgan and Henry Ford founded a secret club which 'endowed certain researches which persist to this day' (116). Commenting on the terrorism of Coalhouse Walker, the narrator writes that 'Even at this date we can't condone the mayhem done in his cause' (140), and later in *Ragtime* the narrator derives his knowledge of Younger Brother's exploits from a diary that he kept 'from the day of his arrival in Harlem to the day of his death in Mexico' (181). The narrator also knows about Harry Houdini because he has read 'the magician's private, unpublished papers' (233).

There is textual evidence to connect this historical consciousness with a fictional character of Doctorow's text, Little Boy, who meets Harry Houdini in chapter 1 and says to him 'Warn the Duke' (17) as if already cognizant of Houdini's meeting with Archduke Franz Ferdinand and the historical significance of Ferdinand's death. Houdini is oblivious to the Little Boy's prophetic insight when he eventually does meet Ferdinand (84) but in the novel's final chapter Houdini performs a spectacular outdoor feat: 'He was upside down over Broadway, the year was 1914, and the Archduke Franz Ferdinand was reported to have been assassinated. It was at this moment that an image composed itself in Houdini's mind. The image was of a small boy looking at himself in the shiny brass headlamp of an automobile' (233). This is a remarkable correspondence; the Little Boy experienced his moment of prescience while 'gazing at the distorted macrocephalic image of himself in the shiny brass fitting of the headlight' (17). That this critical connection finds its focus and expression in an image of the motor car is brilliantly appropriate for Doctorow's novel because it is so studiously devoted to the great modern immigrant proletariat and 'the awful fate industrial America had prepared for them' (96). It is fitting that an image which connects the novel's first and last chapters and transforms it into a moment of historical epiphany is one in which the narrative's historical consciousness is reflected in the new consumer technologies of modern America.

The Little Boy might be identified as the novel's narrator in other ways that are equally important to its central ideas. *Ragtime* is a text devoted to the extraordinary social changes that were brought about by technological developments at that defining moment in the history of the United States. Jacob Riis studied and photographed the immigrant proletariat: 'They waited for life to change. They waited for their transformation' (21). The idea of transformation is something that Little Boy is especially alert to, having learned it at an early age from his classicist grandfather:

he would sit in the parlor and tell the boy stories from Ovid. They were stories of people who became animals or trees or statues. They were stories of transformation. . . . The boy did not know he was hearing Ovid, and it would not have mattered if he had known. Grandfather's stories proposed to him that the forms of life were volatile and that everything in the world could as easily be something else. The old man's narrative would often drift from English to Latin without his being aware of it, as if he was reading to one of his classes of forty years before, so that it appeared nothing was immune to the principle of volatility, not even language. (90–1)

The principle of Ovid's *Metamorphoses* informs every aspect of the novel, as if the Latin text had been subjected to the pressures of modern industrial society, and the idea of change in all its various guises dominates the conduct of Doctorow's novel. The boy's interpretation of *Metamorphoses* is necessarily informed by his own historical moment and he comes to believe that 'the world composed and recomposed itself constantly in an endless process of dissatisfaction' (92). The boy is also central to the novel's structure because he has a special relish for 'unexpected events and coincidences' of which *Ragtime* is constituted (he 'was never surprised by a coincidence', (196)), and because he is an avid collector of that which is thrown away, of remnants or rags: 'The boy treasured anything discarded' (89). It is the boy, for example, who retrieves the silhouette portraits abandoned by Mother's Younger Brother which were executed by Tateh at Evelyn Nesbit's command, another of the novel's remarkable connections. In the context of the conduct of the narrative, the emergence of a first-person narrator is completely unexpected: 'Poor Father, I see his final exploration. He arrives at the new place, his hair risen in astonishment, his mouth and eyes dumb. His toe scuffs a soft storm of sand, he kneels and his arms spread in pantomimic celebration, the immigrant, as in every moment of his life, arriving eternally on the shore of his Self' (235). The narrator takes possession of his artistic voice at the point of the death of Father, and in language strongly reminiscent of the final line of *The Great Gatsby*, *Ragtime* offers itself as a narrative of self and nation in which the author is 'born' at the moment it articulates the idea of self-renewal that the novel proposes as quintessentially American.

Of all the changes dramatized by *Ragtime* the transformation of Tateh's identity is among the most striking. The question of Tateh's politics is also very important because the novel ends with his assimilation into an American bourgeois society that he had previously been antagonistic to, and also because it is Tateh's vision of a twentieth-century American multiculturalism that the novel offers as the future. Tateh's metamorphosis begins in Lawrence, Massachusetts, during a labour strike in the mill town when 'in the middle of brotherhood in action' he catches himself momentarily 'thinking like some bourgeois from the shtetl' (97). Tateh's disillusionment with the strike is such that 'From this moment, perhaps,

Tateh began to conceive of his life as separate from the fate of the working class' (101). Soon afterwards Tateh sells his first movie book for twenty-five dollars and commits himself to the 'flow of American energy' (102), which results ultimately in his rebirth as Baron Ashkenazy the movie producer who is so completely immersed in the entrepreneurial spirit of the new film industry that he is very closely identified with the glass rectangle through which he now views the world 'a tool of the trade which he could not forbear using even when on vacation' (189). Baron Ashkenazy, whose new identity as a European aristocrat is entirely ersatz, submits himself to the necessary cultural compromises and becomes a function of the entrepreneurial business ethos and its technological developments; he is 'no more than a silhouette' (189) and says of himself 'I have become a company' (191). Tateh's rebirth is also a kind of loss; he succumbs to a transformation which makes him a function of modernity, his individuality and its particular cultural history is sacrificed to the corporate commercial and technological innovations that facilitate his success. Simultaneously, Baron Ashkenazy is at the rubicon of the old and the new, occasionally discovered 'bent over in defeat like the old Tateh' (192) but more usually 'a voluble and energetic man full of the future' (192). The vaudeville artist Houdini suffers a similar anxiety: 'every development in technology made him restless' (31). Tateh's metonymic depiction as Baron Ashkenazy dramatizes the cost to the individual of success in this technological and business enterprise.

Tateh's narrative dramatizes the threat to the very idea of individuality that is rampant in the society of *Ragtime*, where the fate of many characters is determined by the indiscriminate energy of industrialization and the whims of figures such as J. P. Morgan 'the most important individual of his time' (199). The novel is full of images of mechanistic repetition and mass production, forces that are inimical to the concept of individuality, in a culture where 'The value of the duplicable event was everywhere perceived' (103). Henry Ford's technological innovation, the assembly line, is heralded as the pinnacle of achievement because 'He had caused a machine to replicate itself endlessly' (104). J. P. Morgan is impressed by Ford's breakthrough and comes to believe in 'universal patterns of order and repetition that give meaning to the activity of this planet' (112). Again the Little Boy might be especially characteristic of his historical moment, playing

the same records over and over 'as if to test the endurance of a dupli-
cated event' (91) and having a special enthusiasm for baseball because
'The same thing happens over and over' (172).

In this dialectic between the individual and industrialization, the
technological forces of modernity become synonymous with history;
this dialectic is at work in the narrative of Coalhouse who demands
recognition and acknowledgement as an individual (especially in his
divergence from the political stance of Booker T. Washington) but
who finds for the focus of his struggle a Model T. Ford, one of a million identical products. The determination of Coalhouse to have his
particular Ford restored is indicative of the futility of his aspirations in
this society at this historical moment. The theme is seen again in the
metamorphosed identity of his followers, 'So transformed as to speak
of themselves collectively as Coalhouse' (183). The defeat of J. P.
Morgan's belief in 'special people born in each age' (113) is revealed in
the great pyramid at Giza where he encounters only a bedbug and 'He
paced from the west to the east, from the north to the south, though
he didn't know which was which' (229). The individuals of *Ragtime* are
powerless to overcome their mortality or achieve the knowledge of
the forms of absolute certainty that they strive for, whether this is
Theodore Dreiser searching for the 'proper alignment' of a chair (28),
or the explorer Peary who, near the North Pole, finds that 'On this
watery planet the sliding sea refused to be fixed' (66).

In the tumult of commodification the bodies of women and children are not exempt. Emma Goldman tells Evelyn Nesbit that she has
been forced by capitalist society to exploit her body as a resource in a
way that is equal to the entrepreneurial skills of John D. Rockefeller
(47). Not only does Nesbit use her body as a commodity, but businessmen recognize that 'Evelyn's face on the front page of a newspaper sold out the edition' (69), and they begin the proliferation for
profit of images and myths which appropriate and nourish American
appetites. *Ragtime* is attentive to the reification that individuals must
suffer in the service of new forms of industrial manufacture and dis-
tribution, and the novel perceives that the reducing of individuals to
market commodities is equally at work in this society's proliferation
of images and modes of representation. This is true not only of
Nesbit's image but of the movie on the novel's last page which, as a
fiction, becomes a part of the myth of American nationhood which is

peddled back to American citizens as an integral and authentic part of their cultural identity: 'The businessmen wondered if they could create such individuals not from the accidents of news events but from the deliberate manufactures of their own medium. If they could, more people would pay money for the picture shows' (69). This process, the autonomy of the medium, is seen at work in the creative strategy of the novel itself: the Coalhouse narrative which is such a major component of *Ragtime* is a reinterpretation of a novella by Heinrich von Kleist called 'Michael Kohlhaas' (1808), a work of fiction with its own problematic relation to 'real' history. This process takes place not only at the narrative level but at a meta-narrative level as if that process of reducing something to a representation of a representation had occurred to the novel's narrator also, and who, from the perspective of the 1970s, has undergone a transformation by which he has become no more than a function of his own fiction. The problem that this interpretation has in accommodating the narrator's arch, self-reflexive and self-conscious internalization of its self as a character is that the novel's sense of its own textuality fundamentally conditions everything to be found in the novel. This innovation in particular has encouraged critics to write about *Ragtime* not as a novel of modernity, its ostensible subject, but as a novel of postmodernity, one which addresses, in the predicament of its historical consciousness, the cultural and economic conditions of the late twentieth century. Fredric Jameson, for example, argues that *Ragtime* is 'the most peculiar and stunning monument to the aesthetic situation engendered by the disappearance of the historical referent. This historical novel can no longer set out to represent the historical past; it can only "represent" our ideas and stereotypes about that past'.[3] For Jameson then, postmodernism is that precise and specific technical innovation of the form of the novel by which the position of its narrator is subject to the economic pressures of the medium by which the narrative is conducted. It is not the purpose of this chapter to debate the nature or value of 'postmodernity', but it is important to note that such debates are predicated on issues of economics, of technological processes, of the medium and means of representation.

---

[3] Fredric Jameson, *Postmodernism, or, The Cultural Logic of Late Capitalism* (London: Verso, 1991), 25.

The political ideology of the novel's historical consciousness is especially valuable for its sensitivity to economic forces which shape modern America not only at the turn of the century, but at the end of it too. *Ragtime*, published in 1975, uses a particular historical moment to mark the birth of American modernity, but simultaneously in 1975, by its stylistic innovations *Ragtime* becomes a crucial text in the advent of something that has come to be known as postmodernity.

Don DeLillo **White Noise**

At one point in *Ragtime* Sigmund Freud visits New York and is appalled by its chaotic energy: 'What oppressed him about the New World was its noise' (35). Don DeLillo's *White Noise* (1984) is also an ironic comedy about the mass replication of images in modern America and the anxiety that technology engenders in its characters' precarious sense of identity.[4] Both Doctorow's and DeLillo's novels focus on the family as a vehicle for ideas about the veracity of historical narratives and the status of 'information' about contemporary America. Both novels (by New Yorkers) have a structure of exactly forty short chapters and consider the impact on the family unit and the individual of technology, consumerism, and the media. *White Noise* is routinely cited as an important postmodern novel, and has attracted more attention than DeLillo's other eleven novels because of it, despite having none of the technical or structural innovations that, for example, Jameson attributes to *Ragtime*. Those innovations belong to DeLillo's later novel *Mao II*. Frank Lentricchia argues that *White Noise* was successful because it was DeLillo's first domestic novel and that the domestic milieu is particularly appealing to American audiences; *White Noise* was thus welcomed home 'to the cultural power of domestic realism'.[5] Lentricchia edited a collection of essays devoted to *White Noise* for reasons to do with the novel's critical reception, although *Libra* seems to deserve our attention equally because Lee Harvey Oswald and John F. Kennedy 'are the founding characters of

---

[4] All page references are to the Picador edition.

[5] Frank Lentricchia (ed.), *New Essays on White Noise* (Cambridge: Cambridge University Press, 1991), 12.

postmodern America'.[6] The term 'postmodern' then is problematical and should be used with care if it is to have any critical purchase on these texts.

What is it that encourages critics to write about *White Noise* under the auspices of postmodernity? The answer lies in the way the novel addresses the media, and, more subtly, the idea of mediation as it occurs in a wide range of guises. *White Noise* is not simply concerned with the power of the media to invade consciousness ('"Were people this dumb before television?"', (249)) but with the idea that all contemporary American experience is crucially informed by modes of representation which determine consciousness at every level. One of the central questions of the novel is the dilemma of an ethical response to this phenomenon: does *White Noise* lament the passing of an earlier historical moment when Americans were in touch with something that could credibly be called 'authentic', or does the novel relish the freedoms that the new technologically determined image culture seems to offer? Is DeLillo's novel nostalgic for the historical moment that *Ragtime* appears to celebrate?

White Noise is a first-person narrative, an important distinction from the other novels of this chapter because it locates the anxieties of postmodern America in its protagonist Jack Gladney, a Professor of Hitler Studies at an American university. Jack Gladney's life is saturated at every point with images; driving his son to school he sees a crossing guard: 'A woman in a yellow slicker held up traffic to let some children cross. I pictured her in a soup commercial taking off her oilskin hat as she entered the cheerful kitchen where her husband stood over a pot of smoky lobster bisque, a smallish man with six weeks to live' (22). Here Jack's perception is governed by a generic cliche from advertising, he sees the world in terms of a banal fictional stereotype derived from a television commercial designed exclusively to encourage him to buy soup; the marketing fictions of business life fundamentally inform his experience: 'I pictured her'. The pressure of representations such as this is felt by Jack even in the most intimate moments of his life and is often related to a consumer product. One of his daughters whispers the words 'Toyota Celica' in her sleep (155), her unconscious mind colonized by brand-name inanity. Jack's sexual

---

[6] Ibid. 11–12.

relationship with his wife Babette is mediated in a different way, by the act of reading erotic passages to each other: ' "Do you want to read about Etruscan slave girls, Georgian rakes? I think we have some literature on flagellation brothels. What about the Middle Ages? We have incubi and succubi. Nuns galore" ' (29). Here Jack and Babette have complete freedom to appropriate any historical period and any kind of sexual indulgence, but it is a freedom of reading only, and in this sense it is about the mediation of texts, no different from the textuality of soup commercials which intervene between the novel's characters and their experience of something authentic or 'unmediated'. In this scene Jack chooses to read in the twentieth century and his erotic experience is further deferred through textuality; he reads from a magazine which features letters from readers that detail their sexual experiences: 'This struck me as one of the few things the modern imagination has contributed to the history of erotic practices. There is a double fantasy at work in such letters. People write down imagined episodes and then see them published in a national magazine. Which is the greater stimulation?' (30). The experience of sex has been erased by new forms of textual mediation, replaced by forms of representation of it, and it is precisely that mediating process which has become primary; Jack's incipient erection suddenly seems 'stupid and out of context' (29). The intervention of the text reduces experience to a function of the publishing genre. Is this postmodern? The eponymous protagonist of Barry Hannah's *Ray* says at one point: 'there's something so deeply elegant to the erotic that you've got to look into *Penthouse* after you've finished making love to be sure it really happened',[7] and American fiction is full of examples of characters' awareness of the presence of the media in their lives. Are Fitzgerald's *The Last Tycoon* or Nathanael West's 'The Day of the Locust' and 'Miss Lonelyhearts' also postmodern? In *White Noise* this reversal is ubiquitous; the character Orest wants to break the record for sitting in a cage of poisonous snakes, 'risking death for a couple of lines in a paperback book' (207), and deriving his identity from a sense of his action's publicity: 'creating an imperial self out of some tabloid aspiration' (268). The subjectivity of the novel's characters is fashioned

---

[7] Barry Hannah, *Ray* (New York: Knopf, 1980), 94. See also Ray's other comment on the media: 'Pick up a *Cosmopolitan* magazine at the drug. Women read it to find out who they ought to be and then that's who they are' (68).

for them by the imperatives of consumer culture and its media images and narratives.

It is remarkable how often this occurs in *White Noise*, and how often the scenes which dramatize the intervention of mediating texts include multiple references to the primacy of representations. In chapter 18, for example, Jack meets his daughter Bee at the airport in Iron City; a man in a down vest tells him that there has been a near-disaster in which a plane lost power in three engines. This man's account of the incident, 'We're a silver gleaming death machine!' (90), is full of references to textual mediation. A stewardess begins to read the relevant passage in a handbook titled 'Manual of Disasters' (90); the co-pilot laments the inadequacy of his training's 'death simulator' (90); the passengers cling to the grain of hope that seems to be offered in the semantic distinction between 'crash' and 'crash landing' because 'They saw how easy it was, by adding one word, to maintain a grip on the future' (91). Perhaps because of this subtle shift of language 'the two forms of flight termination were more or less interchange-able?' (91). This incident, in which the passengers' close personal experience of the proximity of sudden violent death is removed from them by the languages which represent it, is itself represented to them by the man in the down vest; he tells the story on their behalf and they are entirely passive in its reception: 'They trusted him to tell them what they'd said and felt' (91). The man's audience passively accept his account of their experience as if they need a narrative of it to understand it; the extreme degree of their detachment from their own lives completely disables them: 'It was as though they were being told of an event they hadn't personally been involved in' (91). The passengers need a narrative to authorize their experience, even though it removes them from that experience. This idea of the media giving authority and authenticity to an event which it would other-wise lack, is nicely caught in the final exchange between Jack and his daughter:

Where's the media?
There is no media in Iron City.
They went through all that for nothing? (92)

This is the final irony, that it is necessary for the characters of *White Noise* to see themselves as the subjects of a news item for their

experience to be validated, given the proper recognition and authority. In the absence of the media, the passengers have the narrative of
the man in the down vest who shapes and organizes their experience
for them. Only when experience is mediated is it authenticated; this
paradox is at the centre of many of the novel's dramatic scenes and it
is the source of much of the novel's comic irony. Sex, death, culture,
history: without the presence of their distinctive forms of representation, how can the characters acknowledge them as authentic?

'The Most Photographed Barn in America' is the apotheosis of this
phenomenon. Jack is taken to see the barn by Murray Siskind; it is
famous only because it is the most photographed, the most represented, and once Jack has seen the signs which tell him this, there is
no longer any need to see the barn itself, indeed 'Once you've seen
the signs about the barn it becomes impossible to see the barn' (12).
Jack cannot experience even a perception of the barn independently
of the barn's mediated image, he is completely removed from the
privilege of a first-hand experience by the concept of mediation:
'They are taking pictures of taking pictures' (13). The barn disappears
altogether and becomes irrelevant to the real experience, which is one
of mediating not the barn but other acts of mediation; the referent
has gone, and contemporary Americans can only record representations of the barn's exclusively representational status. It is significant
too that the object of cultural attention here is a barn, an image of
lost pastoral America among 'meadows and apple orchards' in the
countryside near *Farm*ington.[8]

White Noise is a novel constituted of such moments; Jack's daughter
Steffie sits in front of the television 'attempting to match the words as
they were spoken' (84). Jack has a dialogue with his son Heinrich
which begins with the question 'Is it raining?' (23) but finds that the
boy trusts the radio reports more than his own immediate senses.
Even the most simple issues become problematical in the presence of
mediation: Heinrich argues that the concept of temporality exists
'Only in our verbs' (24). During the technological disaster which
threatens the Gladney neighbourhood (itself designated an 'event'),
his family suffer from déjà vu; during the evacuation which ensues,

---

8 The Boone Hall Plantation in Charleston, South Carolina, advertises itself as
'America's Most Photographed Plantation'.

the Gladneys are aided by a man from SIMUVAC who sees the toxic waste cloud as 'a chance to use the real event in order to rehearse the simulation' (139), and Murray appears to inform Jack that 'it is possible to be homesick for a place even when you are there' (257).

This kind of transaction takes place in *White Noise* not only at the domestic level but in the larger narratives of culture and history which shape the particular kind of America that the Gladney family inhabits. Jack is a Professor of Hitler Studies but it is important to note that what he teaches is not Hitler but representations of Hitler and the creative constructions of the media that made Hitler into an image. The Hitler of Jack Gladney has nothing to do with morality, ideology, politics, or the industrialized forms of death associated with the Nazis. Hitler here has been reduced to a media spectacle of 'propaganda films . . . mystical epics . . . an impressionistic eighty-minute documentary', and this film footage has no narrative voice to offer interpretation or analysis 'Only chants, songs, arias, speeches, cries, cheers, accusa-tions, shrieks' (25–6). Gladney's Hitler has also been neatly confined within the tidy units of academic structure, 'three credits, written reports' (25). Here the novel flirts with the tentative suggestion that Gladney's students are a crowd of susceptible acolytes in their 'limited-edition T-shirts, in their easy-care knits' (26), an amorphous mass who in their own way are subject to essentially the same forms of control and manipulation as the voters of Hitler's Germany. This is the sharp political edge of DeLillo's social satire, and it is easy to see why some American critics are hostile to its implications. Gladney himself does not even speak German, although like dozens of DeLillo characters from *End Zone* to *Underworld* he is fascinated by its special quality: 'There's something about German names, the German lan-guage, German things. I don't know what it is exactly. It's just there' (63).[9] Unable to speak German and captivated by the visual images by which Hitler was represented, Gladney's Hitler is merely a kind of media celebrity, and in one of the novel's most audacious satirical gestures, Gladney's Hitler is offered alongside Elvis Presley. In chapter 15 especially, Hitler and Elvis are subjected to the same kind of inter-pretative discourse and are presented similarly as cultural icons. It is a

---

[9] In an interview, DeLillo once said that 'Wittgenstein is the language of outer space' (T. LeClair and L. McCaffery (eds.), *Anything Can Happen: Interviews with Contemporary American Novelists* (Urbana: University of Illinois Press, 1983), 85).

scene reminiscent of *Bill and Ted's Excellent Adventure*, a film that dramatizes the appropriation of history by two Californian adolescents for the purposes of a high school performance of history in which there is no significant difference between Ghengis Khan, Sigmund Freud, and Socrates. History is reduced to a performative spectacle of famous people devoid of cultural specificity. This is what one critic, writing about *Ragtime*, has called 'the carnivalisation of history'.[10]

It is easy to imagine a moral perspective on this phenomenon which is one of regret, of nostalgia for an earlier time before this postmodern entropy where mediation has become the sole authorizing practice and individuals are merely the function of modes of representation beyond their knowledge or control and yet which have the power to manipulate their views of themselves, the world, and everything in it. Here at times, subjectivity is itself the function of an anonymous trans-global economics for helpless consumers whose every desire is determined for them by corporate America. As one critic expressed it, 'The propositions are monstrous, but only because we find it so hard to believe in the true and central awfulness of capitalism'.[11] Such is the view of Baudrillard, who argues that Americans live only in a world of simulations. *White Noise* resists that ideological position. After the toxic cloud the sunsets are not diminished but augmented and 'had become almost unbearably beautiful' (170). The forces of consumer economics in *White Noise* facilitate new modes of being and new ways of experiencing something authentic; the word 'authentic' occurs in a surprising context when Jack visits an autoteller: 'The figure on the screen roughly corresponded to my independent estimate. . . . What a pleasing interaction. I sensed that something of deep personal value, but not money, not that at all, had been authenticated and confirmed' (46). Of course, DeLillo's irony makes easy judgements impossible, but there are many scenes like this where Jack derives something genuine and meaningful from these transactions with technology, at least valuable for him. Jack's phrase here 'not money' prompts consideration of the importance of shopping: 'I traded money for goods. The more money I spent, the

10 J. G. Parks, *E. L. Doctorow* (New York: Continuum, 1991) 56.

11 John Frow in F. Lentricchia (ed.), *Introducing Don DeLillo* (Durham, NC: Duke University Press, 1991) 185.

less important it seemed. I was bigger than these sums. These sums poured off my skin like so much rain. These sums in fact came back to me in the form of existential credit' (84). Not only does the experience of shopping help Jack to discover 'new aspects of myself' (84), but it also unites him with his family in a special way that brings them together, 'My family gloried in the event. I was one of them, shopping, at last' (83). Consumerism offers new ways to experience both the self and the social unit, it can facilitate something important and meaningful; when Jack hears his daughter Steffie murmur the words 'Toyota Celica' in her sleep, he is not appalled that her unconscious mind has been colonized by commercial brand names, but 'The utterance was beautiful and mysterious, gold-shot with looming wonder . . . the utterance struck me with the impact of a moment of splendid transcendence' (155). This paragraph is not entirely ironic; DeLillo's characters have consistently demonstrated a powerful interest in the mystical properties of language for its own sake, whether in German or Latin, but usually as a form of romantic epiphany beyond rational comprehension. In the contemporary consumer world of *White Noise* this mysticism attaches itself to commercial brand names but it is no less significant for that; such words are 'the site of a magical plenitude',[12] and however ersatz they might appear out of context, their utterance by his daughter is nevertheless a source of some comfort in Jack Gladney's media-beleaguered life.

Brand names occur throughout the text of *White Noise*, sometimes, but not always, spoken by the novel's characters; it is Murray who says '*Coke is it, Coke is it, Coke is it*' (51), but elsewhere such words appear in the text apparently free from its first-person narrator's speech: 'I watched light climb into the rounded summits of high-altitude clouds. Clorets, Velamints, Freedent' (229). Is this a momentary glimpse of Jack's mind, a signal that his subjectivity like Steffie's has been colonized by the language of commerce? Is this always the way that brand names function in the text, to give an impression of the narrator's subliminal life: 'the neon spectacles in the window of the optical shop cast a gimmicky light on the sidewalk. Dacron, Orlon, Lycra Spandex' (52). Not all such incidents appear to have an association with the text's narrative or dramatic moment: 'The

[12] Ibid, 187.

Airport Marriot, the Downtown Travelodge, the Sheraton Inn and Conference Centre' (15). This comes as an incongruous intrusion while Jack watches children running round a cinder track. It might be proposed that brand names are themselves a form of white noise which, in its strategic positioning outside the conduct of Jack's first-person narrative, becomes a voice which interpolates itself at certain random moments as a reified omniscient discourse which disturbs the reader's sense of Jack's control over his narrative: 'It isn't that she doesn't cherish life; it's being left alone that frightens her. The emptiness, the sense of cosmic darkness. Mastercard, Visa, American Express' (100). This is perhaps the novel's only postmodern structural feature, and it is a tentative one at that; neither the text's interest in the 'postmodern sunset' (227) nor its eclectic synthesis of genres (campus novel, detective novel, domestic social satire) makes *White Noise* a postmodern novel. If the voice of the brand name is not Jack's voice and not Jack's mind but the utterance of white noise, then the text itself is disrupted by the forms of incursion that it dramatizes, like the structuring principle of Doctorow's *Ragtime* uttering an incantation beyond the control of its narrator 'with the heavy breath of the machine' (236). One of DeLillo's working titles for *White Noise* was 'Panasonic', an appropriately contemporary analogue to Doctorow's syncopated ragtime.[13]

Again such arguments are predicated on interpretations of the meaning and value of the term 'postmodern'. The narrative of *White Noise* centres on two manifestations of contemporary technology, the toxic cloud and Dylar, one of which threatens death and the other which promises to assuage the fear of death. The phenomenon of white noise is alluded to six times in the novel: it is 'a dull and unlocatable roar' (36); it is a 'sublittoral drone' (168); it is 'nothing but sound' (198); it is 'insistent but near subliminal' (258); and it is 'faint, monotonous' (306). Only once in the text of the novel does the expression occur, when Jack meets Willie Mink in the motel room with the fire-retardant carpet: 'White noise everywhere' (310). One critic has argued that Jack's narrative moves toward the confrontation with Dylar's manufacturer, in a parody of heroic narrative, because Willie

---

13 Arnold Weinstein, *Nobody's Home: Speech, Self, and Place in American Fiction from Hawthorne to DeLillo* (Oxford: Oxford University Press, 1993), 303.

Mink is himself the embodiment of postmodernity, 'a representative and embodiment of a postmodern informational world of networks and circuits . . . associated both with informational flow and transnational monopoly, a new world of multinational capitalism whose channels of control are so widespread and dispersed that no single authoritative father figure is necessary for its operation'.[14] This is a persuasive argument, one in which DeLillo's novel does not itself 'exhibit the ahistoricism and pastiched depthlessness often associated with postmodernism'.[15] Jack's narrative is a deeply ironic and satirical encounter with the pressures of postmodern America, but unless it is conceded that white noise occurs as a feature of the text, then Jack's narrative is not itself postmodern and *White Noise* is not a postmodern novel, simply a brilliant interrogation of the conditions of postmodernity; this is a fundamentally different thing.

Don DeLillo **Mao II**

In Jack Gladney's eclectic documentary of Hitler footage 'Crowd scenes predominated' (25), and such scenes become the centre of DeLillo's interest in *Mao II* (1991), a novel that is notable for its international range; the action of *Mao II* takes place in New York, London, Beirut, Athens, and there are references to important incidents in China, Tehran, and Sheffield.[16] The novel's major theme, the pernicious effects of mass culture on the solitary individual, is dramatized as global, and in this culture Americans are not immune to the totalizing ideologies of the east. *Mao II* concerns what it means to be an American citizen or subject in a world culture where some people are inimical to America. The novel is also an examination of the idea that the world is moving towards millennial apocalypse in which individuals will be annihilated by ideological movements and that 'only those sealed by the Messiah will survive' (153). Characteristically for DeLillo, this interest in mass movements is closely associated with a corresponding interest in the way they are represented; what relation

---

[14] Leonard Wilcox, 'Baudrillard, DeLillo's *White Noise*, and the End of Heroic Narrative', *Contemporary Literature*, 32: 3 (1991), 359–60.

[15] Ibid. 362.

[16] All page references are to the Jonathan Cape edition.

does the narrative of the individual have to the narratives of historical forces which subsume individuals? What place is left for the very concept of 'individuality'? Is it true that 'The future belongs to crowds'? (16). Most importantly for *Mao II*, does the proliferation of images in a post-industrial world culture, and the ready and immediate accessibility of the mediated spectacle, make more likely the advent of a totalizing culture which will obliterate the narrative of the American individual?

Mao II concerns a reclusive novelist, Bill Gray, and his assistants Karen and Scott, who constitute something of an unconventional family, in hiding from the world (like Pynchon and Salinger) and wary of the incursion of Brita whose arrival precipitates the novel's dramatic action. In the photo shoot with Brita, Bill's image becomes a consumer product, the intervention of the photographer represents a different kind of language of identity from the one that Bill creates himself by writing fiction. Bill has control over his book in deciding not to publish it, but not over the photographer's image: 'I've become someone's material. . . . There's the life and there's the consumer event' (43). In agreeing to the photo session Bill is complicit in his surrender to the image-saturated world, one which is necessarily inimical to his writing, because it will contribute to the myth of visual representations and vitiate the need for his product, his writing. This is why the photo session, the shoot, is his assassination and the beginning of his death: 'Nothing happens until it's consumed. Or put it this way. Nature has given way to aura' (44). Ultimately the novel leaves Karen and Scott with pictures of Bill, not even knowing he has died, and in complete anonymity, robbed of all forms of personal identification, 'anything with a name and a number' (217).

The central character in this respect is not the novelist Bill Gray but the disciple of the Reverend Moon, Karen, the young woman who carries the virus of the future. Karen is the willing worker for the Moonies, the character who begins the novel by marrying the unknown Korean in that most American of places Yankee Stadium. Surely for DeLillo this is some kind of anathema, the sacred site of the New Yorker's team, a place full of associations with history and democracy, now occupied by 6,500 anonymous couples identically dressed and chanting inanely in unison as they are married by Moon and become part of the total family. It is a spectacle that fills Karen's watching parents with horror, and seems, to many Westerners, an affront to concepts of individuality and intimacy associated with romance and marriage. But Karen is a willing American disciple; there is no evidence in the novel that she is coerced to join the Moonies against her judgement. At the same time Karen is the character most in tune with the image-saturated media culture of late twentieth-century America, and for DeLillo these two points, totalitarianism and mediation, are often convergent. Karen is kidnapped by her parents and they attempt to convince her that she has been brainwashed by the Moonies, but the novel avoids any simple moral opposition: 'Other times she hated everyone involved and thought it was the logical brutal extension of parent-child, locked in a room and forced to listen to rote harangues. Of course this is what they said the church had been doing to her all along' (79). With this surprising reversal DeLillo suggests that Karen's American home life is no less a form of brutal socialization than the indoctrinating techniques of the Moonies. The two lifestyles become simply alternative narratives of how the individual is socialized, and the moral distinction between them is erased. Karen is stirred, not by the abduction but by 'the drama of abduction' (79), a drama full of 'tabloid-type reassurances about love and mother and home' (79) in which the players fall into 'their scripted roles' (81). This is the characteristic invasion of experience by what might be called narratives of represented experience, which puts a (nostalgic) distance between many of DeLillo's characters and their mediated lives. But why is this young American woman susceptible to this tendency and what relation does she bear to the international context of the narratives of *Mao II*?

Karen appears to come from an ordinary American home, but it is her fate to dramatize the dialectic between rival forms of socialization and especially rival narratives of family. Karen has a longing to belong to a mass movement, to be subsumed by a totalizing ideological system, and Moon fulfils this longing; Karen's willing dedication 'unburdens them of free will and independent thought' and 'totalized their attachment to true father' (7, 13). It also completely infantilizes all of those who are married by Moon: 'The blessed couples eat kiddie food and use baby names' (6). Through her devotion and dedication to the ideology of Moon, Karen will be 'immunized against the language of self' (8). Karen's abduction by her parents is no less characteristic of a particular conception of family, and the law of the father, which seeks to colonize her subjectivity. Karen's family demand that she conform to their conception of her place in the family and to a system of belief that accompanies it; her father, for example, is eager to get a photograph of Karen's wedding, 'I want to document it' (5), by which she will be reduced to an image; or, as Karen expresses it herself, ' "They bring us up to believe but when we show them true belief they call out psychiatrists and police" ' (8).

Karen believes that to be part of the authentic spirit of future history, to be saved, the individual must derive her subjectivity from the imagery of contemporary media culture, and Karen is uniquely suited to this task; she has a talent for 'uncanny mimicry' (13) which is derived from her special affinity with the media, and especially from visual spectacles of human death and disaster such as Hillsborough and Khomeni's funeral (33, 188). Karen can only imagine Brita's life in terms of clichés and stereotypes, ' "Do you have children that are still torn up over the divorce so that everybody's tense around each other and you can see the resentment lurking far back in their eyes even after all this time?" ' (57), and Karen's model of reality is entirely dependent on its correspondence with representations: her husband, for example, has black hair 'with a Sunday-comics look. It is the thing that makes him real to her' (8). Karen derives her consciousness of the world from watching television: 'She was thin-boundaried. She took it all in, she believed it all, pain, ecstasy, dog food, all the seraphic matter, the baby bliss that falls from the air' (119). The uncritical way in which Karen imbibes the culture of the media makes her especially susceptible to forms of control, and her desire is merely a function of 'brand-name ubiquity'.[17]

Yet Karen still harbours the potential to be rescued from totalitarianism, even if in a diminished form. Even amid the crowd scene of her wedding Karen utters the key word ' "Baseball" ' (8) and she also notices and interprets a road sign erected for the benefit of the one deaf child in the neighbourhood: ' " I thought the state that erects a sign for one child can't be so awful and unfeeling. . . . I'm enlivened by the road sign every time I see it" ' (72–3). Most important is Karen's ability to recognize the individual's plight in Brita's photograph of

---

[17] Douglas Keesey, *Don DeLillo* (New York: Twayne, 1993), 180.

the refugee camp, and perhaps to see his predicament as analogous to her own, because this shows her the potential for an alternative narrative of the self even within a mediated culture. The man in the crowd of boys 'is part of the mass but lost there' (146–7) and Karen interprets his stance as signifying 'how he might escape before they trample him' (147). Karen subsequently ministers in a direct and practical way to the crowds of derelicts in Tompkins Square Park, specifically described as 'A refugee camp' (149). Just as the singular man's position is staged by the photograph, the people here are living in the Park's bandshell, both figuratively and literally 'staged'. Karen's ability to interpret the individual in the photograph reveals an attenuated but significant attention to people as individuals and this is a sign of her possible redemption, even as it takes place within the context of her interpretation of a mediated image in Brita's photograph. It is here too that Karen strikes up a meaningful personal relationship with Omar Neeley as an individual, and an individual without family: 'She used to think siblings were strictly white and middle-class due to something in the nature of the word' (179).

To understand the aesthetic of Bill Gray's artistic life it is necessary to interpret the line 'Measure your head before ordering. It was the line that says everything' (170). This quotation from a Sears catalogue about buying hats has 'the mystery and power he'd felt nowhere else but in the shared past of people who had loved each other . . . so the line was not one voice but several . . . all the better finally because there was nothing to understand' (170). The key elements of Bill's artistic creed as it is given here are the family, the democratic multiplicity of voices in a shared experience, and the fact that the quotation's importance and precise significance is meaningless outwith the narrative which shapes it as part of a grammar. Also, crucially, the quotation comes from a commercial document, and this too is part of Bill's American aesthetic legacy. It is this meaninglessness beyond the parameters of the private family joke which appeals so strongly to Bill. It is a counterpoint to the banal accessibility of ubiquitous global images which flood contemporary culture. At the moment of his death, Bill's artistic aesthetic is given further expression in quotations from his parents, 'I like it better with the sleeves rolled down. . . . We need to have a confab, Junior' (216). This enigmatic language of private family associations has little value outwith the family's knowledge but retains an authenticity for Bill which he strives to be faithful to in his fiction. This idea of a mysterious language of authenticity has been a constant feature of DeLillo's fiction, and finds major expression in *Underworld* (1997).

Another fundamentally important aspect of Bill's aesthetic can be seen in his attitude to baseball, as he explains to Brita: ' "When I was a kid I used to announce ballgames to myself. . . . And I've been trying to write toward that kind of innocence ever since. The pure game of making up. . . . It's the lost game of self, without doubt or fear" ' (46). The imaginary baseball commentary, reminiscent of Coover's novel *The Universal Baseball Association* (1968), is a nostalgic return to inno- cence, a purely ludic and private creative game completely without market value, and its value to the individual lies precisely in its lack of marketability as an imaginative activity. At the moment of crisis in his writing about the hostage when he can see no point in continuing to write fiction, Bill finds himself suddenly saying ' "Keltner takes his time, tipping a glance at the baseball. Hey what a toss. Like a trolley wire, folks" ' (198). Here for a moment Bill recovers the pleasure and spontaneity of a purely imaginative act and reminds himself of his aesthetic creed and its association with baseball. There is a similarly epiphanic moment embedded in the middle of the description of writing with the body: 'In his sleeplessness he went down the batting order of the 1938 Cleveland Indians. He saw them take the field in all the roomy optimism of those old uniforms. . . . The names of those ballplayers were his night prayer, his reverent petition to God, with wording that remained eternally the same' (136). The democratic space of the ballpark is combined with the sacred litany of the players' names in a powerfully nostalgic moment which survives the ravages of history and bears endless comforting repetition. It is reminiscent of the scene in *Ragtime* in which the young boy claims to love baseball because 'The same thing happens over and over' (172). It is no coinci- dence that Karen's marriage takes place in a ballpark, the importance of which she expresses to her partner: ' "Baseball", she says, using the word to sum up a hundred happy abstractions . . . she only means to suggest the democratic clamor, a history of sweat and play on sun- dazed afternoons, an openness of form that makes the game a kind of welcome to my country' (8–9). It is interesting to note that when this part of *Mao II* was first published as an extract in *Granta* in 1990, that final phrase was given as 'a kind of welcome-to-my-country', a textual distinction that has important implications for the question of the novel's narrator, and therefore some bearing on the novel's 'postmodernity'.[18]

The narrative of *Mao II* works a studied analogy between the imprisoned Swiss poet and the American novelist, not only in terms of their pain, isolation, and imprisonment, but in terms of their bodies, and this material is an integral part of their value and importance as writers. Bill's writing is characterized as 'the scant drip, the ooze of speckled matter, the blood sneeze, the daily pale secretion, the bits of human tissue sticking to the page' (28). The physical presence of the body of the artist is a crucial component of the finished work and a fundamental aspect of any true understanding of the writer's life: 'He felt a mass of phlegm wobbling in his throat . . . he swallowed the whole nasty business, a slick syrupy glop. This was the texture of his life. If someone ever writes his true biography, it will be a chronicle of gas pains and skipped heartbeats. . . . He was a sitting industry of farts and belches. This is what he did for a living, sit and hawk, mucus and flatus' (135–6). When Bill subsequently begins to write about the Swiss hostage, he writes in terms which closely emulate the novel's depiction of the hostage, and Bill's imagination maintains a close focus on the poet's body, on 'his face and hands . . . his eyes and ears' (160) and especially on the 'particles' of matter of which his experience is constituted, his kidneys, his urine. An intimate knowledge of the material conditions of the artist's body, the artist's physical presence, is essential to the integrity and authenticity of his art. This is a contrast to the mass reproduction of Warhol images that has no relation to Warhol himself: 'he didn't seem dead because he never seemed real' (62). This is why 'Warhol, like Mao, is the spiritual enemy of everything that Bill Gray has stood for in his life'.[19] At the end of the novel when Bill has disappeared, Scott is scrupulously dedicated to removing all trace of Bill's presence, and the line 'He put his face to the keys and blew' becomes a refrain (141, 142, 143, 144) by which Bill's body is removed from his typewriter, 'the mark-making thing that contained his life experience' (160). It is this sense that Bill Gray, a fictional character of

---

18 Don DeLillo, 'At Yankee Stadium', *Granta*, 34 (Autumn 1990), 218.

19 Robert Towers, 'History Novel', *New York Review of Books*, 27 June 1991, 18.

the novel, is writing the account of its other fictional characters, that distinguishes *Mao II* from *White Noise* (the narrative of which is entirely conventional) and aligns it with *Ragtime* as a novel with a claim to be postmodern.

Don DeLillo **Underworld**

DeLillo's *Underworld* (1997) begins in October 1951 with a baseball game, but it is also the day of the discovery by Americans of Russian atomic capacity.[20] The front page of the *New York Times* which was DeLillo's starting point for the novel carried two headlines, one commemorating the New York Giants' win at the Polo Grounds, and the other declaring 'Soviets Explode Atomic Bomb'. This was a technological breakthrough which was a defining moment in Cold War politics, one which had, according to *Underworld*, a crucial impact on the lives of all American citizens, and which helped to define post-war American culture. As one of the novel's characters expresses it, 'every thought in your mind depends upon the ability of the two great superpowers to hang a threat over the planet' (182). *Underworld* plots the course of American history from 1951 to 1992, and especially the importance of the late twentieth-century turn from regarding weapons as threat, to weapons as waste. The idea of the technology of waste disposal, its significance, history, and cultural value, is central to the novel. The technology of the arms race has become the technology of the disposal of radioactive material, especially 'After Chernobyl' (802). In the 1960s and 1970s 'They were awed by the inner music of bomb technology' (404) and the pressure of the arms race dictated that 'All technology refers to the bomb' (467). But since the dissolution of the Cold War the vanguard of technological innovation has turned its attention to the challenge of dealing with the planet's garbage. The novel's central character Nick Shay is an executive with a waste management company and very much alert to the presence of garbage and all its cultural significations: 'This is Nick, the technology, the logic, the esthetics' (163). The novel is not only about the technology of waste disposal, but also how a culture might be

---

[20] Page references are to the Scribner edition.

interpreted by means of its discarded remnants and its daily detritus, how culture might be analysed anthropologically in terms of how it deals with waste and how future historians might carry out archaeological investigations of twentieth-century America by studying its refuse. The history of waste, its anthropological and artistic value, is also central to the novel's representation of American culture since the Cold War. There is a great deal of continuity here in DeLillo's anthropological fictions. In a key scene in *White Noise* Jack rummages through the household garbage for clues to the family's authentic character: 'I felt like an archaeologist about to sift through a finding of tool fragments and assorted cave trash. . . . I picked through it item by item, mass by shapeless mass, wondering why I felt guilty, a violator of privacy, uncovering intimate and perhaps shameful secrets. . . . Was this the dark underside of consumer consciousness?' (258–9). This too is reminiscent of the Little Boy in *Ragtime* who collects abandoned remnants for their future cultural value, scraps and rags, 'the boy treasured anything discarded' (89).

There are many scenes in *Underworld* where the anthropological importance of waste is dramatized. Brian Glassic compares the scale and ingenuity of Fresh Kills landfill to 'the Great Pyramid at Giza' (184); Nick imagines the dumpsite of discarded and redundant military aircraft in the desert in Arizona to be 'the land art of some lost Andean people' (126), and Albert Bronzini tells his friends about the 'ancient Mayans' who 'did not bury their dead with gleaming jewelry and other valuable objects. . . . They used the dead as a convenient means of garbage disposal' (767). The Russian, Viktor, tells Nick that 'Waste is the secret history, the underhistory, the way archaeologists dig out the history of early cultures' (791). Future historians might interpret twentieth-century America in terms of the history of its waste products, and this is part of the narrative project of *Underworld*, interpreting America's Cold War legacy by gathering and analysing its marginal, broken, or discarded remnants, the fragments at the periphery which are not obviously part of any authorized historical account—Lenny Bruce's monologues, or a lost baseball's circulation. These things are recuperated by *Underworld*, brought back for our attention as revealing and important signifiers of their culture.

The importance of the abandoned remnants of a culture is that they provide a way to interpret that culture; this is as true of contemporary urban America as it is of ancient civilizations, and this is dramatized by the novel's depiction of New York's south Bronx, a place characterized by the massive accumulation of urban detritus, 'years of stratified deposits' (238). In this desperate community where people are dumped by American society and become part of the wasted landscape ('"red-bag waste. Hospital waste, laboratory waste"', (249)), Ismael the graffiti artist salvages something of value from abandoned cars, his crew are 'foragers and gatherers' (the language of anthropology), and they redeem garbage in order to survive. The municipal authorities come to this place to 'excavate' and they leave behind further deposits of their own exploratory endeavours, pizza cartons and styrofoam cups. The south Bronx also becomes a tourist site, destination of 'South Bronx Surreal', where people come to view the spectacle of the most extreme forms of American urban dereliction. The tourists come here for the same reason that Sister Edgar went to Rome to view 'bombed-out terrain, for the moss-grown memory of torture and war' (248), and to see a chapel in a Capuchin church stacked to the roof with skeletons; these artefacts tell the history of a culture and its practices as much as any other cultural landmark. *Underworld* shows how the history of dumping and archaeological recovery stretches back to the Italian renaissance, and that modern technological waste disposal is also a key signifier of our culture, one which should encourage us to pay more attention to the social practices of society's cultural margins.

There is also an important aesthetic quality that attaches itself to waste in *Underworld*. In its dramatization of technology and refuse, the novel shows that contemporary waste can be redeemed artistically, and this too is a means by which we can interpret our history. Klara Sax is engaged in a creative project to transform the discarded aircraft of 'the boneyard' of the Pima Air Museum near Tucson into a work of art, in which the desert landscape of Arizona becomes the frame for something spectacular and beautiful. The materials are described as 'castoffs' (70), and Klara has acquired the moniker 'Bag Lady' (70) because her career 'had been marked at times by her methods of transforming and absorbing junk' (102). Klara characterizes her artistic impulse as 'a graffiti instinct' (77) and this wording immediately associates her with the other artist of the novel Ismael Munoz, who decorates subway trains in New York: 'The whole point of Moonman's tag was how the letters and numbers told a story of backstreet life' (434). This 'backstreet' aesthetic of urban detritus, and the social and political agenda that accompanies it, is part of the novel's democratic ideological freight, characteristic of DeLillo's tendency to write against the grain of received narratives of history, to recuperate the leftovers, to focus on what has been neglected or discarded. Watts Towers in Los Angeles is a magnificent architectural structure, regardless of 'the cast off nature of the materials' (277), and the narrative of *Underworld* aspires to the same artistic condition, 'a sense of repeated themes and deft engineering', constructed from apparently useless materials.

Waste has further important cultural significance because Nick believes that 'Waste is a religious thing. We entomb contaminated waste with a sense of reverence and dread. It is necessary to respect what we discard' (88). It is important to interpret this comment in the context of Nick's Jesuitical training, 'to examine things for second meanings and deeper connections' (88), and it is notable that Nick is not treated with DeLillo's characteristic irony. The religious significance of waste is dramatized in the scene in which Nick takes his granddaughter Sunny to the landfill in Phoenix where 'We feel a reverence for waste, for the redemptive qualities of the things we use and discard . . . the aura of sacred work. It is like a fable in the writhing air of some ghost civilization' (809–10). The visit to the landfill is an important social ritual, a place of community bonding where members of society come together to marvel in awe at the technology that their age has created: 'Sunny loves this place and so do the other kids who come with their parents or teachers to stand on the catwalk and visit the exhibits' (809). The gathering together of the community around the sacred site is emotionally satisfying: 'We all feel better when we leave' (810). The social importance of the supermarket in *White Noise* has been replaced by the landfill as a site of routine, ritual, and social recognition. Waste gives Nick 'a faith to embrace' (282).

The mystical reverence for waste has serious religious connotations for Nick's colleagues in the business, Brian Glassic and Jesse Detwiler. Brian has a genuine moment of epiphany at Fresh Kills landfill on Staten Island where he sees all civilization and all human history as culminating at this point, and 'knew for the first time what his job was all about . . . he saw himself for the first time as a member of an esoteric order, they were adepts and seers' (184–5). Brian's epiphany is a

conflation of his sense of desire and his sense of faith, and it is characterized as an extraordinary compression of all history and all of civilization's desires:

Brian found he could create a flash infatuation, she is dark-eyed and reads
the tabloids and paints her nails and eats lunch out of molded styrofoam,
and he gives her gifts and she gives him condoms, and it all ends up here,
newsprint, emery boards, sexy underwear, coaxed into high relief by the
rumbling dozers—think of his multitudinous spermlings with their history
of high family foreheads, stranded in a Ramses body bag and rollered snug
in the deep-down waste. (185)

The 'flash infatuation' that Brian momentarily imagines here includes
the entire history of his genetic makeup, but that too is only the
imagined garbage of the future. Brian's epiphany telescopes backwards and forwards to bring every element of human desire in all its
minute constituent particles to this moment of visionary wonder at a
dumpsite. The moment also dramatizes the novel's repeated insistence that the concept of waste includes the human body. Marvin
Lundy's bowel movements are given extended attention on his journey through Eastern Europe, 'the stuff came crashing out of him,
noisy and remarkably dark . . . he grunted on the seat until all the
elements issued . . . he unleashed a firewall of chemical waste' (309–13),
and other bodily fluids and the HIV virus constitute waste at its most
basic level: 'All waste defers to shit. All waste aspires to the condition
of shit' (302). In associating waste with all the achievements and
desires of civilization Brian is the disciple of Detwiler, the 'visionary'
of waste (285) who argues that nuclear waste is particularly valuable
because it 'becomes a remote landscape of nostalgia . . . Nostalgia for
the banned materials of civilization' (286), and Detwiler eulogizes shit
in these terms: 'Civilization did not rise and flourish as men ham-
mered out hunting scenes on bronze gates and whispered philosophy
under the stars . . . garbage rose first, inciting people to build a civilization in response. . . . Garbage pushed back . . . it forced us to develop
the logic and rigor that would lead to systematic investigations of
reality, to science, art, music, mathematics. . . . Consume or die.
That's the mandate of the culture' (287).

The language of Bill Gray's aesthetic creed in *Mao II*, 'the line that
says it all', is derived from a *Sears* catalogue and accompanied by a

secular liturgy of the batting order of the 1938 Cleveland Indians which becomes his nightly prayer. Nick Shay shares with Bill a mystical reverence for forms of words that approach the revelation of God and which express his faith in a sense of mystical presence. Nick tells his wife that ' "there's an Italian word or Latin word that explains everything . . . Lontananza. Distance or remoteness" ' (275), and he tells his colleague Sims in the same chapter ' "There's a word in Italian. Dietrologia. It means the science of what is behind something. . . . The science of dark forces" ' (280). DeLillo's fiction has consistently articulated a particular interest in German as a language, and in *Underworld* the key German word is *Weltanschauung*: 'I use this grave and layered word because somewhere in its depths there is a whisper of mystical contemplation that seems totally appropriate to the subject of waste' (282). The important phrase here is 'mystical contemplation' because it betrays Nick's Jesuitical training, and because it expresses a sense of a hidden esoteric language of being which many parts of the novel strive towards articulating. There are several scenes in the novel in which Nick ponders the significance of a word which seems to him to approach metaphysical presence, words which he treasures for their own sake because they're part of a language of mystical revelation. The scene with the Jesuit Father naming the parts of a shoe is the origin of this propensity for linguistic contemplation for Nick, and his discussion with Donna at Mojave Springs is his most thorough explication of it (540, 295). The Jesuit Father tells Nick ' "You didn't see the thing because you don't know how to look. And you don't know how to look because you don't know the names. . . . These names are vital to your progress" ' (540–2). Knowing the correct and precise terminology for things is morally educative, the cornerstone of what Stephen Daedalus' Jesuit teachers call 'the ineluctible modality of the visible' or the inescapable materiality of the physical world. To know anything, Nick must begin by knowing the words for things; language is the gateway to metaphysical essence. Nick adopts this philosophy of language, believing that it is 'the only way you can escape the things that made you' (543). Language is the means by which his material circumstances can be transcended; it is the lost language of the father. Explaining this creed to Donna, Nick tells her that God cannot be known and that his 'unknowability' is the source of his power; language however can enable Nick to 'edge closer to

God's unknowable self' (296). Nick's gnostic phrase becomes 'Todo y Nada', glossed as 'The best sex' (297), a piece of language that Nick repeats as an incantation of esoteric spiritual knowledge. This is not treated by *Underworld* with the kind of austere and distancing irony with which Bill Gray was depicted in *Mao II*, or Jack Gladney in *White Noise*. Nick is consistently characterized as seeking to know the essence of things by naming them and by understanding the meaning of precise technical terms: 'Residents of Phoenix are called Phoenicians' (120); 'A hawser is a rope that's used to moor a ship' (102). This is a consistent refrain of Nick's interior world, and it shows him to be striving for an authentic language of things in which there is no gap between the world and its forms of representation.

This idea of faith in language is part of the wider investigation of the forms that faith takes in a post-nuclear society where faith might appear to have been superseded by technological advances which make faith redundant. What is the place of faith, what does the idea of faith mean, in a contemporary technological world full of 'The faith that replaces God with radioactivity' (251)? Forms of faith persist even in the most quotidian contexts: 'You come to a city and you go where the driver takes you—you go on faith' (304), and in the dramatic incidents of the novel technology is often deeply implicated in late twentieth-century forms of religious belief. There is a woman in the Ukraine 'who says she is the second Christ. . . . Fifteen thousand followers. Educated people. Look very normal' (802). This is a phenomenon specifically 'After Chernobyl'. Simultaneously in Normal, Illinois, there is a woman who 'showed the symptoms of whatever illness Elizabeth Taylor was suffering at a particular time, or John Wayne, or Jackie Onassis, or name your star . . . doctors sponsored by the tabloids were studying her' (378). The miracle of the Angel Esmerelda is also closely associated with, or even the product of, urban consumer culture, her image appearing on an advertising hoarding when subway trains illuminated the undersheet. Sister Edgar's enigmatic epiphany on the world wide web is a conflation of nuclear explosion and divine revelation which takes place in cyberspace while Sister Edgar both watches and participates following her mortal death: 'try to imagine the word on the screen becoming a thing in the world' (827).

DeLillo's interest in the media in *Underworld* is dramatized principally by the Texas Highway Killer, Richard Gilkey. The death of one of Gilkey's victims is accidentally recorded on video by a girl out of the rear window of her parents' car as he randomly shoots dead a lone driver. The girl becomes in media parlance 'The Video Kid': 'The tape is famous and so is she' (159). Gilkey's notoriety is similarly inseparable from the mediation of the death of his tenth victim because his is a crime 'designed for random taping and immediate playing' (159) and the novel proposes a curiously modern affinity between the random killing and the manner of its simultaneously random recording, 'the serial murder has found its medium, or vice versa—an act of shadow technology' (159). The Texas Highway Killer is also associated with the media in his infatuation with the television anchorwoman Sue Anne, who 'made him feel real' (269). Gilkey speaks to her on the telephone while watching her on the television and it is this technological connection which 'was the waking knowledge that he was real' (270). Gilkey is also authenticated by reading about his victims in the media, 'He lived in their histories, in the photographs in the newspaper . . . lived on, merged, twinned, quadrupled' (271), and in this way his subjectivity is predicated on media representations of his numerous victims' lives. But by the end of the novel the Killer has gone 'You never hear the name' (807), his effervescent notoriety has evaporated, at least temporarily. But Gilkey still exists while the Texas Highway Killer does not, and in this way he continues to be a function of media culture, because his identity as the Killer is not controlled by him but conferred upon him, and so it can be taken away. On the other hand, 'The Thomson homer continues to live because it happened decades ago when things were not replayed and worn out' (98). The historical memory of a culture is dependent upon its technological methods, but in an inverse relationship; while the subjectivity of the Texas Highway Killer is multiplied by his knowledge of his victims, the Swiss hostage of *Mao II* feels his identity to be seriously depleted by the spread of information about him.

Underworld does not disclose whether the baseball of Bobby Thomson's homer (the history of which allegedly holds the narrative together) is really the same ball that Nick pays for, and similarly the novel withholds the definitive answer to the mystery of Nick's father's disappearance, although, like the ball, there is a proliferation of competing narratives about him. Ultimately *Underworld* does not resolve these central matters because it is structured around an interest in subjects that are beyond its narrative language: 'He did the unthinkable Italian crime. He walked out on his family. They don't even have a name for this' (204). Once again the idea of naming, and the grammar of signifying practices, is central to DeLillo's fiction, and has implications for the status of the texts that he writes. This novel's title, for example, is as important as those of *White Noise* and *Mao II* to its major concerns: it might refer to Jimmy Costanza's sudden disappearance, but it is equally important that the word has textual precedents: 'the legendary lost film of Sergei Eisenstein, called *Unterwelt*' (424), and if this film is difficult to visualize 'All you have to do is think of the other *Underworld*, a 1927 gangster film and box office smash' (431). It is significant that the word 'underworld' has multiple referents because the novel of that name concerns those epistemological questions that cannot be definitively resolved.

Po Bronson **Bombardiers**

There is a host of younger writers who have taken up this area of cultural enquiry and written about the excesses of consumer society and its new and rapidly changing technological forms. The novels of Kathy Acker, Douglas Rushkoff, Bret Easton Ellis, Douglas Coupland, and the later Jay McInerney dramatize the new freedoms and perils of American corporate enterprise and the sometimes violent personal alienation that can accompany it. Future students of the *fin de siècle* zeitgeist will read with particular attention novels with titles such as *In Memoriam to Identity*, *Media Virus*, *American Psycho*, and *Microserfs*. These are also texts that are self-consciously aware of their own status as market commodities, to be merchandised, advertised, promoted, packaged, and shifted as so many units of 'product', and their narratives have attracted countless inappropriate (i.e. lazy) uses of the word 'postmodern' as a synonym for 'contemporary'. These novels deal with surfaces, and there is sometimes little to say about them other than the obvious point about the apparent depthlessness of the society that they satirize. The crisis of value that such novels dramatize is also the central subject of Po Bronson's *Bombardiers* (1995). This novel is the story of the Atlantic Pacific Corporation and its employees, of how the company mutates into another trading company with a new name following the collapse of its attempted sale of billions of dollars of shares in the stock of the Dominican Republic. In its most ambitious sales effort in its history, APC overextends itself, the shares cannot be offloaded by its overburdened salesforce, and the US government is forced to bail out the company by purchasing the stock that the free market cannot be persuaded to invest in. This is appropriate because as sales manager Coyote Jack argues in the chapter called 'Patriotism': ' "Hell, the French sold us Louisiana and the Russians sold us Alaska—what was so strange about the Dominicans selling us their country at a discount?" ' (237).[21] In this way, nation states become merely market commodities to be entirely devoured by the voracious appetite of capitalism which is forever seeking out new markets in a relentless search for a trading profit regardless of the product: 'Democracy was indeed an obsolete form of management, and time and again the American public had voted for less of its tiresome workings. In its place they proposed the orthodoxy of Capitalism, and they rallied for their cause like devout patriots' (236–7). This is part of the novel's satirical investigation of the concept of value in a rampant and uncontrolled free-market economy where everything is subject to purchase and sale and everything has its price. The novel's brilliant young prodigy Eggs Igino establishes a market in lecture notes, and he trades in breakfast foods on the company's trading floor before the working day begins. Nothing escapes the indiscriminate energy of the market: 'Deals were done when they could be sold, not when they made sense. Making sense had never been a prerequisite for doing a deal, and Atlantic Pacific wasn't going to break with precedent' (109). The novel is set in California, but it could be anywhere in the world, 'Sid Geeder looked out John White's forty-first-floor window. There was nothing but fog and they were the only spaceship in the sky. There was no way to tell they were in San Francisco—they could be flying over Tokyo or London or Bonn and they wouldn't even know, they were so tuned in to the market' (8). Corporate anonymity is an expression of submission to the power of the market, and APC's protean identity is a manifestation of the market in its purest form: relentless, uncompromising, totally unscrupulous.

---

[21] Page references are to the Secker and Warburg edition.

Beyond the frenetic trading activity and the comic energy of the novel is a military metaphor reminiscent of the black humour of Joseph Heller's *Catch 22*. The traders of *Bombardiers* are the foot soldiers of capitalist artillery, decked out in the camouflage of late twentieth-century corporate America and hunkering down in the foxholes of their trading posts in anticipation of the first exchanges at dawn. The novel's characters enjoy none of the profits that they work so hard to generate for their unknown employers, but they are ready to do battle with financial institutions that would outwit and defeat them with superior and more up-to-date trading information. The seasoned veteran of five years of combat is Sid Geeder, 'The King of Mortgages', who leads his troops by example, and who is himself cajoled and harassed in the front line by his ruthless sales manager Coyote Jack. Behind Jack in this chain of command is the figure of White, and beyond him lies Cornwall, in a hierarchy of authority that is quasi-military: 'They were the foot soldiers in the trenches of information warfare. The enemy was out there in the mist, behind the buildings, hidden in the computers, camouflaged by numbers, ready to ambush the wires and the cable and the wavelengths. They wore the uniform, they wore the face paint' (179). This is the contemporary form that American colonial expansion takes, and the modern technological association of information and consumerism ensures that the United States will be able to use its economic power to disseminate American cultural values. The Cold War might be over, but the struggle to establish a world-dominant cultural language now takes the form of an information war, 'The military has found a role to play in the post-Cold War economy.... Once those Azerbaijanis start watching American television, their government will never be able to get control of the people again' (143–4). The military metaphor is not entirely comic. Before APC trades in the stock of the Dominican Republic (as 'a perfect corporate warrior', (217)) the company has been active among the countries previously dominated by communism in Eastern Europe: 'Romania's twenty-first century belonged to Wall Street. Eastern Europe was the last frontier' (107). Thanks to the United States' world economic power 'Romania's going to be an American cultural colony in a blink of an eye' (145). Capitalism seeks to take over the world, reducing everything to questions of profit and price and trading to make American corporations richer, and less worldly nations economically dependent and culturally subordinate in a financial system that the United States has developed to its apotheosis. The US government is 'a bloated, gargantuan, scarfing pig' (21) and the RTC eats money 'like Godzilla ate Tokyo' (22). This is the logical and inevitable consequence of the irresistible energies that *Ragtime* is so attentive to.

The apparent pointlessness of profit-driven transactions and the alienation that the salesforce suffers in its service is often given in references to insanity. When Eggs stops work briefly to consider the ways in which his colleagues have become the functionaries of the APC even down to the company's possession of their minds, he concludes that 'one would have to classify this arrangement as insane' (305). Sid Geeder is forced to accept a similar logic because he realizes that the grasp of the company is inescapable 'Going crazy is the only sane reaction to everything that's happened' (227). The collapse of value in their economy of values is neatly dramatized by Eggs's curiosity to see a real bond. Although he is responsible for the sale of millions of bonds, Eggs has never actually seen one, and neither has anyone else. In desperation, Coyote Jack goes to the Federal Reserve Bank to buy a bond, only to discover that they cannot be purchased in this way. Jack receives instead a receipt, like a credit card carbon, 'It could have been Monopoly money' (171). No one knows any better; in the information economy, real products and commodities disappear, and it is the persuasive or rhetorical quality of the knowledge about bonds that is important, not necessarily the information's truthfulness and certainly not the bonds themselves. The traders buy and sell money with other kinds of money because there is money to be made from money as long as transactions continue. *Bombardiers* is full of absurdist moments that exemplify the emptiness of purely financial enterprise: 'They sold predictions for the direction of money and they sold financial instruments designed to take advantage of that direction. There would always be money, and as long as there were markets, money would always have a direction, and a speed, and an acceleration, all of which could be sold' (10). One of Eggs's colleagues is Regis Reed: 'In college he had illegally taken out student loans, which he had invested in the futures market to try to beat the interest he was paying on the loans' (52). All of the novel's characters are dedicated to this kind of sterile and self-serving circle of trade, it is an addiction to the market in which they become a function of the economy and the concept of value evaporates: 'They paid for the money they had bought with the money they had sold' (67). Money is devoid of value because it is a market commodity that only generates value by its circulation; that value, however, is expressed in terms of further sums of money which contribute to the acceleration of the circulation but which do not signify value in any terms that can be expressed beyond the system of circulation.

The question arises then, is anything resistant to the universal appeal of commerce which spreads through the fabric of the novel like a computer virus? The answer lies with the novel's hero Eggs, who begins life at APC as a novice but who soon becomes an innovative genius and the company's most valuable asset. Eggs's new ideas give fresh impetus to trading activity and they are adopted by management as part of a new commercial rhetoric, 'The Third Law of Information Economy', which helps to establish it as a market leader. Eggs's sales exploits acquire mythical status when he is reported in the *Wall Street Journal*, the ultimate distinction and its textual reward. Eggs's disappearance is almost the only narrative event in the novel, but it is crucial because it dramatizes his disregard for the systems of value that APC enshrines. Ultimately his absence from the text leads to the company's collapse, and when he finally returns it is only to steal away its greatest remaining asset Sid Geeder. Here too *Bombardiers* is closely indebted to the absurdist humour of *Catch 22*: after five years' service Sid is owed four million dollars worth of company shares, but he cannot collect his commissions unless he stays another two years. This extension of service will be repeated endlessly, so that Sid's anticipated financial payoff will be endlessly deferred; he sells 'futures', so it is appropriate that he can only ever be rewarded at some point in the future that can never be realized.

As an individual Sid is irrelevant to the workings of the market, 'The individuals just didn't matter—the organization lived on' (312). The economy makes all of its subjects merely a function of its irrevocable progress: 'In the end, when the dust cleared, only Sidney Geeder was left standing, and everything was different except the market, which was the same, because it was normal to rub out everything human' (306). Only Eggs can appeal to Sid to escape, because only Eggs lives outside the novel's systems of value, having discovered (in Mexico) an alternative system of value and the love of a good woman. This cliche is appropriate to the novel's satirical genre (as is the same cliche to McInerney's *Bright Lights, Big City*) and should not be taken seriously. Eggs's life in Mexico is something that lies outside the system of pricing, like the museum in Aberdeen that Sue Marino once visited: 'She kept thinking about this museum she had been to in Aberdeen where, among the landscape paintings and stringed instruments, five live sheep were kept on pedestals. From afar they looked stuffed, but they weren't—they were chained to their pedestals and they seemed perfectly happy to be scratched by the visitors' (76-7). Sid Geeder too has the germ of his redemption, it is seen in his sensitivity to the mountain of garbage three miles across in the Dominican Republic where gangs of youths kill for the right to scavenge for recyclables (44). Sid cannot imagine himself existing outwith the systems of value that he is in the service of, nor that he has any value himself beyond the market economy of American capitalism, but the novel's final moment is Eggs's appeal to Sid's awareness of something outside trade: ' "You're not worthless. You're Sid Geeder. *The* Sid Geeder. The only model and make in the whole world. You're rarer than diamonds. Scarcer than uranium. You're priceless Sid. Nobody can buy you" ' (314). Hokey as this may sound, in the context of the novel it is a rare assertion of human value in a world where the idea of value is absent. For too long Sid has derived his sense of identity from corporate rhetoric, and his subservience to its language has almost rubbed him out. Eggs's final appeal is to something unique, but it is also an appeal for a new kind of language, one that can replace the exhausted and bankrupt currency of their commercial idiom. This is why the novel ends with a witty play on Sid's colloquial 'So, what's the word, kid?' (318), a question that Eggs cannot answer because Sid has to discover for himself his own language beyond commercial enterprise. The collapse of language is dramatized by APC's inability to find the rhetoric with which to shift the shares in the Dominican Republic, and it results in an absence that Sid must fill with his own words, not the words of commerce. *Bombardiers* is a novel about the failure of the word to signify in a world where the concept of value is in crisis, and it ends with its protagonists driving off into the sunset in search of a new life and a new language. The chapter of *Bombardiers* that is called 'Language' begins with the words, 'Theirs was a bastard language, the illegitimate offspring of technical financial terminology and forty years of pop Americana, littered with ill-chosen metaphors and living acronyms' (122). Can there be an alternative American language beyond that of the systems of commerce that *Ragtime*, *White Noise*, *Mao II*, *Underworld*, and *Bombardiers* investigate? Is there a manner of speech outwith its influence, another idiom, in other words? *Bombardiers* cannot imagine one, but ends with Sid's response ' "Let's go find out" ' (319).

5

Language and Power

One might in turn become less diffident,
Out of such mildew plucking neater mould
And spouting new orations of the cold.
One might. One might. But time will not relent.

Wallace Stevens,
'The Man Whose Pharynx Was Bad'

Above all modern societies the United States is an immigrant society,
and one in which a common language becomes an important mark of
recognition and even a requisite for social membership. There are
important ideological implications involved in the acquisition of a
particular language, and fundamental consequences for the sense of
identity that the newcomer to America must negotiate. Surrendering
the native language helps to perpetuate the ethos of 'one nation, one
language'. Issues of language can be both unifying and divisive at a
political level and an individual level; the national anthem, for
example, is sung in English even though there are substantial communities in America where English is not the first language of the
majority of the population, and there have even been recent calls for
Spanish to be made the national language of the United States. On the
other hand, many Americans believe that speaking English is a basic
requirement of social membership and commitment to America.
These are issues about power, both the empowerment of individuals
who seek to be accepted as a part of American culture, and the social
and political power of groups of American citizens. The novels of
this chapter all investigate the nature of a particular language and
examine the relationship between language, culture, and power.

Furthermore, recent theoretical criticism has emphasized the subtle and sophisticated ways in which language underpins all forms of social organization and has shown how the social sciences are predicated on language as a system of signification in fundamental ways that encode values and have important political implications. This linguistic turn gives a special place to the importance of language and narrative and has had an impact on many different fields of cultural enquiry. The Marxist Louis Althusser, for example, has shown how individual citizens are 'interpellated' into their culture by the ideology of its dominant discourses, and made a 'subject' of it. Language is a crucial part of this process because it carries ideological values that circumscribe the individual's understanding of who they are, and language can be said to inscribe individuals within their culture in ways that make them functions of it. This is the politics of language, the ways in which we are written by it, and one of the primary ways that a culture institutionalizes its values. Recent political struggles over the word 'Squaw', for example, have shown that a term which is an integral part of everyday usage is, and always has been, deeply offensive to many American Indians who understand the word as being strongly derogatory.

At the same time of course the novels of this chapter are texts, pieces of language that are minutely involved in negotiating their own relationships with culture. These novels are often self-conscious about their own status as linguistic constructions or artefacts, and this self-reflexive quality becomes an important part of what they are as texts, metafictional enquiries into the nature of creative language and its political implications. Asian-Americans, Afro-Americans, white metropolitan Americans, and southern rural Americans each have their own specific history and language, and the doppelgängers that are a frequent feature of this chapter's novels reveal the structural self-examination that they are engaged in. These are novels that offer 'new orations' of what American language can consist of, and they advertise the diversity of languages that is a function of the heterogeneity of the United States.

Gish Jen **Typical American**

Gish Jen's *Typical American* (1991) is a novel that explores the ideological pressures of Americanization by dramatizing their impact on a
Chinese family who come to New York in the early 1950s.[1] The novel
is principally concerned with examining the commercial and material
ethos of American culture at that time, and the immigrants' need to
succeed and to be socially accepted in a world of post-war consumer
opportunity. This is perhaps especially true for Asians in the time of
McCarthyism and during the Korean War.[2] But *Typical American* also
scrutinizes significant ethical challenges that Ralph, Helen, and
Theresa face, especially as they are represented by Grover Ding, a fully
Americanized Chinese man who dupes Ralph into business criminality, and Ralph's wife (almost) into infidelity. Often in the novel, the
commercial and the moral are closely associated so as to make the
point that 'Americanization' is for the Changs a process of submitting
ethical standards to the imperative of mercantile values. The Changs'
knowledge of the English language, so different from their native
Shanghainese, is an important part of this process.

Typical American accomplishes this by conjuring subtle psychological tensions from an economical prose style which dramatizes
rather than expounds its moral dilemmas. Ralph's entanglement in
the intricacies of American cultural life begins with his relationship
with Cammy, the secretary at the Foreign Student Affairs Office; his
desire for her is based on a sense of her value: 'Ralph had noticed by
then that she was very pretty, or figured she must be, as about half the
men with affairs to discuss with her didn't seem to be foreign students' (12). Ralph is alert to questions of status and commerce from
the beginning of his American narrative (note the pun on 'figured'),
and he quickly learns to make decisions based on financial considerations: 'Now he went to a new cheaper grocery, even though the first
grocer was friendlier than the second' (14). In the novel's third chapter, ironically called 'Love', Ralph is told that ' "That's all anyone
understands in this country. Dough" ' (17), and he begins to buy

---

[1] All page references are to the Plume Contemporary Fiction edition.
[2] Senator Joe McCarthy: 1908–57; Senate hearings, Apr.—June 1954. Korean War:
1950–3.

Cammy presents in the belief that he has found the way to court her. Here Ralph thinks that he has understood a simple correspondence between his native culture and America's: 'Presents paved roads in China too; this was a type of construction he understood' (18). Ralph is predisposed by his upbringing in China to buy presents, but he does not understand the American code; the cultural interpretation of those presents is quite different in America, and Ralph fails to win Cammy's attention because he buys her inappropriate gifts such as a can opener. He realizes later that 'He ought to have bought her diamonds' (20), and from this point on the importance of money and social status is central to Ralph's narrative. Furthermore, Ralph is blind to the signals of Cammy's duplicity, and she has her sights on bigger presents, 'houses and cars' (19) which she will elicit from her lover: 'the dean had a house and a car, and had had a wife, until the papers finally came through' (20). Ralph is mortified and chastened by his romantic liaison with Cammy, but she leaves a legacy which informs his view of life in America, especially as regards desire and economics; she provides him with his English name too, one which replaces his Chinese name 'Intent-on-the-Peak' with the name of one of her ex-boyfriends, and a name which he looks up in the dictionary: Ralph, 'A kind of dog' (11). Ralph's attempt to understand his new name by reference to the authority of the dictionary is indicative of his dilemma in trying to interpret the language of his new culture. It is important for the politics of this novel to note that the idea of aspiration expressed by 'Intent-on-the-Peak' is something that Ralph brings with him from China; it signifies a predisposition to some of the 'American' values that he will learn. Ralph shares his name with Ralph Waldo Emerson. One critic has argued that Ralph's narrative is one in which he 'discovers romantic individualism, that raft on which both immigrants and the native-born shoot the white rapids of American life',[3] and his name is perhaps chosen to signal that incipient individualism exemplified by Emerson.

These formative experiences of American commercial and moral values establish the pattern of Ralph's narrative, in which questions of commerce and ethical decisions will often be closely associated. Even before Ralph arrives in New York the reader knows that the

---

[3] P. Storace, 'Seeing Double', *New York Review of Books*, 15 Aug. 1991, 9–10.

novel will concern itself with cultural value; in China, Ralph's father announces that he is going to write about ' "Degeneracy! Stupidity! Corruption!".. "America", his mother says then' (5). But the novel is not simply about the collapse of Chinese moral imperatives in the face of Western decadence; Ralph adapts very readily to certain ideological values of personal freedom and individual self-determination epitomized by the America of the 1950s. Ralph writes a manifesto of self-improvement ('I will cultivate virtue . . . I will bring honour to the family') which, although Confucian, unwittingly emulates Jay Gatz's plan of personal salvation written on the flyleaf of *Hopalong Cassidy* in Fitzgerald's *The Great Gatsby*, and Ralph also emulates Gatsby's migration east to New York when he takes a train across the United States from San Francisco, oblivious in his scholarly preparations, to 'the whole holy American spectacle' (7). The language of Ralph's conversion to the new economic culture is also strongly reminiscent of Fitzgerald's expression of the birth of a uniquely American sense of identity: Ralph reads *The Power of Positive Thinking* by Norman Vincent Peale, and one morning in church he has an epiphany: 'he stared up into the multicolored air, and knew: he wanted to be like that man-god. More realistically, he pictured a kind of assistant to the man-god, say a half-step up from an apostle. He pictured himself able to do what he would' (88). Ralph is converted, in an Emersonian paragraph full of religious language, from an engineer to an 'imagineer', a radical transformation of his subjectivity through the agency of the new pseudo-biblical text. This recalls the birth of Gatsby, a character who 'sprang from a Platonic conception of himself. He was a son of God'.[4] The religious language of this rebirth is made possible by the free-market economy's power to appropriate anything and turn it into a commodity, and belief in the new economic system is consistently characterized as a matter of 'Faith'. There is a willingness to subscribe to an ideology of personal fulfilment which is not just a matter of an East–West opposition in *Typical American*. Ralph's confusion when he is married makes him long for the apparent clarity and simplicity of Chinese social conventions: 'He wishes he were in China, where if there turned out to be something wrong with the marriage he could always take a concubine. That was a better system,

---

[4] *The Great Gatsby* (Penguin edn.), 95.

he thought, more sure' (69). This is a nostalgia for a different system of values, and its difference from Western moral attitudes serves to highlight the relativity of value systems in East and West, and Ralph's dilemma in striving to live by a hybrid of the two. Ralph's narrative is one which demonstrates that the personal freedoms that America can offer bring with them complex and difficult moral problems which must be negotiated with shrewdness, tact, and a full and sensitive moral awareness. The figure of the concubine is one which the novel returns to (at (279)), and it is worth noting, in the context of the novel's explication of cultural relativity and moral judgement, how it is used to delineate Ralph and Theresa's different sense of moral responsibility. Most importantly, *The Power of Positive Thinking* is given to Ralph by a figure of authority, Professor Pierce, and like the authority of the dictionary by which he tries to understand his name, this is a piece of (foreign) language through which he learns the principal narratives of his new cultural environment. The book is 'a divine gift' (87).

The issues of the central dramatic action of *Typical American* are also commercial and moral. Ralph's success in his scholarly career results in his appointment as a tenured professor, but he is quickly dissatisfied with the status that it represents because during his time in America as a student his ambitions have changed, so that now, 'he yearned for a larger tenure than any department could grant' (179). Ralph's desire for something more than the prestige of a professorship is fulfilled by his business connection with Grover Ding, a fully Americanized Chinese con-man who provides an entrepreneurial opportunity but quickly involves Ralph in illegal tax evasion. Ralph's greed blinds him to Grover's criminality and he becomes obsessed with commercial enterprise for its own sake, because he believes it to be the American way, and his profit calculations completely absorb him: 'The numbers began to take on a life of their own, which was at the same time the life he gave them' (220-1). Ralph has the entrepreneur's opportunism but without respect for moral, legal, or social conventions, and in the chapter of the novel called 'Living by the Numbers' he builds a fantasy house of cards based entirely on estimated profit margins and gambles everything on its financial success. The extent of his greed and its moral consequences is nicely illustrated by one throw-away aside which also neatly exemplifies the novel's distinctive style: 'he even knew which meters were jammed, so he could park free' (232-3). Ralph's new-found conception of who he is, or who American enterprise will permit him to be, involves the complete abandonment of his laudable ambitions as an engineer, which are made subservient to his desire to build an extra storey to his house of cards so that he might make more money: 'How much more profitable the store would be! Enough to make the mortgage payments and more. "And the next thing I know, I'm millionaire". Ralph could hear himself telling this story to some lost soul in a diner. He straightened the lapels of his bathrobe, a big shot' (220). The image of the successful businessman replaces the professor and Ralph is happy to be complicit in the corruption and illegality it entails. The power of the economic imperative in this culture transforms Ralph's identity and he becomes a function, willingly, of its financial systems; his bourgeois Chinese upbringing makes him susceptible to these forms of change. It is worth noting that Ralph's avarice is given here in terms of a myth or a fiction about millionaire big shots who tell their tales of success, significantly, 'to some lost soul in a diner'. This is not only depicted as a kind of illusion, but is simultaneously one of loneliness and isolation.

Ralph's wife Helen is no less intrigued by material possibilities than he is, and her ambitions are focused on the family house and its domestic comforts. Grover, who is the agent of Ralph's collapse, almost bankrupts Helen too. It is significant that her interest in him is motivated by the knowledge of what he can provide: 'A man with monogrammed shirts, a maid, a mansion, and all he wanted was to finger her belly button. She felt herself to be someone else' (214). Helen's subjectivity is also open to transformation by consumer pressures, but she has the moral integrity to draw back from the vision of the person that abandonment to those pressures would make her. This distinction must influence the way that readers interpret Ralph. Although Helen is flattered by Grover's attention while Ralph 'saw nothing but the register' (218) and although she appears to be tempted by the life of comfort Grover offers ('She laughed and let him paint her toenails', (214)), Helen has the strength of character not to be corrupted by all the opportunities that American culture makes available. Grover taunts her for having married dutifully when in America marriage is a matter of free and personal choice, but Helen holds true to her loyalty to Ralph and still imagines herself 'sharing a place with him, at the center of things' (215). The narrative of Helen's temptation is coincident with Ralph's, because Grover is the agent of corruption for both of them. It seems likely that Grover precipitates Ralph's commercial collapse immediately following his romantic rejection by Helen. Here *Typical American* pursues that particular imbrication of financial and ethical values which is offered by the novel as the char- acteristically American ethos. Furthermore, their subsequent finan- cial hardship brings them back together (249), suggesting that it is mutual struggle that is emotionally rewarding, not material success.

The dilemmas of American culture as they are experienced by Chinese immigrants are further exemplified by the narrative of Ralph's sister Theresa, a doctor who has an affair with a married man. Ralph cannot countenance such a relationship, but his rejection of her leads directly to his need to increase profits once her financial contribution to his household is lost. Theresa, who has made im- portant sacrifices on his behalf, is the moral centre of the novel, the agent of redemption for Ralph when she meets him in the park in the chapter called 'Deliverance', and she is something of a guardian to him in his quest for professorial tenure. Just as Ralph is flanked by Helen in his dealings with Grover, he is unknowingly protected by Theresa in his power relationship with Henry Chao; in both cases the illicit partnership that his wife and sister have with the important men in his life have a significant bearing on what Ralph deems to be his personal self-determination. In this way the novel shows that the very idea of self-determination is something of an illusion: Ralph's narrative is strongly influenced by the women in his life, even though he does not know this. Theresa is the prospective partner for Grover, but unlike Ralph and Helen she keeps well clear of him, uncomfort- able in the high heels that she buys for meeting him and unhappy with the new person that they make of her. Theresa is a subtle com- bination of innocent and conspirator, using her position with Henry Chao to advise Ralph, but not guilty of the shame that Ralph accuses her of: 'The censure of her family was like a hard shell under which she found a certain freedom' (173). Theresa is more sensitive to the moral complexities of the new country and its apparently liberating potential, and she seems to understand how perilous it can be for a stranger: 'She had always been nice about her morals; she grew nicer still. How dangerous a place, this country! A wilderness of freedoms. She shuddered, kept scrupulously to paths' (142). Theresa is also prophetically alert to Helen's absorption in the luxuries of a suburban lifestyle, warning her when she eulogizes in real-estate jargon, ' "Be careful you don't fall in love" ' (152). Here again the novel deliberately confuses material and emotional languages, but Theresa's shrewdness shows her to be a moral touchstone; she is morally educated by the choices American culture offers, and her sense of freedom is a response not to money or power but to other moral positions such as 'The censure of her family', and a sensitivity to the feelings and position of Henry's wife. Theresa remains faithful to certain moral codes: 'In China there were concubines—not what she wanted to be at all, but which proved human nature capable of different sorts of marriage' (279). The uncharacteristic difficulty of the syntax here is a stylistic signal of the intimate association between language and ethics in the process of assimilation that *Typical American* dramatizes.

The moral and financial compromise of Helen and Ralph brings Theresa back into the family, she has 'come to save us' now that 'Her exile was over' (265). Theresa's focus on 'honesty' in her dealings with Henry Chao and his wife brings about a transformation in him, one in which the Western religious imagery of Ralph's economic conversion is given an Eastern reprise in Chao's 'meditative looks' which 'reminded Helen of a monk' (268). It is Theresa's near-death that brings about Ralph's final redemption: 'a gradual thickening. A change of blood. That brought with it a change of thought— imagineering giving way to nostalgia. . . . He was like a nation in crisis, looking back, and back, and back—its history might be ugly, but its past shone perfect' (285). This is the beginning of Ralph's atonement and salvation, and it is significant that the novel's final image is of Ralph's vision of his sister's happiness and fulfilment with Henry Chao. Here too Ralph has learned the cost of American choices: 'He was not who he made up his mind to be. A man was the sum of his limits; freedom only made him see how much so. America was no America' (296). Ralph feels betrayed by Grover, Theresa, Helen, and even Chao, but it is his own investment in American commercialism which lets him down. This is the end of his dream of living in 'the legendary America that was every wish come true' (237). But Ralph is still fooling himself even here, and denying the degree of responsibility that he always had for his own moral choices; America is not some fixed and monolithic entity, it is what he chose to make of it and what he chose to become there. Theresa's nemesis comes in the form of Grover the dog, final confirmation that the fully Americanized Chinese con-man is the agent of destruction for all of them. The novel leaves Theresa's future uncertain; she is a sacrifice to Ralph's moral integrity and the agent of Ralph's happiness and salvation, but her personal fulfilment remains at the end nothing more than a function of his imagination. The gender politics of this suggests that while the women are the touchstones of spiritual virtue it is still the man whose fortunes the reader invests in and the man whose efficacy the women are subordinate to. This is perhaps part of the novel's Eastern ideological legacy.

Ralph has been forced to revalue himself by his recognition of American social inequality, in terms of his position in the new commercial system. Theresa recognizes as he does that 'to be nonwhite in this society was indeed to need education, accomplishment, some source of dignity. A white person was by definition somebody. Other people needed, across their hearts, one steel rib' (200). This pressure is subtly hinted at throughout the novel in one-line asides about 'Japs' and, during the Vietnam war, 'Gooks' (260). In the 1950s too the Changs' perception of themselves is profoundly influenced by American hostility; they watch baseball on television: 'the one time they went to an actual game, people had called them names and told them to go back to their laundry' (127). This sense of the Changs' ethnic difference contributes to the multiple ironic resonances of the novel's title. Theresa points out that their expression 'typical American good-for-nothing' was used by them *because we believed we were* good for nothing' (126); this is a retrospective gloss on the family's use of the phrase earlier in the novel where it is uniformly a term of disparagement: ' "Typical American no-good. . . . typical American no-morals. . . . Typical American just-dumb!" ' (67). The novel's title is not simply a question of whether in the course of their narrative the Changs become typical Americans, but of how the phrase is used first against the new culture as a way to defend and define themselves, and then against themselves as they internalize a feeling of ethnic inferiority that they learn from their American culture. This is a part of the wider drama of language acquisition in the novel; the prose style of *Typical American* is economical, clipped, telegraphic, at times epigrammatical, as if in enactment of the characters speaking English as a second language. Simultaneously the text is full of phrases from Chinese which carry the remnants of their native culture: 'Ting de jian' (4), 'Shuo bu chu lai' (296). This is not simply a matter of translation, but of transliteration (as the author's note points out), not only a shift from a different language but a different alphabet. Thus the drama of immigration and Americanization is also the drama of transforming the Chinese subjectivity, the language of the self, into another language, and *Typical American* shows how those two narratives take place simultaneously. The end of the novel leaves the Changs stranded between two languages, and this is depicted as a fundamental condition of the kind of Americans they are.

Chang-rae Lee **Native Speaker**

What does 'typically American' mean? For the father of the narrator of Chang-rae Lee's novel *Native Speaker* (1995), it is clear: ' "typically American, crazy, self-indulgent, too rich in time and money" ' (43).[5] *Native Speaker* is the first-person narrative of Henry Park, a second-generation immigrant born in the USA after his father moved to New York from Korea in the 1950s. The New York of this novel is a multicultural and politicized urban community in which Koreans like Henry's father take their place with Latvians, Haitians, West Indians, Africans, Poles, and Chinese, each with their own cultural legacy and their own immigrant narrative of the struggle to assimilate. In this context of a plural, shifting, heterogeneous and ethnically sensitive community, Henry Park attempts to define his identity and his place in the culture and to articulate something of what it means to be American, and what it means to become American. In his Oedipal struggle with his father, Henry establishes his difference from the first-generation immigrant's story; his father runs a grocery store, works long hours, and protects his wife from the knowledge of some of the hardships he suffers in order to be successful. Like the characters of *Typical American*, he 'considered the only unseen forces to be

5 All page references are to the Granta edition.

those of capitalism and the love of Jesus Christ' (44). To be American is again synonymous with commercial success and social status, with free-market economics and Christianity. Where *Typical American* acknowledges the importance of Emerson, the epigraph of *Native Speaker* is from Whitman: 'I turn but do not extricate myself / Confused, a past-reading, another / but with darkness yet'. It is through economic success that Henry's father earns respect in the new society where the pressures of social class are felt most keenly by those whose new life in America begins at the bottom. Henry's father was, like Ralph, a university-educated engineer: 'my father had to retool his life to the ambitions his meagre knowledge of the language and culture would allow, invent again the man he wanted to be' (309). Henry's father can only be successful if he adapts quickly to the conditions of the new culture and the language of commercial advancement, and his story is about metamorphosis, 'that daily survival he came to endure, the need to adapt, assume an advantageous shape' (297).[6] When prompted, Henry's father offers his personal history in terms of 'the classic immigrant story' which is one of marvellous self-determination flourishing in the economic freedoms of the United States, 'the heroic newcomer, self-sufficient, resourceful' (46). But he only subscribes to this myth because he knows that it is 'what every native loves to hear' (46), because it is a narrative which exonerates and valorizes the American dream and so Henry's father repeats it and it becomes the first element of his Americanization. The erasure of his true history is the first sacrifice to his desire to become American. The truth is that 'I never learned the exact reason he chose to come to America' (52). Henry's position in relation to the new culture is necessarily different from his father's because he was born in the USA and therefore is naturalized by American culture from the beginning, but his relationship with his father still marks a crucial point of departure and difference which informs his personal and cultural identity. In particular Henry inherits special qualities of restraint and secrecy from his father which are crucial to his subjectivity as a Korean-American man, and those 'amazing properties of emotional recovery' (201) which he attributes to his father are also the cornerstone of

---

6 One of the epigraphs to *Mona in the Promised Land* (1996) is a translation from Ovid: 'all things change. The cosmos itself is flux and motion'. One of the other epigraphs is from the *I Ching* or *Book of Changes*.

Henry's personality. Just as Henry's father makes a break with Korea, so Henry struggles to establish his independence from his father, and the terms and conditions of that struggle shape who he is. This Oedipal conflict is revealed sharply in their respective knowledge of the English language; when Henry's father berates his mother, he uses English rather than Korean, as a weapon she does not understand. Henry fights back 'using the biggest words I knew, whether they made sense or not, school words like "socioeconomic" and "intangible"' (58). Henry understands English better than his father does, and this knowledge is power; Henry's father learns as much English as he can in order to be a successful businessman, but Henry is a native speaker.

Henry's relationship with his wife is a further crucial determining factor in defining his personal and cultural identity. It is significant that Leila is a white American, a woman from Massachusetts with Scottish ancestry, whose family represents something of an established American cultural history. Henry's marriage to Leila is a delight to his father because it is an important recognition of the Korean-American's social acceptance. For Henry though, the relationship is more difficult because of the ways that it continues to problematize his sense of identity. The marriage to a Korean-American exposes Leila to racial tensions that she is not accustomed to, challenging her to respond to the bullying that their son receives, and to the racism of American suburbia: '"a chink, a jap, a gook"' (96). Clearly too the accidental death of their son occasions a crisis in their marriage brought about by mutual feelings of guilt and blame. Leila suggests '"Maybe it's that Mitt wasn't all white or all yellow"' (120).

Henry understands his marriage to Leila from the outset in terms of the acquisition of language and the power that language knowledge confers. The couple meet for the first time in El Paso, Texas, a border city: '"Everyone in this town wants to learn English"' (10) and the first thing that Henry admires in Leila is that 'she could really speak. . . . she was simply executing the language' (9). Furthermore, Leila is a speech therapist and something of a poet, so that her personal and professional identities are predicated on her accomplishments in the English language, and for Henry she comes to be defined by this expertise and the cultural status that it confers and signifies. The one poem of Leila's that the novel gives an account of concerns the death of Henry's father and it is a poem which is unable to define his subjectivity in terms other than 'a house strangely unpossessed' (202). The poem then shifts to the man's son, Leila's husband, and expresses her inability to 'call his real name' (203). This of course is Henry, who Leila finds increasingly opaque, distant, secretive. The list of characteristics which she presents to him when she leaves begins with the word 'surreptitious' (5). Leila's insights into Henry's identity, and the authority invested in her observations by her cultural position, are a source of serious anxiety to him because her remarks intensify his sense of uncertainty about himself. It is this idea of absence which Leila identifies when she says that ' "I realised one day that I didn't know the first thing going on in your head" ' (117), and this has become something she diagnoses as his 'condition' (118). There are aspects of Henry's identity that Leila feels shut out from because ' "You live in one tiny part of your life at a time" ' (208). For Henry these comments are disturbing not only because they signify an inability to communicate, but because they seem to confirm a private suspicion that he has a perilously fragile sense of his own identity.

At the heart of the novel's examination of the Korean-American's subjectivity is Henry's job as a spy. Henry is writing himself into the culture of the United States, and all his relationships show the points of conflict, resistance, and assimilation, the tiny subtle moments of change at which he becomes fully 'American'. But his occupation, his double life, exposes the psychic cost of his particular form of Americanization. Henry seems particularly well-suited to the life of the spook but it serves to intensify greatly his alienation from himself, his alter-ego easily assumed and brilliantly maintained (for the most part) but dramatizing the dangerous doubleness of his newcomer's life and the ways that it succeeds in hiding from him a true sense of who he is. In trying to write the story of his own life in America, Henry finds, disturbingly, that at its core there is a fearful absence, a central inability to articulate a subjectivity which he feels is his own. Henry describes his occupation as 'a string of serial identity' (30) for which he is well-suited because it concurs so well with 'that secret living I'd known throughout my life' (163), and he characterizes his daily work in terms of creating 'an unassailable body of cover' (150). But Henry comes to realize that he disguises his identity so well because he has such a precarious sense of himself to disguise, and this absence, what he terms 'my own instant live burial' (188) is the central subject of his text: 'I have always known that moment of disappearance, and the even uglier truth is that I have long treasured it. That always honorable-seeming absence. It appears I can go anywhere I wish. Is this my assimilation, so many years in the making? Is this the long-sought sweetness?' (188). Henry has a natural facility for the adoption of an alias; he is naturally reticent about himself and naturally disposed by his cultural position to take on something of an assumed personality. Paradoxically, this process becomes his American naturalization. But the rhetorical question implies a way out, and at times there is a certain arch quality to the novel's style which must be broken down if Henry is to find for himself an appropriate narrative language; he needs to move beyond the self-consciousness of statements such as, 'I can be positively Edwardian' (186).

Henry's persona begins to unravel when he is assigned to investigate Luzan, the Filipino psychoanalyst who tells him ' "You'll be yourself again" ' (20). Luzan is subsequently murdered, an early warning to Henry of the cost of his duplicity, both to his subjects who become (innocent) victims, but also to himself in terms of his conscience and his sense of identity. The episode with Luzan shows how dangerous his position is, a betrayal of his subject's personal trust, and a betrayal of himself. But embedded within this narrative of Henry's betrayal is yet another; he confesses to Luzan having been unfaithful once to his wife Leila, an incident which is not referred to at any other point in the novel. This infidelity, a special kind of disloyalty in which he has sex with a Chinese woman in order to betray her husband to his rivals, has almost destroyed Henry: 'for years I felt disordered by it, sickened, until I released the secret to him' (193). Henry uses Luzan doubly, first to absolve his sense of guilt at his own betrayal, and then to betray Luzan to the Filipino agents who murder him. It is painfully ironic that Luzan should be the one to tell Henry that his problem is partly to do with where he lives ' "and who you are within that place. Or believe yourself to be. We have our multiple roles like everyone else" ' (124). Henry's problematic subjectivity is partly a function of the culture, institutions, and social practices that he seeks to inscribe himself within.

An important aspect of the novel's exploration of the immigrant experience is revealed in Henry's doppelgänger relationship with his

Korean subject John Kwang. Henry begins by impersonating the Korean politician, 'I played John Kwang' (85), and gradually becomes involved in a close relationship with him, 'I suppose you could call ours a kind of romance' (129). Kwang is the public and political face of Henry's identity crisis, he wants to be accepted as American and to represent the newest generation of ethnic minorities in New York, the 'neo-Americans' (16), and Henry sees, in his immigrant's desire to assimilate, important correspondences between them, that 'one was an outlying version of the other' (129). Kwang reminds Henry of his father, and he reminds him too of himself as his father did, part of the novel's theme of Oedipal struggle with 'elders' and the importance in Korean culture of deference and respect for them. Kwang is also like Henry in his reserve, formal restraint or self-discipline which is also, in this novel, part of a Korean cultural legacy. Most of all, Henry recognizes in Kwang his own precise cultural condition: 'where he began to think of America as a part of him, maybe even his, and this for me was the crucial leap of his character, deep flaw or not, the leap of his identity no one in our work would find valuable but me' (196). Henry shadows Kwang in order to betray him but becomes oppressively conscious of betraying only himself; he cannot write the necessary reports to indict Kwang because they would be about Henry as much as Kwang, and self-revelation is inimical to him. This is one point at which Henry's opaque and sometimes arch narrative voice begins to crack, and his persona begins to 'steadily unravel from the inside out' as he becomes anxiously self-conscious of 'my fraying mesh of self' (292). Kwang is finally betrayed, but not by Henry, and Kwang is guilty of the murder of the man who betrayed him. Henry knows this, and his fidelity to Kwang, his 'final honoring' (292) is to keep the secret of Kwang's guilt. This is the means by which Henry redeems himself.

Henry's relationship with Kwang demonstrates that there is a violence in assimilation into a new culture, not simply in murderous betrayal or in the beating his father receives from black shoplifters, but in the very process of learning the language. Violence characterizes Henry's remedial speech classes, his wife's language therapy sessions, and every aspect of the grammar of the new American culture; to Henry, 'English is a scabrous mouthful' (217) but his text is dominated by the imperative of learning it:

At their height, the Romans lived among all their conquered, the outer peoples brought to the city as ambassadors, lovers, soldiers, slaves. And these carried with them their native spice and fabric, rites, contagion. Then language. Ancient Rome was the first true Babel. New York City must be the second. No doubt the last will be Los Angeles. Still, to enter this resplendent place, the new ones must learn the primary Latin. Quell the old tongue, loosen the lips. Listen, the hawk and cry of the American city. (220)

Henry submits to this history lesson, and he wanted 'a life univocal' for his son so that Mitt might not suffer the painful doubleness of his father. But the politics of language acquisition and the pressure of the dominant culture is such that his soul frets in the shadow of a predetermined narrative:

But I and my kind possess another dimension. We will learn every lesson of accent and idiom, we will dismantle every last pretence and practice you hold, noble as well as ruinous. You can keep nothing safe from our eyes and ears. This is your own history. We are your most perilous and dutiful brethren, the song of our hearts at once furious and sad. For only you could grant me these lyrical modes. I call them back to you. Here is the sole talent I ever dared nurture. Here is all of my American education. (297)

Henry's narrative language (and by implication the language by which Chang-rae Lee makes his contribution to the vanguard of contemporary fiction) is dictated to him by his cultural history and necessarily spells an indictment of the dominant white culture from which he must appropriate his 'lyrical modes'. Like *Typical American*, *Native Speaker* interrogates the close association between language and ethics as a fundamental part of its drama.

John Edgar Wideman **Philadelphia Fire**

Henry comments at one point that white Americans have the advantage in the United States because 'The talk somehow works in their favor' (227) and he remembers how his father used to show off his son's command of English by prompting him to recite ' "some Shakespeare words" ' (49). This idea of language as discourse and the process of erasure and loss that accompanies the learning of a language in

America is central to John Edgar Wideman's *Philadelphia Fire* (1990),[7] where the double-voiced quality of *Typical American* and *Native Speaker* becomes a multiple-voiced predicament, full of linguistic perils and political consequences. The protagonist of this novel, Cudjoe, has also married a white woman and, like Henry, suffers from the tensions of an interracial marriage and the attendant anxieties of identity that it brings. Also like Henry, Cudjoe is separated from his wife, finds the absence or loss of his son to be a source of considerable pain, has difficulties with father-figures, lives in an urban America with a history of serious racial tension, and is often absorbed by thoughts of racial fidelity and betrayal. Most importantly, Wideman's narrative, like Chang-rae Lee's, attributes the power relations and conditions of contemporary multiculturalism to the machinations of language, and, like Henry, Cudjoe seeks to be the historian of a lost culture and to recover its proper history in its own cultural language. *Philadelphia Fire* is a history text at many different levels, but it is principally concerned with the history of writing and the idea of history as a discursive text constructed from an ideological position which necessarily encodes cultural value. The novel also proposes that language itself is an instrument of power, not only as it functions within historical narratives, but in its own right as a unit of signification. Cudjoe seeks to be the historian of the Osage Avenue bombing and to recover Simba and write the narrative of the boy who escaped (an expression of his sense of guilt at the loss of his own son). Along with these stories is the story of Cudjoe himself, a black person trying to negotiate a relationship with white America, the history of the black community in west Philadelphia, and the history of the African race, not only in America but as it has been written and institutionalized by texts such as Shakespeare's *The Tempest*. In each aspect of this political and aesthetic enterprise the narrator is acutely conscious of writing in a language which is the language of a dominant culture and which is in some respects inimical both to him as an individual black person and to attempts to write a history against the grain of the received and authorized one. *Philadelphia Fire* is a novel that attempts to find a fresh narrative language with which to write the authentic history of Afro-Americans, and in this project it has something in

---

[7] All page references are to the Penguin edition.

common with many contemporary black American texts, most notably Toni Morrison's *Beloved* (1987).

The fire of the novel's title occurred on 13 May 1985, in west Philadelphia, and eleven Afro-Americans, apparently members of a group called MOVE, were killed by it. No charges were brought against the public officials who planned the bombing from a police helicopter. It is believed that one young boy escaped, Simba, and Cudjoe/Wideman returns from exile (in Greece, in Laramie) to style himself as the historian of this terrible incident and the author of the lost story of Simba: 'Story of a fire and a lost boy that brought him home' (7). Cudjoe feels he has a duty to find him, having been in exile for ten years following his separation from his wife Caroline, mostly spent on the Greek island of Mykonos. The narrator 'Wideman' also saw the CNN coverage of the fire from his home in Laramie, Wyoming, 'That's how I learned about the Philadelphia fire' (103). Cudjoe recognizes immediately the importance of this incident and what it signifies for black Americans and their history; in writing about the fire, he makes a decision to write about himself and his race because the fire is 'about us too' (82). *Philadelphia Fire* also includes the history of how Wideman wrote the text, and its self-consciousness is part of the novel's sophisticated agenda of scrutinizing the relationship between history, language, and power. For example, Cudjoe remembers the incident in April 1947 when the Brooklyn Dodgers were turned away from a hotel in Philadelphia, the City of Brotherly Love, because one of their players, Jackie Robinson, was black. Cudjoe the cultural historian asks, 'Was that the beginning of the fire?' (108).

Cudjoe begins his research by interviewing Margaret Jones and recording her testimony as evidence, but she is suspicious of his motivation and she senses the distance of his exile, his decision to leave Philadelphia, 'and she held it against him' (9). Margaret also suspects that Cudjoe has returned to the community in Philadelphia to write the story of the fire '"so you can sell it"' (19). The act of writing has immediate political and aesthetic anxieties for Cudjoe which Margaret makes him acutely sensitive to, and her resentment compounds his existing sense of betrayal at having married a white woman and failed both her and their children; Cudjoe feels that Margaret knows 'that his betrayal was double, about blackness and about being a man' (9-10). Cudjoe's sense of himself as a traitor to his gender and to his race is something that he hopes to remedy in writing his text, and that pressure informs every aspect of his writing; he wants to break the silence about the fire and about himself, to bear witness and take responsibility as a writer. In returning to Philadelphia, Cudjoe hopes to reintegrate himself, but also to acknowledge properly the cultural auspices which have determined who he is, and this cultural positioning of himself is part of the novel's analysis of the larger historical narratives in which individuals are inscribed. Cudjoe's analytical skill, self-consciousness, and honesty in revealing his cultural determinants is remarkable, and so is his ability to extend that analysis to those forms of historical discourse which inform communities and cultures.

One of the key precepts here is that no man is an island ('entire of itself', John Donne), and the novel is full of references to islands and attendant ideas of individual consciousness and personal spheres of government. The source of these figurative islands is the island in Shakespeare's *The Tempest*, which Prospero is cast out upon, usurping Caliban. In Shakespeare's play Caliban is the indigenous inhabitant of the island and Prospero is the European nobleman, using his magic powers derived from his books to colonize and subordinate Caliban and making him his slave. Many recent critics have interpreted *The Tempest* as a play about colonialism, most notably Stephen J. Greenblatt, who argued that the play dramatizes 'the startling encounter between a lettered and an unlettered culture in the relationship between a European whose entire source of power is his library and a savage who had no speech at all before the European's arrival'.[8] Cudjoe considers Caliban's idyllic situation before Prospero's arrival: 'Ah. Think of it. Your untouched island. . . . You can't be lonely because you know nothing but yourself. You are like the island. To prosper you don't need another island beside you. You are complete' (146). Cudjoe's contemplation of Caliban turns back on himself as island-dweller on Mykonos, an escapee into himself from the cultural pressures of Philadelphia and interracial marriage. Here the island becomes a symbol of consciousness but also of authority, circumscription, dominion. In this respect the island is an image of

---

[8] S. J. Greenblatt, *Learning to Curse: Essays in Early Modern Culture* (London: Routledge, 1990), 23.

both captivity and freedom, a sphere of self-government and self-enclosure, but especially to do with power and knowledge, as in the image of 'the dispossessed urban proletariat surrounding the island of University' (112). Cudjoe considers this again in relation to the island of his imprisoned son's consciousness, his mental illness, his solitary confinement: 'If I draw a line around who I am, who I can be, you are inside the circle. I have no choice. Don't want a choice. To be who you are you must draw your own circle' (151). Cudjoe's son's divided consciousness is possibly a form of 'sanctuary' (110) which cannot be broached by language.

The text of Wideman's novel declares that the production of the play organized by Cudjoe in Philadelphia in the late 1960s is 'the central event' of the novel: '*The Tempest* sits dead center, the storm in the eye of the storm, figure within a figure, play within play, it is the bounty and hub of all else written about the fire' (132). This production was to have been all black, a lesson to the adolescent actors that something as cultured and canonical and apparently distant as Shakespeare was within their grasp, and a signal to the wider community that black children could appropriate Shakespeare, a political demonstration of the black community's talents and desire for serious recognition, 'your lives are vindicated. The play was the thing' (132). At the heart of Cudjoe's staging of the play and of Wideman's contemplation of its importance is the scene between Caliban, Prospero, and Miranda in which Caliban is admonished and berated for his desire for Miranda, and chastised for his rejection of the colonizer's language in the speech beginning 'Abhorred slave' (Act 1, scene ii).

But before the text of the novel comes to this speech, which it quotes in full, Caliban is allowed the last word on how he feels about Prospero and about the play; the author of *Philadelphia Fire*, commenting as ever on his own imaginative and creative strategies, allows Caliban to appeal to the audience and to articulate his own point of view in his own language:

Think of this play this man done. Him broken my island all to pieces. White folk weeping and wailing cause all lost. Ship lost. Fader lost. Storm taken ebryting away. . . . All fall down on golden sand of this island mine. Or was mine. Once pon time. As that fancy one dere does testify. Mine by way Queen Sycorax my mother. Him say all dat and say my mother am witch. Why him play dozens now? Say island belong to him now. Say my mother dead in nother country. Why he swoop down like great god from the sky, try make everybody feel high? Take ebryting. Den ebryting give back. Go off teach at University. Write book. Host talk show. Jah self don't know what next dis dicty gentleman do. (121)

It is important that the novel permits Caliban to speak first so that his perspective is recovered and given priority, and it is important that the novel gives Caliban a language 'queerly accented' (120) which bears some resemblance to the language with which Cudjoe appeals to his students in an attempt to make clear to them the relevance of this play to their lives. When first reading the play to his pupils at school, Cudjoe casts himself as Prospero, 'the good tyrant, protector of his island children' (125) and hoping that they will take his imprint from the power of his black language, just as Caliban took his imprint from Prospero's. Cudjoe seeks to provide them with a role model to compensate for 'the inadequacy of your background, your culture' (128) and he offers them an 'authentically revised version of Willy's con' (131) especially as regards 'your greater than god grandfather Caliban' (131). Announcing that the play is about 'colonialism, imperialism, recidivism' (127) Cudjoe speaks to the children in a language they will recognize and understand, a language which has correspondences with the language that the novel has already attributed to Caliban:

The lingo is English landwich. Quack of the baddest, biggest Quacker. King's English. Pure as his tribe. . . . But the lingo mi buckos, my sweet oreos, the talk they talked, the Queen's English to be more exact, was down, especially in the pen of this one, the master blaster, bad swan from Avon, number one voice and people's choice, scratcher and fixer and sweet jam fixer, ripsnorter and exhorter, cool as a refrigerator prestigitator, have no fear, Mr. Auctioneer is here super pitchman mean as a bitch man, pull my goat and milk my goat ding-dong pussy-in-the-well wheeler dealer and faith healer, record changer dog-in-a-manger platter pushing poppa of the rewrite righteous doo-wopping, skin-popping, hip-hopping got all the ladies drawers dropping. (129)

These languages, Caliban's, Cudjoe's, are two different varieties of a distinctively black vernacular that Wideman employs in the novel to articulate the authentic voice and perspective of black characters whose identities would be radically different if given in the language of white European standard English. Furthermore, as one critic has pointed out, 'The English language is a language that consumes, "landwich", that eats up the language of the slave. It is a language of the slavemaster'.[9] Wideman uses different types of black vernacular at many points in *Philadelphia Fire* in order to create a text that is composed of black voices and which conveys the energy, inventiveness, and creative wit of a black oral tradition. These black voices represent an aesthetic and cultural position which, like Caliban's, speak of racial politics in an authentic black voice different from the writerly texts of European modernism.

Cudjoe takes issue with editors who have attributed the 'Abhorred slave' speech to Prospero and argues that it belongs to Miranda, describing it as 'The spurned woman speech' (139) and arguing that 'She offered the word. Caliban desired flesh' (140). The text of *Philadelphia Fire* quotes the whole speech and the central quotation is 'I endowed thy purposes / With words that made them known' (139) from Act 1, scene ii. Miranda's position here, and Cudjoe's determination to set her at the centre, is crucial because of the way it presents her as the product of her father's instruction, of how she is hostage to 'A language which Xeroxes image after image of her father. . . . which is also confirmed and claimed in the words he taught her and she taught Caliban. . . . signified in the small print' (141). Thus, Miranda becomes in Cudjoe's reading the means by which Prospero ensures his position in the future, his ideological values encoded in the language he teaches her, and so 'Her womb perpetuates his property' (141). Caliban becomes the victim of this too, his independence and autonomy doubly erased, his subjectivity inscribed within the language that Miranda teaches, 'All her civilization whispered in his ear' (141). Prospero's language, and the racist ideology that it carries, is the means by which he ensures authority and control for future generations of his race, class, and gender: 'To him it's just a matter of staying on top, holding on to what he's got. Power' (142). *The Tempest* is a text which in its canonicity culturally institutionalizes a false history of Africans and emburdens them with a false sense of cultural inferiority. Cudjoe forges a connection between Prospero's subjugation of Caliban and the low self-esteem of black children in west Philadelphia

---

[9] D. D. Mbalia, *John Edgar Wideman: Reclaiming the African Personality* (Selinsgrove: Susquehanna University Press, 1995), 110.

who seem to have no future and live impoverished lives in poor neighbourhoods and are always part of a black underclass. This connection lies in language, in the discourse of racism that they internalize from their American culture and which is valorized through the agency of canonical texts such as *The Tempest*.

Cudjoe's close textual examination of this particular moment in the play is central to everything valuable in *Philadelphia Fire*; he perceives himself on occasions as Caliban or as Prospero, as an island dweller on Mykonos, as having inherited from Caliban a common attitude to women and the knowledge that their bodies signify, and as suffering the anxieties of fatherhood in his relationship with his imprisoned son ('This thing of darkness / I acknowledge mine', (105)). Most of all, as a writer he has himself imbibed the language of Prospero, and seeks to create an alternative that will recover Caliban's position and create a text of *Philadelphia Fire* which is experimental, innovative, and distinctively black, but without relinquishing the qualities of high European modernism. These aesthetic and cultural agendas are politicized by historical narratives of oppression such as slavery and the holocaust, and given urgent political focus by moments such as the fire in Philadelphia in 1985. *The Tempest* does not feature only in part II of the novel where Miranda's speech is interrogated, but occurs at moments throughout the novel's text, much of which is preoccupied with considering Shakespeare's play as a paradigm for the position of Afro-Americans, in multiple and various linguistic and political ways. Of course, the novel is acutely conscious that in committing acts of close textual analysis and cultural interpretation it is creating another text, *Philadelphia Fire*, and the novel's self-consciousness about the politics of this is one of its most difficult features.

The episode in which Cudjoe recalls visiting his artistic mentor Sam, for example, is full of associations with *The Tempest*. Sam is a successful writer, prosperous, who lives on an island described as 'Sam's island' (61) and Cudjoe visits him to seek the approval for his language in the form of the manuscript of his novel. Cudjoe is distracted by the sight of Sam's naked daughter Cassandra (the prophetess of doom whose warnings were never heeded), he lusts after her, and he debates in his imagination her father's reaction to his desire for the daughter. The key associations here are between language, authority, and the body, as they are configured in Shakespeare's text and in Wideman's. Cudjoe asks himself at one point, 'What was he looking for in women's bodies?. . . . The mystery persisted' (27) and part of the answer lies with Miranda, whose body offers the potential for multiple interpretations and some kind of hermeneutic pluralism. This is a crucial point: Cudjoe sees her speech as 'an opportunity for Miranda to talk for once . . . the many meanings she suggests with, among other things, what's secreted between her thighs' (141). Perhaps it is partly Cudjoe's marriage to a white woman that encourages him to configure himself as Caliban to Caroline's Miranda, and Caroline's fastidiousness about her body would support this interpretation. Cudjoe remembers from their five-year marriage Caroline's 'vulnerable urinary tract' (56), and how she would 'shut her knees if she noticed his eyes straying from his book, peering between her naked legs' (56). Caroline's fastidiousness contrasts with Cudjoe's 'funk', an indulgence in physicality, and a key word used to define an essential black characteristic in Morrison's novel *The Bluest Eye* (1970): 'The dreadful funkiness of passion, the funkiness of nature, the funkiness of the wide range of human emotions' (64). At many points the text of *Philadelphia Fire* dwells on the features of a woman's body, intrigued by the knowledge it represents, and especially the text has a tendency to regard women in terms of an orifice: the woman in the park with 'the dark hinge between her legs' (26); Rachel, with the 'smell of moon trapped in her blood once a month' (70); Cynthia and 'her sopping wet twat' (169). The woman who lives across the block from Cudjoe seems to synthesize these bodies because 'She was the body of woman. No beginning, middle, end to her life. All women. Any woman' (54). The important association here is between Cudjoe's attitude to women and Caliban's desire for Miranda, an association which figures Cudjoe as a twentieth-century Caliban who believes that knowledge and power reside in a woman's body rather than in the slavemaster's language.

It is a woman, of course, Margaret Jones, who holds the secret of Simba's whereabouts, and Margaret is also important for the change of heart she experiences in her relationship with the MOVE leader King. At first she is painfully aware only of his 'funk', but gradually she becomes conscious of her cultural conditioning and undergoes a transformation: 'By then stink wasn't really stink no more. Just confusion. A confused idea. An idea from outside the family, outside the teachings causing me to turn my nose up at my own natural self. Felt real ashamed when I realised all of me wasn't inside the family yet' (15). This acceptance of an African cultural heritage is important because the text of *Philadelphia Fire* strives to accomplish a corresponding literary breakthrough, to become part of the generic family of African-American texts both in its language and its ideology. If there is the possibility of some form of redemption that consists in a woman's body and in the heterogeneous interpretative secrets that it holds (distinct from the phallocentric discourse of white European colonialism), then the 'Wideman' character who intervenes in the text appears to have learned this and accommodated a multiplicity of voices and languages in the body of *Philadelphia Fire*, which becomes, in part III especially, polysemous, multivalent, multivocal. The final part of the novel is the narrative of J.B., a black derelict in contemporary Philadelphia who raps his way through 'the everyday runaway chaos of an ailing urban landscape' (111) and who discovers the ur-text of Kaliban's Kiddie Korps, the Book of Life, in the briefcase of the suicide Richard Corey. This is yet another scenario in which a white man appears to be the author of the language taken up by (black) youths, and therefore the architect of the ideology it espouses. The narrative of J.B. is only one element of the conflation of voices and languages in this part of the novel; J.B.'s urban street language is combined with that of Timbo, Caliban, Cudjoe, Simba, and perhaps even the 'Wideman' character, in the novel's final dramatic representation of the political value of writing as a response to the material circumstances of the impoverished black urban lives that *Philadelphia Fire* depicts. The novel becomes a polyphony of voices as it asks what is the place of art, what is the political effectiveness of writing, and can it be useful (fighting fire with fire) to write back against texts such as *The Tempest* and its colonizing language? The final part of the novel is extremely self-conscious in its metafictional enquiry into the power of language and its importance as an instrument of political agency, as it must be if it is to negotiate a challenge to existing creative languages.

Caliban's voice is present in the allusion to 'secret springs of potable water, the edible roots and berries' (167) which he revealed to Prospero when the European first arrived on Caliban's island. But here his voice becomes part of a confession of betrayal in which he 'Revealed all our good hiding places', and 'squealed on my former soul mates', and worse still 'Translated our secrets. . . . into the grunting, rooting, snarly pig tongue' (167) and in this way was complicit in and responsible for the betrayal of MOVE leader King. The text conflates Caliban's voice with Timbo's, who emerges recognizably as assistant to 'My friend the Mayor' (168). Timbo is the childhood friend of Cudjoe's from 'those thrilling days of yesteryear and shit' (75) who is now cultural attaché to the Mayor of Philadelphia. Timbo undergoes a direct reversal of the change Margaret Jones experienced in her attitude to King: 'you feel dirty, like stink's painting you a nasty color' (79–80), and he learns to be ashamed of his colour, race, family. Timbo's association with power and authority has corrupted him and he has betrayed both his black brothers and the idealism of the 1960s which he shared with Cudjoe in making of Philadelphia a 'Black Camelot' (159). Cudjoe is not excused here, as the reference to Wyoming acknowledges (82) because when the situation began to deteriorate Cudjoe 'exited for goddamn parts unknown' (82). The voice here is also Richard Corey's at the moment of his suicide from a window ledge above the city streets; Richard is thinking about ideas to do with writing, 'wiping the slate clean. A slate it dirties with each line of fiction' (167), which recalls the 'carte-blanche' of the narrator's final interpretation of the politics of Philadelphia: 'carte-blanche, white power to whip whatever heads need to roll. Carte-blanche and the black Mayor's dark blessing' (157). Carte-blanche: literally, blank paper or full discretionary power. Note too that Richard Corey takes his name from a famous poem by E. A. Robinson, called 'Richard Corey'. These voices are only one part of the polyphony of *Philadelphia Fire*, a text which includes references to high European culture (Sophocles, Giacometti, Derrida, Joyce) but also has many allusions to modern American popular culture, 'Roadrunner', James Brown, Superman, and 'the rusty tin woodsman clanking after Dorothy' (50) in *The Wizard of Oz*. The novel's accommodation of high and low cultures complements its dialectic between an African oral tradition and a European written one, so that any simple metaphor, such as a musical one of jazz, for example,[10] cannot entirely account for everything that the novel accomplishes.

[10] Ibid. 107

Paul Auster The New York Trilogy

At one point in his analysis of *The Tempest* and the text's relation to the material world, Cudjoe refers to his exposition in terms of 'Derridian diddley-bop' (131), and although *Philadelphia Fire* articulates an ideological position closer to post-colonialism than post-structuralism, it does certainly have qualities of self-consciousness and self-reflexivity about its own narrative strategies which might be termed 'metafictional'. The word 'metafiction' was coined by the contemporary American novelist William Gass in the late 1960s to describe fiction whose subject was fiction. Metafiction internalizes the relationship between authors and readers so that the text itself, its own narrative, is devoted to its own fictional conduct, and so metafictional texts 'subvert their own referential illusion'.[11] The word is appropriate to Paul Auster's novel *The New York Trilogy* (1987) a collection of three novellas, 'City of Glass', 'Ghosts', and 'The Locked Room', originally published separately in the mid-1980s.[12] This work's engagement with language and power is different in its politics from that of Jen, Lee, and Wideman but it is still principally devoted to an interrogation of the nature of antecedent texts and their ability to inform or determine contemporary acts of writing and, therefore, contemporary states of being. Like *Philadelphia Fire, The New York Trilogy* internalizes some interpretative practices of recent literary theory, especially post-structuralism, but Auster's text does this to the extent that it actually has these practices as the very subject of its narrative, and this has important consequences for the ideological values which Auster's text articulates.

'City of Glass', for example, concerns a man called Quinn who writes detective novels under the pseudonym William Wilson. This name is taken from a story by Poe called 'William Wilson', a macabre short story from 1839 in which Wilson is driven to murder his alter ego.[13] Quinn's William Wilson has created a fictional detective called Max Work. So Quinn has cut himself off from the world outside his books and his writing to the extent that 'he no longer existed for

---

[11] M. Currie, *Metafiction* (London: Longman, 1995) 5.

[12] All page references are to the Faber and Faber edition.

[13] 'William Wilson' was published in *Tales of the Grotesque and Arabesque* in 1840.

anyone but himself' (4). In his absorption in writing detective fiction, Quinn, we are told, has become both a 'private eye' and a private 'I', a fictional detective but also a profoundly isolated individual, and we are told that 'for five years now Quinn had been living in the grip of this pun' (9). Quinn has come to inhabit a world of texts rather than a material world, and again Auster's text comments on this directly: 'What interested him about the stories he wrote was not their relation to the world but their relation to other stories' (7). This quotation is of central importance to *The New York Trilogy* because it is as true of Auster's text as it is true of the texts written within Auster's text by Quinn. This is typical of the metafictional self-consciousness of 'City of Glass'. The narrative itself is no less self-reflexive in its metafictional enquiry, which begins by depicting Quinn reading a book by Marco Polo, which is quoted directly: 'We will set down things as seen, things heard as heard, so that our book may be an accurate record, free from any sort of fabrication' (6). This is a strategically chosen quotation because it concerns the text's claims to authenticity, claims that Auster's text will interrogate minutely, not simply for Polo's text, but for all texts. Quinn, who writes under an assumed identity about matters of detection that he has only read about in other books, is here depicted as reading a book which claims to be free from the artifice of imagination. It is this concept of artifice or 'fabrication' which *The New York Trilogy* sets out to explore.

The dramatic action begins when, just as Quinn is reading the quotation from Polo, the telephone rings unexpectedly and someone asks to speak to Paul Auster; this stranger not only asks Quinn if he is Paul Auster, but if he is the Paul Auster of the detective agency. This is a curious conflation of several textual matters at once: Quinn is now a fictional character who is being mistaken for someone that many readers imagine to be 'real', Paul Auster. Furthermore, Quinn's assumed identity as William Wilson is here being tacitly invoked in the reference to detective work, and the unexpected late night call from a mysterious woman is a standard cliche of the detective fiction genre, and precisely the kind of generic moment with which Wilson's fiction might begin. Here then, the fiction of Wilson has become in some sense the authentic real-life experience for Quinn, who is himself the fiction of Paul Auster, who, Auster, is introduced here as a fictional character. Clearly 'City of Glass' is a text which begins by exploding the humanist distinction between that which is 'real' and that which is merely fictional, and it takes great delight in finding a multitude of sophisticated textual means by which to challenge the reader's assumptions about the status of textual representations. The quotation from Marco Polo concerning textual 'fabrication' is by no means accidentally placed, and is only one of a substantial number of important intertextual references which serve to undermine the reader's faith in a sense of a material world which is anterior to textual representation.

The fictional Quinn decides to pretend that he really is Paul Auster when the mysterious woman next calls, and he subsequently goes to meet her pretending that he is a detective agent. The woman introduces Quinn to a man called Peter Stillman, who is a very odd person, for two reasons: Stillman was brought up by his father for nine years without speech. Stillman's father wanted to know if God had a language, and so as an experiment he deprived his son of exposure to language in any way; he wanted to know if, given that language is a learned system, a social construct, what would happen if a child was raised entirely without it? The language of Stillman junior is very strange, and he has a precarious sense of identity which is related to the language experiment of his father. Stillman repeats 'I am Peter Stillman. That is not my real name'. This is also true of Quinn, of course, who usually writes under an assumed name and here finds himself acting under a further assumed identity, so that Quinn can answer Stillman's phrase with a parallel one of his own: 'My name is Paul Auster. That is not my real name' (40). Furthermore, Stillman's language as it is given in *The New York Trilogy* is very similar to the language of the characters of Samuel Beckett, almost imitative of them. This is not acknowledged by the text, but it is clear that Auster is indebted to Beckett, and especially to that trilogy of works composed of 'Molloy', 'Malone Dies', and 'The Unnameable', otherwise known collectively as *The Beckett Trilogy*. This is a further metafictional reference, one in which a text about language, writing, and identity, derives some of its own sense of textual identity by allusion to another text about language, writing, and identity. This is one of the ways that *The New York Trilogy* reveals how identity (of a person, of a text) is predicated on language acquisition, and it has a lot in common with *Typical American*, *Native Speaker*, and *Philadelphia Fire* in its

self-conscious exposition of the particular conditions and circumstances of that language-knowledge. One critic has argued that the
special achievement of Auster's fiction 'is to combine an American
obsession with gaining an identity with the European ability to
ask how, and under what conditions, identity is stolen or lost',[14]
and like Wideman, Auster deploys both American and European
canonical texts at that metaphysical juncture. *Typical American* and
Native Speaker show that this dilemma is not only a circumstance of
European heritage.

In investigating the case of Peter Stillman, whose demented father
has recently been released from prison and now threatens to murder
his son, Quinn is led to investigate several propositions which are of
fundamental importance to *The New York Trilogy* and its own textual
status as a piece of writing. First, the novel shows that the opposition
between the 'real' world and the world of fiction is a false one. The
real world is composed of stories, of fictions, of narrative, and ultimately of language in the same way that the fictional world of a novel is
constructed. The 'real' lives of Auster's characters are comprised of the
language of fiction. Second, a character's identity is created by the
acquisition of language and any sense of that character's subjectivity
is determined by the language they use. Furthermore, this is true of
'real' characters as much as it is of fictional ones because language
speaks us—it is a social system already in place when we are born and
we learn how to articulate our sense of ourselves entirely through our
use of it; we become in fact a function of the language that we use.
Third, history, and especially perhaps the history of America, is a form
of fiction, and like other fictions it is dependent upon the narrative
devices that are found in imaginative works such as novels. History is
not ontologically given but is linguistically and textually constructed,
and it is therefore subject to the same textual and hermeneutic
uncertainties as fiction. *The New York Trilogy* dramatizes each of these
theoretical ideas about the representational nature of reality even
while calling into doubt its own narrative procedures.

In desperation at not being able to solve the mystery of detection
that he has embarked upon, Quinn decides to contact the real Paul

---

[14] C. Baxter, 'The Bureau of Missing Persons: Notes on Paul Auster's Fiction',
Review of Contemporary Fiction, 14: 1 (Spring 1994), 41.

Auster that he has been impersonating. This decision should be interpreted as an appeal to authority to resolve the epistemological crisis
that the text has uncovered. Quinn contacts Auster, but discovers
only that the real Paul Auster is not a detective at all but a writer, and,
in an extraordinarily self-conscious piece of metafictional narcissism,
Quinn, no longer pretending to be Paul Auster, is told by the text's
real Paul Auster that 'I'm afraid you've got the wrong Paul Auster', to
which Quinn replies 'You're the only one in the book' (94). This is only
the beginning of the metafictional joke, because Paul Auster is writing
an essay on Cervantes, and he explains to Quinn that Cervantes, the
author, went to great lengths to convince the reader that he is not the
author of *Don Quixote*. Paul Auster is writing an essay which argues
that *Don Quixote* is an attack on the dangers of make-believe, and that
Cervantes had to claim that it was real in order to do this because,
after all 'he couldn't very well offer a work of imagination as an attack
on the dangers of the make-believe' (98).

The strategic employment of Cervantes here, and especially the
way that Auster's interpretation turns back on the narrative of 'City of
Glass', is characteristic of a wider tactic of textual allusion at work
throughout *The New York Trilogy*, which is packed full of significant
references to canonical writers: Hawthorne, Melville, Thoreau, Poe,
Milton, Defoe, Stevenson, The Bible, Raymond Chandler, and Lewis
Carroll. 'The Locked Room' also includes a synopsis of a film called
Out of the Past, a Robert Mitchum movie of the 1950s which is part of
the film noir genre that 'The Locked Room' imitates, parodies, and
subverts. These allusions are never gratuitous but occur at points
where they have an important bearing on the Auster text's sense of its
own precarious fictionality, its sense of its own fragile status as a
product of antecedent writing. The literary allusions constitute a
canon of previous texts many of which exhibit similar anxieties about
the referential nature of language. In this sense the real subject of
Auster's novel is its own relation to previous writing and expresses 'a
canonical hunger to construct a justifying tradition'[15] from the books
to which it is most indebted. There are many good examples of this;
Auster's novel is about this. *The New York Trilogy* takes this technique

[15] M. Bradbury, *The Modern American Novel* (Oxford: Oxford University
Press, 1992), 259.

to vertiginously self-reflexive limits. In the final novella 'The Locked Room', there are references to the two previous novellas of the Trilogy, and the narrator informs us that 'These three stories are finally the same story' (294). The narrator also meets a character called Peter Stillman, whose significance can only be appreciated by reference back to a reading of 'City of Glass'. In this way Auster's novel creates its own canon and its own tradition of itself by making an interpretation of it dependent upon a knowledge of antecedent parts of itself. This is remarkably solipsistic and has led one critic to characterize the novel as being pervaded by 'a sense of infinite regression'.[16] Paul Auster becomes one of the authors that *The New York Trilogy* employs to construct a tradition to show where the author Paul Auster has come from; like a serpent devouring its own tail, the novel is simultaneously self-consuming and self-consummating. Where in *Typical American*, *Native Speaker*, and *Philadelphia Fire* questions of language and the inscription of individuals within a particular narrative are shown to be a function of the material conditions of Americans' lives and social relations, *The New York Trilogy* reduces these issues to questions of language which are devoid of material consequences or ideas of personal freedom or political inequality. In Auster's text it becomes a game without consequences, a textual solipsism, a self-consuming linguistic conundrum. Where the multiple-voiced quality has a political purpose, for *The New York Trilogy* there is no explicit politics, only poly-texts, unless it is allowed that here too there is a political ideology at work. One critic has argued, for example, that 'City of Glass' can be seen 'to contain traces of a counter-hegemonic cartography, rather than being automatic capitulations to the logic of late capital'.[17] Furthermore, readers can ask a similar question of Auster's text as should be asked of *Ragtime*, *White Noise*, and *In Country*: is it nostalgic for a time when there was an epistemological certainty that only the 'postmodern' lacks? This too is a question about the politics of postmodernity that has important implications for these novels' language.

---

[16] M. Alexander, *Flights from Realism* (London: Edward Arnold, 1990), 190.

[17] Brian Jarvis, *Postmodern Cartographies: The Geographical Imagination in Contemporary American Culture* (London: Pluto Press, 1998), 88.

Barry Hannah **High Lonesome**

The doppelgängers of Lee (John Kwang), Wideman ('John Wideman', Cudjoe) and Auster (William Wilson, 'Paul Auster'), are part of their texts' self-analysis, and Barry Hannah too has an obsessive interest in doppelgängers, or 'wretches and their duplicates' as they are called in *High Lonesome* (1996). Hannah's fiction is full of losers and creeps whose language is of special interest and the story 'Ned Maxy, He Watching You' provides a usefully succinct introduction to them.[18] Ned Maxy is in his forties as the end of the twentieth century approaches, and he looks back on the 1970s with great relief that the decade has passed. From the isolated vantage point of his room he uses an old pair of opera glasses to spy on a young woman across the street. Ned's voyeurism is given religious language as if it were a rite, a formal or ceremonial act customary in religious devotion; he is a 'penitent' who devotes his time to 'weeping, fasting and praying' (93). This ritualistic aspect of his voyeurism is an integral part of his detachment, both from the young woman he spies on and from the terror of the 1970s when he 'would have been teaching her the needs of his famished world, her body a naked whirlwind of willing orifices' (95). Ned Maxy has crossed a watershed and is now free of 'the lifetime monster of lust' (94) which terrorized him in the 1970s; the desire from which he suffered has passed and he watches the woman across the street 'in high admiration, goodwill, and with no panic' (94). The relinquishing of desire is necessary to Ned's socialization, which takes place tentatively in the story in the form of his attendance at the woman's wedding. Ostensibly the isolated voyeur is integrated into the community at the religious ceremony, itself an act of union, and in the shade of 'a tall brothering sycamore' (96) where the wedding guests greet him felicitously with the phrase 'Well howdy, stranger, I guess' (96). There is something peculiarly western about Ned Maxy's recently discovered freedom and its accompanying socialization: 'howdy' is conventionally a western form of greeting, and Ned 'like a stranger in town', embraces the southern landscape by putting his arm out 'to the west' (93). Is it possible that Ned interprets his

---

18 All page references are to the Atlantic Monthly Press edition.

predicament in terms of western fictional stereotypes and that his tendency to fantasize contributes to his continuing paralysis? Ned's invitation to the wedding is given in the form of a 'whisper' which he hears at a distance of 'a hundred yards' (94) although 'He had spoken to the woman only once' (94) and the greeting of the guests is also heard by Ned 'as if each one was whispering' (96). These whispers are associated in Ned's mind with the dying whisper of his friend Drum, so that desire and death and the intimate act of verbal communication are all closely connected in Ned's drama, a psychological drama of his consciousness which resolves itself in the story's central enigmatic phrase 'a whisper of some weight' (95). The story permits an interpretation in which Ned is entirely delusional, in which even his dreams of social integration are a sad fantasy, a projection of his debilitatingly fixated desire for a woman he does not know, fed by western myths he has only read about. The story is a chilling dramatization of Ned's pathological condition, one in which he remains beyond the possibility of socialization except in his dreams; his story's title 'Ned Maxy, He Watching You', is crude and ungrammatical because Ned remains outside the structures of social communication.[19]

Ned Maxy's story is creepy in its claustrophobic interiority, and the narrator of 'The Ice Storm' describes himself as 'an aging creep' as he too has a special interest in voyeurism, not with opera glasses but a video camera that he uses to film his wife (190). The story begins with the description of violent weather, the narrator's exhilaration at its immense energy, but also the loss that ice storms cause, here the loss of ancient trees that are so integral to the southern landscape as to seem like family; they are dead uncles losing their limbs and 'family in the act of dying' (188) which is precisely the narrator's mother's condition in this story. The loss of the trees and the loss of family are used to signify the end of history and community, and this story, like Ned Maxy's, is deeply informed by an elegiac tone, over-dramatized here by the narrator as 'the end of the world' (188). The idea of exaggeration is very important to 'The Ice Storm'; the story's severe weather is 'the storm of the century' (187), a remarkable and rare event, a spectacle of nature's havoc, a special occasion to bear witness to and

---

[19] It is possible that Ned derives his name 'Maxy' from his status as the epigone of an earlier Hannah protagonist *Captain Maximus* (1985).

create fables from. This exaggeration extends to the narrator's depiction of himself as 'Like a Jeremiah' and 'an addict' (187), someone exceptional, someone with a story to tell.

The narrator's story concerns another ageing creep, the film-maker Hood, who experienced an earthquake in California and was injured by a tree that fell on him in his shower and broke his leg, an oak tree 'about the age of the Civil War' (189). It can be no coincidence for a writer who once claimed 'I know the Civil War like the back of my hand',[20] that John Bell Hood (1831–79) was a Confederate General, disastrously defeated at the Battle of Nashville in 1864. Hannah's fictional Hood suffers his injury in an absurd and ridiculous way which has nothing to do with heroism, glorious defeat, or traditionally masculine pursuits, he is simply whistling in the shower 'all loose in an orgy of steam' (189) and can have no claim to the status enjoyed by even defeated Confederate Generals. Hood is psychologically bitter about his broken leg, 'his body, not just the leg, was poisoned' (189) and this, according to the narrator's dying mother, is proof that Hood is not much of a man. Even the narrator admits 'There was a real whine in his voice' (190). Hood, of course, is an artist of sorts, probably the director of cheap pornographic films full of 'lively girls' (191) like Shannon who want to escape the small-town South and move to California to become stars. Hood's dramas are sordid and degenerate, a contrast to the real drama of the story's violent weather storms, but he is an artist nevertheless, one who has lost his creativity since his accident, 'His art vision was gone' (191) and he is confined to a wheelchair. Hood's claim to be an artist is tawdry and pathetic, but it is this aspect of his identity that appeals so strongly to the story's narrator: 'I'd liked Hood's peculiarity' (190), and sordid though it might seem, the narrator strives to emulate Hood's creativity:

I bought a video camera, my first, because I felt like life was getting away from me and wanted to shoot scenes of my wife naked or nearly so in compromising positions. I know this is the act of an aging creep who cannot understand his good luck, but I had ceased to care. I paid a great deal for this thing but what I could not buy was any desire to use it once it was in my hands. The first time I raised it I felt like an idiot and my wife ran away

[20] L. McCaffery and S. Gregory (eds.), *Alive and Writing: Interviews with American Authors of the 1980s* (Urbana: University of Illinois Press, 1987), 119.

raving into the backyard. I just toiled there, whispering about my tender aims. Maybe I was in Hood's world, a deeply wretched place. (190)

This is the story's confessional heart, a statement of the narrator's abject dissolution, his impotence and detachment, like Ned Maxy's, taking the form of a diminished desire to capture something before it is gone forever. The key word here is 'creep', a word learned from a British rock band of particularly striking adolescent affectation, Radiohead: 'I wish I was special! But I'm a creep! The defeated tenor of Radiohead howls. "I don't belong here!" God what freedom in that statement. I just adore it and am terrified too' (109). This quotation from 'Through Sunset into the Raccoon Night' is important to 'The Ice Storm' and to most of the stories of *High Lonesome*, because it articulates both the isolation of the romantic outsider and the source of his creative impetus ('genius' seems hardly the word). Among late twentieth-century rock songs those of Radiohead are some of the more manifestly bogus in their sentiments, and it is precisely this bogus quality, the staged moment of teen angst, that excites the imagination of Hannah's narrators. Hood, for example, is a complete charlatan:

One afternoon I noticed a man in a cape and a beret rolling down in a chair. Across the arms, too, he held a cane. This was a lot of costume for early fall or I'd not have noticed. Under the beret was a long blond face, very surly. It was Hood. Before I knew this, I'd had in mind one of the great wounded artists of the fin de siecle. He was enrolled in yet another workshop. But I have it on witness by his last vixen, a nurse, that, in truth, there is nothing wrong with him. (191–2).

Hood's imitation of a wounded war veteran is pure performance, he might be defeated in some sense, but he has turned this into theatre and contrivance. Even here Hood's status as a figure who inspires creativity is emphasized, if not in Hood's mind then certainly in the narrator's with the image of 'one of the great wounded artists of the fin de siecle'. Hood romanticizes and exploits his banal domestic mishap and the narrator is complicit in this performance because he too likes to portray himself as a debilitated creative talent of the end of the century. It is even possible that he might have someone specific in mind, like Ernest Dowson. But if there is nothing wrong with Hood, then perhaps there is nothing wrong with the narrator either, and it is possible to read his confessional moment as a staged act of drama, one which emulates Hood's dramatic performance in being contrived for the purposes of artistic creativity. In this interpretation of 'The Ice Storm' the narrator is completely degenerate, his story is a simulation of romantic confession which seeks to imitate the bogus theatrical posing of Hood, which he acknowledges to be spurious. The figure of Hood and the story's sense of an ending are used to bring about a painful acknowledgement of the narrator's own abject condition, but like the confession of Robert Lowell's 'Skunk Hour' (which is also one specifically of sexual voyeurism), the central moment 'I myself am hell' is, at its most intimately revealing, a direct quotation from Milton's *Paradise Lost*. Lowell's confessional subjectivity is a confession principally of literary indebtedness; Hannah's narrator performs a similar sleight-of-hand, contriving a moment of romantic revelation for the purposes of a *fin de siècle* creativity which is in fact simply affectation. In doing so, the narrator writes himself into a southern narrative of defeat that both his and Hood's creative enterprises self-consciously acknowledge to be ersatz. What is remarkable is that the self-conscious theatricality of Hannah's story becomes its central dramatic subject.

Hood is a loser and a creep but he inspires creativity nevertheless; such are the conditions of the contemporary South where to be a creative artist and a man it is necessary to be sick, and to make art from one's sickness. The cultural memory of the Civil War is important to 'The Ice Storm' where 'A vast pile of debris burned like the end of a war out on the west edge of town' (188) and 'this place looks bombed all over again' (187). The narrator's mother, who, in tune with the theatrical imagery of the story, is not dying but 'in the act of dying' (190), articulates the stoicism of an earlier generation in her attitude to Hood's injury 'That's not a man, then, son' (191) and her very language simultaneously invokes the narrator's immaturity. Hood and the narrator can only ever be the epigone of the heroically defeated, or even the unheroically defeated like John Bell Hood whose theatre of war at least had some credence and stature. The 'confidence' of the South which precipitates its 'comeuppance' (188, 189) is dramatized by the attenuated high spirits of Hood's whistling, whether 'whistling about his luck' (189) or 'whistling in his shower' (189) but such are the vestiges of the southern cultural inheritance, both for its men and its artists. Hood is described as 'a bitch' (191) which truly emasculates him, but neither this word nor the word 'vixen' (192) have the true 'old-timey' (190) qualities of the language of the previous southern generation, and in this respect 'The Ice Storm' is a story which laments the poverty of its own creative strategies, even while prosecuting them. Hannah's metafiction is extraordinarily accomplished because it evokes a nostalgic desire for the language of the past, and yet fashions its own unique creative enigmas as characteristic of the language of the present, and, simultaneously, this is offered as the distinctive crossroads of the old South and the new South.

The narrator of 'The Ice Storm' takes a vicarious pleasure in Hood's behaviour and this idea of vicariousness is important to 'The Agony of T. Bandini' where Bandini and the story's narrator also have an interesting relationship and where the delayed introduction of the first-person singular narrator is a significant feature of the story's drama. 'The Agony of T. Bandini' is also about storytelling, myth-making, and romanticizing, of finding the appropriate language to transform oneself into a character with a storied reputation. Like Hood, Bandini does not appear to have much to recommend him, and yet the story's narrator is crucially affected by Bandini's narrative. Bandini is a Yankee who accidentally kills someone in a road crash while drunk, an act of stupid and thoughtless irresponsibility, but one in which he believes he becomes the victim of some sort of tragic blight. Bandini feels that he is a suffering outcast 'in the world of pain and ruin' (128) and his supposed affinity with 'the southern boys' (128) is one which gives his life a fated tragic quality because 'the only worthy subjects were coiled up and crossed like nylon fishing line' (128). Bandini moves from upstate New York to the South, specifically to the home town of William Faulkner in Mississippi, which seems 'a sad and wonderful place' (129) befitting his new condition, and where Bandini discovers that he has 'a free wide heart for the vanquished' (130). This is however, a pathetic, self-indulgent, and adolescent attitude, nothing more than a ridiculous pose, as Bandini's escapades amply demonstrate: he shoplifts two lobsters, is beaten by a college professor in public, and makes an exhibition of exposing himself at the dance. All this is trivial stuff; Bandini has no agony and has never truly suffered, his vulnerability seems to consist of having nothing more than an extraordinarily attenuated narrative of defeat. For example, Bandini can only approach the feet of the Confederate statue at the courthouse on which he dotes; he is infatuated with this image, as he is with other narratives of defeat such as Vietnam, Faulkner, and Elvis Presley in Las Vegas (131). Bandini's desire for the Confederate soldier is phony and ridiculous: 'He scaled toward the man, all fours engaged, in an act of hunching and embracing. The policeman had driven up to witness this remarkable love, as Bandini almost reached the boots of the defeated. The policeman heard the man cry out like a thing impaled and then it was too ugly for him to watch anymore. The odor of rank sea and a low hissing brought the officer to kneel with his light. Above him, Bandini was going nowhere'(130). The language of religious allegory has a double effect on this scene, exaggerating its comic potential but at the same time rendering it strangely authentic and transformative for the observer, the policeman. In the drama of adoration, the policeman becomes an audience and he is brought to kneel by Bandini's piece of abject theatre. The important point here is the vicarious transference that takes place between the statue and Bandini (which is 'an act'), and then between Bandini and the policeman. This scene enacts in miniature the central major drama of the story that takes place between Bandini and the story's narrator.

Bandini meets a man in jail, Cruthers, who claims to have been a sergeant in Vietnam, and Cruthers later tells Bandini a story of his experience there which forms the narrative's central transformative moment:

I could sleep and make myself little but I always woke up the second anything anybody in range. I could smell them, my nose wake me up. I was on that tree crotch and had me a good limb with my honey and I start fucking her. They come over a hill five black pajamas in a row across like they was hunting rabbits. I blow all they heads off. Then I let myself down and each and every one I stomp they balls. But one of them a teenage girl just the top of her head blown back. I commence giving it to her mouth when I hold her up by the shoulders. That was the best I ever had. (135–6)

This brief and enigmatic story has a remarkable effect on Bandini, hypnotizing and captivating him. Furthermore, Bandini's equally cryptic interpretation of the story has a remarkable effect on our story's narrator who is 'stunned by the new deep voice of Bandini, and this whole language' (136). This double incidence of being transformed by narrative language recalls the three-way relationship between the solider, Bandini and the policeman in its vicarious and its performative aspects, but what is 'this whole language'? The answer is some arcane conflation of sex, violence, and masculinity; the line 'I blow all they heads off' associates darkly the violence of shooting with the act of oral sex as if Cruthers puns on the word 'blow' in a macabre and sadistic way, as he does with the one girl in the company of Vietcong, the 'five black pajamas', when he is 'giving it to her mouth'. He also has sex with his weapon, the M-60 described as 'his sweet big baby' (131) which here becomes his 'honey'. Bandini takes vicarious pleasure in the violence of the story, just as he takes vicarious pleasure in the violence of football players as 'pure cruising crushing meat, a kind of express ham' (132). Bandini's vicarious interest in the violence of others is a pun also, on the word 'crush' in which he is enraptured in a mildly homoerotic way by accounts of masculine physical action. As with Hood, this is a symptom of Bandini's impotence.

Bandini ends the story 'in love', not necessarily with Cruthers, but in rapt attention to the dark mysteries of Cruthers's narrative language with its 'turning' and 'twistings' (136) which seem to speak to Bandini's own predicament like the nylon fishing line of all 'worthy subjects' (128). There is of course a great deal of delusional self-mythologizing to this, just as there is for Hood and the narrator of Hood's story. Bandini's desire to regard himself as a Faulknerian character is bogus and self-aggrandizing, and so might be the story of Cruthers; this does not seem to matter, either for Bandini, or for the story's narrator who is so strongly impressed by Bandini's interpretative voice. Just as the authenticity of Bandini's desire for the Confederate soldier is not important for the policeman to be impressed, neither is the verisimilitude of Cruthers's story to Bandini, or of Bandini's interpretative language to the narrator. As with Hood, the important thing is for the performance to be convincing; such is the debility of Hannah's southern men. The word 'Agony' then is not entirely ironic.

There are further subtleties to this story: Bandini's agony is associated with the legacy of the Civil War because 'He read up on Bruce Catton and could account for the Northern agony' (131); the story holds out the possibility that its narrator and the 'town writer who specialized in the burden of history' (130) are the same person; the story's attention to homoeroticism, male-bonding, and ethnicity combine with its depiction of sex, violence, and the language of religion in a way that contributes to a particularly surreal version of southern gothic which is simultaneously authentic and parodic. The lives of Hood and Bandini might be a sham, but Hannah's narrators testify to their redemptive potential, and above all Hannah's language transforms them utterly into something compelling. There is an extraordinary drama in Hannah's language, even though little narrative action takes place in his stories; as one critic claimed, 'Barry Hannah writes the most consistently interesting sentences of any writer in America today'[21].

The performative element by which Hannah interrogates ideas about creativity and art takes a different form in 'Repulsed', but it is still associated with a narrative of defeat from which some kind of aesthetic victory is retrieved. The narrative of 'Repulsed' is reasonably clear: the adolescent narrator has a defining moment in his youth when he sees a woman from his window; this is no ordinary act of voyeurism, as the story will testify. He leaves the South for New York City where he witnesses a street bum begging and he suddenly discovers his own voice. He returns to the South and becomes a successful trumpet player; he goes to look for the woman from his window again, but she is older now and the moment has gone. He plays at the window for her, and she dies. The story ends with the detective accusing the narrator of having killed her, because 'the whole point of her later life was to escape where horns were' (163–4). The detective's accusation is corroborated by the narrator's mother who 'caught me in the act going about various manipulations at the window' (161), but he is probably a scapegoat for others unknown, and therefore becomes 'merely a squalid pile they could talk around' (165) and someone who has suffered 'a tragic humiliation from which there was no recovery' (165). The narrator is thus repulsed, and at the same time has become repulsive to others because of his behaviour. What ideas about aesthetics can be salvaged from this?

Like Bandini, the narrator of 'Repulsed' is in search of an inter-

---

21 Sven Birkerts, *New Republic*, 10 Feb. 1997, 40.

pretative language that can do justice to the enigma of revelatory moments, and that moment bears some resemblance to Cruthers's: 'I saw her through the bare limbs of the tree—next to my house in its March agony ... A buttered French bread afloat there at her lips' (153-4). This is the vision that the narrator makes attempts to articulate, and his story concerns his search for exactly the right form of artistic expression to do justice to its unique qualities. It is a moment of bliss, of revelation and of ecstasy, and that ecstasy is religious, sexual, and artistic because it includes the suggestion of oral sex (again), and the association of sex and death. It is also perhaps 'a Daliesque vision of the Eucharist'[22]. The moment itself seems beyond rational explication, but this is less important than the narrator's search for the proper artistic expression of it, expression which enables him to carry out an extended double entendre on the word 'horn' to signify both his trumpet and his burgeoning sexuality. His horn was 'partner to my vision through the naked tree' (156).

As with most of the stories of *High Lonesome*, there is a double drama at work here which elevates Hannah's story to the subtlety of metafiction. The ostensible subject of 'Repulsed' is the narrator's *Bildungsroman*, but the real subject is the challenge of representing that *Bildungsroman* in language which does justice to its own narrative subtleties. This gives the story a doubleness that extends from the doppelgänger relationships of the story's characters, to the narrative strategies and structures of the story itself, a story about 'wretches and their duplicates' (160-1). Even while the story is obsessed with history, there is an acutely dramatic quality to the conduct of its narrative. For example, the narrator asks rhetorically: 'what ecstasy holds a candle to the sudden intelligence one is granted years, whole cycles of war and famine, after viewing a rare event in ignorance? The collision of mind and flesh, all your veins pumped with light. Your own sweet innocence brings tears to your eyes, which see again revised, nostalgia on you like a barrel of walnuts' (154). This might seem simple enough, but 'Repulsed' is a story which is constantly interrogating and revising its own narrative language; the walnuts here have already been alluded to: 'I had while an urchin begged the walnut orchard to let go

---

[22] Ruth Weston, *Barry Hannah: Postmodern Romantic* (Baton Rouge: Louisiana State University Press, 1998), 127.

and smite me with those heavy nuts in their pods' (153). At one moment the narrator longs for maturity, and at another he is filled with a desperate nostalgia for the time before it fell upon him. This is typical of how Hannah's stories, extraordinarily sophisticated investigations into the subjective apprehension of history, dramatize by their own narrative strategies the very historical conundrums that they examine. In its uniquely southern way, this is no less ambitious and complex an achievement of creative language than the linguistic self-examinations of the other novels of this chapter.

In a further interrogation of what it means to become an artist, the narrator ventures to New York City to find his horn and meets the street bum whose begging is the definitive dedication to the craft, and the narrator is overwhelmed by admiration for the beggar's devotion to pure form, 'I began to love the man' (157). The narrator interprets the beggar as some version of himself, 'His old teenagehood shared with mine' (157) and 'Maybe he was me in my old age' (158). But as the narrator begs the beggar for the return of his horn the beggar collapses and 'broke down in a sickness of decomposition' (157). It is here, inadvertently murdering the creative mentor, that the narrator finds his voice, 'and I was free to see my youth again' (158). He returns to the South and becomes a successful trumpet player now that he can do justice to his vision of the woman, 'I used this mystery in my horn and had new tones' (160). The narrator and the beggar might be vilified outcasts, but they are guardians of creative expression, sharing both a commitment to a vision and the craft that can articulate that vision. In this way 'Repulsed' addresses the enigma of creative inspiration and articulates its own unique prose language in the process. One critic wrote of Hannah's lyrical style that 'Tom Waits couldn't sing it any better', and a musical metaphor is appropriate, perhaps even necessary: 'What Hendrix did with the guitar, Hannah does with prose: invent a whole new American music'.[23] The title *High Lonesome* (which bears no significant relation to the 1962 Louis L'Amour novel of the same name) is derived from a distinction between country music and bluegrass (although the elevation and detachment of 'high' and 'lonesome' are consistent themes of the stories) and Hannah often uses musicians as vehicles for explorations into the

23 Will Blyth, 'Hannah and his Sentences', *Esquire*, Mar. 1993, 55

nature of language, narrative, and the empowerment of the vanquished creeps and losers of his fiction. Hannah's fiction has a long history, since *Geronimo Rex* (1970) of exuberance, exaggeration, and a particular brand of linguistic resourcefulness. Bluegrass is an especially improvisational form, suitable as an analogy for Hannah's southern riffs: when a girl in 'Uncle High Lonesome' shouts '"Hey Cracker, eat me!"', she is characterized as 'Already deep into sin, weathered like a slut at a bingo table, from a neighborhood that smelled like whisky on a hot bus exhaust' (229).

The best story that Hannah has written is the first story of *High Lonesome* 'Get Some Young', a story that is impossible to do justice to, even at the level of narrative exposition. To offer a synopsis of what happens in 'Get Some Young' would not come remotely close to what it is as a text because the language of this story is an extraordinary and eclectic synthesis of many different styles, lexicons, and genres. 'Get Some Young' is characterized by a pathology of language in which the circumstances of the story's protagonists are dramatized by the condition of the story's language, and the impotent rage of the contemporary southern male, Tuck, is given dramatic expression by the shifting linguistic styles of the text. The story is constructed in terms of a tableau of static visual moments, moments that concern visual fixation, voyeurism, witness and rapture, and the language of 'Get Some Young' changes in creative fidelity to the transformative energy of those moments. There are moments of religious awe in which Swanly and Bernadette are discovered 'in a condition of the Pieta' (38), where Tuck joins them in bed 'like adepts in a rite' (35), where Swanly becomes 'the boy savior' (33), and where 'this trinity' are figured as 'ignorant animals amongst the fruit of Eden just hours before the thunder' (35). At other points the story self-consciously mimics the compression of historical perspectives that it dramatizes: Sunballs is appalled by the spectacle of 'two smoky old queers availing theyselve' (20), Walthall is defeated in love 'and he was sore in gloom' (31), and Tuck says of Bernadette 'Why, my wife, she's a right holy wonder' (21). Elsewhere 'Get Some Young' describes its staged moments of drama by deploying the language of the theatre: wrestling is a spectacle 'where operatic goons in mode just short of drag queens grappled in the city auditorium' (12), and Tuck is overcome by desire 'like something in a storekeeper's costume activated by a pullstring and thrust into a playhouse by a child' (27). Inevitably the story's language also parodies southern gothic, in the figure of Swanly who 'had felt his own beauty drawn from him in the first eruption of sperm, an accident in the bed of an aunt by marriage whose smell of gardenia remained wild and deep in the pillow' (6). Elsewhere the language of the story is imitative of Joycean syntactical compression, 'Eden in the bed of Eros, all Edenwide all lost' (39), or satirically misquotes the language of the classics: 'Send not to ask for when the bell tolls. I refuse to mourn the death by fire of a child's Christmas on Fern Hill. Do not go gently in my sullen craft, up yours' (23), or the story parodies the language of popular American song lyrics 'Uh found your high school ring in muh baby's twat' (7), or the voices of 'AM teenage castrati' on the radio singing 'You are muh cuntshine, muh only cuntshine' (7). This is not all of Hannah's virtuosity; some of the story's metaphors are remarkable: Swanly regards the future as a dark prospect 'like bad fish heaved into the outer dark' (6), Tuck as storekeeper is guardian of 'a fantastic dump of road offal brought in by a stranger' (22) and who regards married life as a case of 'get some partner to stoop down to that tiny peephole look at all the little shit' (17). Despite the associations of Sunballs' name 'Nothing in him vouched for parts solar. More perhaps of a star gray and dead or old bait or of a sex organ on the drowned' (17). Hannah combines all this linguistic resourcefulness with a sometimes acute dramatic simplicity; when Tuck observes his wife's desire for Swanly, he comments 'You are desperate. I sort of like it' (28). 'Get Some Young' is the most densely allusive of Hannah's stories, and its multiple narrative perspectives are given an analogue in the richness and diversity of its languages.

This is more than just ludic experimentation, it is a parasitical linguistic energy in which a variety of cultural discourses are appropriated as part of the project of articulating the morbid stagnation of the contemporary southerner's historical predicament. 'Get Some Young' is given a further retrospective turn for example by the final paragraph which looks back from a perspective of fourteen years. Walthall revisits the store to find that Tuck is dead, but Bernadette, wearing a fragment of Swanly's old shirt, raves for the loss of her teenage son (in Vietnam?) and also her youthful lover. The trauma of her loss is the story's final image, but it is important that Walthall is similarly disturbed by the experience of witnessing Bernadette's demented anguish: 'the vision was so awful he fled almost immediately and was not right in Boca Raton nor much better when he came back home' (41). In this way the central dramatic scenes of witness, loss, and emotional trauma are repeated beyond the immediate temporal moment and replicated in the future in a further cycle of formative emotional encounters. This is an important feature of the story's southern cultural identity, its 'Civil War ghoulments' (25) revived from the river where the action takes place, and the characters trapped by cycles of historical repetition, condemned even in the future to be imprisoned by events from the past. History is the vanquished Tuck's consummation: 'I am a vampire I am a vampire' (13), and the language of his story feeds on the languages of southern history to sustain itself. The remarkable success of 'Get Some Young' consists of its ability to turn this to a form of cultural analysis which is a landmark in contemporary American fiction while preserving its southern character. The narrator of 'Uncle High Lonesome' looks back on his southern history and laments, 'there was plainer language then, there had to be' (222), but Hannah's fiction testifies to the artistic achievement that linguistic attention to the contemporary moment can accomplish.

6

Sport

The crowd at the ball game
is moved uniformly
by a spirit of uselessness
which delights them.

William Carlos Williams,
'At The Ball Game'

For a variety of social and historical reasons, sport occupies a different place in American culture than it does in Europe. In the United States sport is the distillation of that competitive spirit that is integral to a free-market culture and it dramatizes vividly the ethos of success that is central to American life. As the Washington Redskins' George Allen put it, 'Every time you win, you're reborn; when you lose, you die a little', or as Leo Durocher of the Brooklyn Dodgers said 'Nice Guys finish last'.[1] Sport is also part of the democratic spirit of American society, a revered arena of the rags-to-riches narrative regardless of social or ethnic background, and sport is important because it tells a story of how 'a frontier people becomes the richest industrial nation in the world. . . . The real descendants of Davy Crockett and Mike Fink are Babe Ruth and Dizzy Dean'.[2] This sense of sport's cultural import-ance underwrites its contemporary forms. When David Remnick's book about Muhammad Ali, *King of the World* was published in 1999 its subtitle was 'The Rise of an American Hero', and it used Ali's fight with Sonny Liston partly as a way to provide an analysis of America in

[1] Cited in E. Fawcett and T. Thomas, *The American Condition* (New York: Harper & Row, 1982), 395.
[2] C. K. Messenger, *Sport and the Spirit of Play in American Fiction: Hawthorne to Faulkner* (New York: Columbia University Press, 1981), 2.

the 1960s. Ali is still honoured, still mythologized, and widely written about as part of a morality tale about the individual sportsman and society in the United States. Sport is also big business, more closely associated with family entertainment and show business, more often predicated on television schedules and advertising opportunities, and more subject to the vicissitudes of corporate life than sport is in Europe. One writer has attributed the recent proliferation of sports fiction to the increasing involvement of business in the 1960s and 1970s, 'a period which has seen unprecedented growth in the commercial value of sport'.[3] Successful sportsmen become businessmen, movie stars, celebrities, politicians, respected for their achievements beyond the limits of their game because the ethos of success has bestowed on them a special status which can carry them into other areas of American public life (Johnny Weismuller, O. J. Simpson, Joe DiMaggio, Bill Bradley, and the present Governor of Minnesota, ex-professional wrestler, Jesse 'The Body' Ventura).

A collection of essays published in 1970, *Sport and American Society*,[4] showed the ways in which sport has been put to a variety of cultural uses, and the novels of this chapter provide support for some of its sociological and philosophical arguments. American fiction investigates the myth of the gifted individual, what it means to be successful, sport as a means to examine masculinity and the male body, to interrogate epistemologies of history, to consider the history of racial politics, to analyse the structure and organizing principles that lie behind social systems and the passage of time, and to examine questions of morality and aesthetics. In fact, American writing has a long history of using sport as a means of cultural commentary, ever since Fitzgerald characterized Tom Buchanan as a restless and violent man forever seeking 'the dramatic turbulence of some irrecoverable football game' in *The Great Gatsby*. American sports has an illustrious history in fiction that might include: Bernard Malamud *The Natural* (1952); John Updike, *Rabbit Run* (1960); Fredrick Exley *A Fan's Notes* (1968); Philip Roth, *The Great American Novel* (1973); E. J. Gaines, *A Gathering of Old Men* (1983); Barry Hannah, *The Tennis Handsome*

---

[3] N. D. Berman, *Playful Fictions and Fictional Players* (New York: Kennikat Press, 1981), 4.

[4] G. H. Sage (ed.), *Sport and American Society: Selected Readings* (Reading, Mass./ London: Addison Wesley, 1970).

(1983); James Welch, *The Indian Lawyer* (1990); and Don DeLillo's novel about hockey published under a pseudonym *Amazons* (1980). In non-fiction also, eminent American writers have addressed sports as a serious field of cultural enquiry, for example, Norman Mailer, *The Fight* (1976); Joyce Carol Oates, *On Boxing* (1987); and John Irving's book about college wrestling *The Imaginary Girlfriend* (1997). These writers are well known for their achievements in fiction. There is very little British literature about twentieth-century sports that can match this American pedigree, suggesting perhaps that sport is fundamental to American life rather than ancillary to it. F. R. Leavis dismissed *Wuthering Heights* as unworthy of inclusion in *The Great Tradition* because it is merely 'a sport'.

The novels of this chapter consider sport as a predominantly male sphere of enterprise, as a male space; John Hawkes's female protagonist is sensitive to this when she observes that to enter a gun shop 'was to enter the dark caves of male endeavor, male dauntlessness, a space and darkness so serene and severe . . . that it brooked no woman' (*Adventures in the Alaskan Skin Trade* (1985), (62)) and James Dickey noted that the American tradition of hunting, fishing, and shooting is very much about subscribing to a particular type of masculinity which the use of weapons appears to facilitate: 'all men were once boys and boys are always looking for ways to become men' (*Deliverance* (1970)). Modern spectator sports also offer a means for male camaraderie ('Men don't trust a man who missed the Super Bowl', *Bright Lights, Big City*, (85)) and a way for men to communicate and to form relationships based upon a common identification and all that it signifies: 'They were both Mets fans, and the hopelessness of that passion had created a bond between them' (*The New York Trilogy*, (37)). American sports is a space in which anything might be possible within structured limits, and it is capable of bearing narratives that have wide cultural application. As one writer commented: 'The playing field is the holiest of American grounds because it is the place where time past retains the light of time present . . . The great good American game takes place in the American garden of Eden . . . If only the game could be made to go on forever, then everybody's best hope still might remain plausible, and nobody would ever die.'[5] The

5 Lewis Lapham, *Harpers*, June 1991, 12.

language of religion here suggests that American sports are a sacred ritual, and the ludic impulse that they dramatize is a serious and important part of American life.

Richard Ford **The Sportswriter**

Richard Ford's *The Sportswriter* (1986)[6] has as its protagonist 38-year-old Frank Bascombe, a man who is experiencing a mid-life, post-divorce crisis of identity in which he feels alienated and 'dreamy', and the novel charts 'the bearable shambles of Bascombe's life.'[7] Frank is unable to establish social relationships, he is not good at communicating, and he distrusts closeness or intimacy ('full disclosure') because of his experience of divorce. Frank is from Biloxi, Mississippi, and he tells us that he has 'grown up in the South, full of betrayers and secret keepers;'[8] his ex-wife is consistently characterized as a northerner and often disparaged by him for her specifically northern qualities: she is described as expressing 'a perfect Michigan attitude' to his friend, Walter's, suicide. In diagnosing Frank's problems, his ex-wife remarks that 'All that originated . . . with the outcome of the Civil War' (19). Frank's new girlfriend Vicki is from Texas, and she prides herself on her sense of southern cultural identity. It is Vicki who reminds Frank of his deracination and displacement from a sustaining culture and identifies a fundamental aspect of his malaise: 'You don't fit in at all, you know that' (263). Frank is a *Babbit* for the 1980s, a White Man Without a Clue, cut off from his culture, exiled from his family, and distant from his own emotional life; he wanders the suburbs of contemporary America completely adrift from anything that might wake him from his 'dreaminess' or help establish meaningful social contact. Frank is depicted as seeking small consolations in retreat from existential despair; he falls back on a defensive faith in sports and in writing about sports, from which he creates a

---

6 All page references are to the Flamingo edition.

7 Elizabeth Hardwick, 'Reckless People', *New York Review of Books*, Aug. 1995, 13.

8 There is an important minor character in *The Great Gatsby* who comes from Biloxi, and the critic Arnold Weinstein has some crucial things to say about his name ('Blocks Biloxi') and his dramatic function in relation to Gatsby's self-mythologizing in *Nobody's Home* (Oxford: Oxford University Press, 1993), 144.

belief system which preserves him in his struggle for emotional survival and cultural connectedness. Ford however, invites us to see through the self-censorship of his first-person narrator, and to interrogate myths of writing and identity which expose problems about American cultural life more fundamental than the social surface of the novel might suggest.

Frank Bascombe in his bewilderment and uncertainty finds comfort in ordinary things, and ordinary things are present throughout the novel as mysterious and magical: 'There is mystery everywhere, even in a vulgar urine-scented suburban depot such as this. You have only to let yourself in for it' (348). Frank creates a lyricism of the ordinary as his aesthetic credo; he lives in Haddam, New Jersey, because 'it is not an interesting town' (56), and claims that 'none of us could stand it if every place were a grizzled Chicago or a bilgy Los Angeles' (109). Frank describes his girlfriend's naked body as revealing 'altogether an ordinary nakedness' (175), and he remembers 'the abundance of the purely ordinary. . . . I loved those ordinary good American faces', and he describes how 'the literal can become the mildly mysterious' (202) in the catalogues from a PO box in Nebraska which in his somnambulant way are therapeutic reading after his son's death. Frank says of his possible future life with Vicki: 'it could be a damn good ordinary life' (278). This paean to ordinariness has its lyrical moments in which the diurnal and prosaic are given a mystical reverence: 'it is a dreamy, average, vertiginous evening in the suburbs—not too much on excitement, only the lives of isolated individuals in the harmonious secrecy of a somber age' (333). Ordinariness is valorized as remarkable, reliable, trustworthy, and aesthetically valuable in a modern world of the random, contingent, and precarious. As Frank says in Detroit, 'I love the television in other cities, the assurance of looking up from my chair in some strange room to see a familiar newscaster talking in his familiar Nebraska accents . . . these comprise a comfort I would not like to do without' (139). Frank tends to think of Nebraska specifically as epitomizing all that is most stable in American life. Wyoming receives similar plaudits (50) as if the West represents to Frank some sort of nostalgic pastoral idyll. Much of *The Sportswriter* is a celebration of what Frank takes to be ordinary, and this accounts for its saturation of banal details about the suburbs. There is a kind of security to this, the assurance of stability and familiarity which is crucial to Frank's emotional health: 'a good sense of decorum can make life bearable when otherwise you might be tempted to blow your brains out' (40). This is significant, of course, because of the fate of fellow Divorced Man's Club associate, Walter Luckett, who commits suicide after his wife leaves him. What though, of the place of sport and the function of writing? How is Frank's Carveresque celebration of the everyday associated with sports writing? Why is this novel not called *The Postman*?

The idea of sport as a retreat from the precariousness and duplicity of modern American life is important to Frank's survival; he is asked in chapter 10 by Vicki's father, Wade, 'How can you stay isolated from events on a grand scale?' Frank replies simply, 'I write sports' (285). It is precisely 'events on a grand scale' that Frank is in retreat from. In his defensive post-divorce condition he is happy only with the ritualized formal relations that sports and sports commentary provide. It is a code of social exchange between men, 'the perfect lingua franca for crabwise advances between successive boyfriends and husbands who might otherwise fall into vicious fistfights' (141). The language here makes it plain that Frank thinks of sports as an exclusively male discourse, a way for men to communicate, and a discourse that accommodates their masculinity and social differences. Frank's editor tells him when he first starts writing that it is important to write in such a way as to 'overcome the irrelevancy of sports itself' (47), and this is a lesson that Frank takes easily to heart, coming to believe that, 'sportswriting is not a real profession but more an agreeable frame of mind, a way of going about things rather than things you exactly do or know' (318). This vagueness about writing and the absence of an engagement with real sports contributes strongly to Frank's sense of defeat in *The Sportswriter*. Despite his belief in sports as a male discourse, and one which requires no knowledge of real sports for its maintenance, Frank's ex-wife is a golfer who gets on with the business of improving her game as the novel progresses, and the scene which precipitates his separation from Vicki occurs while they are playing croquet. Both women are game players who defeat and then abandon Frank. During the game of croquet he confesses to Vicki: ' "I'm no good at games, not since I was little" ', and Vicki responds with great insight: ' "You don't play games, but you write about 'em all the time. That's backwards" ' (262). This reversal, the replacement of playing by writing, is the real source of Frank's psychological malaise; it signals a tendency to romanticize and sentimentalize not only sports but other aspects of his life, and it is a habit of thinking through writing which for him is profoundly debilitating.

For Frank, writing about sports is an escape from writing fiction, which for him is necessarily more complex and difficult. Sports is a non-fiction which in its simplicity is more reassuring. Writing about sports is 'more like being a businessman, or an old-fashioned travelling salesman, than being a genuine writer. . . . Real writing is something much more complicated and enigmatic than anything usually having to do with sports' (48). Frank has abandoned a very promising career as a writer of fiction: he had one book of short stories published called *Blue Autumn* (43) culled from the text of an abortive novel called *Night Wing*, the plot and first line of which are produced from memory by Frank in chapter 2. The success of *Blue Autumn* encouraged Frank to begin another novel, called *Tangier*, the first line of which is given by Frank from memory, but which is never completed.[9] This possible life as a creative writer is abandoned because, 'I didn't know with certainty what to say about the large world, and didn't care to risk speculating' (58). For Frank, writing about sports is a way to protect himself from the epistemological anxieties of 'the large world', and a clear renunciation of the exoticism of his earlier prose with its extravagantly dramatic narrative and its overblown language. Frank's new style is a direct economical non-fictional reportage ('My name is Frank Bascombe. I am a sportswriter'), and he writes about a masculine activity founded on a faith in reliable rules and laws. He is especially anxious to avoid sentimentality, and this explains his antipathy to Walter Luckett, who later commits suicide 'In what could be called a sentimental confusion, for that is his nature.'[10]

Behind Frank Bascombe is the shadow of Raymond Carver, and beyond Carver, Ernest Hemingway. The rigour and simplicity of Frank's credo, and especially his mystical faith in the value of that which goes unspoken, owes a debt to Hemingway's ethos of the aesthetics of sporting endeavour. If this seems too simplistic a summary

---

[9] 'Autumn came later that year to the rif of the Low Atlas, and Carson was having an embarrassing time staying publicly sober' (44).

[10] Elizabeth Hardwick, 'Reckless People', *New York Review of Books*, Aug. 1995, 13.

of Hemingway's oeuvre (and it is), then *The Sportswriter* provides the reader with a more specific textual reference:

> 'How long has it been since you read *The Sun Also Rises*, Frank?'
> 'It's probably been a while now.'
> 'You should re-read it', Delia says, 'there're important lessons there.
> That man knew something.' (219)

Frank professes that the novel is not one of his favourites, although he knows it well enough to identify its exact date of publication, 1925, and admits 'it might have been a better time back then'. Frank's nostalgia for the world of 1925 might again be interpreted as a retreat from the complexity and contingency of contemporary American life, but why is *The Sun Also Rises* relevant to Frank Bascombe, and what 'important lessons' does it contain?

The protagonist of Hemingway's novel, Jake Barnes, is impotent. Jake was injured in the war, and now pursues a relationship with the androgynous Brett Ashley which can never be fulfilled because of his sexual injury. This sexual impotence finds a close parallel in Frank Bascombe's life, rejected by his wife, and now by his new girlfriend in the most unequivocal terms. Frank, like Jake, has little sense of control in his relationships, knowing that his impotence is the badge of his permanent defeat, his bewildered emotional indeterminacy. This is not the only insight that the Hemingway allusion offers. Jake, like Frank, is fond of sports, and *The Sun Also Rises* is partly a celebration of the aesthetics of bull-fighting, and of the special adversarial intimacy to be shared in sporting engagement. The Hemingway novel also contains important textual allusions, especially to W. H. Hudson's *The Purple Land*, to the short stories of A. E. W. Mason,[11] and to Ivan Turgenieff's *A Sportsman's Sketches*. Jake's writing constitutes a canon of sports writing, and an ur-text of adventure narratives which bears significant relation to his own text. Like *The Sportswriter*, *The Sun Also Rises* is self-conscious about its protagonist's recourse to an ethos of masculine toughness which is founded on textual allusion; Jake comments in chapter 4, 'it is awfully easy to be hard-boiled about everything in the daytime, but at night it is another thing'. It is the failure of the hard-boiled which Hemingway's novel dramatizes, not

[11] The Mason text is probably *The Cook and the Captain Bold* (1924).

its success. *The Sun Also Rises* exposes the empty social dialogue of its characters as a ritualized form of defence against larger existential anxieties brought on by the war. Hemingway's novel depicts a deracinated lost generation enjoying with quiet desperation a holiday (*Fiesta*) from the serious problems of their disordered lives, and Frank Bascombe parallels their aimlessness and occasional desire for oblivion. Ford's protagonist complains in a pathetic and defeated moment reminiscent of the nihilism of *The Sun Also Rises*: 'give us all a good night's sleep until it's over' (58). Frank's strategies of survival, like those of his predecessor, are strategies learned from, and fed by, fiction. Jake's reading in *The Sun Also Rises* has important bearings on the conduct of his narrative, just as Frank's reading of *The Sun Also Rises* in *The Sportswriter* has an important bearing on his. Paradoxically, part of that 'important lesson' is a warning of the dangers of reading: in chapter 2 Jake describes *The Purple Land* as 'a very sinister book if read too late in life'. That Frank's ex-wife is a golfer reminds us of Jordan Baker, and perhaps Ford's reading of *The Great Gatsby* (also published in 1925) is most poignantly invoked in his pathetic final plea to his ex-wife in their final scene together: 'I just wanted to be a good sport' (336). The echo of Gatsby's language here ('old sport') is combined in *The Sportswriter* with ideas of the potential of fiction to provide a means of rebirth and reinvention which are quintessentially American. Both *The Great Gatsby* and *The Sportswriter* dramatize the failure of characters to sustain a sense of identity which originates in abstraction and fictionalization.

English literature also has its monuments to manly stoicism, and Frank knows his English well; he takes a copy of an A. E. Housman poem when he meets X at the grave of their son. This poem from *A Shropshire Lad* (1896) is, appropriately for a sportswriter, 'To an Athlete Dying Young'. It is a poem which offers comfort to the sportsman whose career is ending prematurely by arguing that the dead athlete never sees his records broken, and that his glory will never fade with time because he dies while he is still a champion, and that is preferable to the defeat and relegation which is the inevitable trajectory of the ageing sportsman's career: 'Smart lad, to slip betimes away / From fields where glory does not stay / And early though the laurel grows / It withers quicker than the rose'. Housman's poem offers a stoicism which is yet sentimental: it is better to die young than to suffer the defeats of time. Frank recognizes that the poem is inappropriate: 'it was much too literal and dreamily so about real athletes' (23), and besides, his son 'had not been much of an athlete'. The poem shows the failure of fiction about sports, especially for Frank's purposes. As a sports writer he is guilty of the same kind of sentimentality as Housman's poem. Frank's ex-wife sees clearly the gap between a writer and his idealized sportsmen, and she articulates this bluntly: ' "Housman" ', she says, ' "was an old pederast" ' (23). Fictions about sport are a source of conflict between Frank and his wife, and the duplicitous falsehoods of fiction are partly to blame for their separation: 'she thought she'd married a young Sherwood Anderson with movie possibilities' (15). More literally, Frank's estrangement from his girlfriend Vicki is precipitated by the rumour that X is having an affair with Fincher Barksdale (Frank Bascombe/Fincher Barksdale: the interloper appropriates both his wife and his name). This fiction is also exploded: X explains at the end that she was only helping him to improve his golf game in the run up to a college reunion tournament. Again Frank's encounter with real sports is made treacherous by his preference for fictions about it. Fictions about sport then, are not simply literary allusions but function as an integral part of the novel's narrative structure, and provide fundamental insights into Frank's character.

The real defeat of Frank Bascombe's ethos of sports writing stoicism comes in his meeting with the one genuine sportsman in the novel, Herb Wallagher, whom he interviews in a Detroit suburb. Herb has been forced to retire early from professional football and is now in a wheelchair. Frank is hoping to write 'a little inspirational business on the subject of character for people with their own worries', something upbeat with 'a touch of optimism', but he is quickly disappointed because, 'it is hard to think of Herb as an athlete'. Herb is concerned only with death. In fact, he is an athlete dying young. Moreover Herb has been reading Ulysses Grant, who felt that his life had become an act, 'and that act was dying' (163). Frank is completely disconcerted by this preoccupation of the sportsman's (despite its origin in his reading) and he is also disconcerted by Herb's interest in questions of aesthetics: 'Do you have any theories about art Frank . . . of how what the artist sees relates to what is finally put on the canvas?' Of course, Frank has no such theories, because they are inimical to his philosophy of stoicism. Herb's theory of art, of painting it as it is, is lost on

Frank, who approaches Herb as a kind of fiction himself and is incapable of learning a lesson from his meeting with a real sportsman. Frank concedes: 'I have expected a different Herb Wallagher from the Herb Wallagher I've found' (164). Herb tries in a blunt and confrontational way to awaken Frank from his dreaminess, ' "this is goddamn *real life* here Frank" ' (163), but Frank learns nothing from his meeting with Herb and at the end of the novel admits, 'I never properly wrote about Herb Wallagher and had to accept defeat there' (375). Herb will not conform to the comforting platitudes that Frank hopes to glamorize him with, and, unable to indulge the kind of consoling rhetoric of the poem 'To An Athlete Dying Young', he is rendered speechless: 'just nothing to say' (375).

It is significant that Frank's relationship with Vicki comes to an abrupt and unequivocal end during a game of croquet, and one which is accompanied by a further reference to writing. In this scene (the language of which is full of connotations of sexual power and conquest) Frank confesses that he can't concentrate on the game because 'I'm a tinge dreamy now', and Vicki follows up this allusion to dream worlds: 'When I was a lil girl I saw *Alice in Wonderland*, Cade and me. You know? In the part where they played croquet with ostriches' heads, or whatever those pink birds are, I cried bloody murder' (262). It is specifically writing about games which is depicted in *The Sportswriter* as constitutive of the individual's identity: 'I hated to see anything get hurt even then. That's why I'm a nurse'. Vicki makes the most concerted effort in this chapter to awaken Frank from his dream world of mediating fictions. As he pleads with her, Frank senses that his faith in a narrative language is failing him: 'Words, my best refuge and oldest allies, are suddenly acting to no avail, and I am helpless. In the wind, in fact, words hardly seem to clear my mouth. It is like a dream in which my friends turn against me and then disappear' (300). Even at this point of crisis in their relationship, the only way that Frank can imagine a closeness to Vicki is through the literature of her profession: 'I'll read some books and we can talk about nursing all the goddamn time' (300). It is through a further sporting reference that Vicki finally concludes this encounter and ends their relationship: 'She busts me full in the mouth with a mean little itchy fist that catches me midstride and sends me to the turf' (301). This punch is for Frank an unequivocal 'But a proper end' because he recognizes it as sportingly apposite. His immediate conceptualization of the scene in the language of boxing shows how profoundly he inhabits his writerly dream-world; but the punch fails to wake him from his absorption in a sporting rhetoric with which he continues to mystify his own emotional dilemma.

Frank receives numerous warnings of the deadly falsity of his fictionalized nostalgia for sports. On his way to play croquet with Vicki he stops at a roadhouse called 'Sweet Lou's Sportsman's Bar', owned by a famous ex-Giants player. Frank imagines writing a feature on Sweet Lou, a kind of *Where Are They Now* article in which the player buys a bar so that 'friends and fans could come and reminisce about the old glory days' (246). But Sweet Lou himself is absent; in fact, he's dead: ' "some gangsters drove over here from Mount Holly and walked him into the parking lot out there like it was friends and shot him twenty or thirty times. That did it" '. Frank is told this story by Lou's ex-wife, who warns him (more aptly than she realises) 'I don't wanna ruin your dreams' (247). Frank has reinvented himself as a sports writer, he participates in the American project of taking on a new identity when his old one has served its purpose. His change of identity from a fiction writer to a sports writer is an exercise in the freedom of what is called 'the American dream'. But Frank's use of the word 'dream' throughout *The Sportswriter* to signify his confusion and loss of volition reveals the novel's ambivalence about ideals of American self-determination. Frank Bascombe has written himself into a new social role, but its reliance on ideas which exist only in fiction and its faith in an ideal which is itself a fiction, undermine repeatedly the new freedom which Frank hopes to find. It is here that *The Sportswriter* is at its best, interrogating American issues of social identity and individual aspiration which are exposed as existing only in writing, even while Frank himself depends on writing for his identity.

It is significant that Walter Luckett's suicide note in the penultimate chapter includes a proposal to write a novel. Walter's first line is dramatic in the style of Frank's abandoned novel, and he claims that his fictional protagonist is a representation of himself: 'Eddie Grimes woke up on Easter morning and heard the train whistle far away in a forgotten suburban station. His very first thought of the day was, "You lose control by degrees" ' (355). The reference to the suburban train and to losing control strongly suggests Frank's situation: he has just jumped a train, he is at his wits' end, and now finds himself reading Walter's suicide note. The implication of the metafictional reference is that writing about writing is synonymous with death. Walter thinks that, 'Maybe a good way to start a novel is with a suicide note', but immediately discovers that it is a cul-de-sac and commits suicide rather than write the projected novel. In the same way *The Sportswriter* at its conclusion approaches very closely a certain kind of self-conscious textual cancellation which annihilates the novel's narrator. Frank employs a detective to find Walter's hidden daughter, as if to locate her in the final chapter would be to come upon a satisfactory narrative solution, a point of origin. But the story of Walter's daughter is not true, only 'a novelistic red herring', and it cannot provide what Frank calls 'a natural convincing closure' (372). Even more self-consciously, Frank begins to think of himself in the final chapter as 'a character at the end of a good short story' (375) and for a moment he returns to the possibility of writing fiction: 'If I could write a short story, I would' (376). At this point (where the ex-writer imagines himself as a character in fiction who is writing fiction) Frank finally comes upon the story Wade told him about the man who disappeared in the landslide. This apocryphal story of annihilation and rebirth is dramatized by Frank in his relocation to Florida and a new world of exotic possibilities where he stands on the edge of the Gulf of Mexico and gazes out to Cuba. It is one of a number of crucial incidents in Frank's narrative where he finds himself perilously close to the seductions of various kinds of storytelling. It is surely no coincidence too that Florida and Cuba appear in the text here, reminding us again of Hemingway, of horizons coloured by literary association. Frank does not disappear to Florida, he evaporates in a plethora of textual self-consciousness and metafictional self-referentiality in which Ford writes Frank out of his own narrative. Writing and reading are synonymous with death; *The Sportswriter* articulates a scepticism about playful fictions which ultimately extends to its own narrative progress, and in writing about a writer Ford finds an excellent vehicle for anxieties about the ability of fiction to maintain myths of personal identity. This extends to the interpretative strategies that we bring as readers to Ford's novel; as Vicki expresses it more succinctly in Detroit, 'I shouldn't read . . . it always gets me in trouble' (179).

The culmination of Frank's association with sports comes not at the end of *The Sportswriter* but at the end of its sequel *Independence Day* (1995) in which Frank takes his son Paul on a visit to the Baseball Hall of Fame at Cooperstown in upstate New York. Cooperstown was founded by Fenimore Cooper, a coincidence of writing and sport which is not lost on Frank. Frank sets out on this journey to Coopers-town 'staring like Jay Gatz at a beacon light that lures you' (288). Even here he is incapable of relinquishing the comforting remedies of fiction. At the Hall of Fame, Frank and his son practise on a baseball simulator which pitches balls into a cage at 75 mph. But a ball hits Paul full in the face and he is rushed to hospital in danger of losing an eye. This disastrous conclusion to Frank's attempt to bring himself closer to Paul precipitates a deeper alienation from both his son and his ex-wife. This final harrowing scene dramatizes the continuing failure of sport's sustaining myths and demonstrates again the crisis of masculinity attendant upon ideas about sports and the valorization of those ideas by writing.

William Kennedy **Billy Phelan's Greatest Game**

Ideas about sport are also fundamentally important to the characters of *Billy Phelan's Greatest Game* (1978) by William Kennedy, a novel in which 'sport' covers a wide range of gaming activities, including dice, darts, horses, baseball, pool, bowling and cards.[12] The novel is set in 1938 in a town in upstate New York called Albany, ' "The asshole of the northeast" ' (273), among a community of gamblers for whom sport is a way of life. For these particular Albany citizens sport is not simply a pastime but a matter of extreme importance, and for Billy Phelan it is his livelihood. From their dependence on gambling and their love of gaming the characters of the novel are bound together in a code of sporting honour which has nothing to do with the law but which is a very sensitive web of knowledge, indebtedness, and reputation with its own rules and its own severe punishments for those who contravene them. The concept of sporting integrity which governs the Albany of Kennedy's novel is a sensitive and intricate one; obser-vance of it is crucial to the survival of the novel's characters in this

---

[12] All page references are to the Penguin edition.

closely-knit gaming tribe, and transgression of it occasionally becomes a matter of life and death. To be 'a good sport' in this novel means to participate in a certain tribal cohesion which comes from a recognition of the rules of the game, whether that be sporting, political, or familial. Kennedy's novel is full of pointed reminders of the importance of this knowledge: Billy advises George 'if they say pay, just pay and shut up about it' (160); Lemon has been 'around the rackets all his life and he never learned how the game was played' (120), and Martin Daugherty urinates on the feet of a Cuban who is pimping his sister because 'Transgressors of good fame are punished for their deeds' (192). Through the novel's network of gaming contacts, tribal allegiances are established, and a character's trustworthiness becomes the mark of his reputation; this extends from sport to Albany politics in which the McCall family wields deistic power over police and newspapers as well as private citizens in what one character describes as 'the awareness of the truth of mobs' (113). This sporting affinity transcends ethnic difference: 'Billy thought of Morrie as a gambler not as a Jew. Morrie was a hustler who knew how to make a buck. He was all right. One of Billy's own kind' (139). This idea of a sporting fraternity with its own code of honour is analogous in Albany to family, a brotherhood of common interest which binds together the fate of the community, and inscribes the individual in a tight and formally observed social contract.

The idea of sporting loyalty is crucial to one of the central themes of the novel, Oedipal struggle. Both Martin Daugherty and Billy Phelan, aged 50 and 31 respectively, are depicted as negotiating relationships with their fathers which are fragile and precarious. Billy has not seen his father Francis for twenty years since the old man fled town after accidentally killing a strike breaker by throwing a rock; Martin tells Billy that 'Any one of us might have done what he did, but your father had that ball-player's arm' (226). Francis Phelan returns to Albany during the course of this novel and so offers Billy a chance to come to terms with his father's legacy. Martin too must come to terms with his father 'in whose humiliating shadow he had lived all his years' (24), and whose reputation as a writer and womanizer is so disabling that Martin 'never seemed to his wife to have grown up like other men' (27). Martin also has a problem with his only son Peter who has been removed from the ways of the world by 'pederast priests' who have duped him, Martin feels, with 'that windy God shit' (15). Kennedy's novel then, bears more than a casual resemblance to Joyce's *Ulysses* (1922) in which Stephen and Leopold cross each other's paths as potential fathers and sons to each other. Martin expresses this succinctly when he comments 'I know how it is to live in the inescapable presence of the absence of the father' (7), and he understands that Billy has taken to the gambling fraternity in the absence of Francis Phelan. The issue of paternity is of great significance to Kennedy's novel because it is analogous to the structures of indebtedness and autonomy which govern the sporting life of Albany in the 1930s.

The central narrative of *Billy Phelan's Greatest Game* is one of betrayal and redemption which brings together the sporting and the Oedipal dramas with great subtlety and wit. Following the kidnapping of Charlie Boy McCall from his father's dynasty, Billy becomes involved in the attempt to redeem the son within the terms of the Albany gaming community's system of honour. At the same time, he finds himself owing Martin seven hundred dollars, and he is also confronted by the spectre of his father who holds out to him the prospect of becoming a derelict, alcoholic has-been. Billy is merely 'a two-bit pool hustler' (272) but Martin as surrogate father sees his potential 'to make a heroic piccaro out of a simple chump' (7). To do this, Billy must negotiate several systems of sporting honour simultaneously, and somehow still retain his integrity and reputation as a trustworthy member of the Albany fraternity; it was 'Billy in the middle, a new game' (149). In refusing to inform on Morrie Berman for the McCalls, Billy sets himself outside the protection of their power and he becomes an outsider in Albany. But he understands that to have played the informant would have been to tarnish his reputation irrevocably; this system of political patronage is an extension of Albany gambling life: 'All anybody on Broadway needed to hear was that Billy was finking on Morrie . . . who'd trust him after that? . . . the McCalls were asking him to risk that' (156). Such is the McCalls' power that when Billy refuses to play their game he is ostracized by the entire community upon which his livelihood depends. This calamity occurs at the point where he needs to work to pay back Martin, and also find four hundred dollars to bail his father out of prison.

Billy's dilemma reaches a crisis in chapter 18 where, completely isolated, he is befriended by the black piano-player Slopie Dodds.

Slopie enables him to pay back his debt to Mike the Wop, and to get a drink in Albany: 'And he'd never used a nigger bootlegger before' (255). It is Slopie who tells Billy that ' "shootin pool aint how to get where you're goin" ' (257), and in a moment of despair Billy thinks of throwing himself in the river. It is important to recognize the significance of Billy's encounter with the black man: 'The knowledge of what was valuable in his life eluded him, except that he valued Slopie now as much as he valued his mother' (257). This broadening of Billy's community to include blacks, while clearly not a sentimental humanism (' "How is it being a nigger Slope?" "I kinda like it" ') is nevertheless crucial to Billy's redemption. It is no coincidence that this brotherhood of stigmatized groups is one which Morrie Berman's father Jake told a story about in chapter 6: 'It was a moment of monstrous ethnic truth in American history my friend, the persecuted Irish throwing a persecuted Jew out the window in protest against drafting Irishmen into the Union Army to help liberate the persecuted Negro' (113). Equally important in Billy's time of crisis is his response to social isolation: 'Maybe they wanted Billy to run. Maybe they thought if he got shut out of a joint like Becker's, he'd pack his bag and hop a freight. But his old man did that, and all he got was drunk' (258). In rejecting the precedent of his father, Billy becomes his own man and throws off the legacy of his father's cowardliness and failure. At the same time, in giving his last few dollars to his father who lies paralytic in a squalid Albany tavern, Billy honours his father while breaking free of the responsibility to be like him. It is Martin who recognizes Billy's remarkable talent in this respect, arguing that Billy is 'a gamester who accepts the rules and plays by them' but who also plays above them,' (252). It is Billy's generosity towards other game-players that earns him special respect, a generosity that marks him out from Scotty Streck, a brilliant bowler who 'wouldn't give a sick whore a hairpin' (12) and who dies as a direct result of hexing Billy's luck; he has a heart attack from dishonour: 'Scotty: Game over' (12). Martin sees the hero in Billy's fidelity to sporting integrity and in his extraordinary respect for other players, even cheaters. These personal qualities mark out Billy Phelan as exceptional, and the novel is really 'a triumph for self-development' (2) in which a sporting code of honour is used to govern and regulate the identity of individuals and the politics of the community.

Leonard Gardner **Fat City**

Where Frank Bascombe in *The Sportswriter* is disabled by the deadly falsity of sentimentalized sporting myths (and Ford's novel's success lies in its investigative use of this as a form of cultural analysis), Billy Phelan finds that a code of honour derived from sports is a stringent but vitally enabling mode of survival and fulfilment. For both prot-agonists sport is a value-system that offers the individual a way to define themselves by sporting rules which are also social rules. Cer-tain ideas about masculinity are necessarily associated with this, because Frank and Billy acknowledge codes of social definition which are about being a certain type of man. They are also protagonists who are used to examine closely what it means to be a failure. Masculinity is a prominent theme of Leonard Gardner's *Fat City* (1969), a novel which is devoted to one sport only, boxing, and which, like *The Sportswriter* and *Billy Phelan's Greatest Game*, uses sport to examine what it means to be a success or a failure as a man. *Fat City* tells the stories of two boxers, Billy Tully and Ernie Munger, who work with the same trainer/manager.[13] Billy is nearly 30 but he is encouraged to attempt a comeback after he floors a man in a bar room brawl and begins to believe that he can still be a success. Billy is haunted by memories of earlier victorious bouts when he was young, and by memories of the wife who left him when he began to lose. Ernie is a young fighter whose career is similarly entwined with the story of his relationship with a woman, his wife Faye, for whom he likes to think that he is fighting. Both boxing narratives are combined with accounts of sexual relationships. *Fat City* is a novel that uses boxing specifically to address ideas about masculinity and the male physical body, perhaps because boxing is above all sports 'a celebration of the lost religion of masculinity'.[14]

Billy Tully's ex-wife, the redhead Lynn, represents to him some-thing both physical and psychological from the past that he struggles to recapture; she had accompanied him to his winning bouts, and when he began to lose, 'he had looked to his wife for some indefinable

[13] All page references are to the Vintage Contemporaries edition.
[14] Joyce Carol Oates, *On Boxing* (1988). See also Gary Wills review of Oates's book in 'Blood Sport', *New York Review of Books*, 18 Feb. 1988, 5.

endorsement, some solicitous comprehension of the pain and sacrifice he felt he endured for her sake, some always withheld recognition of the rites of virility' (11–12). But Lynn leaves Billy for a bartender in Reno and he degenerates into alcoholism and petty crime. The loss of this woman is bound up in his mind with the loss of his athletic prowess, and without Lynn, Billy lacks the sustaining emotional spirit that would help him to be a winner. Instead, the physical punishments of boxing are replaced by those of gruelling farm labour, picking cherries, onions, walnuts, weeding tomato plants: 'Of all the hated work he had ever done, this was a torment beyond any, almost beyond belief, and so it began to seem this was his future, that this was Work, which he had always tried to evade and would never escape now that his wife was gone and his career was over' (75). With his life in a state of terminal decline, Billy's romance with the lush Oma quickly degenerates into sexual paranoia, bickering antagonism, and still he fails to escape the torments of his body; Billy lies in bed beside her 'excruciatingly aware of his structure, of each troubled limb, each restless joint, that he longed to thrash about in search of some position of ease' (114).

It is precisely such a 'position of ease' that the characters of *Fat City* cannot discover, and the novel dramatizes their anguished restlessness with forensic attention, especially as it is given physical expression. Boxing is used to examine the weaknesses of the male body, and also the extent to which a man's conception of his self is bound up with an investment in it. The boxing ring is a small symbolic space in which to test the prowess of the body. Chapter 5, for example, is given over to a conversation between two trainers in which one claims that at the doctor's, where Ernie has gone to have the veins burned out of his nose to stop nosebleeds, a needle could not penetrate Ernie's skin because it was like leather. Then the doctor finds that Ernie's blood is nearly black, and finally, that the blood turns solid in the test tube within moments of being given, 'like gelatin'. Unperturbed, the other trainer replies nonchalantly: 'Manny Chavez had the clearest piss of any man I ever seen. He'd take a specimen and the piss in that bottle would be just as clean and pure as fresh drinking water' (30). This is characteristic of the scrutiny to which the body is subjected in *Fat City*; devoid of a purpose and direction other than a vague notion of success, the boxers are reduced to anatomical components, the brutality of their physical lives made more acute by the total and comprehensive absence of showbiz glamour. When Ernie Munger first starts boxing he hides his bruises from his mother by using her makeup: 'With a bowl and a carton of salt dabbling and snuffling' (25–6). The body's ability to withstand various physical pressures is closely connected with the loss of a sustaining emotional spirit. Feeling no real affection for his girlfriend Faye, Ernie can only think of her in material terms: 'Faye had a short fleshy body that seemed to Ernie impervious to stimulation' (31). The women at the strip club that Billy attends are also devoid of glamour and reduced to physical components:

Calves sinewy, thighs dimpled, scars tucked in the fat of bellies, the women rocked and heaved, beckoned with tongues, crouched and rose with the edge of the curtain between their legs. Mouths open, they trotted out on the runway in high heels, squatted, shook, lay on the floor, lifted legs, caressed themselves, rose and ran off with little coy steps, wriggling dusty buttocks. (152)

Fat City is a novel full of failure, loss, regret, and 'all the desolate reality of defeat' (51) in which men and women alike are reduced to anatomical components; the novel's characters are exposed in all their desperate impoverishment, isolation, and loneliness. Ernie Munger concludes the novel ditched while hitchhiking home to California from Salt Lake City, in the middle of the desert at night, his ideas about women defeated by the unconventional behaviour of women drivers. The physical actions of boxing, sex, labouring, and drinking take place in cheap hotels and squalid gyms set amid an uncompromising landscape where the 'trunks and limbs and stumps' of amputated trees match 'the maimed bodies of the derelict characters who sought shade from a remorseless sun'.

Fat City is written with great directness and economy and has very little interpretative exposition; rather, the characters' emotional lives are crowded out by the material details of mundane daily routines, the narrative using boxing to highlight their physical endurance and the body's work-rate in a struggle for survival which informs every aspect of their lives. The style is reminiscent of Nathanael West in its evocation of despair, in its use of the grotesque to dramatize physical alienation, and in its poignant perception of the ugly gap between material reality and emotional fulfilment. The text is punctuated with references to the vacuity of the modern American commercial world, and Gardner's style is also reminiscent of West's in being entirely devoid of pity or hope for its hapless characters; the novel's vision of the brutalization of boxing and the life that goes with it is direct and uncompromising:

In the midst of a phantasmagoria of worn-out, mangled faces, scarred cheeks and necks, twisted, pocked, crushed and bloated noses, missing teeth, brown snags, empty gums, stubble beards, pitcher lips, flop ears, sores, scabs, dribbled tobacco juice, stooped shoulders, split brows, weary, desperate, stupefied eyes under the lights of Center Street, Tully saw a familiar young man with a broken nose. (116)

The alienation from their bodies that the characters of *Fat City* endure is accompanied by a trenchant depiction of the squalid and tawdry modern commercial world that they inhabit, the reification of their physical components becoming an internalization of the desperately fragmented and commodified society that they are part of. Nathanael West captured this spirit in the 1930s in *The Day of the Locust*:

He got out of bed in sections, like a poorly made automaton, and carried his hands into the bathroom. He turned on the cold water. When the basin was full, he plunged his hands in up to the wrists. They lay quietly on the bottom like a pair of strange aquatic animals. When they were thoroughly chilled and began to crawl about, he lifted them out and hid them in a towel.[15]

Homer Simpson, in his murderous distance from his own body parts, prefigures precisely Gardner's presentation of the body as a collection of inanimate material pieces which, in their fragmentary nature, reflect the collapse of any meaningful narrative that would hold society and the individual together. In this sense *Fat City* uses sport to dramatize the failure of a particular mode of aspiration, and it is worth noting too that *Fat City* is set in California, a common focus for western ideas of success and reinvention from *The Day of the Locust* and *The Grapes of Wrath* through to the present day (Tobias Wolf's novel *This Boy's Life*, for example).

---

[15] Nathanael West, *Complete Works* (Picador Classics, 1988), 289.

Don DeLillo **End Zone**

Don DeLillo's *End Zone* (1972) is a first-person comic novel set in west Texas, nominally about a college football team (hence the title) but also concerned with ideas about language in many different aspects.[16] Gary Harkness has found himself playing football in west Texas after leaving several more prestigious colleges and having discovered that 'my life meant nothing without football' (22). It must be remembered (and Keesey sometimes forgets[17]) that *End Zone* is a comic novel, and that despite the seriousness of some of DeLillo's themes in this novel, there is a pervasive and very dry irony which informs everything in it. Coach Creed, for example, is a man of destiny: 'He sits up nights, he has piercing eyes. You never see him in a phone booth' (57). One particularly fearsome sporting opponent is described as 'an oblong monument to the virtues of intimidation' (119), and after the game against West Centrex Biotechnical Institute the players discuss injuries on the bus on the way home: 'Bobby Iselin, pulled hamstring. Terry Madden, broken nose. Ron Steeples, mild concussion. Len Skink, worms' (147). The team coach recruits a public relations officer to promote the excellence of the college team; he is a man more used to promoting acts such as 'Two sword swallowers on a trampoline' (178), and he remarks that 'what I know about football you can inscribe with a blunt crayon around the rim of a shot glass' (152). Gary Harkness, the narrator, has a voice full of ironic detachment, the other players cannot tell when he is joking, and he confesses that 'my examinations of life sometimes ended in oblique forms of self-mockery' (65). Before one game, a player prepares himself by trying to vomit: 'It was a poignant sound, monumentally hoarse, soulful, oddly lacking in urgency. A herd of seals' (172). Despite the austerity of the comic irony with which everything is treated in *End Zone*, the novel has a consistent interest in forms of language and modes of discourse, and this interest originates in the language of football: 'Football is the one sport guided by language' (112), and 'Much of the appeal of sport derives from its dependence on elegant gibberish' (113). It is here that

[16] All page references are to the Penguin Contemporary American Fiction edition.

[17] Douglas Keesey, *Don DeLillo* (New York: Twayne, 1993), chapter on *End Zone*, 34–47.

DeLillo's novel is radically different from those of Ford, Kennedy, and Gardner, but it still retains a consistent focus on the fundamental importance of the material details of sport as a means of cultural analysis.

End Zone is as much about the language of football as it is about football itself, and the crucial game at the centre of the novel reveals DeLillo delighting in the technical jargon of the game in dense rhetorical paragraphs of closely-detailed field plays: 'Twin deck left, ride series, white divide. Gap-angle down, 17, dummy stitch. Bone country special, double-D to right' (141). These paragraphs are complemented by reports of the language of the players in the scrimmage: 'Nigger kike faggot. Kike fag. Kike. Nigger fag. Nigger kike faggot' (119). At the same time, the novel parodies the language of sports commentary: ' "What's going to happen up there on the banks of the Fox River in little Green Bay when the big bad Bears come blowing in from the windy city?" ' (139). In this way different kinds of language are contrasted against one another, modes of speech are punctuated by different types of specialized language, and *End Zone* scrutinizes sport as if it were simply a mode of technical discourse; this is especially true of football because 'Each play must have a name. The naming of plays is important. All teams run the same plays. But each team uses an entirely different system of naming. Coaches stay up well into the night in order to name plays. They heat and reheat coffee on an old burner. No play begins until its name is called' (118). It is the act of naming which confers power to the team coach, and the relationship between things and the names for things is DeLillo's real focus of interest in *End Zone* (as in so much of his later fiction). American football provides DeLillo with a metaphor by which he examines almost everything else in the novel: it consistently asks, what is the relationship between words and the things that those words appear to signify? This conceptual enquiry colours the depiction of everything in *End Zone*, moving from the depiction of a football match to the language of nuclear war, to the nature of an individual's sense of identity, racial difference, and the ontological status of all material things. Football provides *End Zone* with a conceptual tool by which to interrogate culture and its language and to demonstrate the ridiculousness of both.

The football coach Creed is endowed with power because he has control over the language of the game: 'This was his power, to deny us the words we needed. He was the maker of plays, the name-giver. We were his chalk scrawls' (135). The players become merely the function of the language that Creed devises for the plays that they will enact, and their identity is annihilated when they submit themselves properly to the discipline of his game plan. DeLillo's interest here is in how the language of football dictates the individual's identity: the players become the subjects of a language which is already written. Gary Harkness is aware of the perilous eradication of himself by another's language, and he seeks to discover another language by which he can escape it: 'in some form of void, freed from consciousness, the mind remakes itself. What we must know must be learned from blanked out pages. To begin to reword the overflowing world. To subtract and disjoin. To re-recite the alphabet. To make elemental lists. To call something by its name and need no other sound' (89). Gary's dedication to football has taught him that he is the subject of its language, and this gives him a fascination with all forms of language and discourse and the power they have to inform and determine the identity of the individual inscribed by those discourses. Gary recognizes too, that his subjugation to language is an intensely violent process, not only in the football scrimmage, but everywhere; he has therefore an obsession with the language of nuclear holocaust:

It started with a book . . . assigned reading for a course I was taking in modes of disaster technology. . . . I liked reading about the deaths of tens of millions of people. . . . Fifty to a hundred million dead. Ninety percent population loss. Seattle wiped out by mistake. . . . I liked to think of huge buildings toppling, of firestorms, of bridges collapsing, survivors roaming the charred countryside. Carbon 14 and strontium 90 . . . Titan, Spartan, Poseidon. People burned and unable to breathe. . . . Two hundred thousand bodies decomposing on the roads outside Chicago. I read several chapters twice . . . I became fascinated by words and phrases like thermal hurricane, overkill, circular error probability, post-attack environment, stark deterrence, dose-rate contours, kill-ratio, spasm war. Pleasure in these words. (20–1)

It is important to recognize that it is the language of technological warfare which Gary relishes: the words are entirely separated from any sense of the concepts they refer to, the violence here is abstract and theoretical. But the violence of the individual's subjection to the language of football is authentic and painful, and so is the violence by which other individuals are inserted into their culture. Three important characters in *End Zone*, Bloomberg, Myna, and Taft Robinson, all seek to throw off the language of their inherited culture in ways that are analogous to Gary's rejection of the discourse of football. Anatole Bloomberg is attempting to 'unjew' himself by rejecting the inherited culture of his ethnic origin, and by renouncing its language: 'You take out the urbanisms. The question marks. All that folk wisdom. The melodies in your speech. The inverted sentences. You use a completely different set of words and phrases' (46). This is a parodic dramatization of the young Jewish man attempting to escape what he perceives to be his cultural history, more openly satirized later as 'a hunchbacked Talmudic scholar in a woolly black coat and shoes without shoe laces' (187). Bloomberg also tries to escape this inheritance by changing his name from 'Anatole' to 'EK17'. Bloomberg's rejection of a cultural language that inscribes him is paralleled by Myna's, she is a young woman who adopts the cultural language of ugliness in order to escape the feminine 'responsibilities of beauty'. Myna's ridiculous clothes, pimply face, and gross overweight, are a rejection of the received stereotype of the attractive young woman of the 1970s. Ultimately however, she too comes to realize that this self-violence is as destructive and harmful as that of her dominant culture; it is simply another cultural language, no more original than any other.

Taft Robinson also rejects the language by which culture inscribes his personal identity. The only black player on the team ('They got him for his speed', (3)) Robinson is entirely mute throughout the novel, but suddenly becomes garrulous when he decides to quit football altogether, to abandon his skill as an athlete: 'Less of white father watching me run. Prefer to sit still' (233). Taft Robinson is the key to *End Zone*, and he is accompanied by an important reference to Wittgenstein (whose philosophy of language is often evoked by the novel), and Robinson remarks at the end: 'A new way of life requires a new language' (234). The text of *End Zone* is in part a search for such a language, one by which individuals might strive to be individuals rather than the mindless functionaries of an already written cultural language such as football players are. One such player is renowned for saying that he would ' "go through a brick wall for coach Creed" ';

Gary cannot understand this sporting rhetoric: 'Maybe the words were commissioned, as it were, by language itself' (54). Yet at the same time, if we are not to be spoken by our culture in a hackneyed and redundant language, a comparable violence to the self is required; Gary's asceticism in the west Texas desert combines the self-denial of religious devotion with the landscape of a nuclear test site. Ultimately, the novel's self-mocking narrator rejects football altogether for a different kind of physical discipline: 'High fevers burned a thin straight channel through my brain. In the end they had to carry me to the infirmary and feed me through plastic tubes' (242).

Robert Coover **The Universal Baseball Association, inc. J. Henry Waugh, PROP.**

End Zone is an early DeLillo novel, and although there are scattered comments about sport throughout his subsequent novels (golf is referred to in *Players* as 'That anal round of scrupulous caution and petty griefs. Watching golfers being massacred . . . an occasion for sardonic delight'), it was not until 1992 that DeLillo returned to sport as a central vehicle with the novella 'Pafko at the Wall', the short story that later became the first chapter, in a revised form, of *Underworld* (1997). Here DeLillo's chosen vehicle is not American football but baseball, beloved of DeLillo, Doctorow, and Coover alike. Baseball has a special place in the heart of the narrator/novelist of DeLillo's *Mao II* (1991), who comments that 'the word [baseball] has resonance if you're American, a sense of shared heart and untranslatable lore . . . an openness of form that makes the game a kind of welcome to my country' (9). There is an interesting question about American sports here, a question asked by S. J. Gould: 'Why is baseball so different from other sports in its symbolic status and impact upon America? . . . why is baseball alone among sports (with some challenge, perhaps, from boxing) the subject of a distinguished literature?'.[18] Robert Coover's novel *The Universal Baseball Association, inc. J. Henry Waugh, PROP.* (1968) is one which, like *End Zone*, takes sport as a language by

[18] S. J. Gould, 'Dreams That Money Can Buy', *New York Review of Books*, 5 Nov. 1992, 41.

which to interpret American culture, and offers an answer to these questions.[19] In this novel a 56-year-old bachelor plays out a baseball league he has invented using a variety of numerical charts and the roll of three dice. This league, the universal baseball association, is a complex and sophisticated one which accommodates in its intricacies many variable factors of the 'real' game, and Henry Waugh presides over it, deciding the play with a roll of the dice and keeping a formal record of the details of every game: 'From the bathroom door he could see the kitchen table. His association lay there in ordered stacks of paper. The dice sat there, three ivory cubes, heedless of history yet makers of it' (16). The story has 'The Secret Life of Walter Mitty' as an antecedent in its depiction of a private fantasy world, and Henry does once momentarily remark that 'this was sure a helluva thing for a grown man to be doing at dawn on a working day' (125). On the surface it might appear that Henry's Association is a retreat from the world, a private obsession devised as an escape from his job as an accountant. But the special pleasure that Henry derives from his league is in keeping a close historical record of every pitch, every innings, every game and every season: 'the accountability—the beauty of the records system which formed a place to keep forever each last action' (19); it is this which makes baseball for Henry 'The Great American Game'.

Henry's pleasure in maintaining precise historical records of each Association season is symptomatic of an intellectual enquiry into ideas of historiography and power. On the bus on the way home from work in chapter 2 Henry reads the newspaper and observes that 'without numbers or measurements there probably wouldn't be any history' (49), and this remark leads him to consider how history is constituted: 'You have to accept certain assumptions or ground rules about what's left in and what's left out' (49). Henry is aware of the ideological freight of historical accounts and makes his point to his friend on the bus: ' "At 4.34 on a wet November afternoon, Lou Engel boarded a city bus and spilled water from his hat brim on a man's newspaper. Is that history?" ' (50). Most importantly of all, Henry's consideration of what constitutes history leads him to ask, who decides, or as he expresses it, 'Who's writing it down?' (50). In this

[19] All page references are to the Minerva edition.

brief comic exchange, Henry identifies the central conceptual issues of Coover's novel: what is history, and who has the power to decide what is historically significant?

An interrogation of historiography is not the only use to which Coover puts Henry's Baseball Association; the novel works a subtle pun on historical accounts and business accounts exploiting Henry's daytime job as a clerk in a firm of bookkeepers. The history of baseball is an analogue to other kinds of historical record, but also intersects with another crucial aspect of American culture, as Henry's boss points out: ' "what do *both* baseball and business need, Mr Waugh? Somebody to keep the books" ' (138). Henry's boss describes baseball as the great American game, 'after business of course' (138), and then adds ' "This is the *American* way, Mr Waugh!" ' (139). Henry's fastidious records of his baseball games are a parallel to double entry bookkeeping, the very fabric of American commercial life. This helps to explain the significance of the abbreviations in the novel's title, 'inc' and 'prop', emphasizing the commercial and the proprietorial as an integral part of the game's nature. The connectedness of American business life and American sport is part of the novel's project in offering a critique of that which is quintessentially American.

Henry takes the details of his game to extraordinary lengths, inventing not only names for his players but also individual personalities, racial identities, personal histories and speech patterns. Much of the novel is devoted to dialogue between players during the games, and especially to their quarrels over the sporting history of which they are a part. This aspect of the novel contributes significantly to the impression of each game's authenticity, and through their disputes about baseball culture the novel comprises a kind of oral history, mythology, and folk lore which gives Henry's statistical account of their games a living texture and enables the novel to dramatize a whole social and cultural existence, a way of life and a particular community. In one especially self-reflexive paragraph in which players in a game comment on the possible significance of numerology, Waugh introduces a player 'who's discovered that the whole damn structure from the inning organization up and double entry bookkeeping are virtually identical' (219). Coover's playfulness in switching between Waugh's inner and outer worlds suggests that precisely such a simple binary opposition is spurious and redundant.

Furthermore, Waugh is no aberration but a product of his culture, and his baseball association is fundamentally akin to his particular American milieu in a way which enables Coover to use sport to write about important constituents of American life. At one point Henry leaves his oppressive office and steps out into the world beyond:

Motion. The American scene. The rovin' gambler. Cowpoke and trainman. A travelin' man always longs for a home, cause a travelin' man is always alone. Out of the east into the north, push out to the west, then march through the south back home again: like a baserunner on the paths, alone in a hostile cosmos, the stars out there in their places, and him trying to dominate the world by stepping on it all. Probably suffered a sense of confinement there in the batter's box, felt the need to strike forth on a meaningful quest of some kind. (141)

Here Coover evokes a quintessentially American ethos in a moment of lyrical reflection, one which combines key elements of American history with the spirit of baseball and a sense of America's restless commercial enterprise. The frontiersmen and the cowboy become the spirited individuals of American sport, heroic in their aspiration to conquer not simply the four points of the compass but even 'the stars' in a hostile cosmos. This paragraph encapsulates much that is central to Coover's novel and shows succinctly how baseball is integral to the novel's vision of what America is. Henry's intimations lead him shortly to announce that, 'Ball stadiums and not European churches are the real American holy places' (166). This pronouncement expresses the democratic spirit of baseball that is so cherished by DeLillo and Coover.

Both *End Zone* and *The Universal Baseball Association* put sports to sophisticated and far-reaching uses. Both novels are comedies which use sport to write about the grammar of American culture, its language and its structures. Both novels interrogate the idea that sport provides an illusion of order, and in both novels the act of naming is crucial because of the way in which it confers the power to determine meanings and to assign cultural value. Where coach Creed names the plays that his team must execute in *End Zone*, Henry Waugh names his players and constructs their identities around those names. Furthermore, this power to name is not restricted to the Baseball Association. When one of his most successful pitchers, Damon Rutherford, has an exceptional game to end an inning, Henry goes out to a bar to celebrate; he meets Hettie and invites her home with him, 'not sure it was himself talking' (25). At his apartment as they undress, Henry whispers to her 'Call me . . . Damon', and his sexual empowerment is facilitated by his taking on the name of 'The greatest pitcher in this history of baseball' (29). This comic climax to chapter 1 uses sporting metaphors to dramatize ideas about how the individual relates to his broader culture, or as one critic expresses it:

The capacity to construct meaning is made evident by Henry's insight into the power of naming: 'In the name. Or rather: in the naming'. The power to confer names is the power to assign meaning, especially when this is institutionally underwritten: if meanings are to gain currency and authority, they must be officially inscribed, ritualised, functions which Henry meticulously performs.[20]

This power enables both Coover and DeLillo to joke about the apparently deistic status of football coaches and baseball association proprietors. As Gary Harkness asks incredulously: ' "this shit about the man upstairs. Is the man upstairs supposed to be synonymous with God or what?" ' (98). Similarly, Henry hovers beneath the light bulb over his kitchen table while his players suffer a crisis of faith: ' "Look up, good men, cast your eye on the Ineffable Name . . . "What does it say?" "100 Watt" ' (231–2). Such illusions of omnipotence are satirized and dismantled in both novels, and in *End Zone* coach Creed in particular ends a broken man. DeLillo has commented on this directly: 'Most games are carefully structured. They satisfy a sense of order and they even have an element of dignity about them . . . Games provide a frame in which we can try to be perfect. Within sixty minute limits or one hundred yard limits . . . we can look for perfect moments or perfect structures'.[21]

It is this idea of sport as a structure of knowledge, an epistemology, that the novels of this chapter have in common: the textuality of sporting myths, the sporting code of honour and integrity, the human body as a sporting instrument, dreams of glamour and

---

[20] P. Maltby, *Dissident Postmodernists* (Philadelphia: University of Pennsylvania Press, 1991), 231

[21] L. McCaffery (ed.), *Anything Can Happen* (Urbana: University of Illinois Press, 1987), 81.

success, the language and the grammar of sport, and sport as a mode of historiography which marks time by recording significant achievements. All of these things are represented by sport in the contemporary American novel, and it is testimony to the place of sport in American culture that these writers use it as a serious field of enquiry in its own right and as a means to examine important aspects of American life.

7

Imagining Subjectivity

> When I was younger
> it was plain to me
> I must make something of myself.

> William Carlos Williams,
> 'Pastoral'

The novels of this chapter are principally devoted to the dramatization of a particular individual's life story, especially their career and their romantic history, and each of them is a retrospective narrative of their development, or autobiography, in which their author explains how they came to be who they are. These novels are a kind of confession or revelation in writing of their authors' consciousness of themselves as Cartesian 'subjects' and they provide an account not only of the material circumstances of their lives but of the prevailing conditions that constitute them as individual American citizens. This romantic narrative has a prestigious American history with notable landmarks in Whitman's 'Song of Myself' and Melville's *Moby Dick*: 'Call me Ishmael'. It is a process of representation that is intimately associated with imagination and with language, because any written account of a character's consciousness must necessarily be predicated on the language that it employs and the larger cultural narratives that it subscribes to. The novels of this chapter are forms of self-representation, and they are notable for scrutinizing their respective languages of representation even while they tell their story. The French cultural critic Michel Foucault is one of a number of writers who theorized this area. In *The Order of Things* (1966) and *The Archaeology of Knowledge* (1969), Foucault refuted the subjectivity of humanism and formulated instead what he termed the 'author function' in which subjectivity was exposed as an affect of certain social discourses and institutional practices. For Foucault, in any piece of writing the first person singular 'I' is not a natural or spontaneous entity but a product of a socially sanctioned discourse that is determined by the language that it deploys or engages with. This theory, which has been widely influential in the social sciences, diminishes the role of human agency in narratives of subjectivity and emphasizes the importance of cultural institutions by which the subject is written or 'subjected to'.

The interpretations of this chapter, while not thoroughly Foucauldian, are alert to the linguistic games that writers play in creative attempts to produce on the page a sense of subjectivity that is natural or 'authentic'. If the reader's sense of the subject is produced by language, then what are the figurative devices that these writers employ to render that subject convincingly, and what are the struggles and tensions in the social discourse that those subjects discover? Three of this chapter's novels, for example, are written by male fictional protagonists who tell of their rise to success and their respective romances, and in several important ways Louise Erdrich's novel is different from them; these differences help to illuminate the significance of gender in the act of imagining subjectivity, and they highlight a distinction between oral and written narratives. The novels of this chapter scrutinize their own language as part of the conduct of their narrative, in some very direct and archly self-conscious ways they are each characterized by a self-reflexive questioning of the narrative strategies by which they imagine their own fictional characters. Furthermore, they have an obsessive interest in origins and in the body, and they situate their subjects in the conflicts of a particular historical moment. They all to some degree show the legacy of the Puritan confession of how the penitent found the way to God and so became the masterful author of the text that the reader holds. In this they have all heeded that particularly American lesson 'I must make something of myself'.

John Updike **Memories of the Ford Administration**

In *Memories of the Ford Administration* John Updike creates a narrator, Alfred Clayton, who is writing his recollections of the spirit of the days of the Gerald Ford presidency (1974–7) for a New England historical society.[1] At this time in his life Clayton was a history professor at Wayward College and was writing (and had been writing already for ten years) a book on the fifteenth President of the United States, James Buchanan (1791–1868). Updike's novel thus negotiates a parallel historical narrative between the 1970s and the period leading up to the Civil War, broadly 1820–65. Clayton's interest in recovering his personal domestic history during the Ford era is closely associated with his attempt to retrieve the life of Buchanan, so that it is pertinent to ask at the outset if there is an analogy for Updike between the two historical moments, and what is the significance of his narrator's attempt to write adjacent historical narratives in the same text?[2]

While Gerald Ford is completely absent from the novel as a character, Clayton is obsessed with the personality of Buchanan, 'I love him' (14), and admits that Buchanan took over his life during the years of the Ford presidency: 'His life had become an incubus stealing strength from mine' (281). Clayton even sees possible correspondences between himself and the President: 'I wondered if that was my bond with Buchanan—a helpless standing by' (144). But although his mistress Genevieve claims that Clayton is emasculated by his marriage to Norma ('how disempowering of you Norma was', (100)) there is little dramatic evidence that either Clayton or Buchanan are passive or victimized men. Here, as elsewhere, Clayton is disingenuous about his own character and motivations during the 1970s, even while he strives to appear candid. Clayton is always trying to discover analogies between the characters of his two historical narratives; he is strongly infatuated with the historical image of Ann Coleman, for example, the woman Buchanan nearly married. At one point during the Ford years, Clayton recalls having sex with a student's mother primarily because her name was Ann, and so he

---

[1] All page references are to the Penguin edition.

[2] For an indication of Updike's long-term interest in fellow Pennsylvanian Buchanan, see his play *Buchanan Dying* (1974).

recognized the romantic opportunity as 'a chance to rescue lonely Ann' (222).

This is part of a wider strategy in which Clayton's eagerness to recover Buchanan is associated with his equally scholarly preoccupation with recalling the details of his sexual adventures during the Ford years, and especially the cultivation of his almost forensic interest in the woman's body (Norma's, Genevieve's, Mrs Ann Arthrop's). Historical investigation is sexually motivated; for Clayton there is a very close association between historical narratives and erotic desire. The extraordinary focus and detail of Clayton's research into Buchanan's life is exemplified by his eagerness to locate an editorial of Horace Greeley's at the Boston Public Library; Clayton can still remember in vivid detail the room 'where six of the crapulous homeless dozed' (324). Here as elsewhere (he offers to go to Washington to find the exact date of a dinner Buchanan held, (337)), Clayton has forgotten, in his obsession with Buchanan, that his true narrative remit is a recollection of the Ford years. Gradually Clayton's reanimation of Buchanan takes over his reminiscence of the 1970s almost entirely. Following the final rejection by Genevieve (who returns to her husband), Clayton's narrative of the Ford years is consumed by his attachment to Buchanan and the drama of impending Civil War. Thus, Clayton's crisis of affections, loyalties, and desires (mistress Genevieve, wife Norma) is paralleled by the nineteenth-century American domestic crisis. This is part of a broader political correspondence between the turmoil of the Nixon resignation with which the novel begins (and the agony for Americans of its ugly circumstances) and the crisis of nationhood that was attendant upon the Buchanan administration. It might also be the case that there is something quintessentially American about the Buchanan years which Ford's administration and Clayton's personal history in the 1970s still adhere to; it is as if Buchanan's time and culture set the parameters of modern American selfhood and in some sense represent a moment of origin. Writing about the 1970s Clayton observes,

Young American men and women, sons and daughters of corporation lawyers, had sinned against the Holy Ghost, and got up the next morning to take a piss and look in the mirror, to see if there was a difference. There didn't seem to be. Everything was out of the closet, every tabu broken, and still God kept His back turned, refusing to set limits. A President had been shot, a war had been lost, our empire had been deemed evil, our heavenly favored-nation status had been revoked, the air had been let out of our parade balloon, and still we bumped on, as we had in 1865, with wandering steps and slow, as out of Eden we took our solitary way. (247–8)

Clayton's attempts to conflate the innocence of pre-Civil War days with the innocence pre-Nixon (a mythical and strongly nostalgic narrative of a prelapsarian America) is tentative and provisional. As one contemporary reviewer wrote of Buchanan, 'We remember him as the futile occupant of the White House who came before Lincoln, just as we are likely to remember Gerald Ford in the White House because of Nixon'.[3] Clayton finds occasional and fleeting points of association between the characters of Buchanan's narrative and the characters of the 1970s (himself as Buchanan, Genevieve as Ann Coleman, Ann Arthrop as Ann Coleman, Buchanan's running mate Floyd as the betrayer and deserter Genevieve) but none of these correspondences, like those of the wider temporal horizons, are satisfactory. Crucially for Updike's novel, Clayton is aware of this. Any analogy is merely a function of the project of attempting to situate the individual human subject in narrative language, and analogies (like other rhetorical tropes and devices) are simply and finally devices of imaginative language. It is this central idea of articulating the self in narrative language and at a precise historical moment which is the most urgent project of Updike's novel. The true subject of the novel is the impossibility of writing an authoritative narrative of subjectivity, and Clayton discovers this to be as true of himself as it is of Buchanan, who is only ostensibly more remote. Despite his scorn for what he terms 'deconstruction', Clayton learns some of the lessons of contemporary literary theory, and what he has learned contributes significantly to the writing of his own text about subjectivity and textuality which becomes *Memories of the Ford Administration*. After all, the novel's epigraph is a quotation from Heidegger in *The Question of Being*, which is in turn cited by Derrida in the preface to his *Of Grammatology*, which is, as Updike well knows, one of the sacred texts of Clayton's post-structuralist arch-rival, Brent.

The inadequacy of narrative language to capture or convey the enigmatic history of the individual's desire is dramatized often by

---

[3] Alfred Kazin, 'The Middle Way', *New York Review of Books*, 17 Dec. 1992, 45.

Clayton's scholarly frustration. Again and again the historian is confronted by absence, gaps and empty spaces which only speculative conjecture can fill. Clayton is either thwarted by the loss of crucial documentation, or bewildered by the proliferation of conflicting historical records: 'And still we don't know exactly what happened: Buchanan's state of mind varies from hysterical to coolly determined depending on the source and slant; a crucial document like the rejected final letter of the South Carolina Commissioners is missing; more basically, the quotidian fluff has evaporated.... The past is as illusory as the future' (313). Here Clayton is reminded again of how text-dependent history is; although committed to writing an authoritative account, he learns the lesson of his 'deconstructionist' colleague that there is no history which exists, as Brent might have put it, anterior to textuality. This is not only true of particular historical narratives, but, Clayton finds, characteristic of the very idea of narrative language itself: 'How dismayingly, arriving at this climactic crisis of my tale and of Buchanan's life, did I find nothing but dried old words, yards of them strung together from accounts of suspect authenticity' (331). The authenticity of narrative language is itself called into doubt by Clayton's research; the authenticity of the historical moment and the subjectivity situated at that moment cannot be given by a language which indefinitely evades and defers. But to return to the dual historical narrative, is this as true of Clayton's 1970s as it is of Buchanan's nineteenth century?

At one point in characterizing the last few months of Buchanan's administration in 1861, Clayton suddenly exclaims, 'I *hate* history! Nothing is simple, nothing is consecutive, the record is corrupt. Further, the *me* inside these brackets appears no wiser than the one outside them, though he (the former) is fifteen years older' (307). Clayton despairs at his inability to learn from history, even (or especially) his own history; in his anxiety to recover an authentic sense of himself, he divides his narrative into that of two subjectivities, one parenthetically contemporary experiencing a crisis of identity in trying to articulate a sense of his former self. Clayton writes about the two selves as if they were entirely separate, and not acknowledging that the Clayton of the 1970s is the product of the contemporary Clayton's narrative designs. Thus, the inability to recover a definitive

Buchanan is paralleled by a sense of the hopelessness of recovering the definitive Clayton. As the crisis in Buchanan's administration reaches a dramatic culmination, so too does the crisis in Clayton's attempt to recover himself. Just before the quotation cited above, Clayton interrupts his nineteenth-century history to offer another parenthetical observation about his own motivations and desires: 'speaking of embarrassment, what follows is fragmentary, unsatisfactory. After my break with Genevieve, I realised that my attempt to complete my book and my attempt to marry her had been aspects of a single vain effort to change my life' (303). In the context of the novel, this comes as a surprise; Clayton's desire to change his life is not actually articulated by his text but 'discovered' here retrospectively in the form of a footnote to his own emotional development. It is as if, like the elusive details of Buchanan's life, the crucial psychological motivations and impulses of Clayton's life lie beyond his narrative grasp. The absence of expressions of Clayton's desire is revealed starkly by the style in which he recalls his separation from his wife Norma: 'All I had to do was dispose of my own wife and children. They had been deconstructed, but didn't know it yet. I would have to tell them. The wife, the kids' (52). The unemotional tenor of this, its pragmatic outlook on the syntax of marital reconfiguration, is coldly expressive of Clayton's own inability to recover his personal sense of desire. This crucial moment in Clayton's life is, like the letter that Ann Coleman sent to Buchanan summoning him to reconciliation on the eve of her death, a lost message of desire which can never be authentically retrieved. Clayton's use of the word 'deconstructed' here is also significant, because it reveals the extent to which his subjectivity has been colonized (apparently against his will) by the language of academia, and that colonization is synonymous with a kind of emotional loss or death. That the word should also be used as part of a quest to understand a point of origin is appropriate because deconstruction is a methodology that has a particular interest in origins.

The one aspect of desire that Clayton recovers successfully and repeatedly in vivid technicolour is his sexual life, the details of which are scattered through the 1970s narrative, a time of 'terrifying permissiveness' (248). Clayton has a forensic and prurient interest in the bodies of women, an interest which matches the obsessive quality of his intellectual research on Buchanan, as if there is a correlation between the body of a woman and a body of texts. This is also perhaps a displacement or reification of emotional desires into physical encounters. Here is Clayton on the subject of female genitalia for example: 'The two sets of lips, major and minor. The *frilly* look of it, climaxing in a little puckering wave of flesh around the clitoris. Its livid, oysterish, scarcely endurable complexity, which all but gynecologists used to spare themselves, along with the visual ordeal of parturition' (15–16). Clayton's fascination with the woman's body, the technical language of his descriptions of it, and his forensic delight in finding exactly the right word and the most evocative image, sometimes have the effect of reducing his female partners to an orifice ('her thrusting muff the no-color of pewter', (23)) and of diminishing his interest in women purely to an objectification of their physicality: 'Cunts are as individual as faces, and seating oneself inside a new one is a violent chemical event. Her wetness has become so extreme I kept slipping' (19). This interest in the physical processes of the woman's body goes beyond the sexual: 'As I followed her into the bathroom in the mornings, my nostrils were struck by the chthonian after-scent, spicier than Norma's spoor, of what had just passed from one of her seven sacred orifices' (170). The image is one in which Clayton tracks Genevieve like an animal, newly sensitive to the different scent that her body waste emits. Note again the technical language ('chthonian', 'spoor') by which Clayton attempts to do justice both to the woman's body and to his relish in its processes. This aspect of Clayton's characterization provides the novel with some extraordinary images: 'By the time of our New York trip, Genevieve and I knew each other a bit too well for her to gulp me up brainlessly, at the mucky bottom of the carnivorous sea, while I at an extremity of invertebrate bliss ran a trembling tentacle around and around the crenelated waxy hole at the center of her rhythmically lifting ear' (176–7). The couple here are hardly even animals, so complete is their regression to submarine oblivion; Clayton is a mollusc and Genevieve is merely a hole. There is a kind of obliteration of subjectivity in these descriptions of sex which is of course at the same time a transformation into a different kind of narrative language where the tropes and devices of historiography are annihilated: 'the act felt like a singularity, a unique trip to the edge of self-obliteration by a woman possessed, her needs and mine fused. In retrospect it seems as though I came not in her mouth so much as in the room, the black space limited by eight unseen corners, my body being the only one present, Genevieve transformed for this interval into pure fierce spirit' (176). In this quotation Clayton retreats from the exasperating intellectual struggle to articulate historical knowledge in a definitive scholarly language, in favour of a figurative language of sex that is ostensibly a refuge from intellectual rigour. Both of these languages are forensic in their attempts to imagine subjectivity, and together they constitute a representation of Clayton's consciousness of himself which is simultaneously a complaint against the limits of its language.

Philip Roth **American Pastoral**

The narrator of Philip Roth's *American Pastoral* (1997) is a novelist rather than a historian, but one who, like Clayton, is self-conscious about his narrative's claims to authenticity and to its necessary textual provisionality.[4] Nathan Zuckerman is prepared to concede that in attempting to recover the history of Seymour Levov he might simply have imagined 'an outright fantastical creature' (76) or a 'dazzling illusion' (35). Roth's narrator is, like Updike's, embroiled in the retrieval of the hidden life of an individual at a particular historical moment, and at the same time anxious about the value of his own textual record: 'Is everyone to go off and lock the door and sit secluded like the lonely writers do, in a soundproof cell, summoning people out of words and then proposing that these word people are closer to the real thing than the real people that we mangle with our ignorance every day?' (35). The status of Zuckerman's text and its authenticity is bound up with questions about the nature of history which are of fundamental importance to *American Pastoral*; Zuckerman concludes provisionally that in writing this kind of narrative 'it's up for grabs, it seems to me, as to whose guess is more rigorous than whose' (77), but it is worth looking closely at the inception of Zuckerman's portrait of Levov because, unlike Clayton's, it is given in significant detail.

Zuckerman's imagination begins to formulate the narrative of

---

[4] All page references are to the Vintage edition.

Levov while he is dancing at a high school reunion to the Johnny Mercer song 'Dream'; he proposes 'This is where it must begin' (88) and, searching imaginatively for a point of origin in Levov's tribulations, he claims 'I dreamed a realistic chronicle' (89). But Zuckerman's narrative of Levov has in fact already begun, and its true origin lies as much in fiction as it does in the real Levov that the novelist knew in high school. Zuckerman and Levov were both avid readers of John R. Tunis's baseball books, and especially *The Kid From Tomkinsville*, a story about a country boy whose dream is to pitch for the Brooklyn Dodgers; the Kid makes it, and as a rookie his pitching helps to pull the team out of a slump when suddenly a freak accident ends his career. But the Kid summons enough determination to forge for himself another place on the team. So close is the association that Zuckerman makes between Levov and the fictional ballplayer that 'I thought of the Swede and the Kid as one' (9). Sports writing is of crucial importance because of its power to elevate sportsmen to the level of myth; through the agency of the mythmaking of sports fiction, Levov is remembered from the very beginning as an imaginary figure: 'through the Swede the neighborhood entered into a fantasy about itself and about the world, the fantasy of sports fans everywhere' (3). Sixty years later Zuckerman sets out to recover this archetypal American hero's true story and to imbue it at every moment with the flavour of authenticity: 'Where was the irrationality in him? . . . Where were the wayward temptations? . . . What did he do for subjectivity? What *was* the Swede's subjectivity?' (20). There are several elements here which are fundamental to Roth's novel: the function of memory; the historical verisimilitude of the imaginative creation; the authenticity of the recovered personal subject; the search for origins and causes; the act of writing and fantasizing and mythmaking; the idea of dreaming, which is itself given in the form of a text by the reference to Johnny Mercer's 'Dream': 'You'll find your share / Of memories there'.[5] These elements occur together at many points in Zuckerman's narrative and they underpin the investigation of the recovery of subjectivity in imaginative prose. The terms and conditions upon which Roth's narrator begins to imagine Levov are important because of the

---

[5] 'Dream, when you're feeling blue / Dream, that's the thing to do / Just watch the smoke rings rise in the air / You'll find your share / Of memories there'.

ways in which they determine the theoretical and cultural parameters of his subsequent exposition. It is also worth noting that Zuckerman rejects Tolstoy's example of being contemptuous of the ordinary (Levov is 'blessed with all the attributes of a monumental ordinariness', (81)), and that he does so partly by allusion to a further text: 'Swede Levov's life, for all I knew, had been most simple and most ordinary and therefore just great, right in the American grain' (31). As part of his democratic American enterprise Zuckerman invokes William Carlos Williams's *In the American Grain* (1925) a volume of essays which includes sketches of figures such as Columbus, Poe and Franklin, but also includes many more minor characters in an attempt to discover the essential qualities of the American character.

American Pastoral begins as an attempt to understand why the novelist Zuckerman became interested in Levov as a promising subject of enquiry in the first place. Zuckerman is fascinated by his own memory of Levov as a high school celebrity. This is because Levov begins as a mythical figure and *American Pastoral* is a novel about mythologies. When he meets Levov in 1995 the novelist comments: 'I kept waiting for him to lay bare something more than this pointed unobjectionableness, but all that rose to the surface was more surface. What he has instead of a being, I thought, is blandness—the guy's radiant with it. He has devised for himself an incognito, and the incognito has become him' (23). Levov's conflation with myth is so complete that a sense of his individuality is erased; Roth's novelist seeks to recover both the true subjectivity of Levov, and at the same time to locate precisely the source of his own childhood beguilement. Zuckerman is deeply self-conscious about this imaginative enterprise, and his authorial self-consciousness is an important aspect of his text, a text fraught with anxieties about misreading and misrepresenting. At the high school reunion, for example, Zuckerman meets Ira Posner and discovers to his surprise that in remembering their childhood together 'what I had missed completely took root in Ira and changed his life' (55). In creating a retrospective narrative of subjectivity the novelist (like Updike's historian Clayton) finds himself re-creating his own; this is inextricable from writing Levov's secret history (as Clayton's is impossible to disentangle from Buchanan's). When he begins to get a glimpse of Levov's real story, Zuckerman is astonished at how completely he has misread his protagonist: 'the revelation of the interior life that was unknown and unknowable, the story that is tragic and awful and impossible to ignore, the ultimate reunion story, and I missed it entirely' (80). The story of Levov, and the story of each of the characters of the novel, is bound up with an anxious self-consciousness concerning the storyteller's responsibility. Levov's story is Zuckerman's too; when the novelist meets Levov by accident at a ball game in New York in 1985, Zuckerman's companion remarks to him, 'I saw just what you looked like as a boy' (17). This is important because it signals one of the consistent themes of the novel, a powerful desire to return to childhood innocence.

That innocence is represented variously in the novel, by ideas of pastoral, by the historical moment that Zuckerman and Levov shared, and by a nostalgia for the figure of Levov which is simultaneously a nostalgia for the novelist's former self. When he remembers Levov playing football in 1943 Zuckerman becomes poignantly conscious of 'how seriously I'd fallen in love with him', and he recalls significantly 'How captivatingly that innocence spoke to my own' (70). Levov comes to signify mythological proportions, not only for Zuckerman, but through him for American self-mythologizing; the broader political implications of Roth's novelist's manner of dreaming move him from *The Kid from Tomkinsville* to another American hero who acquired mythical status: 'But of course. He is our Kennedy' (83).

Zuckerman's narrative is simultaneously Levov's and his own, and it is one which is obsessive in its search for points of origin or key formative moments which determine the progress of history; it is also one which is deeply conscious of its own provisionality because any beginning is revealed subsequently to be only one of a number of possible beginnings. This is also true of Levov's daughter's narrative, the one which violently disrupts all other narratives, personal, political, and pastoral. The innocent kiss on the mouth which Levov gives his daughter Merry, for example, interests the novelist because it might be perceived as transgressive and therefore a point of origin (Marcia, although savagely satirized, returns to this idea at the end of the novel when she argues flippantly that 'without transgression there isn't very much knowledge', (360)). The kiss is offered as a possible explanation for the events which followed, a 'strange parental misstep' in which Levov 'kissed her stammering mouth with the passion that she had been asking him for' (91). Levov is doomed to find for the rest of his life that 'when he went obsessively searching for the origins of their suffering, it was that anomalous moment . . . that he remembered' (92). Ten years later Levov can still focus on 'That foolish kiss' which he still insists was 'innocent' (240). Although there are shades of *Lolita* in the 11-year-old American girl's humorous French (Nabokov's language, or Humbert's, is invoked in the novel's 'precious lighthearted jokester', (90)), neither Levov nor the novelist privilege this 'anomalous moment' over other equally anomalous moments. It is also possible that Merry's aberrant behaviour is the result of the mismatch between her father's Judaism and her mother's Catholicism (386). It is equally possible, they believe, that the eleven-year-old Merry was profoundly affected by witnessing the self-immolation of Buddhist monks on the television news in the early 1960s, 'he struck the match, and a nimbus of ragged flames came roiling out of him' (153). This event, 'a ghastly tv spectacle that had imbedded itself in her impressionable mind' (157), traumatized Merry for weeks, and is interpreted by Levov as the formative moment of his daughter's commitment to the anti-war movement: 'he is sure he has unearthed the reason for what happened' (152). But ultimately there is no single point of explanation for Merry's violence; in the search for origins and causes, for an aetiology of all these narratives, 'People looking to her childhood for some clue about her alleged violent act remained stymied' (171). This observation is quoted from a newspaper report that is cited in the text, and like other key moments in the novel, it defers authority to other forms of textual representation which are simultaneously both messages of explanation and texts which demand our further critical scrutiny. This is true also of *The Kid from Tomkinsville*, Johnny Mercer's 'Dream', the numerous myths of American self-determination which proliferate throughout the novel, and the whole genre of 'pastoral'.

The story of how Merry became the Rimrock Bomber is opaque and enigmatic; it is no more susceptible to misinterpretation than other characters' narratives. Merry's mother Dawn, for example, had been Miss New Jersey in 1949, but 'Dawn couldn't stand people who made that story the whole of her story' (341). There is a curious correlation here between the two roles, the women entrapped by narratives which have a mythology which functions independently of them. Levov complains of the reductiveness of these ways of interpreting a

life when he remarks with dismay that 'A bomb tells the whole fucking story' (340). Dawn repeatedly insists that she only entered the
beauty pageant to win money to send her brother to college, and she
argues 'I never wanted to be Miss America!' (178). But despite her
efforts to convince Levov that she only married him because after the
pageant 'I wanted something that seemed normal' (180), Levov insists
that Dawn 'was nothing like the girl she portrayed as herself in those
tirades', and he draws great comfort from remembering her 'sheer
delight in being herself' at that time (181). One of the novel's remarkable achievements lies in showing that the very idea of 'being herself'
is never really available to Dawn, at least while she is perceived and
represented by the narrative language of others. This is true of all the
characters of *American Pastoral* because the novel repeatedly challenges the possibility of an authentic subjectivity being articulated by
language, even while the novel strives to dramatize its characters'
subjectivity with remarkable energy and verisimilitude.

This is the problem of retrospective narratives that Zuckerman self-
consciously poses himself at the beginning of the novel: how can the
reader adjudicate between Dawn's memory of herself, Levov's reminiscence of the woman he courted, and the role of imagination in
constructing a kaleidoscope of perspectives in the challenge to
account for Levov's catastrophe and Merry's violence? The novel
focuses on Dawn's participation in the Miss America contest in 1949
(won by Miss Arizona), as the defining moment in Dawn's history,
and Levov fleetingly glimpses the significance of this: 'he sometimes
wondered if it wasn't better for her to identify what had happened to
her in 1949, not what had happened to her in 1968, as the problem at
hand' (179). This is true: Dawn's elevation to the status of myth
has determined how she is interpreted by others, but such roles and
functions entail a serious personal cost. At various points (69, 95)
American Pastoral entertains the possibility that Merry's violence is a
response to the success of her parents. Rita Cohen, for example,
claims that Merry despised her mother and was inhibited by her
inability to aspire to Dawn's standards and expectations of her. But
this analysis of Merry's motivation is also provisional, partial, and
unreliable.

Levov too finds his life articulated by references to American myths
which make him larger than life; he begins the novel as a version of

the fictional sports hero *The Kid from Tomkinsville* and he ends the novel in the guise of another mythical figure Johnny Appleseed (based on the real person John Chapman, 1774–1845), leading his daughter home to utopian innocence (420). Johnny Appleseed is only one of a number of myths *American Pastoral* employs to characterize an ideal of American selfhood and nationhood; the novel reveals the origin of that ideal in dreaming and imagining, and it dramatizes that ideal's demise. The end of the novel is crowded with pastoral references, to Appleseed, to the Swiss farms of the Levovs' holiday ('a big fiesta down in the square', (414)), Merry's identification with the settlers and the pioneers (419, 420), the references to Thanksgiving ('the American pastoral par excellence', (402)), and Lou teaching Jessie to eat apple pie at the kitchen table with a glass of milk. The idea of pastoral (itself a literary genre which has mythological origins in the lyrics of romanticized shepherds) floods the culmination of the novel as Levov fantasizes about Merry's return, and his dream is interrupted by the stabbing of his father with a kitchen fork. The evocation of pastoral is associated with the novelist's nostalgic depiction of a pre-1960s American idyll, and with Levov's stubborn insistence on his daughter's innocence. Merry's father consistently believes that 'she is being used by radical thugs, she is innocent' (152), that her interest in science did not contribute to her bomb-making but 'was totally innocent' (149), and that 'No one in his family was going to fall into doubt about Merry's absolute innocence, not so long as he was alive' (365). The wilfulness of Levov's faith in innocence is shared by Roth's narrator because it is an expression of a central American theme, the idea of a tragic departure from a state of grace. Nor is this novel the first time that Roth has written at length on the subject of pastoral. In *The Counterlife* (1986) Zuckerman recalls watching on television a piece of microphotography that depicted 'the whole sexual act leading to conception, from the point of view of the innards of the woman', and he describes this scene as 'The pastoral landscape par excellence': 'According to one school, it's where the pastoral genre that you speak of begins, those irrepressible yearnings by people beyond simplicity to be taken off to the perfectly safe, charmingly simple and satisfying environment that is desire's homeland. How moving and pathetic these pastorals are that cannot admit contradiction or conflict!' (368). Pastoral then is the generic language of innocence and prelapsarian grace, and it has a uniquely American inflection that is not simply about a particular historical moment but which claims the United States as 'desire's homeland'. *American Pastoral* writes itself, or is written into, this narrative of America as the Promised Land, and the novel's artistic success lies partly in its self-reflexive acknowledge-ment of the infinitely textual nature of that enterprise. William Carlos Williams's 'Pastoral', from which this chapter's epigraph is taken, concludes with the belief that 'No one / will believe this / of vast import to the nation', and his poem, like Roth's novel, is attentive to the ways in which the individual is shaped by the larger narratives of their culture and their subjectivity strongly influenced, if not determined, by those narratives' institutionalization.

One of the things that makes *American Pastoral* remarkable is the self-consciousness with which it treats American dreaming as a fic-tional narrative and shows the rupture in Levov's fortunes to be part of the collapse of an American meta-narrative. Throughout the novel there is a profound acknowledgement of the extent to which Ameri-can social and political aspiration is itself a function of a particular narrative language. For example, Merry's emergence from a child-hood interest in Audrey Hepburn into an awkward adolescent's polit-ical consciousness is described as being 'like some innocent in a fairy story who has been tricked into drinking the noxious potion' (99–100). This figuring of Merry's life as a fairy story is entirely consonant with Levov's conception of his own life, which was to have been, 'a simple story tangibly unfolding, a deeply unagitating story . . . or so it had all seemed to him *once upon a time*, back when the union of beauti-ful mother and strong father and bright bubbly child rivalled the trinity of the three bears' (413). The italicized phrase calculatingly draws attention to the pressures of storytelling and its association with childhood innocence. Such idealized fantasies have political connotations which help sustain the domestic narrative; Levov con-templates the security of the words First Fidelity Bank, 'the most reassuring words in the English language' (236) and laments their decline into nothing more than 'A sign in a fairy tale' (237). The lawyer who advises Levov on his daughter's legal position is not interested in dreamy narratives but sees her predicament without illusion, 'This man did not deal in fairy tales' (339). Levov's narrative is doomed because it seeks to recover an innocence that has gone forever, and his attempt to retrieve his daughter can only be 'an absurd fairy-tale hope' (141–2).

Like Updike's protagonist, Levov has an experience of a woman's body which is very important to his narrative in his attempt to recover his daughter. Levov is blackmailed by Rita Cohen who promises to take him to his daughter, but first she meets him in a hotel room in New York and taunts him sexually: 'She edged her two hands down onto her pubic hair, "Look at it", she told him and, by rolling the labia lips outward with her fingers, exposed to him the membranous tissue veined and mottled and waxy with the moist tulip sheen of flayed flesh' (145). Rita's display of her body is her attempt to wake Levov from his dream life and make him confront what she terms 'reality'. This scene in Zuckerman's text is given in terms of an opposition between two kinds of language, a male narrative language of order and control, and a female language of the body which, to Levov/Zuckerman is anarchic and fantastically different. Levov is shocked by Rita because 'He was prepared for the verbal violence . . . he had not counted on being assailed by something *other* than the verbal violence' (144). Rita's body, and all its intimate material details ('the fecund smell released from within', (146)), is offered by her as the key to what happened to Levov's daughter: ' "It's a jungle down there", she said. "Nothing in its place. Nothing on the left side like anything on the right side . . . Don't you see what this has to do with what happened?" ' (145). To Levov, Rita's behaviour and the message she tries to offer him are utterly incomprehensible: 'All his thinking seemed to be taking place in a foreign language' (147), and the incident ends with his complete defeat; Rita takes his ten thousand dollars and leaves him with nothing; Levov flees the room when Rita offers herself as a brutally parodic imitation of the body of his daughter: 'He'd bolted not from the childlike cruelty and meanness, not even from the vicious provocation, but from something that he could no longer name. Faced with something he could not name, he had done everything wrong' (147). What Rita offers is something that lies outside the parameters of Levov's experience and something beyond the ability of Zuckerman's language to articulate entirely; this is curious because, of course, the whole episode is still part of Zuckerman's imagined narrative of Levov, or as one reviewer expressed it: 'What Rita represents is brought into question when Merry later says that she did not know her and perhaps Rita is part of Zuckerman's dream, as his knowledge of the details of the story is explained'.[6] In other words, it can be argued that the episode with Rita is perhaps provided exclusively by Zuckerman as part of his attempt to account fully for the narratives of Merry and Levov, which otherwise would be as fraught with gaps and silences as Clayton's narrative of Buchanan. Rita's repeated assertion that her body will 'unlock the mystery' suggests that there is a female language of subjectivity that is closely associated with the body and which neither Levov nor Zuckerman can be completely cognizant of, a form of knowledge which is not language-dependent and which is associated by them with abandon, anarchy, terror, and horror. In this context it is some testimony to Zuckerman's narrative talents that he provides a place for it at all in his imagined account of Levov's ordeal.

E. L. Doctorow **Billy Bathgate**

E. L. Doctorow's *Billy Bathgate* (1989) is a *Bildungsroman* which shares many central characteristics with Updike's novel and Roth's.[7] Clayton and Zuckerman both articulate a nostalgic regret for the crossing of a particular historical rubicon, and Billy's narrative too occupies a watershed moment in the 1930s and dramatizes its own version of a fall from innocence. 'Innocence' is as important a word to Billy's text as it is to Zuckerman's. All three novels are concerned with writing the book of the self and in the ideas of the self being realized in conjunction with historically specific social pressures, and all three narrators look back on themselves at a particular historical moment and construct the tale of how they came to be who they are. This idea of the discourse of subjectivity is handled with great self-consciousness by each of the novels' narrators, artfully and subtly, and is associated with dreaming, with reading and interpretation, and with living in an American culture saturated with representations, and with violent struggle and conflict which marks the transitional historical moment. Each of these male narrators also has a particular interest in the body

---

6 Elizabeth Hardwick, 'Paradise Lost', *New York Review of Books*, 12 June 1997, 14.
7 All page references for *Billy Bathgate* are to Picador edition.

of a woman, or women, which is important to their view of history, desire, and control.

Billy is both a narrator and a juggler and these skills are closely associated. The street urchin of the Bronx, living in hardship but 'a capable boy', first catches the attention of mobster Dutch Shultz while juggling, a theatrical performance which earns him his first real money. Thereafter Billy uses the idea of juggling as a key metaphor, his life becoming a trick of dexterity as he negotiates the various pressures he is subjected to while keeping all the balls in the air. From the outset of his remarkable career, juggling was 'something that marked me' (23) a special ability of sleight of hand in which dexterity is the fundamental attribute. These are qualities, the reader soon will learn, that Billy the juggler shares with Billy the writer; this is not only a matter of sleight of hand but, 'the art of the thing is in creating a flow nevertheless, maintaining the apogee from a kind of rhythm of compensating throws, and it is a trick of such consummate discipline that the better it is done the easier and less remarkable it looks to the uninitiated' (25). This association between juggling, magic, and the dextrous illusions of creating a retrospective narrative of the self is made again and again in *Billy Bathgate*. Billy is conscious of an analogy between the writing practices of newspapermen and the illusions of his own text: 'You could only guess about reporters, they never wrote about themselves, they were just these bodiless words of witness composing for you the sights you would see and the opinions you would have without giving themselves away, like magicians whose tricks were words' (212). Telling his story is a way for Billy to sustain a sense of identity; the trajectory of his career is dependent for its teleology upon his skill as a narrator to keep the story moving along at a pace which masks the illusions of its flashbacks and other literary sleights of hand. Again, Billy's is a self-conscious narrative in this respect; this is made clear by his comment at the end of Bo Weinberg's death song: 'The song was clearly over, as in juggling when the ball you throw up finds the moment to come down, hesitates as if it might not, and then drops at the same speed of that celestial light. And life is no longer good but just what you happen to be holding' (160). Storytelling, whether Bo's or Billy's, becomes an interlude prior to death, a way to conjure an illusory sense of being which displaces and defers the consciousness of death. As one critic argues,

'Bo's death seems to bring him to the verge of this true understanding: that the world is inescapably fictional'.[8] Billy is also closely associated with fictional characters; where Zuckerman thinks of his protagonist as *The Kid from Tomkinsville*, Billy is christened 'Mandrake' after the magician in the 'New York American' comics. In this way, identity becomes a function of narrative language, of the resources available to the storyteller. It is worth noting, for example, that the gangster's real name is not used by newspapermen because 'Dutch Shultz is a name that fits in the headline' (203). Identity is a function of the vicissitudes of narrative and linguistic form, and Billy is conscious of himself as a fictional character throughout the course of his self-created narrative. Billy acknowledges the analogy between writing and living when he remembers the death of Bo Weinberg: 'every moment that we had lived since that night was my hallucination, a moment's reprieve from the great heaving sea lunging up from itself to gulp at the night's prey' (234). Billy's life begins as a dream and is conducted as a temporary effect of the hallucinatory qualities of narrative.

This kind of magic transformation of a character's identity through the agency of fiction is part of the project of American dreaming; Gatsby, for example, writes his projected image of himself on the inside cover of *Hopalong Cassidy*.[9] Billy soon learns that he has skills of dissembling which he shares with his mentors Berman and Shultz, both of whom are portrayed as magicians in their own way. Berman is a magician of hidden numerical shapes and patterns; he goes by the name 'Abbadabba'. The identity of Shultz is masked by his public image; he advises Billy, 'if you don't run and you don't hide and you are on the lam then you are there all the time, you are simply controlling people's ability to see you and that is a very potent magic' (48). What Billy learns in 'that moment in the history of the Bronx' (25) is a talent for understanding the value of performance in American

---

[8] C. Morris, *Models of Misrepresentation: On the Fiction of E. L. Doctorow* (Jackson: University Press of Mississippi, 1991).

[9] The analogy with Fitzgerald's novel was made in a different way by one contemporary reviewer who argued that 'Nick, already an adult, meets a Gatsby who has covered up his criminal past. Billy, a streetwise boy but still a boy, meets Dutch Shultz at the height of his lawlessness. Yet Billy is in some way less dazzled than Nick by the glamour of the man beyond rules'. (Garry Wills, 'Juggler's Code', *New York Review of Books*, 2 Mar. 1989, 3).

commercial life. Billy learns ideas about disguise, control, and transformation which are central to his self-determination as one of the
founding fathers of American culture; these ideas are also fundamental to his ability to write the retrospective narrative of success
which is the novel *Billy Bathgate*.

Doctorow's novel is composed of competing systems of signification or narrative languages which Billy must negotiate if he is to succeed Dutch Shultz; it is his ability to interpret correctly which gives
Billy his prescience and which enables him to write so deftly. In the
hotel room in Onondaga, for example, Billy becomes aware of
'another presence which was making itself known' and he has a
moment of recognition of 'certain expectations of the society that
were trying to represent themselves to me' (118). Billy realizes at an
early stage that Berman's obsession with numbers is 'a system of
understanding' (60) and his audacity and confidence are founded on
his talent for shrewd and discriminating observation. Billy is
instructed from the outset 'to become the person who would always
be watching and always be listening' (4). Following the barber-shop
murder, for example, Billy scans the papers searching for 'the personal
message for me in this news' (104) and he is able to stay ahead of the
pressures that might overwhelm him because 'I knew more than what
was going on, I knew what was going to happen next' (107). This must
always be true, because he is writing his account of events in
retrospect.

Billy is the coming man, the man of the future, and he recognizes it
as his destiny to be the successor to Dutch Shultz. Although he characterizes himself as merely 'a simple boy trying to get ahead and make
something of himself' (61), Billy's emergence at a precise historical
moment facilitates his success; it is clear that he writes himself into a
particular narrative genre, but also into a particular economic one.
Billy is quick to recognize 'the first representations of the new world
coming' (186) and not only does he see his commercial opportunities
as part of this, but many of the other characters interpret him in the
same way. Berman, for example, comments that 'the times change
and looking at you I see what's in the cards, you're the upcoming
generation and it's possible what is required of you will be different'
(143). Billy has talents and a special opportunity to learn that will
enable him to masquerade as respectable more successfully than

Shultz who understands that ' "that outlaw shit ain't in the economic mainstream" ' (126) but is still old-style enough to be victim to 'the murderous rages of the disordered spirit' (13). As a juggler, Billy has more self-control and a better ability to dissemble; most importantly, he 'could discern Mr Shultz's inarticulate genius and give it language' (187). Billy is the new commercial language of twentieth-century America, and his ascent coincides with Shultz's decline: 'the Dutchman's life with me was his downfall' (281). It is characteristic of the self-consciousness of Billy's text that the novel dramatizes his ascent through a play on words. Shultz's confusion of the words 'progeny' and 'prodigy' adroitly identifies Billy's position: Miss Drew glosses 'prodigy' as 'child genius' (128) and Billy is also the progeny of Shultz in being the natural issue of his criminal career. It is also worth noting that Bo Weinberg tells Billy 'He's obsolete kid' (156) and that Billy himself uses precisely this word at the moment of Shultz's death, describing the gangster's style of urinating as 'terribly obsolete' (301). In these ways the education of Billy is linguistic as much as it is economic, and he becomes a master writer by the end of his text as much as he becomes a father and the inheritor of Shultz's money.

Like Clayton and Levov, Billy Bathgate also has an experience of a woman's body that is crucial to his education; he drives Drew Preston to Saratoga, and en route they take a detour into the woods:

she was covered with this invisible slime, her body was slimed as mine was, and we lay in this mud and I punched into her and held her blond head back in the mud and pumped slime up her and we lay there rutting in this foul fen . . . and I found the primeval voice in her, like a death rattle, a shrill sexless bark, over and over again as I jammed into her . . . as if time had turned in her and she had passed back into infancy and reverted through birth into nothingness. (217)

As with some of Clayton's sexual encounters, this is both a form of regression and a recourse to a different kind of language from that which characterizes most of the narrative, one of flight from the adult language of conjuring a retrospective myth of the self. It is similarly presented as annihilation and oblivion, as an animalistic physicality that is both terrifying and liberating. The woman again is an orifice, she seems to disappear altogether in Billy's ecstasy, merely the agent of his development; the experience of the woman's body is for Billy, as for Clayton and Levov, about absence and loss: 'you can't remember sex. You can remember the fact of it, and recall the setting, and even the details, but the sex of the sex cannot be remembered, the substantive truth of it, it is by nature self-erasing' (226). This 'splurge of being' as he describes it, is an escape from the complexities of his linguistic juggling, and as with the texts of Clayton and Zuckerman, Billy valorizes it as having special qualities of authenticity: 'the quickest thinking is the thinking of the body, and the body thinks surely, errorlessly, because it is not soaked in character as the brain is' (230). Sex is the point at which the juggling which constitutes Billy's entire narrative comes closest to collapse: 'my hand was shaking, I, the juggler extraordinaire' (231). The woman's body is the means to another kind of knowledge and another kind of language, but one which threatens to overthrow the creative artistry of male narrators who bring their subjects too close to it.

Comparing Doctorow's novel with Toni Morrison's *Song of Solomon* (1977) in terms of how 'Milkman's identity is not his own but is bound up with the cultural system of which he has just become an adult member', Jay Clayton argues that in Doctorow's novel 'Billy shows himself to be equally aware of the intricate ways his identity has been constructed by tradition, even hackneyed stories: internationalised stories of orphanhood, criminality, romance, and redemption that structured his experiences as he had them and that join seamlessly in the autobiographical fabric he weaves'.[10] In other words Billy is self-consciously alert to the ways that his apparently spontaneous or 'natural' story has already been written for him by the genres of narrative that are available, and his subjectivity is the product of a synthesis of these narratives even as he appears to write something personal, individual. Billy is aware of this and strives to take advantage of the opportunities that it affords. Like Clayton and Zuckerman, Billy is embroiled in a struggle with existing languages of the self which write his narrative for him. In writing about the bodies of women, the three male narrators attempt to, or purport to, escape the anxieties of subjectivity this precipitates; the language with which they do so reveals such an escape to be merely a recourse to a different

---

[10] J. Clayton, *The Pleasures of Babel: Contemporary American Literature and Theory* (Oxford: Oxford University Press, 1993), 34, 51.

language, and one which is equally institutionalized in the genres of writing.

Louise Erdrich **Tales of Burning Love**

The novel *Tales of Burning Love* (1996) by Louise Erdrich has little of the self-consciousness about writing which characterizes the novels of Doctorow, Roth, and Updike, partly because its narratives are oral and perhaps also because they are given by women rather than men.[11] The narrative structure of Erdrich's novel is reasonably clear: Jack Mauser has been married five times to different women; four of Jack's ex-wives become stranded in his truck in a ferocious snowstorm in North Dakota one night in January. Believing him to be dead, the women tell stories of their relationships with Jack in order to stay awake and to survive the terrible cold which threatens to kill them. The women, Eleanor, Dot, Candice, and Marlis, take turns to give accounts of how they became involved with Jack, how their romance and marriage was conducted, and how the marriage ended. Sharing these stories, the tales of burning love, helps them to survive the night. Meanwhile, Jack has in fact cheated death and sets out in the same storm to rescue his son John, the only child he has fathered by any of his wives. The novel is an investigation of the enigmatic nature of love, and especially how love is capable of transforming the subjectivity of those who are possessed by it: 'They had all at one time been married to the same man. Each woman had seen the others as usurpers and killers, as thieves, as sluts driven by the same lusts that she treasured as sublime in her own heart, but despised emanating from any other source' (199). It is Eleanor who points out to the other women that their perceptions of Jack are likely to be very different, that their sense of him will be dependent on the different romances and relationships that they each had with him at different points in his life: ' "Jack probably showed a separate facet of himself to each one of us. Or we brought it out in him. Made him as different as we are different from one another. In fact, it isn't entirely far-fetched to say that we each married a different man" ' (200).

---

[11] All page references are to the Flamingo edition.

This question of the transformation of subjectivity, and of the relativity of perceptions of it, is important to Erdrich's novel, much of which is devoted to dramatizing sudden and irrevocable changes in identity brought about by love. It is worth proposing, provisionally, that the experience of love in this novel functions as something of a parallel to the experiences of sex in the novels of this chapter's male narrators, it radically shifts the individual's sense of their identity and simultaneously calls up a fresh narrative language by which to do justice to it. But where do these languages originate?

The narratives of all of the women of Erdrich's novel are marked by death or by near-death experiences, by some form of serious loss, as if their initial involvement with Jack is accompanied by the sloughing away of a subjectivity they have outgrown, and in each case Jack is the catalyst for a radically altered sense of identity. The proximity of death in their meetings with Jack is literal, and figuratively it represents the end of a subjectivity which their love for Jack has rendered redundant. The symbolic death also facilitates a rebirth into a subjectivity which is in itself a form of self-fulfilment. This pattern of death and rebirth has its structural parallel in the novel itself, in which the women save themselves from death by sharing their stories about Jack, while Jack himself miraculously escapes death and is reborn with a sense of paternal responsibility.

Dot's relationship with Jack, for example, takes place in the absence of her husband Gerry Nanapush who is serving two life sentences in prison. Dot is Jack's fifth and current wife, but her desire for him is a function of the loss of Gerry: 'I just want the chance to hold someone until I can hold Gerry again' (91). As Dot describes it 'our first real date' is the incident in which Jack fights with Caryl Moon, a violent and cathartic encounter involving the near-death of Dot when, in her compact car, she tries to run Moon's Mack truck off the road. Dot risks death, and her reward is Jack. Like all of the women, Dot is struck by the irrationality of her involvement with Jack: ' "If you try to analyse this or anything it could drive you crazy" ' (96). It is Eleanor who explains that the origin of Dot's relationship with Jack was about 'Abandonment. Being left. Loss' (96). Dot knows about none of Jack's former wives when she marries him, but in driving the women out into the winter wilderness in Jack's truck, she is the catalyst who brings the others together.

The relationship between Candice and Jack also defies rational explanation, it is, she explains, 'nothing that I could name or that truly had a rational basis' (280), and it is also associated with death because she meets Jack just as he is about to shoot his dog. Candice intervenes and saves the dog's life, but her relationship with Jack is doubly marked by death when she accompanies him on a hunting trip and he kills a deer. The death of the dog too on the same day signifies the end of their relationship because their attitude to it also served as a barometer of their feelings for each other: '"when my dog's cold eye opened, blinked wide and fixed me in a flat beam of understanding, I saw deeper than the moment. Wider than the street. I saw farther than my marriage, straight to its end, into the heart of helpless things"' (295). The moment of death and the mystery of desire become synonymous here, as elsewhere in women's relationships with Jack, and an inexplicable attraction turns to an equally inexplicable antagonism. But in the course of her involvement with Jack, Candice's subjectivity is crucially altered and she subsequently becomes the lover of one of Jack's ex-wives, Marlis. In turn, Marlis meets Jack when she nearly dies from an electric shock: 'He is the guy who saves me' (300), and Jack can truthfully claim 'You would have died if I hadn't done something' (301). The irrationality of Marlis's desire for Jack often takes violently destructive forms of expression, she becomes obsessive (315) and her desire is closely associated with revenge, money, and control. Marlis's love is intensely adolescent, a function of ersatz ideas about love affairs she has watched on television ('"pretend we're insane about each other"', (311)) and even her changing sense of identity has a bogus quality in contrast to the other women: '"I am entirely a new person and Jack has paid for the works. The look I am aiming for is a combination of Thelma and Louise"' (313). Clearly, Marlis's identity is strongly influenced by media representations, and the language of her subjectivity is derived from the clichés of romance in ways that are easy to recognize.

Marlis's desire is powerful, and sometimes she is powerfully antagonisic to Jack; in their romance she soon becomes 'this grasping menace he has to appease' (310), and her feelings are symptomatic of unresolved feelings for her father by which Jack becomes 'Dad' and, equally self-deluding, 'I am his goddess' (304). Marlis describes herself as 'manic depressive' (332), and she says to the other women in the truck ' "You don't know the first thing about me. I live outside what you know" ' (202), but it seems equally true that Marlis's impulses are beyond her own comprehension until after the birth of her son and the guiding influence of Candice. Marlis describes herself as ' "a survivor" ' (202), thus connecting the battle against death in the truck with the violent tribulations of her relationship with Jack, which she also survives even to the extent of using him for sex after their marriage is over and she is living with Candice. But for Marlis the antagonism of love and its violent incidents and episodes does not dissipate; even her partner Candice describes Marlis as 'a pathetic *nutcase*' (199).

It is important to note how closely Eleanor's tale about Jack is bound up with her mother Anna's, even to the extent that they might have both been his lover. Anna saves Jack's life by using her body heat to prevent him from dying of hypothermia, and saving Jack's life suddenly causes a dramatic change in her own fortunes as she is immediately abandoned by her husband and the life of security and comfort she had built with him. Here again love is accompanied by loss, suffering, salvation, and redemption. Anna also undergoes a symbolic death and rebirth: Eleanor describes her as ' "coming back to life. . . . By saving Jack my mother erased the past. She was herself again, her original self" ' (224), and although Anna suffers a desperate decline in her life, she nevertheless enters a 'state of grace' (228). Eleanor's subsequent involvement with Jack also begins with an act of violence (231) which initiates a cathartic shift in her character: 'It was as though I were another person suddenly, as though I inhabited my old skin but was bursting out of my personality with surprising power' (232). The radical shift of subjectivity is a re-enactment of her mother's and a parallel to that of all of Jack's wives. Anna's story also holds the key to the idea of falling in *Tales of Burning Love*; Anna was a Montana barrel rider who later became 'the surviving half of a blindfold trapeze act' (210) and her thoughts on falling (literal, figurative) are important to all the women's stories and are again closely associated with death when her trapeze partner falls to his death during their act at the moment of kissing. Lawrence Schlick, Eleanor's father, falls in love with Anna at the hospital; the novel makes the connection explicit, falling in love is a kind of death which can lead to the rebirth of a new subjectivity and a new life of self-fulfilment. This is a process of violent and painful struggle: Anna's life is transformed by her husband's abandonment, she falls again, this time in terms of her social status, but through her suffering she discovers a new conception of herself, and eventually Lawrence returns.

In *Tales of Burning Love* death is postponed by storytelling (as for Bo Weinberg singing 'Bye bye blackbird' as the liquid hardens in his concrete overshoes), and the subject of the women's stories is Jack Mauser. Jack's narrative is also characterized by the proximity of death and a symbolic rebirth; after he escapes the fire he realizes that, 'He could vanish, and he knew just where, he'd always fantasized it anyway' (180). While his ex-wives attend what they believe to be his funeral, Jack has the opportunity to disappear north to Winnipeg, but he decides to stay in Fargo and face the consequences, and he stays because of his son and his mother. Jack's symbolic rebirth is given in terms of the birth of his son: 'He was sleeping like a newborn, it occurred to him. The way Marlis's baby must have slept at first. . . . He wondered if women felt this way in labour, if Marlis had, bearing his son' (179). The shift in Jack's subjectivity is brought about by his escape from death and the subsequent birth of a sense of paternal responsibility and love. But equally important is the visitation of the spirit of Jack's mother in the form of an owl: 'An owl preens its young with the finest touch of a beak sharp as a razor and strong enough to open cans. Her touch was like that, so tender, of stanched power. . . . She had periods of catatonia in which, it was told to him later, she re-experienced the loss of her parents as a child' (184–5). The visitation of this owl, and its symbolic associations with death and desire, recalls the owl that visited Eleanor's father at a particular moment in his relationship with Anna. Lawrence's mortuary business survives while the rest of his empire collapses, and when he is preparing the dead he is watched over by an owl which he has not seen. Lawrence's familiarity with the postures of death 'intensified his lover's yearning' (252), but he still harbours a jealousy for Jack Mauser for which he has no rational evidence, 'only the cry of the owl to go on' (253). Lawrence returns early from Minneapolis on the chance of catching his wife with Jack and he sits up all night accompanied by the unseen presence of the nocturnal bird of prey and eventually greets his wife in the morning: 'Bitterness. Tender lust. The softest feathers brushed his throat' (256). The owl again signifies love and violent death,

Lawrence's jealousy finally absolved, the shift in his subjectivity represented by the visitation of the owl which reminds him of his vulnerability. When Anna dies Lawrence climbs into the mortuary oven with her body and disappears in 'a thick roar of consuming fire' (435).

All of the novel's characters are between life and death in a state synonymous with desire and each of them struggle with the challenges to subjectivity that love brings. But Jack's subjectivity is also somewhere between native American and northern European, his cultural heritage a combination of Ojibwa and German, and he shifts between them not properly understanding his liminal status and not fully understanding himself: 'Sometimes Ojibwa words snared his tongue. Sometimes German' (102). Jack is displaced from his native culture, and Eleanor is right to characterize him as a painting by Magritte with a sky full of holes. This idea of gaps and blank spaces is seen best in Jack's attitude to land: 'The Ojibwa part of him was so buried it didn't know what it saw looking at the dirt or sky or into a human face. . . . Since the Ojibwa part of Jack was inaccessible he was a German with a trapdoor to an inner life still hidden to him' (152–3). Again this idea of being between two states, caught in a double sense of identity, is characteristic of the land in a wider sense because of the particular location of Fargo, North Dakota: 'there is a flavor to it of the West more than the Midwest. This is where the regions meet, where the tallgrass once shaded into mixed-grass prairie and from there the short-grass plains' (164–5). Not only is Jack at the border of Ojibwa and European cultural legacies that constitute his particular form of Americanism, he is between the West and the Midwest, and also on the border between the United States and Canada; it is not only Fargo which could be described as 'a cautious amalgam' (165).

Jack keeps his native American Indian ancestry a secret from everyone 'Even his own wives' (151) but in doing so he remains hidden from himself. This lack of self-knowledge about his identity is an important characteristic of his relationship with his first wife June Morrisey whose absence haunts every subsequent marriage. In the interval of his apparent death, Jack has an important recognition: 'Had she cursed him to die this way because he hadn't even told her his real name?' (161). The legacy of June's death is significant, 'he'd stayed married to a ghost' (381) and his uxorious behaviour is a symptom of a compulsion to repeat, even to the point of re-marrying all of his previous wives (106). This repetition is a form of imprisonment, a kind of entrapment which is cleverly dramatized by the death of June, a death which frames the whole narrative of *Tales of Burning Love*. The novel begins and ends with the story of her death by freezing when Jack failed to save her life; it is, as the novel punningly expresses it, the 'Freeze frame' (106). This quotation has multiple references, not least to the fact that Jack's subsequent wives shape tales about him in order to save themselves from freezing, and it is partly their tale telling that redeems him. The 'cautious amalgam' which is Jack's subjectivity undergoes a transformation on the night of the storm, one in which 'Bits and pieces of understanding he had carefully collected and hidden from himself were magically assembling' (380), and he finds by the end of the storytelling that it was 'as though his whole life had come together without his knowing it' (404). It is worth noting that this magical integration of Jack's sense of himself is indebted directly to the women in his life 'all together like that, talking through the night' (404) and also to the miraculous appearance of June: 'He followed her meekly. She was bringing him home' (385). The man's salvation is dependent on the women's storytelling about him, as if his identity and history were functions of their narrative language.

The religious language here and elsewhere in Jack's narrative, where he becomes 'like a petitioner wearing down the stone steps of a cathedral' (109) and where later he 'began to climb like a petitioner, like a man wearing away the stone steps of a cathedral' (451), corresponds with the language of Eleanor's love for Jack, which is privileged above that of his other wives because of its association with a spiritual quest for divine love. Eleanor is determined to 'discipline herself' and to devote her time to the study of 'saintly hungers' (36), and her determination to rid herself of selfishness and to live a life of self-abnegation is a form of Christian asceticism learned from her mother's devotion to society's outcasts (253). Eleanor has a special affinity with Jack in their mutual recognition of how their history of romantic relationships has the power to teach them something important about subjectivity and desire. Just as Jack humorously imagines remarrying each of his previous wives, Eleanor jokes about spending one night with each of her previous lovers (33); she comments that 'I'd be someone else entirely if I could go back' (33) and when she is finally reunited with Jack she finds him to be 'More himself. . . . Whatever that means' (449). These words are written in Eleanor's notebook, a spiritual diary which the text of the novel quotes in italics and which forms a written counterpoint to the predominantly oral mode of the novel. This written version of Eleanor's subjectivity is private, not shared like the oral narratives, and it provides the reader with a double perspective on her character. This too marks her characterization as exceptional among the women of the novel; Eleanor's spiritual diary gives the depiction of her changing subjectivity a self-reflexive and a written quality that the others do not have.

The predominance of death in the novel is a prophetic adumbration of the real death which will bring the characters to God's love, and Eleanor is granted a vision of this when she meets Leopolda the Catholic nun on the night of the storm. Leopolda anticipates Jack's wives' tales and gives their desire a spiritual turn when she tells Eleanor 'My prayer is a tale of burning love' (53). Eleanor's vision of Leopolda parallels Jack's meeting with June, and is at the centre of the novel's depiction of subjectivity and desire. The resurrected nun tells Eleanor that mortal love of the kind that the novel investigates is a form of suffering which mimics in diminished form the suffering of Christ on the cross, and that, 'We are held upon the cross by our own desires' (372). Romantic love is a pale shadow of the divine love which Eleanor struggles towards and her desire is a mark of her suffering and her Christian vocation, it is ' "The stigma, the blessing" ' (372). Human desire, the central aspect of subjectivity which the novel examines, must be understood as a mark of Christian suffering, as a deferral until the moment of the revelation of divine love after death. This Christian love cannot be found in a man, but all human life is a struggle and a quest towards it: ' "It is a love that is no other thing than pure salvation, and by it, Christ's balancing trick was inspired and foretold" ' (370). This balancing trick is given an ingenious mortal reprise at the end of the novel when everyone's life has been saved. By way of another biblical reference, to Jacob's ladder (by which angels ascend to heaven) Eleanor and Jack make love on the stairway in a sexual balancing trick of their own as they ascend the steps towards heaven. In a final scene loaded with Christian imagery, the novel combines sexual love with divine supplication: 'Then, he suddenly unbuckled his jeans and pushed into her, hard, on his knees, and began to climb like a petitioner, like a man wearing away the stone steps of a cathedral, one step at a time' (451). The body and the spirit are combined here in a way that gives special significance to this act of love because of its divine connotations.

It is notable that sex and death are often closely associated in these novels; in the texts by men the woman's body is antithetical to their self-conscious linguistic games, a material experience which provides a temporary respite from the anxieties of imagining subjectivity. The male narrators offer the woman's body as the place where they are momentarily free from the pressures of dissembling a myth of themselves. These novels are each forms of romance, and romantic novels are particularly appropriate for the investigation of subjectivity; sexual desire disrupts the male language of subjectivity in these novels and results in language's temporary collapse. For each of these writers the vicissitudes of a language-dependent subjectivity are temporarily assuaged by recourse to a language of the body which is offered by them as a radical alternative. In *Tales of Burning Love*, however, although sex and death are still associated, they are transformative and liberating in ways that point to the language of God.

Conclusion

The drive to try to put everything in the covers of a single book is perhaps a uniquely American form of enterprise with a specifically American history, a quintessentially American syntax, a desire to include and account for everything in a single leap of the imagination, part of that project to constitute a taxonomy of the United States, to assess and evaluate at a particular historical moment what the United States now comprises and how far it has come. This has its antecedents in Thomas Jefferson's *Notes on the State of Virginia* (1785), and it is a tradition that is seen in texts such as *Moby Dick*, 'Song of Myself', *U.S.A.*, and 'Paterson'.

Although in a culture as diverse as the United States' there are always texts that can be produced as evidence to confound generalizations that might be made about it, it is still possible to consider many different novels in terms of how they conduct a dramatic negotiation between the individual and various forms of social organization, between who one is and who society wants one to be. Individuals still struggle for autonomy, freedom, and personal fulfilment, and many novels articulate the ways in which that drive is enabled or inhibited by the particular cultures and histories of the United States. Novelists still investigate how identities are shaped by the terms of the interface between personal liberty and social responsibility and commitment. Also, in almost every novel here, the course of the protagonist is marked by the influence of economics. The American market place is a crucial factor in shaping, even determining, the form of American social life and the progress of the individual citizen. The free-market economy and consumer culture are key factors in the kinds of liberty that American individuals are permitted, irrespective of their gender or ethnicity. Economics both enables and inhibits American freedom, and it is an abiding feature of the lives of Americans.

It is worth noting too that for a culture where religion is, at the very least, historically important, where a high proportion of its citizens profess to believing in God and where the national currency bears the words 'In God We Trust', American fiction seems remarkably secular. There is a strong tendency towards epiphany in the short fiction of Hannah, Carver, and Alexie, but this is more a function of their narrative form; their stories often reach towards moments of revelation, and although they might occasionally deploy the language of religious awe, their stories are not about faith or spiritualism or divine conviction and doubt. Even Carver's 'Cathedral' is only tentative in its gesture towards Christian belief. Pynchon's fiction is often underpinned by an obsession with 'the Word' which is indicative of his Puritan legacy, but his fictions of omnipotent guidance are not ones of religious conviction. With the exception perhaps of *Tales of Burning Love*, there are few contemporary novels with a wholly didactic religious purpose.

Perhaps the influence of religious belief is felt in different (secular) ways. It is remarkable how often the characters of these novels dramatize a symbolic death and rebirth, a sloughing away of the old in favour of a new and revivifying sense of identity. Although this is now something of a cliche, it is nevertheless a trope that occurs in many novels that are ostensibly very different from one another; it is an important characteristic of *Tales of Burning Love* (where everyone assumes that Jack Mauser has died in a fire); *The Shipping News* (where Jack Buggit does actually die, only to be miraculously brought back to life); in *The Sportswriter* (where a landslide enables one character who is presumed dead to abandon his whole life and move away to another state to start again under an assumed identity); in *Typical American* (where Ralph's journey across the United States from California to New York effects a transformation in his identity even before he is given his new name); in *A Thousand Acres* (where Ginny moves to Minneapolis and starts again with a radically altered sense of who she is), and in *Ragtime* (where Tateh is dramatically reborn as the displaced European aristocrat Baron Ashkenazy). It is significant that these are all novels that appear under different rubrics in this book. It is a secular 'born-again' phenomenon that has its historical origin in Puritanism as part of the American psyche and is compounded by modern American social mobility and faith in the new. J. Hector St John Crèvecoeur wrote in 1782: 'The American is a new man, who acts upon new principles; he must therefore entertain new ideas, and form new opinions' ('What is an American?', in *Letters from an American Farmer*). The new man and woman is a common motif of the writing of the West, but it is one that occurs in many other spheres of American life and cuts across class, gender, and ethnicity. It is available to everyone in the United States to reinvent themselves. The depiction of some of these characters might be unflinching in showing the cost of that transformation, but rarely does it all go completely and hopelessly wrong. This disastrous outcome is seen in Russell Banks's *Continental Drift* (1985), where Bob Dubois is stabbed to death in the backstreets of Miami at the age of 31, having moved to Florida from New Hampshire in search of a new life, 'This is an American story of the late twentieth century'. *Continental Drift* is an exception that proves the rule; there is still a strong belief in the value of the new, in the freedom of individuals to renovate and refashion their lives and their sense of who they are, one which has its origin in Puritanism and its recent history in modern immigration. These aspirations remain undiminished. Do Americans always look to the future and commit themselves to the dynamic of change? It is as if the very idea of change is central to the United States, and this is particularly true at the end of the twentieth century when innovations in technology are occurring exponentially and will continue to have a significant impact on American social and political culture. Tony Hilfer argues that 'the myth of an American society that allows for relatively unimpeded social mobility gives Americans a sense of identity as fluid and performative'[1] and this might certainly be part of the answer. Adrienne Rich has also provided a way of thinking about this American habit: 'It's a very old American pattern, the pattern of the frontier, the escape from the old identity, the old debts, the old wife to the new name, the "new life". . . . In the desire to be twice-born there is a good deal of self-hatred. Too much of ourselves must be deleted when we erase our personal histories and abruptly dissociate ourselves from who we have been'.[2] The impossible dream of

---

[1] T. Hilfer, *American Fiction since 1940* (London: Longman, 1992), 11.
[2] A. Rich, *Blood, Bread and Poetry* (London: Virago, 1986), 143.

escape from oneself is a form of deliverance that can never be achieved, but it is no less attractive for that. The very title of Gish Jen's novel *Mona in the Promised Land* (1996) suggests the continuity of the ideas of expectation that the United States generates, and also their biblical origins. There are still characters, fictional and otherwise, who are destined to learn the lesson of Hemingway's Jake Barnes: 'You can't get away from yourself by moving from one place to another. There's nothing to that.'

Since the successes of feminism in the 1970s, women have begun to exercise more control over their lives and move towards greater autonomy and independence as they strive for forms of personal fulfilment less dictated to them by old social pressures. Most fiction reflects this, not simply the fiction of women and not simply the novels of this book's 'gender and history' chapter. There has been an attendant crisis of masculinity as men struggle to respond to social changes that fundamentally affect their social roles and their conceptions of themselves as men. The model of manhood that was available to men in the 1970s has changed profoundly, as the narratives of Frank Bascombe and Wade Whitehouse strongly attest. These men have a changed place in the family, at work, and in society; they find themselves lost in a world where women take the initiative, make important decisions, and have aspirations beyond those of their mothers. The men of texts as diverse as *The Bean Trees*, *Northern Lights*, *Typical American*, *American Pastoral*, and the stories of Alexie and Carver, are not able to deal well with children, not especially capable as breadwinners, and not happy and fulfilled as individuals because their status as men has been depleted and diminished. Men are yet to find their feet in this new 'post-feminist' world, and American fiction reflects this. While in some male texts this is presented as a problem, in Mason, Walker, and Phillips, women writers offer a generous analysis of the predicament of men, one which shows how they might learn to free themselves from outmoded roles to their decisive benefit and to the benefit of women too.

There has been an extraordinary amount of writing about history. Recent fiction's interest in the potential of history to offer exciting and challenging avenues for the novel is demonstrable, especially fiction in which an occluded perspective has been recovered and the idea of history as power and privilege is scrutinized. Historiography is not exclusively the province of the academy. Many novels address a historical moment directly: *Libra* and *Oswald's Tale* (Kennedy's assassination); *Dog Soldiers* and *Going After Cacciato* (Vietnam); *The Public Burning* and *The Book of Daniel* (the Rosenbergs), and there are other important texts about history such as Vonnegut's *Slaughterhouse 5* (the bombing of Dresden in the Second World War) and Heller's *Catch 22* (Korean War, Cold War, McCarthy trials). This tendency is not confined to fictional enquiries of the mid-twentieth century, as the following brief list testifies: Russell Banks's *Cloudsplitter*; Alan Gurganus's *Oldest Living Confederate Widow Tells All*, David Bradley's *The Chaneysville Incident*, Thomas Pynchon's *Mason and Dixon*, Gore Vidal's *Lincoln*, Charles Frazier's *Cold Mountain*, T. C. Boyle's *Riven Rock*, and Steve Erikson's *Arc d'X*. Raymond Carver's 'Blackbird Pie' is an extraordinary exposition of the ways in which differences of gender are fundamental to understandings of history and its contents and documents, its 'names and dates, inventions, battles, treaties, alliances, and the like'. This list is a partial rejoinder to the characterization of 'The relentlessly ahistorical consciousness of contemporary American society', if society might be allowed to include its novelists.[3] There is an acute awareness especially of the representational nature of history, of its dependence on the ways of fiction, and this has been used to great advantage by novelists; as the narrator of John Dufresne's *Louisiana Power & Light* (1993) says 'We keep revising our past to keep it consistent with who we think we are' (2). The Warren Commission Report of *Libra* exemplifies for DeLillo's CIA historian the connectedness of fiction and history: 'this was the megaton novel James Joyce would have written if he'd moved to Iowa City and lived to be a hundred' (181). It is seen too in Dutch Shultz's indignant statement about the media in Doctorow's *Billy Bathgate*: 'All the garbage they ever wrote about me is true to people who don't know me' (200). As early as 1973 DeLillo's *Great Jones Street* provided a comic coda in the form of a Professor of Latent History who 'deals with events that almost took place', and who argues that 'Potential events are often more important than real events' (75); it is an idea that acquires some credence in respect of

---

[3] A Cowart, 'Attenuated Postmodernism: Pynchon's *Vineland*', *Critique*, 32: 2, (Winter 1990), 71.

the Cold War's nuclear threat by the time of *Underworld* (1997) where the threat of nuclear war contributes to feelings of national unity and solidarity.

If the twentieth century was 'the American century', then what of the twenty-first? The United States has been examined in this book in terms of the discrete cultures of the continental interior, but the inclusion of a chapter on the American protagonist abroad (omitted due to limitations of space) might have been part of the answer. Such a chapter, investigating how American fictional characters see themselves in the context of international cultures, would have an important antecedent in Henry James, but its arguments would be sensitive to late twentieth-century political circumstances. The reassessment of America's position in the world post-Vietnam, the end of the Cold War, the Iran hostage crisis at the end of the Carter administration, Ronald Reagan's renewed commitment to the arms race in the form of the Strategic Defence Initiative, the Persian Gulf War, the Iran-Contra affair, and American military intervention in Angola, Nicaragua and Grenada: these are just some of the events that have problematized the United States' position as a world leader. One of DeLillo's protagonists feels that he has discovered something authentic in Greece (where East meets West) and he can never return to America: 'I've come to think of Europe as a hard-cover book, America as the paperback version' (*The Names*, (23)), but a thesis about Americans abroad might suggest that America's principal foreign relationship was no longer with Europe but in wider markets that accord with the emergence of Marshall McLuhan's 'global village'. While many novelists feel that there is enough to write about at home, the narrator of T. C. Boyle's *The Tortilla Curtain* is surely prescient when he observes, 'We were all right in America, sure, but it was crazy to think you could detach yourself from the rest of the world, the world of starvation and loss and the steady relentless degradation of the environment'.[4] The arrival of international terrorism suggests that even at home Americans cannot hold to ethnocentric views, and immigration from the South is, as Boyle's novel confirms, an extremely pressing issue in California, Arizona, and Texas.

---

[4] T. C. Boyle, *The Tortilla Curtain* (New York: Viking, 1995), 32.

A thesis about the United States as part of a world culture would have to take account of the global economy, and especially the relentless spread of an American system of free enterprise as American capitalism seeks out fresh international markets. In 1970 Saul Bellow's Mr Sammler noted this trend: 'Of course in a sense the whole world is now U.S. Inescapable. Like a big crow that has snatched our future from the nest' (164) and it could be argued that this is an inevitable consequence of capitalism, that it must always be driven to discover new consumers, and that American values are propagated in the marketing of products such as Coca-Cola, Disney, and Levis, and that a form of imperialism is accomplished by the spread of those values. In an article in *The Times* called 'The Future is Going the American Way', it was argued recently that America 'will come increasingly to set the tone for the rest of the world—not as in bringing McDonald's to distant corners of China, but in driving the pace of global change. This "Americanisation" of the world reflects the increasing power and dominance of the American economy'.[5] Again American novelists have been sensitive to the possibilities of this idea for fiction; both Don DeLillo and Po Bronson suggest that economics is the determining factor in American international relations. In *The Names* (1982) the Greek man Eliades comments that 'it's only in a crisis that Americans see other people', and he makes it clear that such a crisis must involve a commodity, such as oil, in which America has an interest.[6] For Po Bronson's *Bombardiers*, Eastern Europe is the final frontier of American commercial expansion: 'Romania's going to be an American cultural colony in a blink of an eye'.[7] The American novel at the international millennium might also include William Styron, *Set This House on Fire* (1961), Paul Theroux, *The Mosquito Coast* (1981), Joan Didion, *The Last Thing He Wanted* (1996), Norman Mailer, *Ancient Evenings* (1983), Robert Coover, *Pinocchio in Venice* (1991), John Updike, *The Coup* (1978), Robert Stone, *Damascus Gate* (1998), Walter Abish, *How German Is It?* (1980), Alison Lurie, *Foreign Affairs* (1985), William Gaddis, *Carpenter's Gothic* (1985), David Leavitt, *Place I've Never Been* (1990), and Saul Bellow *The Dean's December* (1982). The

[5] Jon Ashworth, 'The Future is Going the American Way', *The Times*, 20 Nov. 1999, 30.

[6] Don DeLillo, *The Names* (New York: Knopf, 1982), 58.

[7] Po Bronson, *Bombardiers* (New York: Random House, 1995), 145.

American protagonist and world culture is a very promising subject in any attempt to work towards understandings of what it means to be American in a late twentieth-century global culture, and even in this electronic age American novelists are still in the vanguard of imagining the future.

Bibliography

Primary works

Abish, Walter

Alphabetical Africa. New York: New Directions, 1974.

Minds Meet. New York: New Directions, 1975.

In the Future Perfect. New York: New Directions, 1977.

How German Is It?. New York: New Directions, 1980.

99: The New Meeting. Providence, RI: Burning Deck, 1990.

Eclipse Fever. New York: Knopf, 1993.

Acker, Cathy

The Adult Life of Toulouse Lautrec by Henri Toulouse Lautrec. New York: T.V.R.T. Press, 1978.

Kathy Goes to Haiti. New York: Rumor Publications, 1978.

Great Expectations. San Francisco: Re/Search Productions, 1982.

Blood and Guts in High School. New York: Grove Press, 1984.

Hello I'm Erica Jong. New York: Contact II, 1984.

Algeria. London: Aloes, 1985.

Don Quixote. New York: Grove Press, 1986.

Empire of the Senseless. New York: Grove Press, 1988.

Literal Madness. New York: Grove Press, 1988.

Young Lust. London: Pandora, 1989.

In Memoriam to Identity. New York: Grove Press, 1990.

Hannibal Lecter My Father. New York: Semiotext(e), 1991.

Portrait of an Eye. New York: Pantheon Books, 1992.

My Mother: Demonology. New York: Pantheon Books, 1993.

Pussycat Fever. San Francisco: Arte Press, 1996.

Pussy, King of the Pirates. New York: Grove Press, 1996.

Bodies of Work. London: Serpent's Tail, 1997.

Eurydice in the Underworld. London: Serpent's Tail, 1997.

Alexie, Sherman

The Business of Fancydancing. Brooklyn, NY: Hanging Loose Press, 1992.

The Lone-Ranger and Tonto Fistfight in Heaven. New York: Atlantic Monthly Press, 1993; London: Vintage, 1997.

Reservation Blues. New York: Atlantic Monthly Press, 1995.

Indian Killer. New York: Atlantic Monthly Press, 1996.

Toughest Indian in the World. New York: Atlantic Monthly Press, 2000.

Allison, Dorothy

Trash. Ithaca, NY: Firebrand, 1988.

Bastard out of Carolina. New York: Dutton, 1992.

Cave Dwellers. New York: Dutton, 1998.

Anaya, Rudolfo

Bless Me, Ultima. Berkeley: Quinto Sol, 1972.

Heart of Aztlan. Berkeley: Quinto Sol, 1972.

Tortuga. Berkeley: Editorial Justa Publications, 1979.

The Silence of the Llano. Berkeley: Tonatiuh — Quinto Sol, 1982.

The Legend of La Llarona. Berkeley: Tonatiuh — Quinto Sol, 1984.

Lord of the Dawn: The Legend of Quetzalcoatl. Albuquerque: University of New Mexico Press, 1987.

Albuquerque. Albuquerque: University of New Mexico Press, 1992.

Zia Summer. New York: Warner Books, 1995.

Jalamanata: A Message from the Desert. New York: Warner Books, 1996.

Angelou, Maya

I Know Why the Caged Bird Sings. New York: Random House, 1969.

Gather Together in my Name. New York: Random House, 1974.

Singin' and Swingin' and Gettin' Merry like Christmas. New York: Random House, 1976.

The Heart of a Woman. New York: Random House, 1981.

All God's Children Need Travelling Shoes. New York: Knopf, 1986.

Antrim, Donald

Elect Mr. Robinson for a Better World. New York: Viking, 1993.

The Hundred Brothers. New York: Crown Publishers, 1997.

The Verificationist. New York: Knopf, 2000.

Askew, Rilla

Strange Business. New York: Viking, 1992.

The Mercy Seat. New York: Viking, 1997.

Auster, Paul

The Art of Hunger. London: Menard Press, 1982.

The Invention of Solitude. Los Angeles: Sun Press, 1982.

Squeeze Play (as Paul Benjamin). London: Alpha-Omega, 1982.

In The Country of Last Things. New York: Viking Penguin, 1987.

The New York Trilogy. London, Faber & Faber, 1987.

Moon Palace. New York: Viking Penguin, 1989.

Ground Work. New York: Viking, 1990.

The Music of Chance. New York: Viking Penguin, 1991.

Leviathan. New York: Viking, 1992.

Mr Vertigo. New York: Viking, 1994.

Timbuktu. New York: Henry Holt, 1999.

Baker, Nicholson

The Mezzanine. New York: Weidenfeld & Nicolson, 1988.

Room Temperature. New York: Grove/Weidenfeld, 1990.

U and I. New York: Random House, 1991.

Vox. New York: Random House, 1992.

The Fermata. New York: Random House, 1994.

The Size of Thoughts. London: Chatto & Windus, 1995.

The Everlasting Story of Nory. New York: Random House, 1998.

Bambara, Toni Cade

The Black Woman: Tales and Stories for Black Folks, An Anthology. New York: New American Library, 1970.

Gorilla, My Love. New York: Random House, 1972.

The Sea Birds Are Still Alive. New York: Random House, 1977.

The Salt Eaters. New York: Random House, 1980.

Raymond's Run. Mankato, Minn.: Creative Education, 1990.

Those Bones Are Not My Child. New York: Pantheon Books, 1999.

Bank, Melissa

The Girls' Guide to Hunting and Fishing. New York: Viking, 1999.

Banks, Russell

Family Life. New York: Avon, 1975.

Searching for Survivors. New York: Fictive Collective, 1975.

The New World Tales. Urbana: University of Illinois Press, 1978.

The Book of Jamaica. Boston: Houghton Mifflin, 1980.

Trailerpark. Boston: Houghton Mifflin, 1981.

The Relation of My Imprisonment. Washington, DC: Sun and Moon Press, 1983.

Continental Drift. New York: Harper & Row, 1985.

Success Stories. New York: Harper & Row, 1986.

Affliction. New York: Harper & Row, 1989; New York: Harper Perennial, 1990.

The Sweet Hereafter. New York: HarperCollins, 1991.

The Rule of the Bone. New York: HarperCollins, 1995.

Cloudsplitter. New York: Harper Flamingo, 1998.

Angel on the Roof: The Stories of Russell Banks. New York: HarperCollins, 2000.

Barth, John

The Floating Opera. New York: Appleton, Century, Crofts, 1956.

The End of the Road. New York: Doubleday, 1958.

The Sot Weed Factor. New York: Doubleday, 1960.

Giles Goat-Boy, or, The Revised New Syllabus. New York: Doubleday, 1966.

Lost in the Funhouse: Fiction for Print, Tape, Live Voice. New York: Doubleday, 1968.

Chimera. New York: Random House, 1972.

LETTERS. New York: Putnam's, 1979.

Todd Andrews to the Author. Northridge, Calif.: Lord John Press, 1979.

Sabbatical: A Romance. New York: Putnam's, 1982.

The Friday Book: Essays and other Nonfiction. New York: Putnam's, 1984.

The Tidewater Tales: A Novel. New York: Putnam's, 1987.

The Last Voyage of Somebody the Sailor. Boston: Little Brown, 1991.

Once Upon a Time: A Floating Opera. Boston: Little Brown, 1994.

Barthelme, Donald

Come Back, Dr Caligari. Boston: Little Brown, 1964.

Snow White. New York: Atheneum, 1967.

Unspeakable Practices, Unnatural Acts. New York: Farrar, Straus, Giroux, 1968.

City Life. New York: Farrar, Straus, Giroux, 1970.

The Slightly Irregular Fire Engine. New York: Farrar, Straus, Giroux, 1971.

Sadness. New York: Farrar, Straus, Giroux, 1972.

Guilty Pleasures. New York: Farrar, Straus, Giroux, 1974.

The Dead Father. New York: Farrar, Straus, Giroux, 1975.

Amateurs. New York: Farrar, Straus, Giroux, 1976.

Great Days. New York: Farrar, Straus, Giroux, 1979.

Presents. Dallas, TX: Pressworks, 1980.

Sixty Stories. New York: Putnam, 1981.

Overnight to Many Distant Cities. New York: Putnam, 1983.

Paradise. New York: Putnam, 1986.

Forty Stories. New York: Putnam, 1987.

The King. New York: Harper & Row, 1990.

Barthelme, Frederick

Rangoon. New York: Winter House, 1970.

War and War. Garden City, NY: Doubleday, 1971.

Moon Deluxe. New York: Simon & Schuster, 1983.

Second Marriage. New York: Simon & Schuster, 1984.

Tracer. New York: Simon & Schuster, 1985.

Chroma: Stories. New York: Simon & Schuster, 1987.

Two Against One. New York: Weidenfeld & Nicolson, 1988.

Natural Selection. New York: Viking, 1990.

The Brothers. New York: Viking, 1993.

Painted Desert. New York: Viking, 1995.

Bob the Gambler. Boston: Houghton Mifflin, 1997.

Trip. New York: Power House Books, 1999.

Double Down: Reflections on Gambling and Loss (with Steven Barthelme). Boston: Houghton Mifflin, 2000.

Bausch, Richard

Real Presence. New York: Dial Press, 1980.

The Last Good Time. Garden City, NY: Dial Press, 1984.

Spirits and Other Stories. New York: London Press/Simon & Schuster, 1987.

Mr Field's Daughter. New York: Linden Press/Simon & Schuster, 1989.

The Fireman's Wife. New York: Linden Press, 1990.

Rebel Powers. Boston: Houghton Mifflin, 1993.

Violence. New York: Vintage Books, 1993.

Rare and Endangered Species. Boston: Houghton Mifflin, 1994.

Good Evening Mr & Mrs America, and All the Ships at Sea. New York: Harpe-Collins, 1996.

Selected Stories of Richard Bausch. New York: Modern Library, 1996.

In the Night Season. New York: Harper Flamingo, 1998.

Take Me Back. Baton Rouge: Louisiana State University Press, 1998.

Someone to Watch over Me. New York: Harper Flamingo, 1999.

A Hole in the Earth. New York: Harcourt, 2000.

Beattie, Ann

Chilly Scenes of Winter. New York: Doubleday, 1976.

Distortions. New York: Doubleday, 1976.

Secrets and Surprises. New York: Random House, 1978.

Falling in Place. New York: Random House, 1980.

The Burning House. New York: Random House, 1982.

Love Always. New York: Random House, 1985.

Spectacles. New York: Ariel Books, 1985.

Where You'll Find Me and Other Stories. New York: Linden Press/Simon & Schuster, 1986.

Alex Katz. New York: B. Abrams, 1987.

Picturing Will. New York: Random House, 1989.

What Was Mine. New York: Random House, 1991.

Another You. New York: Knopf, 1995.

My Life, starring Dara Falcon. New York: Knopf, 1997.

Park City: New and Selected Stories. New York: Knopf, 1998.

Bell, Madison Smartt

The Washington Square Ensemble. New York: Viking Press, 1983.

Waiting for the End of the World. New York: Ticknor & Fields, 1985.

Straight Cut. New York: Ticknor & Fields, 1986.

The Year of Silence. New York: Ticknor & Fields, 1987.

Zero db and Other Stories. New York: Ticknor & Fields, 1987.

Soldier's Joy. New York: Ticknor & Fields, 1989.

Barking Man and Other Stories. New York: Ticknor & Fields, 1990.

Doctor Sleep. San Diego: Harcourt, Brace, Jovanovich, 1991.

Save Me, Joe Louis. New York: Harcourt, Brace & Co., 1993.

All Souls Rising. New York: Pantheon, 1995.

Ten Indians. New York: Pantheon Books, 1996.

Bellow, Saul

Dangling Man. New York: Vanguard, 1944.

The Victim. New York: Vanguard, 1947.

The Adventures of Augie March. New York: Viking, 1953.

Seize the Day and Other Stories. New York: Viking, 1956.

Henderson the Rain King. New York: Viking, 1959.

Herzog. New York: Viking, 1964.

The Last Analysis. New York: Viking, 1965.

Mosby's Memoirs and Other Stories. New York: Viking, 1968.

Mr Sammler's Planet. New York: Viking, 1970.

Humbolt's Gift. New York: Viking, 1976.

To Jerusalem and Back: A Personal Account. New York: Viking, 1976.

The Dean's December. New York: Harper, 1982.

Him with his Foot in his Mouth and Other Stories. New York: Harper, 1984.

More Die of Heartbreak. New York: William Morrow, 1987.

The Bellarosa Connection. New York: Penguin, 1989.

A Theft. New York: Penguin, 1989.

Something to Remember Me By. Three Tales. New York: Penguin, 1991.

It All Adds Up. From the Dim Past to the Uncertain Future: A Nonfiction Collection. New York: Viking, 1994.

Ravelstein. New York: Penguin, 2000.

Bender, Aimee

The Girl in the Flammable Skirt. New York: Doubleday, 1998.
An Invisible Sign of My Own. New York: Doubleday, 2000.

Bender, Karen E.

Parts of Like Normal People. Boston: Houghton Mifflin, 2000.

Benedict, Pinckney

Town Smokes. Princeton, Ontario: Review Press, 1987.
The Wrecking Yard. New York: Doubleday, 1992.
Dogs of God. New York: Doubleday, 1994.

Berendt, John

Midnight in the Garden of Good and Evil: A Savannah Story. New York: Random House, 1994.

Boyle, T. Coraghessan

The Descent of Man. Boston: Little Brown, 1979.
Water Music. Boston: Little Brown, 1981.
Budding Prospects. New York: Viking, 1984.
Greasy Lake and Other Stories. New York: Viking, 1985.
World's End. New York: Viking, 1987.
If the River Was Whiskey. New York: Viking, 1989.
East is East. New York: Viking, 1990.
Collected Stories. London, New York: Granta in Association with Penguin, 1993.
The Road to Wellville. Franklin Center, Pa.: Franklin Library, 1993.
Without A Hero. New York: Viking, 1994.
The Tortilla Curtain. New York: Viking, 1995.
Riven Rock. New York: Viking, 1998.
Friend of the Earth. New York: Viking, 2000.

Bradfield, Scott

The History of Luminous Motion. New York: Knopf, 1989.
The Dream of the Wolf. New York: Knopf, 1990.
What's Wrong with America. New York: St Martin's Press, 1994.
Animal Planet. New York: Picador, 1995.

Bradley, David

South Street. New York: Grossman, 1975.

The Chaneysville Incident. New York: Harper & Row, 1981.

The Lodestar Project. New York: Pocket Books, 1986.

Brautigan, Richard

A Confederate General from Big Sur. New York: Grove, 1964.

Trout Fishing in America. San Francisco: Four Seasons Foundation, 1967.

In Watermelon Sugar. San Francisco: Four Seasons Foundation, 1968.

The Abortion: An Historical Romance 1966. New York: Simon & Schuster, 1971.

Revenge of the Lawn: Stories 1962–1970. New York: Simon & Schuster, 1971.

The Hawkline Monster: A Gothic Western. New York: Simon & Schuster, 1974.

Willard and his Bowling Trophies: A Perverse Mystery. New York: Simon & Schuster, 1975.

Sombrero Fallout: A Japanese Novel. New York: Simon & Schuster, 1976.

Dreaming of Babylon: A Private Eye Novel 1942. New York: Delacorte Press/ Seymour Lawrence, 1977.

The Tokyo-Montana Express. New York: Delacorte Press/Seymour Lawrence, 1980.

So the Wind Won't Blow it All Away. New York: Delacorte Press/Seymour Lawrence, 1982.

Brodkey, Harold

First Love and Other Stories. New York: Dial Press, 1957.

Women and Angels. Philadelphia: Jewish Publication Society of America, 1985.

Stories in an Almost Classical Mode. New York: Knopf, 1988.

The Runaway Soul. New York: Farrar, Straus, Giroux, 1991.

Profane Friendship. New York: Farrar, Straus, Giroux, 1994.

Bronson, Po

Bombardiers. New York: Random House, 1995.

The First $20 Million is Always the Hardest: A Silicon Valley Novel. New York: Random House, 1997.

The Nudist on the Late Shift, and Other Tales of Silicon Valley. New York: Random House, 1999.

Brown, Larry

Facing the Music. Chapel Hill, NC: Algonquin Books, 1988.
Dirty Work. Chapel Hill, NC: Algonquin Books, 1989.
Big Bad Love. Chapel Hill, NC: Algonquin Books, 1990.
Joe. Chapel Hill, NC: Algonquin Books, 1991.
Father and Son. Chapel Hill, NC: Algonquin Books, 1996.

Burke, James Lee

Half of Paradise. New York: Houghton Mifflin, 1965.
To the Bright and Shining Sun. New York: Charles Scribner's Sons, 1970.
Lay Down My Sword and Shield. New York: Thomas Y. Crowell, 1971.
Two for Texas. New York: Pocket Books, 1983.
The Lost Get-Back Boogie. Baton Rouge: Louisiana State University Press, 1986.
The Neon Rain. New York: Henry Holt, 1987.
Heaven's Prisoners. New York: Henry Holt, 1988.
Black Cherry Blues. New York: Little, Brown & Co., 1989.
A Morning for Flamingos. New York: Little, Brown & Co., 1990.
A Stained White Radiance. New York: Hyperion, 1992.
In the Electric Mist with Confederate Dead. New York: Hyperion, 1993.
Dixie City Jam. New York: Hyperion, 1994.
Burning Angel. New York: Hyperion, 1995.
Cadillac Jukebox. New York: Hyperion, 1996.

Butler, Robert Olen

The Alleys of Eden. New York: Horizon Press, 1981.
Sun Dogs. New York: Horizon Press, 1982.
Countrymen of Bones. New York: Horizon Press, 1983.
On Distant Ground. New York: Knopf, 1985.
Wabash. New York: Knopf, 1987.
A Good Scent from a Strange Mountain. New York: Henry Holt, 1992.
They Whisper. New York: Henry Holt, 1994.
Tabloid Dreams. New York: Henry Holt, 1996.
The Deep Green Sea. New York: Henry Holt, 1997.

Canin, Ethan

Emperor of the Air: Stories. Boston: Houghton Mifflin, 1988.
Blue River. Boston: Houghton Mifflin, 1991.
The Palace Thief. New York: Random House, 1994.
For Kings and Planets. New York: Random House, 1998.

Canty, Kevin

A Stranger in This World. New York: Doubleday, 1994.
In the Great Wide Open. New York: Nan A. Talese/Doubleday, 1996.
Rounders. New York: Hyperion, 1998.
Nine Below Zero. New York: Nan A. Talese/Doubleday, 1999.

Carlson, Ron

Betrayed by F Scott Fitzgerald. New York: Norton, 1977.
Truants. New York: Norton, 1981.
The News of the World. New York: Norton, 1987.
Comatose Christianity: A Wake Up Call for Christians. Nashville, Tenn.: Christian Communications, 1989.
Plan B for the Middle Class. New York: Norton, 1992.
The Hotel Eden Stories. New York: Norton, 1997.

Carr, Caleb

The Devil Soldier. New York: Random House, 1992.
The Alienist. New York: Random House, 1994.
The Angel of Darkness. New York: Random House, 1997.

Carver, Raymond

Will You Please Be Quiet, Please? New York: McGraw Hill, 1976.
What We Talk about When We Talk about Love. New York: Knopf, 1981.
Cathedral. New York: Knopf, 1983.
Elephant, and Other Stories. London: Collins Harvill, 1988.
Where I'm Calling From. New York: Atlantic Monthly Press, 1988.
No Heroics Please: Uncollected Writings. London: Collins Harvill, 1991.

Casey, John

An American Romance. New York: Atheneum, 1977.
Spartina. New York: Knopf, 1989.
The Half-life of Happiness. New York: Knopf, 1998.

Castillo, Ana

The Mixquiahuala Letters. Binghampton, NY: Bilingual Press, 1986.

Sapogonia: An Anti Romance. Tempe, Ariz.: Bilingual Press, 1990.

So Far From God. New York: W. W. Norton, 1993.

Loverboys: Stories. New York: W. W. Norton, 1996.

Peel My Love Like An Onion. New York: Doubleday, 1999.

Chabon, Michael

The Mysteries of Pittsburg. New York: Morrow, 1988.

A Model World and Other Stories. New York: Morrow, 1991.

Wonder Boys. New York: Villard Books, 1995.

The Amazing Adventures of Kavalier and Clay. New York: Random House, 2000.

Were Wolves in their Youth: Stories. New York: Random House, 2000.

Cisneros, Sandra

The House on Mango Street. 1984; 2nd edn. revised Houston: Arte Publico, 1988.

Woman Hollering Creek and Other Stories. New York: Vintage, 1991.

Colwin, Laurie

Passion and Affect. New York: Viking, 1974.

Shine a Bright and Dangerous Object. New York: Viking, 1975.

Happy all the Time. New York: Knopf, 1978.

Lone Pilgrim. New York: Knopf, 1981.

Family Happiness. New York: Knopf, 1982.

Another Marvellous Thing. New York: Knopf, 1986.

Home Cooking. New York: Knopf, 1988.

Goodbye Without Leaving. New York: Poseidon Press, 1990.

A Big Storm Knocked it Over. New York: HarperCollins, 1993.

Coover, Robert

The Origin of the Brunists. New York: Putnam, 1965.

The Universal Baseball Association. New York: Random House, 1968.

Pricksongs and Descants. New York: Dutton, 1969.

The Public Burning. New York: Viking Press, 1977.

Spanking the Maid. New York: Grove Press, 1981.

Gerald's Party. New York: Linden Press, 1986.

A Night at the Movies. New York: Linden Press/Simon & Schuster, 1987.

Whatever Happened to Gloomy Gus of the Chicago Bears? New York: Simon & Schuster, 1987.

Pinocchio in Venice. New York: Linden Press/Simon & Schuster, 1991.

John's Wife. New York: Simon & Schuster, 1996.

Coupland, Douglas

Generation X. New York: St Martin's Press, 1991.

Shampoo Planet. New York: Simon & Schuster, 1992.

Life After God. New York: Simon & Schuster, 1994.

Microserfs. New York: ReganBooks, 1995.

Polaroids from the Dead. New York: ReganBooks, 1996.

Girlfriend in a Coma. New York: ReganBooks, 1998.

Miss Wyoming. New York: Pantheon Books, 1999.

Crews, Harry

The Gospel Singer. New York: Morrow, 1968.

Karate is a Thing of the Spirit. New York: Morrow, 1971.

Car. New York: Morrow, 1972.

Gypsy's Curse. New York: Knopf, 1974.

A Childhood: The Biography of a Place. New York: Harper & Row, 1978.

The Mulching of America. New York: Simon & Schuster, 1995.

Crumley, James

The Last Good Kiss. New York: Random House, 1978.

The Mexican Tree Duck. New York: Mysterious Press, 1993.

Bordersnakes. New York: Mysterious Press, 1996.

DeLillo, Don

Americana. Boston: Houghton Mifflin, 1971.

End Zone. Boston: Houghton Mifflin, 1972.

Great Jones Street. Boston: Houghton Mifflin, 1973.

Ratner's Star. New York: Knopf, 1976.

Players. New York: Knopf, 1977.

Running Dog. New York: Knopf, 1978.

Amazons. (A collaboration under the pseudonym Cleo Birdwell). New York: Holt, Rinehart & Winston, 1980.

The Names. New York: Knopf, 1982.

White Noise. New York: Viking, 1985.

Libra. New York: Viking, 1988.

Mao II. New York: Viking; London: Jonathan Cape, 1991.

Underworld. New York: Scribner, 1997.

Dexter, Pete

God's Pocket. New York: Random House, 1983.

Deadwood. New York: Random House, 1986.

Paris Trout. New York: Random House, 1988.

Brotherly Love. Philadelphia: Franklin Library, 1991.

The Paperboys. New York: Random House, 1995.

Dickey, James

Deliverance. Boston: Houghton Mifflin, 1970.

Didion, Joan

Run River. New York: Obolensky, 1963.

Slouching Toward Bethlehem. New York: Farrar, Straus & Giroux, 1968.

Play It As It Lays. New York: Farrar, Straus, Giroux, 1970.

A Book of Common Prayer. New York: Simon & Schuster, 1977.

The White Album. New York: Simon & Schuster, 1979.

Salvador. New York: Simon & Schuster, 1983.

Democracy. New York: Simon & Schuster, 1984.

The Last Thing He Wanted. New York: Knopf, 1996.

Dillard, Annie

Pilgrim at Tinker Creek. New York: Harper's Magazine Press, 1974.

Tickets for a Prayer Wheel. Columbia: University of Missouri Press, 1974.

Holy the Firm. New York: Harper & Row, 1977.

Living by Fiction. New York: Harper & Row, 1982.

Teaching a Stone to Talk. New York: Harper & Row, 1982.

Encounters with Chinese Writers. Middleton, Conn.: Wesleyan University Press, 1984.

An American Childhood. New York: Harper & Row, 1987.

The Living. New York: HarperCollins, 1992.

Doctorow, E.L.

Welcome to Hard Times. New York: Simon & Schuster, 1960.

Big as Life. New York: Simon & Schuster, 1966.

The Book of Daniel. New York: Random House, 1971.

Ragtime. New York: Random House, 1975.

Loon Lake. New York: Random House, 1980.

Lives of the Poets. New York: Random House, 1984.

World's Fair. New York: Random House, 1985.

Billy Bathgate. New York: Random House, 1989.

The Waterworks. New York: Random House, 1994.

City of God. New York: Little, Brown, 2000.

Doig, Ivan

This House of Sky. New York: Harcourt, Brace, Jovanovich, 1978.

English Creek. New York: Atheneum, 1984.

Dancing at the Rascal Fair. New York: Atheneum, 1987.

Ride with Me, Mariah Montana. New York: Atheneum, 1990.

Dorris, Michael

A Yellow Raft in Blue Water. New York: Henry Holt, 1987.

Drury, Tom

The End of Vandalism. Boston: Houghton Mifflin/Seymour Lawrence, 1994.

Dubus, Andre

The Lieutenant. New York: Dial Press, 1967.

Separate Flights. Boston: D. R. Godine, 1975.

Adultery and Other Choices. Boston: D. R. Godine, 1977.

Finding a Girl in America. Boston: D. R. Godine, 1980.

The Times are Never So Bad. Boston: D. R. Godine, 1983.

Land Where My Fathers Died. Winston Salem, NC: Wright, 1984.

Voices from the Moon. Boston: D. R. Godine, 1984.

We Don't Live Here Anymore. New York: Crown, 1984.

The Last Worthless Evening. Boston: D. R. Godine, 1986.

Blessings. Elmwood, Conn.: Raven Editions, 1987.

Into the Silence. Cambridge, Mass.: Green Street Press, 1988.

Selected Stories. Boston: D. R. Godine, 1988.

Broken Vessels. Boston: D. R. Godine, 1991.

Dancing After Hours. New York: Knopf, 1996.

Dufresne, John

The Way That Water Enters Stone. New York: W. W. Norton, 1991.

Louisiana Power & Light. New York: W. W. Norton, 1994.

Love Warps the Mind a Little. New York: W. W. Norton, 1997.

Dybek, Stuart

The Coast of Chicago. New York: Alfred A. Knopf, 1990.

Eidson, Thomas

St Agnes' Stand. New York: Putnam's, 1994.

The Last Ride. New York: Putnam's, 1995.

All God's Children. London: Michael Joseph, 1996.

Elkin, Stanley

Boswell. New York: Random House, 1964.

Criers and Kibitzers, Kibitzers and Criers. New York: Random House, 1966.

A Bad Man. New York: Random House, 1967.

The Dick Gibson Show. New York: Random House, 1971.

The Making of Ashenden. London: Covent Garden Press, 1972.

Searches and Seizures. New York: Random House, 1973.

The Franchiser. New York: Farrar, Straus, 1976.

Early Elkin. New York: Dutton, 1979.

The Living End. New York: Dutton, 1979.

George Mills. New York: Dutton, 1982.

The Magic Kingdom. New York: Dutton, 1985.

The Rabbi of Lud. New York: Scribners, 1987.

The MacGuffin. New York: Simon & Schuster, 1991.

Van Gogh's Room at Arles: Three Novellas. New York: Hyperion, 1993.

Ellis, Bret Easton

Less Than Zero. New York: Simon & Schuster, 1985.

The Rules of Attraction. New York: Simon & Schuster, 1987.

American Psycho. New York: Vintage, 1991.

The Informers. New York: Berzoi, 1994.

Glamorama. New York: Knopf, 1999.

Ellroy, James

Brown's Requiem. New York: Avon, 1981.

Clandestine. New York: Avon, 1982.

Because the Night. New York: Mysterious Press, 1984.

Blood on the Moon. New York: Mysterious Press, 1984.

Killer on the Road. New York: Avon, 1986.

Silent Terror. New York: Mysterious Press, 1986.

Suicide Hill. New York: Avon, 1986.

The Black Dahlia. New York: Mysterious Press, 1987.

The Big Nowhere. New York: Mysterious Press, 1988.

L. A. Confidential. New York: Mysterious Press, 1990.

White Jazz. New York: Mysterious Press, 1992.

Hollywood Nocturnes. New York: Dell Publishing, 1994.

American Tabloid. New York: Random House, 1995.

My Dark Places. New York: Random House, 1996.

Erdrich, Louise

Love Medicine. New York: Holt, Rinehart & Winston, 1984.

The Beet Queen. New York: Holt, 1986.

Tracks. New York: Henry Holt, 1988.

Crown of Columbus. New York: HarperCollins, 1991.

The Bingo Palace. New York: HarperCollins, 1994.

Tales of Burning Love. New York: HarperCollins, 1996.

The Antelope Wife. New York: Harper Flamingo, 1998.

Birchback House. New York: Hyperion for Children, 1999.

Erickson, Steve

Days between Stations. New York: Poseidon Press, 1985.

Rubicon Beach. New York: Poseidon Press, 1986.

Leap Year. New York: Poseidon Press, 1989.

Tours of the Black Clock. New York: Poseidon Press, 1989.

Arc d'X. New York: Poseidon Press, 1993.

Amnesiascope. New York: Henry Holt, 1996.

American Nomad. New York: Henry Holt, 1997.

The Sea Came in at Midnight. New York: Bard, 1999.

Exley, Frederick

A Fan's Notes. New York: Harper & Row, 1968.

Pages from a Cold Island. New York: Random House, 1975.

Last Notes from Home. New York: Random House, 1988.

Finnegan, William

Complicated War. Berkeley: University of California Press, 1992.

Cold New World. New York: Random House, 1998.

Ford, Richard

A Piece of My Heart. New York: Harper & Row, 1976.

The Ultimate Good Luck. New York: Houghton Mifflin, 1981.

The Sportswriter. New York: Vintage, 1986.

Rock Springs. New York: Atlantic Monthly Press, 1987.

My Mother in Memory. Elmwood, Conn.: Raven Editions, 1988.

Wildlife. New York: Atlantic Monthly Press, 1990.

The Granta Book of the American Short Story (ed.). New York: Penguin, 1992.

Independence Day. New York: Knopf, 1995.

Women with Men: Three Stories. New York: Knopf, 1997.

Frazier, Charles

Cold Mountain. New York: Atlantic Monthly Press, 1997.

French, Albert

Billy. New York: Viking, 1993.

Holly. New York: Viking, 1995.

Patches of Fire. New York: Anchor Books, 1997.

I Can't Wait on God. New York: Anchor Books, 1998.

Gaddis, William

The Recognitions. New York: Harcourt, Brace & Co., 1955.

J.R. New York: Knopf, 1975.

Carpenter's Gothic. New York: Viking Press, 1985.

A Frolic of His Own. New York: Poseidon Press, 1994.

Gaines, Ernest J.

Catherine Carmier. New York: Atheneum, 1964.

Of Love and Dust. New York: Dial Press, 1967.

Bloodline. New York: Dial Press, 1968.

The Autobiography of Miss Jane Pitman. New York: Dial Press, 1971.

In My Father's House. New York: Knopf, 1978.

A Gathering of Old Men. New York: Knopf, 1983.

A Lesson Before Dying. New York: Knopf, 1983.

Garcia, Guy

Skin Deep. New York: Farrar, Straus & Giroux, 1988.

Obsidian Sky. New York: Simon & Schuster, 1994.

Spirit of the Maya: A Boy Explores His People's Mysterious Past. New York: Walker, 1995.

Gardner, John

The Resurrection. New York: New American Library, 1966.

The Wreckage of Agathon. New York: Harper, 1970.

Grendel. New York: Knopf, 1971.

The Sunlight Dialogues. New York: Knopf, 1972.

Nickel Mountain. New York: Knopf, 1973.

The King's Indian. New York: Knopf, 1974.

October Light. New York: Knopf, 1976.

Freddy's Book. New York: Knopf, 1980.

The Art of Living and Other Stories. New York: Knopf, 1981.

Mickelsson's Ghosts. New York: Knopf, 1982.

Stillness and Shadows. New York: Knopf, 1986.

Gass, William H

Omensetter's Luck. New York: New American Library, 1966.

In the Heart of the Heart of the Country. New York: Harper, 1968.

Willie Master's Lonesome Wife. New York: Knopf, 1968.

The First Winter of my Married Life. Northridge, Calif.: Lord John Press, 1979.

Culp. New York: Grenfell Press, 1985.

The Tunnel. New York: Knopf, 1995.

Cartesian Sonata and Other Novellas. New York: Knopf, 1998.

Gibbons, Kaye

Ellen Foster. Chapel Hill, NC: Algonquin Books, 1987.

A Virtuous Woman. Chapel Hill, NC: Algonquin Books, 1989.

A Cure for Dreams. Chapel Hill, NC: Algonquin Books, 1991.

Charms for the Easy Life. New York: Putnam's, 1993.

Sights Unseen. New York: Putnam's, 1995.

On the Occasion of My Last Afternoon. New York: Putnam's, 1998.

Gilchrist, Ellen

In the Land of Dreamy Dreams. Boston: Little, Brown & Company, 1981.

The Annunciation. Boston: Little, Brown & Company, 1983.

Victory Over Japan. Boston: Little, Brown & Company, 1984.

Drunk with Love. Boston: Little, Brown & Company, 1986.

The Anna Papers. Boston: Little, Brown & Company, 1988.

Light Can Be Both Wave and Particle. Boston: Little, Brown & Company, 1989.

The Blue-Eyed Buddhist and Other Stories. London: Faber, 1990.

I Cannot Get You Close Enough. Boston: Little, Brown & Company, 1990.

Net of Jewels. Boston: Little, Brown & Company, 1992.

Anabasis. Jackson: University of Mississippi Press, 1994.

Starcarbon. Boston: Little, Brown & Company, 1994.

The Age of Miracles. Boston: Little, Brown & Company, 1995.

Rhoda: A Life in Stories. Boston: Little, Brown & Company, 1995.

The Courts of Love. Boston: Little, Brown & Company, 1996.

Sarah Conley. Boston: Little, Brown & Company, 1997.

The Cabal and Other Stories. Boston: Little, Brown & Company, 2000.

Godwin, Gail

The Perfectionists. New York: Harper & Row, 1970.

Glass People. New York: Knopf, 1972.

The Odd Woman. New York: Knopf, 1974.

Dream Children. New York: Knopf, 1976.

Violet Clay. New York: Knopf, 1978.

A Mother and Two Daughters. New York: Viking, 1982.

Mr Bedford and the Muses. New York: Viking, 1983.

The Finishing School. New York: Viking, 1984.

A Southern Family. New York: Morrow, 1987.

Father Melancholy's Daughter. New York: Morrow, 1991.

The Good Husband. New York: Ballantine, 1994.

Evensong. New York: Ballantine, 1999.

Gordon, Mary

Final Payments. New York: Random House, 1978.

The Company of Women. New York: Random House, 1980.

Men and Angels. New York: Random House, 1985.

Temporary Shelter. New York: Random House, 1987.

The Other Side. New York: Random House, 1989.

Good Boys and Dead Girls. New York: Viking Penguin, 1991.

The Rest of Life. New York: Viking Penguin, 1993.

Gurganus, Allan

Good Help. Rocky Mount, NC: Wesleyan College Press, 1988.

Oldest Living Confederate Widow Tells All. New York: Knopf, 1989.

Blessed Assurance: A Moral Tale. Rocky Mount, NC: Wesleyan College Press, 1990.

White People: Stories and Novellas. New York: Knopf, 1991.

The Practical Heart. Rocky Mount, NC: Wesleyan College Press, 1993.

Plays Well With Others. Rocky Mount, NC: Wesleyan College Press, 1997.

Gustafsson, Lars

The Tale of a Dog: From the Diaries and Letters of a Texan Bankruptcy. New York: New Directions, 1999.

Guterson, David

Country Ahead of Us: The Country Behind. New York: Harper & Row, 1989.

Family Matters: Why Homeschooling Makes Sense. New York: Harcourt, Brace, Yovanovich, 1992.

Snow Falling on Cedars. San Diego: Harcourt Press, 1994.

East of the Mountains. New York: Harcourt, Brace & Co., 1999.

Hagy, Alyson

Madonna on her Back. New York: Stuart Wright, 1986.

Hardware River Stories. New York: Poseidon, 1991.

Keeneland. New York: Simon & Schuster, 2000.

Hannah, Barry

Geronimo Rex. New York: Viking Press, 1972.

Nightwatchmen. New York: Viking Press, 1973.

Airships. New York: Knopf, 1978.

Ray. New York: Knopf, 1980.

Power and Light. Winston-Salem, NC: Palaemon Press, 1983.

The Tennis Handsome. New York: Knopf, 1983.

Captain Maximus. New York: Knopf, 1985.

Hey Jack! New York: Dutton, 1987.

Boomerang. Boston: Houghton Mifflin, 1989.

Never Die. Boston: Houghton Mifflin, 1991.

Bats Out of Hell. Boston: Houghton Mifflin, 1993.

High Lonesome. New York: Atlantic Monthly Press, 1996.

Hansen, Ron

Desperadoes. New York: Knopf, 1979.

The Assassination of Jesse James by the Coward Robert Ford. New York: Knopf, 1983.

Nebraska. New York: Atlantic Monthly Press, 1989.

Mariette in Ecstasy. New York: HarperCollins, 1991.

You've Got to Read This: Contemporary American Writers Introduce Stories that Held them in Awe (ed. R. Hansen and J. Shepard). New York: Harpers Perennial, 1994.

Atticus. New York: HarperCollins, 1996.

Hitler's Niece. New York: Harper Flamingo, 1999.

Hawkes, John

The Cannibal. Norfolk: New Directions, 1950.

The Beetle Leg. New York: New Directions, 1951.

The Goose on the Grave and the Owl. New York: New Directions, 1954.

The Lime Twig. New York: New Directions, 1961.

Second Skin. New York: New Directions, 1964.

The Blood Oranges. New York: New Directions, 1971.

Death, Sleep & The Traveller. New York: New Directions, 1974.

Travesty. New York: New Directions, 1976.

The Universal Fears. Northridge, Calif.: Lord John Press, 1978.

The Passion Artist. New York: Harper & Row, 1979.

Virginie: Her Two Lives. New York: Harper & Row, 1982.

Adventures in the Alaskan Skin Trade. New York: Simon & Schuster, 1985.

Innocence in Extremis. Providence: Burning Deck Press, 1985.

Whistlejacket. New York: Weidenfeld & Nicolson, 1988.

Sweet William: A Memoir of Old Horse. New York: Simon & Schuster, 1993.

Heim, Scott

Mysterious Skin. New York: HarperCollins, 1995.

In Awe. New York: HarperCollins, 1997.

Heller, Joseph

Catch 22. New York: Scribner's, 1961.

Something Happened. New York: Scribner's, 1974.

Good as Gold. New York: Simon & Schuster, 1979.

God Knows. New York: Alfred Knopf, 1984.

Picture This. New York: G. P. Putnam's, 1988.

Closing Time. New York: Scribner's, 1994.

Heller, Ted

Slab Rat. London: Abacus, 2000.

Helprin, Mark

A Dove of East and Other Stories. New York: Knopf, 1975.

Ellis Island and Other Stories. New York: Delacorte Press/Seymour Lawrence, 1981.

A Soldier of the Great War. New York: Harcourt, Brace, Jovanovich, 1991.

Memoir from an Antproof Case. New York: Harcourt Brace & Co., 1995.

Hempel, Amy

Reasons to Live. New York: Knopf, 1985.

At the Gates of the Animal Kingdom. New York: Knopf, 1990.

Tumble Home: A Novella and Short Stories. New York: Scribner, 1997.

Herr, Michael

Dispatches. New York: Knopf, 1977.

Big Room. New York: Summit Books, 1986.

Walter Winchell. New York: Knopf, 1990.

Kubrick. New York: Grove, 2000.

Hillerman, Tony

The Blessing Way. New York: Harper & Row, 1970.

The Fly on the Wall. New York: Harper & Row, 1971.

The Boy Who Made Dragonfly. Albuquerque: University of New Mexico Press, 1972.

Dance Hall of the Dead. New York: Harper & Row, 1973.

Listening Woman. New York: Harper & Row, 1978.

People of Darkness. New York: Harper & Row, 1980.

The Dark Wind. New York: Harper & Row, 1982.

The Ghostway. New York: Harper & Row, 1982.

Skinwalkers. New York: Harper & Row, 1986.

A Thief of Time. New York: Harper & Row, 1988.

Talking God. New York: Harper & Row, 1989.

Coyote Waits. New York: Harper & Row, 1990.

Sacred Clowns. New York: HarperCollins, 1993.

Finding Moon. New York: HarperCollins, 1995.

The Fallen Man. New York: HarperCollins, 1997.

The First Eagle. New York: HarperCollins, 1998.

Hoffman, Alice

Property Of. New York: Farrar, Straus & Giroux, 1977.

Drowning Season. New York: Putnam, 1979.

Angel Landing. New York: Putnam, 1980.

White Horses. New York: Putnam, 1982.

Fortune's Daughter. New York: Putnam, 1985.

Illumination Night. New York: Putnam, 1987.

At Risk. New York: Putnam, 1988.

Seventh Heaven. New York: Putnam, 1990.

Turtle Moon. New York: Putnam, 1992.

Second Nature. New York: Putnam, 1994.

Practical Magic. New York: Putnam, 1995.

Here On Earth. New York: Putnam, 1997.

Local Girls. New York: Putnam, 1999.

River King. New York: Putnam, 2000.

Hogan, Linda

Mean Spirit. New York: Atheneum, 1990.

Dwellings: A Spiritual History of the Living World. New York: W. W. Norton, 1995.

Houston, Pam

Cowboys are my Weakness. New York: W. W. Norton, 1992.

Waltzing the Cat. New York: W. W. Norton, 1998.

A Rough Guide to the Heart. New York: Little, Brown, 2000.

Indiana, Gary

Roberto Juarez. New York: Bellpat Press, 1986.

White Trash Boulevard. Madras, NY: Hanaman Books, 1988.

Horse Crazy. New York: Grove Press, 1989.

Gone Tomorrow. New York: Pantheon Books, 1993.

Rent Boy. New York: High Risk/Serpent's Tail, 1994.

Resentment. New York: Doubleday, 1997.

Three Month Fever. New York: Cliff Street Books, 1999.

Irving, John

Setting Free the Bears. New York: Random House, 1969.

The Water-Method Man. New York: Random House, 1972.

The 158-Pound Marriage. New York: Random House, 1974.

The World According to Garp. New York: Dutton, 1978.

The Hotel New Hampshire. New York: Dutton, 1981.

The Cider House Rules. New York: Morrow, 1985.

A Prayer for Owen Meany. New York: Morrow, 1989.

Trying to Save Piggy Snead. London: Bloomsbury, 1993.

A Son of The Circus. New York: Random House, 1994.

The Imaginary Girlfriend. London: Bloomsbury, 1996.

A Widow for One Year. New York: Random House, 1998.

Janowitz, Tama

American Dad. New York: Putnam, 1981.

Slaves of New York. New York: Crown Publishers, 1986.

A Cannibal in Manhattan. New York: Crown, 1987.

The Male Cross-Dresser Support Group. New York: Crown, 1992.

By the Shores of Gitchee Gumee. New York: Crown Publishers, 1996.

A Certain Age. New York: Doubleday, 1999.

Jen, Gish

Typical American. Boston: Houghton Mifflin/Seymour Lawrence, 1991.

Mona in the Promised Land. New York: Knopf, 1996.

Who's Irish? New York: Knopf, 1999.

Johnson, Charles

Faith and the Good Thing. New York: Viking, 1974.

Oxherding Tale. Bloomington: Indiana University Press, 1982.

Being and Race: Black Writing since 1970. Bloomington: Indiana University Press, 1988.

Middle Passage. New York: Atheneum, 1990.

Jones, Gayl

Corregidora. New York: Random House, 1975.

Eva's Man. New York: Random House, 1976.

White Rat. New York: Random House, 1977.

Jones, Thom

The Pugilist at Rest. Boston: Little Brown, 1993.

Cold Snap. Boston: Little Brown, 1995.

Sonny Liston Was a Friend of Mine. Boston: Little Brown, 1999.

Karlin, Wayne

Crossover. San Diego: Harcourt, Brace, Jovanovich, 1984.

Extras. New York: Henry Holt, 1989.

Us. New York: Henry Holt, 1993.

Rumors and Stones: A Journey. Willimantic, Conn.: Curbstone Press, 1996.

Prisoners. Willimantic, Conn.: Curbstone Press, 1998.

Keillor, Garrison

Happy to be Here. New York: Atheneum, 1982.

The Book of Guys. New York: Viking, 1983.

Lake Wobegone Days. New York: Viking, 1985.

Leaving Home. New York: Viking, 1987.

Wobegone Boy. New York: Viking, 1987.

We Are Still Married. New York: Viking, 1989.

Kenan, Randall

A Visitation of Spirits. New York: Grove Press, 1989.

Let the Dead Bury their Dead. San Diego: Harcourt, Brace, Jovanovich, 1992.

Kennedy, William

The Ink Truck. New York: Dial Press, 1969.

Legs. New York: Coward, McCann & Geoghegan, 1975.

Billy Phelan's Greatest Game. New York: Viking, 1978.

Ironweed. New York: Viking, 1983.

Quinn's Book. New York: Viking, 1988.

Very Old Bones. New York: Viking, 1992.

Flaming Corsage. New York: Viking, 1996.

Kesey, Ken

One Flew Over the Cuckoo's Nest. New York: Viking, 1962.

Sometimes a Great Notion. New York: Viking, 1964.

The Day Superman Died. Northridge, Calif.: Lord John Press, 1980.

Demon Box. New York: Viking, 1986.

Further Inquiry. New York: Viking, 1990.

Sailor Song. New York: Viking, 1992.

Last Go Round. New York: Viking, 1994.

Kingsolver, Barbara

The Bean Trees. New York: HarperCollins, 1988.

Homeland and Other Stories. New York: HarperCollins, 1989.

Animal Dreams. New York: HarperCollins, 1990.

Pigs in Heaven. New York: HarperCollins, 1993.

High Tide in Tucson. New York: HarperCollins, 1995.

The Poisonwood Bible. New York: HarperFlamingo, 1998.

Kingston, Maxine Hong

The Woman Warrior: Memoirs of a Girlhood among Ghosts. New York: Vintage, 1976.

China Men. New York: Ballantine, 1980.

Through the Black Curtain. Berkeley: University of California Press, 1987.

Tripmaster Monkey: His Fake Book. New York: Knopf, 1989.

Kosinski, Jerzy

No Third Path. Garden City, NY: Doubleday, 1962.

The Painted Bird. Boston: Houghton Mifflin, 1965.

Steps. New York: Random House, 1968.

Being There. New York: Harcourt, Brace, Jovanovich, 1971.

The Devil Tree. New York: Harcourt, Brace, Jovanovich, 1973.

Blind Date. Boston: Houghton Mifflin, 1977.

Passion Play. New York: St Martin's Press, 1979.

Pinball. Toronto: Bantam Books, 1982.

Cockpit. New York: Arcade Publishers, 1989.

Leavitt, David

Family Dancing. New York: Knopf, 1984.

The Lost Language of Cranes. New York: Viking, 1986.

Equal Affections. New York: Viking, 1989.

A Place I've Never Been. New York: Viking, 1990.

While England Sleeps. New York: Viking, 1993.

Italian Pleasures. London: Fourth Estate, 1996.

Arkansas: Three Novellas. London: Abacus, 1997.

Lee, Chang-rae

Native Speaker. New York: Riverhead Books; London: Granta, 1995.

A Gesture Life. New York: Riverhead Books; London: Granta, 2000.

Leithauser, Brad

Hence. New York: Knopf, 1989.

Leonard, Elmore

Hombre. New York: Ballantine, 1951.

The Bounty Hunters. Boston: Houghton Mifflin, 1953.

The Law at Randado. Boston: Houghton Mifflin, 1955.

Escape from Five Shadows. Boston: Houghton Mifflin, 1956.

Last Stand at Saber River. New York: Dell, 1959.

The Big Bounce. New York: Fawcett, 1969.

The Moonshine War. New York: Doubleday, 1969.

Valdez is Coming. London: Hale, 1969.

Forty Lashes Less One. New York: Bantam, 1972.

Fifty-Two Pickup. New York: Delacorte, 1974.

Mr Majestyk. New York: Dell, 1974.

Swag. New York: Delacorte, 1976.

The Hunted. New York: Delacorte, 1977.

Unknown Man No. 89. New York: Delacorte, 1977.

The Switch. New York: Bantam, 1978.

Gunsights. New York: Bantam, 1979.

City Primeval: High Noon in Detroit. New York: Arbor House, 1980.

Gold Coast. New York: Bantam, 1980.

Cat Chaser. New York: Arbor House, 1982.

Split Images. New York: Arbor House, 1982.

LaBrava. New York: Arbor House, 1983.

Stick. New York: Arbor House, 1983.

Glitz. New York: Arbor House, 1985.

Bandits. New York: Arbor House, 1987.

Touch. New York: Arbor House, 1987.

Freaky Deaky. New York: Arbor House, 1988.

Killshot. New York: Arbor House, 1989.

Get Shorty. New York: Delacorte, 1990.

Maximum Bob. New York: Delacorte, 1991.

Rum Punch. New York: Delacorte, 1992.

Pronto. New York: Delacorte, 1993.

Riding the Rap. New York: Delacorte, 1995.

Lesley, Craig

Storm Riders. London: Picador, 2000.

Lethem, Jonathan

Motherless Brooklyn. London: Faber, 2000.

Louie, David Wong

The Barbarians Are Coming. New York: Putnam, 2000.

Lurie, Alison

Love and Friendship. New York: Macmillan, 1962.

The Nowhere City. London: Heinemann, 1965.

Imaginary Friends. New York: Coward McCann, 1966.

Real People. New York: Random House, 1969.

The War between The Tates. New York: Random House, 1974.

Only Children. New York: Random House, 1979.

Foreign Affairs. New York: Random House, 1984.

The Truth about Lorin Jones. Boston: Little, Brown, 1988.

Women and Ghosts. London: Heinemann, 1994.

The Last Resort. New York: Henry Holt, 1998.

McCarthy, Cormac

The Orchard Keeper. New York: Random House, 1965.

Outer Dark. New York: Random House, 1968.

Child of God. New York: Random House, 1973.

Suttree. New York: Random House, 1979.

Blood Meridian, or, The Evening Redness in the West. New York: Random House, 1985.

All the Pretty Horses. New York: Knopf, 1992.

The Crossing. New York: Knopf, 1994.

The Gardener's Son: A Screenplay. Hopewell, NJ: Ecco Press, 1996.

Cities of the Plain. New York: Knopf, 1998.

McCorkle, Jill

The Cheer Leader. Chapel Hill, NC: Algonquin Books, 1984.

Tending to Virginia. Chapel Hill, NC: Algonquin Books, 1987.

McCracken, Elizabeth

Here's Your Hat, What's Your Hurry? New York: Turtle Bay Books, 1993.

The Giant's House. New York: Dial Press, 1996.

McGuane, Thomas

The Sporting Club. New York: Simon & Schuster, 1969.

The Bushwacked Piano. New York: Simon & Schuster, 1971.

Ninety-Two in the Shade. New York: Farrar, Straus, Giroux, 1973.

Panama. New York: Farrar, Straus, Giroux, 1978.

Nobody's Angel. New York: Random House, 1982.

Something to be Desired. New York: Random House, 1984.

To Skin a Cat. New York: E. P. Dutton/Seymour Lawrence, 1986.

Silent Seasons: Twenty-one Fishing Stories. Livingston, Mont.: Clark City Press, 1988.

Keep the Change. New York: Vintage, 1990.

Nothing But Blue Skies. Boston: Houghton Mifflin/Seymour Lawrence, 1992.

Live Water. Stone Harbor, NJ: Meadow Press, 1996.

The Longest Silence. New York: Knopf, 1999.

Some Horses. New York: Lyons Press, 1999.

McInerney, Jay

Bright Lights, Big City. New York: Vintage Books, 1984.

Ransom. New York: Vintage Books, 1985.

Story of My Life. New York: Atlantic Monthly Press, 1988.

Brightness Falls. New York: Knopf, 1992.

The Last of the Savages. New York: Knopf, 1996.

Model Behaviour. New York: Knopf, 1998.

Maclean, Norman

A River Runs Through It. Chicago: University of Chicago Press, 1976.

Young Men and Fire. Chicago: University of Chicago Press, 1992.

McMillan, Terry

Mama. Boston, Houghton Mifflin, 1987.

Disappearing Acts. New York: Viking, 1989.

Waiting to Exhale. New York: Viking, 1992.

How Stella Got Her Groove Back. Rockland, Mass.: Wheeler Publishers, 1996.

McMurtry, Larry

Leaving Cheyenne. New York: Harper & Row, 1963.

The Last Picture Show. New York: Dial Press, 1966.

Terms of Endearment. New York: Simon & Schuster, 1975.

Lonesome Dove. New York: Simon & Schuster, 1985.

Texasville. New York: Simon & Schuster, 1987.

Buffalo Girls. New York: Simon & Schuster, 1990.

The Streets of Laredo. New York: Simon & Schuster, 1993.

Dead Man's Walk. New York: Simon & Schuster, 1995.

Mailer, Norman

The Naked and the Dead. New York: Rinehart, 1948.

Barbary Shore. New York: Rinehart, 1951.

The Deer Park. New York: Putnam's, 1955.

Advertisements for Myself. New York: Putnam's, 1959.

An American Dream. New York: Dial, 1965.

The Short Fiction of Norman Mailer. New York: Dell, 1967.

Why Are We in Vietnam? New York: Putnam's, 1967.

The Armies of the Night. New York: New American Library, 1968.

Maidstone: A Mystery. New York: New American Library, 1971.

The Executioner's Song. New York: Little, Brown, 1979.

Ancient Evenings. Boston: Little, Brown, 1983.

Tough Guys Don't Dance. New York: Random House, 1984.

Harlot's Ghost. New York: Random House, 1991.

Oswald's Tale: An American Mystery. New York: Random House, 1995.

The Gospel According to the Son. New York: Random House, 1997.

Mamet, David

The Village. Boston: Little Brown, 1994.

The Old Religion. New York; Free Press, 1997.

Boston Marriage. New York: Vintage, 2000.

Marshall, Paule

Brown Girl, Brownstones. New York: Random House, 1959.

The Chosen Place, the Timeless People. New York: Harcourt Brace, 1969.

Praisesong for the Widow. New York: Putnams, 1983.

Daughters. New York: Atheneum, 1991.

Mason, Bobbie Anne

Shiloh and Other Stories. New York: Harper & Row, 1982.

In Country. New York: Harper & Row, 1985.

Midnight Magic: Selected Stories of Bobbie Anne Mason. Hopewell, NJ: Ecco Press, 1988.

Spence + Lila. New York: Harper & Row, 1988.

Love Life. New York: Harper & Row, 1989.

Feather Crowns. New York: HarperCollins, 1993.

Clear Springs: A Memoir. New York: Random House, 1999.

Maupin, Armistead

Tales of the City. New York: Harper & Row, 1978.

More Tales of the City. New York: Harper & Row, 1980.

Further Tales of the City. New York: Harper & Row, 1982.

Baby Cakes. New York: Harper & Row, 1984.

Significant Others. New York: Perennial Library, 1987.

Sure of You. New York: Harper & Row, 1989.

28 Barbary Lane. A Tales of the City Omnibus. New York: HarperCollins, 1990.

Maybe the Moon. New York: HarperCollins, 1992.

Millhauser, Steven

Edwin Mullhouse. New York: Knopf, 1972.

Portrait of a Romantic. New York: Knopf, 1977.

In the Penny Arcade. New York: Knopf, 1985.

From the Realm of Morpheus. New York: Morrow, 1986.

The Barnum Museum. New York: Poseidon Press, 1990.

Little Kingdoms. New York: Poseidon Press, 1993.

Martin Dressler: The Tale of an American Dreamer. New York: Crown, 1996.

Knife Thrower. New York: Crown, 1998.

Enchanted Night. New York: Crown, 1999.

Mohr, Nicholasa

Rituals of Survival: A Woman's Portfolio. Houston, Tex.: Arte Publico Press, 1985.

Momaday, N. Scott

House Made of Dawn. New York: Harper & Row, 1968.

The Way to Rainy Mountain. Albuquerque: University of New Mexico Press, 1969.

The Gourd Dancer. New York: Harper & Row, 1976.

The Names. New York: Harper & Row, 1976.

The Ancient Child. New York: Doubleday, 1989.

Moody, Rick

The Ice Storm. Boston: Little Brown, 1994.

The Ring of Brightest Angels around Heaven. Boston: Little Brown, 1995.

Garden State. Boston: Little Brown, 1997.

Purple America. Boston: Little Brown, 1997.

Moore, Lorrie

Self-Help. New York: Knopf, 1985.

Anagrams. New York: Knopf, 1986.

The Forgotten Helper. New York: Kipling Press, 1987.

Like Life. New York: Knopf, 1990.

Who Will Run the Frog Hospital? New York: Knopf, 1994.

Morrison, Toni

The Bluest Eye. New York: Holt, Rinehart & Winston, 1970.

Sula. New York: Knopf, 1973.

Song of Soloman. New York: Knopf, 1977.

Tar Baby. New York: Knopf, 1981.

Beloved. New York: Knopf, 1987.

Jazz. New York: Knopf, 1992.

Paradise. New York: Knopf, 1998.

Mosley, Walter

Devil in a Blue Dress. New York: Norton, 1990.

A Red Death. New York: Norton, 1991.

White Butterfly. New York: Norton, 1992.

Black Betty. New York: Norton, 1994.

R. L.'s Dream. New York: Norton, 1995.

A Little Yellow Dog: An Easy Rawlins Mystery. New York: Norton, 1996.

Gone Fishin': An Easy Rawlins Mystery. Baltimore: Black Classic Press, 1997.

Always Outnumbered, Always Outgunned. New York: Norton, 1998.

Blue Light. Boston: Little Brown, 1998.

Walkin' the Dog. Boston: Little Brown, 1999.

Wakin' on the Chain Gang. New York: Ballantine Publishing, 2000.

Mukherjee, Bharati

The Tiger's Daughter. Boston, Houghton Mifflin, 1971.

Wife. Boston: Houghton Mifflin, 1975.

Darkness. Markham, Ontario: Penguin, 1985.

The Middleman and Other Stories. New York: Viking Penguin, 1988.

Jasmine. New York: Grove Weidenfeld, 1989.

The Holder of the World. New York: Alfred A. Knopf, 1993.

Naylor, Gloria

Bailey's Cafe. New York: Harcourt, Brace, Jovanovich, 1992.

The Women of Brewster Place. New York: Viking Press, 1982.

Linden Hills. New York: Ticknor & Fields, 1985.

Mama Day. New York: Ticknor & Fields, 1988.

Oates, Joyce Carol

By the North Gate. New York: Vanguard, 1963.

With Shuddering Fall. New York: Vanguard, 1964.

Upon the Sweeping Flood. New York: Vanguard, 1966.

A Garden of Earthly Delights. New York: Vanguard, 1967.

Expensive People. New York: Vanguard, 1968.

them. New York: Vanguard, 1969.

The Wheel of Love. New York: Vanguard, 1970.

Wonderland. New York: Vanguard, 1971.

Marriages and Infidelities. New York: Vanguard, 1972.

The Goddess and Other Women. New York: Dutton, 1974.

The Hungry Ghosts: Seven Allusive Comedies. Los Angeles: Black Sparrow Press, 1974.

The Assassins: A Book of Hours. New York: Vanguard, 1975.

The Poisoned Kiss and Other Stories from the Portuguese. New York: Vanguard, 1975.

The Seduction and Other Stories. Los Angeles: Black Sparrow Press, 1975.

Childwold. New York: Vanguard, 1976.

Crossing the Border. New York: Vanguard, 1976.

The Triumph of Spider Monkey. Santa Barbara, Calif.: Black Sparrow Press, 1976.

Night-Side: Eighteen Tales. New York: Vanguard, 1977.

Son of the Morning. New York: Vanguard, 1978.

All the Good People I've Left Behind. Santa Barbara, Calif.: Black Sparrow Press, 1979.

Cybele. Santa Barbara, Calif.: Black Sparrow Press, 1979.

Unholy Loves. New York: Dutton, 1979.

Bellefleur. New York: Dutton, 1980.

A Sentimental Education. New York: Dutton, 1980.

Angel of Light. New York: Dutton, 1981.

A Bloodsmoor Romance. New York: Dutton, 1982.

Last Days. New York: Dutton, 1984.

Mysteries of Winterthurn. New York: Dutton, 1984.

Solstice. New York: Dutton, 1985.

Marya: A Life. New York: Dutton, 1986.

Raven's Wing. New York: Dutton, 1986.

Lives of the Twins (as Rosamond Smith). New York: Dutton, 1987.

You Must Remember This. New York: Dutton, 1987.

The Assignation. New York: Ecco Press, 1988.

American Appetites. New York: Dutton, 1989.

Soul/Mate (as Rosamond Smith). New York: Dutton, 1989.

Because It Is Bitter, and Because It Is my Heart. New York: Dutton, 1990.

I Lock My Door Upon Myself. New York: Ecco Press, 1990.

Nemesis (as Rosamond Smith). New York: Dutton, 1990.

Oates in Exile. Toronto: Exile Editions, 1990.

Heat and Other Stories. New York: Dutton, 1991.

The Rise of Life on Earth. New York: New Directions, 1991.

Black Water. New York: Dutton, 1992.

Where Is Here? Hopewell: Ecco Press, 1992.

Foxfire: Confessions of a Girl Gang. New York: Dutton, 1993.

Snake Eyes (as Rosamond Smith). New York: Dutton, 1993.

Where Are You Going, Where Have You Been? Selected Early Stories. Princeton: Ontario Review Press, 1993.

Haunted: Tales of the Grotesque. New York: Dutton, 1994.

What I Lived For. New York: Dutton, 1995.

You Can't Catch Me (as Rosamond Smith). New York: Dutton, 1995.

Zombie. New York: Dutton, 1995.

First Love: A Gothic Tale. Hopewell: Ecco Press, 1996.

We Were the Mulvaneys. New York: Dutton, 1996.

Will You Always Love Me? New York: Dutton, 1996.

Double Delight (as Rosamond Smith). New York: Dutton, 1997.

Man Crazy. New York: Dutton, 1997.

Collector of Hearts: New Tales of the Grotesque. New York: Dutton, 1998.

My Heart Laid Bare. New York: Dutton, 1998.

Unspeakable. New York: Dutton, 1998.

Broke Heart Blues. New York: Dutton, 1999.

Blonde. London: Fourth Estate, 2000.

O'Brien, Tim

If I Die in a Combat Zone, Box Me Up and Ship Me Home. New York: Delacorte/Seymour Lawrence, 1973.

Northern Lights. New York: Delacorte/Seymour Lawrence, 1975.

Going After Cacciato. New York: Delacorte/Seymour Lawrence, 1978.

The Nuclear Age. New York: Knopf, 1985.

The Things They Carried. Boston: Houghton Mifflin/Seymour Lawrence, 1990.

In the Lake of the Woods. Boston: Houghton Mifflin/Seymour Lawrence, 1994.

Tomcat in Love. New York: Broadway Books, 1998.

Olmstead, Robert

River Dogs. New York: Vintage Books, 1987.

Soft Water. New York: Vintage Books, 1988.

A Trail of Heart's Blood Wherever We Go. New York: Random House, 1990.

America by Land. New York: Random House, 1993.

Stay Here with Me: A Memoir. New York: Metropolitan Books, 1996.

Ozick, Cynthia

Trust. New York: New American Library, 1966.

The Pagan Rabbi and Other Stories. New York: Knopf, 1971.

Bloodshed and Three Novellas. New York: Knopf, 1976.

Levitation: Five Fictions. New York: Knopf, 1982.

The Cannibal Galaxy. New York: Knopf, 1983.

The Messiah of Stockholm. New York: Knopf, 1987.

The Shawl. New York: Knopf, 1989.

The Puttermesser Papers. New York: Knopf, 1997.

Palahniuk, Chuck

Fight Club. New York: Norton, 1996.

Invisible Monsters. New York: Norton, 1999.

Survivor. New York: Norton, 1999.

Paley, Grace

The Little Disturbances of Man. Garden City, NY: Doubleday, 1959.

Enormous Changes at the Last Minute. New York: Farrar, Straus, Giroux, 1974.

Later the Same Day. New York: Farrar, Straus, Giroux, 1985.

Patchett, Ann

The Patron Saint of Liars. Boston: Houghton Mifflin, 1992.

Taft. Boston: Houghton Mifflin, 1994.

The Magician's Assistant. New York: Harcourt Brace, 1997.

Peck, Dale

Fucking Martin. New York: Farrar, Straus, Giroux, 1993.

The Law of Enclosures. New York: Farrar, Straus, Giroux, 1996.

Now It's Time to Say Goodbye. New York: Farrar, Straus, Giroux, 1998.

Percy, Walker

The Moviegoer. New York: Knopf, 1961.

The Last Gentleman. New York: Farrar, Straus, 1966.

Love in the Ruins. New York: Farrar, Straus, 1971.

Lancelot. New York: Farrar, Straus, 1977.

The Second Coming. New York: Farrar, Straus, 1980.

The Thanatos Syndrome. New York: Farrar, Straus, 1987.

Perry, Phyllis

Stigmata. New York: Hyperion, 1998.

Phillips, Jayne Anne

Sweethearts. Carrbora, NC: Truck Press, 1976.

Black Tickets. New York: Delacorte Press/Seymour Lawrence, 1979.
How Mickey Made It. St Paul, Minn.: Bookslinger Editions, 1981.
Machine Dreams. New York: Dutton/Seymour Lawrence, 1984.
Fast Lanes. New York: Dutton/Seymour Lawrence, 1987.
Shelter. Boston: Houghton Mifflin/Seymour Lawrence, 1994.
Motherkind. New York: Knopf, 2000.

Piercy, Marge

Going Down Fast. New York: Trident, 1969.
Dance the Eagle to Sleep. Garden City, NY: Doubleday, 1970.
Small Changes. Garden City, NY: Doubleday, 1973.
Woman on the Edge of Time. New York: Knopf, 1976.
The High Cost of Living. New York: Harper, 1978.
Vida. New York: Summit, 1980.
Braided Lives. New York: Summit, 1982.
Fly Away Home. New York: Summit, 1984.
Gone to Soldiers. New York: Summit, 1987.
Summer People. New York: Summit, 1989.
He, She, and It. New York: Knopf, 1991.
The Longings of Women. New York: Fawcett, 1994.

Pirsig, Robert

Zen and the Art of Motorcycle Maintenance. New York: Morrow, 1974.

Power, Susan

The Grassdancer. New York: Putnam's, 1994.

Price, Richard

Breaks. New York: Simon & Schuster, 1973.
The Wanderers. Boston: Houghton Mifflin, 1974.
Bloodbrother. Boston: Houghton Mifflin, 1976.
Ladies Man. Boston: Houghton Mifflin, 1978.
Clockers. Boston: Houghton Mifflin, 1992.
Freedomland. New York: Broadway Books, 1998.

Proulx, E. Annie

Heartsongs and Other Stories. New York: Scribner, 1988.

Postcards. New York: Scribner, 1992.

The Shipping News. New York: Scribner, 1993; London: Fourth Estate, 1993.

Accordion Crimes. New York: Scribner, 1996.

Close Range. New York: Scribner, 1999.

Pynchon, Thomas

V. Philadelphia: J. B. Lippincott, 1963.

The Crying of Lot 49. Philadelphia: J. B. Lippincott, 1966.

Gravity's Rainbow. New York: Viking Press, 1973.

Slow Learner. Boston: Little Brown, 1984.

Vineland. Boston: Little Brown, 1990.

Mason and Dixon. New York: Henry Holt, 1997.

Reed, Ishmael

The Free-Lance Pallbearers. New York: Doubleday, 1967.

Yellow Back Radio Broke-Down. New York: Doubleday, 1969.

Mumbo-Jumbo. New York: Doubleday, 1972.

The Last Days of Louisiana Red. New York: Random House, 1974.

Flight to Canada. New York: Random House, 1976.

The Terrible Twos. New York: St Martin's Press, 1982.

Reckless Eyeballing. New York: St Martin's Press, 1986.

The Terrible Threes. New York: Atheneum, 1989.

Japanese by Spring. New York: Atheneum, 1993.

Richard, Mark

The Ice at the Bottom of the World. New York: Knopf, 1989.

Fishboy. New York: Doubleday, 1993.

Charity. New York: Doubleday, 1998.

Roth, Philip

Goodbye, Columbus. Boston: Houghton Mifflin, 1959.

Letting Go. New York: Random House, 1962.

When She Was Good. New York: Random House, 1967.

Portnoy's Complaint. New York: Random House, 1969.

Our Gang. New York: Random House, 1971.

The Breast. New York: Holt, Rinehart & Winston, 1972.

The Great American Novel. New York: Holt, Rinehart & Winston, 1973.

My Life as a Man. New York: Holt, Rinehart & Winston, 1974.

Reading Myself and Others. New York: Farrar, Straus, Giroux, 1975.

The Professor of Desire. New York: Farrar, Straus, Giroux, 1977.

The Ghost Writer. New York: Farrar, Straus, Giroux, 1979.

Zuckerman Unbound. New York: Farrar, Straus, Giroux, 1981.

The Anatomy Lesson. New York: Farrar, Straus, Giroux, 1983.

Zuckerman Bound: A Trilogy and Epilogue. Consists of *The Ghost Writer*, *Zuckerman Unbound*, *The Anatomy Lesson* and *The Prague Orgy*. New York: Farrar, Straus, Giroux, 1985.

The Counterlife. New York: Farrar, Straus, Giroux, 1986.

The Facts. New York: Farrar, Straus, Giroux, 1988.

Deception. New York: Simon & Schuster, 1990.

Patrimony. A True Story. New York: Simon & Schuster, 1991.

Operation Shylock: A Confession. New York: Simon & Schuster, 1993.

Sabbath's Theater. Boston: Houghton Mifflin, 1995.

American Pastoral. Boston: Houghton Mifflin, 1997.

I Married a Communist. Boston: Houghton Mifflin, 1998.

The Human Stain. Boston: Houghton Mifflin, 2000.

Russo, Richard

Mohawk. New York: Vintage, 1986.

Risk Pool. New York: Random House, 1988.

Nobody's Fool. New York: Random House, 1993.

Straight Man. New York: Random House, 1997.

Salter, James

The Hunters. New York: Harper, 1956.

The Arm of Flesh. New York: Harper, 1961.

A Sport and a Pastime. Garden City, NY: Doubleday, 1967.

Light Years. New York: Random House, 1975.

Solo Faces. Boston: Little Brown, 1979.

Dusk, and Other Stories. San Francisco: Northpoint, 1988.

Burning the Days. New York: Random House, 1997.

Schwartz, John Burnham

Bicycle Days. New York: Plume, 1989.

Reservation Road. New York: Knopf, 1998.

Shange, Ntozake

Sassafrass. San Lorenzo, Calif.: Shameless Hussy Press, 1976.

Shepard, Sam

Cruising Paradise. New York: Knopf, 1996.

Shields, Carol

Small Ceremonies. Toronto: McGraw Hill, 1976.

The Box Garden. Toronto: McGraw Hill, 1977.

Susanna Moodie: Voice & Vision. Ottawa: Borealis Press, 1977.

Happenstance. Toronto: McGraw Hill, 1980.

A Fairly Conventional Woman. Toronto: McMillan, 1982.

Various Miracles. Ontario: Stoddart, 1985.

Swann. New York: Viking, 1987.

The Orange Fish. Toronto: Random House, 1989.

Celibate Season. Regina, Saskatchewan: Coteau Books, 1991.

The Republic of Love. New York: Viking, 1992.

The Stone Diaries. New York: Viking, 1994.

Larry's Party. New York: Viking, 1997.

Dressing Up for the Carnival. New York: Viking, 2000.

Silko, Leslie Marmon

Ceremony. New York: Viking, 1977.

Almanac of the Dead: A Novel. New York: Simon & Schuster, 1991.

Simpson, Mona

Anywhere But Here. New York: Knopf, 1986.

Lost Father. New York: Knopf, 1992.

A Regular Guy. New York: Knopf, 1996.

Smiley, Jane

Barn Blind. New York: Harper & Row, 1980.

At Paradise Gate. New York: Simon & Schuster, 1981.

Duplicate Keys. New York: Knopf, 1984.

The Age of Grief. New York: Knopf, 1987.

Greenlanders. New York: Knopf, 1988.

Ordinary Love and Good Will. New York: Knopf, 1989.

Life of the Body. Minneapolis: Coffee House Press, 1990.

A Thousand Acres. New York: Knopf, 1991.

Moo. New York: Knopf, 1995.

The All-True Travels and Adventures of Lidie Newton. New York: Knopf, 1998.

Horse Heaven. New York: Knopf, 2000.

Smith, C. W.

The Thin Men of Haddam. New York: Grossman, 1973.

Country Music. New York: Farrar, Straus, Giroux, 1975.

Vestal Virgin Room. New York: Atheneum, 1984.

Will They Love Me When I Leave? New York: Putnam, 1987.

Buffalo Nickel. New York: Poseidon Press, 1989.

Letters from the Horse Latitudes. Fort Worth: Texas Christian University Press, 1994.

Hunter's Trap. Forth Worth: Texas Christian University Press, 1996.

Understanding Women. Fort Worth: Texas Christian University Press, 1998.

Smith, Lee

Something in the Wind. New York: Harper & Row, 1971.

Fancy Strut. New York: Harper & Row, 1973.

Black Mountain Breakdown. New York: Putnam's, 1980.

Cakewalk. New York: Putnam's, 1981.

Oral History. New York: Putnam's, 1983.

Family Linen. New York: Putnam's, 1985.

Fair and Tender Ladies. New York: Putnam's, 1988.

Me and My Baby View the Eclipse. New York: Putnam's, 1990.

Devil Dream. New York: Putnam's, 1992.

Saving Grave. New York: Putnam's, 1995.

Christmas Letters. Chapel Hill, NC: Algonquin Books, 1996.

News of the Spirit. New York: Putnam's, 1997.

Last Day the Dog Bushes Bloomed. New York: Harper & Row, 1998.

Sontag, Susan

The Benefactor. New York: Farrar, Straus, Giroux, 1963.

Death Kit. New York: Farrar, Straus, Giroux, 1967.

I, etcetera. New York: Farrar, Straus, Giroux, 1978.

The Way We Live Now. New York: Farrar, Straus, Giroux, 1991.

The Volcano Lover: A Romance. New York: Farrar, Straus, Giroux, 1992.

Stone, Robert

Hall of Mirrors. Boston: Houghton Mifflin, 1967.

Dog Soldiers. Boston: Houghton Mifflin, 1974.

A Flag for Sunrise. New York: Knopf, 1981.

Children of Light. New York: Knopf, 1986.

Outerbridge Reach. New York: Ticknor & Fields, 1992.

Bear and His Daughters. Boston: Houghton Mifflin, 1997.

Damascus Gate. Boston: Houghton Mifflin, 1998.

Suarez, Virgil

Latin Jazz. New York: W. Morrow, 1989.

Cutter. New York: Available Press, 1991.

Welcome to the Oasis. Houston, Tex.: Arte Publico Press, 1992.

Havana Thursdays. Houston, Tex.: Arte Publico Press, 1995.

Going Under. Houston, Tex.: Arte Publico Press, 1996.

Spared Angel. Houston, Tex.: Arte Publico Press, 1997.

In the Republic of Longing. Tempe, Ariz.: Bilingual Press, 1999.

Tallent, Elizabeth

In Constant Flight. New York: Knopf, 1983.

Museum Pieces. New York: Knopf, 1985.

Time with Children. New York: Knopf, 1987.

Honey. New York: Knopf, 1993.

Tan, Amy

The Joy Luck Club. New York: Putnam's, 1989.

The Kitchen God's Wife. New York: Putnam's, 1991.

The Hundred Secret Senses. New York: Putnam's, 1995.

Tartt, Donna

The Secret History. New York: Knopf, 1992.

Theroux, Paul

Waldo. Boston: Houghton Mifflin, 1967.

Fong and the Indians. Boston: Houghton Mifflin, 1968.

Girls at Play. Boston: Houghton Mifflin, 1969.

Murder in Mount Holly. London: Ross, 1969.

Jungle Lovers. Boston: Houghton Mifflin, 1971.

Sinning with Annie and Other Short Stories. Boston: Houghton Mifflin, 1972.

Saint Jack. Boston: Houghton Mifflin, 1973.

The Black House. Boston: Houghton Mifflin, 1974.

The Family Arsenal. Boston: Houghton Mifflin, 1976.

The Consul's File. London: Hamish Hamilton, 1977.

Picture Palace. Boston: Houghton Mifflin, 1978.

World's End. Boston: Houghton Mifflin, 1980.

The Mosquito Coast. London: Hamish Hamilton, 1981.

The London Embassy. London: Hamish Hamilton, 1982.

Doctor Slaughter. London: Hamish Hamilton, 1984.

Half Moon Street. Boston: Houghton Mifflin, 1984.

Ozone. New York: Putnam, 1986.

My Secret History. New York: Putnam, 1989.

Doctor DeMarr. London: Hutchinson, 1990.

Chicago Loop. New York: Random House, 1991.

Millroy The Magician. London: Hamish Hamilton, 1993.

Tilghman, Christopher

In a Father's Place. New York: Farrar, Straus, Giroux, 1990.

Mason's Retreat. New York: Random House, 1996.

The Way People Run. New York: Random House, 1999.

Tyler, Anne

If Morning Ever Comes. New York: Knopf, 1964.

The Tin Can Tree. New York: Knopf, 1965.

A Slipping-Down Life. New York: Knopf, 1970.

The Clock Winder. New York: Knopf, 1972.

Celestial Navigation. New York: Knopf, 1974.

Searching for Caleb. New York: Knopf, 1975.

Earthly Possessions. New York: Knopf, 1977.

Morgan's Passing. New York: Knopf, 1980.

Dinner at the Homesick Restaurant. New York: Knopf, 1982.

The Accidental Tourist. New York: Knopf, 1985.

Breathing Lessons. New York: Knopf, 1988.

Saint Maybe. New York: Knopf, 1991.

Ladder of Years. New York: Knopf, 1995.

A Patchwork Planet. New York: Knopf, 1998.

Updike, John

The Poorhouse Fair. New York: Knopf, 1959.

The Same Door. New York: Knopf, 1959.

Rabbit, Run. New York: Knopf, 1960.

Pigeon Feathers. New York: Knopf, 1962.

The Centaur. New York: Knopf, 1963.

Olinger Stories. New York: Knopf, 1964.

Of the Farm. New York: Knopf, 1965.

The Music School. New York: Knopf, 1966.

Couples. New York: Knopf, 1968.

Beck: A Book. New York: Knopf, 1970.

Rabbit Redux. New York: Knopf, 1971.

Museums and Women. New York: Knopf, 1972.

A Month of Sundays. New York: Knopf, 1975.

Marry Me: A Romance. New York: Knopf, 1976.

The Coup. New York: Knopf, 1978.

Problems. New York: Knopf, 1979.

Too Far to Go. New York: Fawcett Crest, 1979.

Rabbit is Rich. New York: Knopf, 1981.

Beck is Back. New York: Knopf, 1982.

The Witches of Eastwick. New York: Knopf, 1984.

Roger's Version. New York: Knopf, 1986.

Trust Me. New York: Knopf, 1987.

Rabbit at Rest. New York: Knopf, 1990.

Memories of the Ford Administration. New York: Knopf, 1992.

Brazil. New York: Knopf, 1994.

Rabbit Angstrom: A Tetralogy. New York: Knopf, 1995.

In the Beauty of the Lilies. New York: Knopf, 1996.

Toward the End of Time. New York: Knopf, 1997.

Bech at Bay: A Quasi Novel. New York: Knopf, 1998.

Gertrude and Claudius. New York: Knopf, 2000.

Vega, Ed

Comeback. Houston, Tex.: Arte Publico Press, 1985.

Mendoza's Dreams. Houston, Tex.: Arte Publico Press, 1987.

Casualty Report. Houston, Tex.: Arte Publico Press, 1991.

Vidal, Gore

Williwaw. New York: Dutton, 1946.

In a Yellow Wood. New York: Dutton, 1947.

The City and the Pillar. New York: Dutton, 1948.

The Season of Comfort. New York: Dutton, 1949.

Dark Green, Bright Red. New York: Dutton, 1950.

A Search for the King: A Twelfth Century Legend. New York: Dutton, 1950.

The Judgement of Paris. New York: Dutton, 1952.

Messiah. New York: Dutton, 1954.

Three: Williwaw, A Thirsty Evil, Julian the Apostate. New York: New American Library, 1962.

Julian. Boston: Little Brown, 1964.

Washington D.C. Boston: Little Brown, 1967.

Myra Breckinridge. Boston: Little Brown, 1968.

Two Sisters: A Memoir in the Form of a Novel. Boston: Little Brown, 1970.

Burr. New York: Random House, 1973.

Myron. New York: Random House, 1974.

1876. New York: Random House, 1976.

Kalki. New York: Random House, 1978.

Creation. New York: Random House, 1981.

Duluth. New York: Random House, 1983.

Lincoln. New York: Random House, 1984.

Empire. New York: Random House, 1987.

Hollywood. New York: Random House, 1990.

Live from Golgotha. New York: Random House, 1992.

Palimpsest: A Memoir. New York: Random House, 1995.

The Smithsonian Institution. New York: Random House, 1998.

Viramontes, Helena Maria

The Moths, and Other Stories. Houston, Tex.: Arte Publico Press, 1985.

Under the Feet of Jesus. New York: Dutton, 1995.

Their Dogs Came with Them. New York: Dutton, 2000.

Vonnegut, Kurt

Player Piano. New York: Scribners, 1952.

The Sirens of Titan. New York: Dell, 1959.

Canary in a Cat House. Greenwich, Conn.: Fawcett, 1961.

Mother Night. Greenwich, Conn.: Fawcett, 1962.

Cat's Cradle. New York: Holt, Rinehart & Winston, 1963.

God Bless you, Mr Rosewater. New York: Holt, Rinehart & Winston, 1965.

Welcome to the Monkey House. New York: Delacorte Press/Seymour Lawrence, 1968.

Slaughterhouse-Five. New York: Delacorte Press/Seymour Lawrence, 1969.

Breakfast of Champions. New York: Delacorte Press/Seymour Lawrence, 1973.

Slapstick; or, Lonesome No More! New York: Delacorte Press/Seymour Lawrence, 1976.

Jailbird. New York: Delacorte Press/Seymour Lawrence, 1979.

Deadeye Dick. New York: Delacorte Press/Seymour Lawrence, 1982.

Galapagos. New York: Delacorte Press/Seymour Lawrence, 1985.

Bluebeard. New York: Delacorte Press, 1987.

Hocus Pocus; or, What's the Hurry, Son? New York: Putnam, 1990.

Walker, Alice

The Third Life of Grange Copeland. New York: Harcourt, Brace, Jovanovich, 1970.

In Love and Trouble: Stories of Black Women. New York: Harcourt, Brace, Jovanovich, 1973.

Meridian. New York: Harcourt, Brace, Jovanovich, 1976.

You Can't Keep a Good Woman Down. New York: Harcourt, Brace, Jovanovich, 1981.

The Color Purple. New York: Harcourt, Brace, Jovanovich, 1982.

Living by the World: Selected Writings, 1973–1987. New York: Harcourt, Brace, Jovanovich, 1988.

The Temple of My Familiar. New York: Harcourt,Brace, Jovanovich, 1989.

Possessing the Secret of Joy. New York: Harcourt, Brace, Jovanovich, 1992.

Everyday Use. New Brunswick, NJ: Rutgers University Press, 1994.

By the Light of My Father's Smile. New York: Random House, 1998.

The Way Forward is with a Broken Heart. New York: Random House, 2000.

Wallace, David Foster

The Broom of the System. New York: Viking, 1987.

Girl with Curious Hair. New York: Norton, 1989.

Infinite Jest. Boston: Little Brown, 1996.

Supposedly Fun Thing I'll Never Do Again: Essays and Arguments. Boston: Little Brown, 1997.

Brief Interviews with Hideous Men. Boston: Little Brown, 1999.

Watson, Larry

In a Dark Time. New York: Scribner's, 1980.

Montana 1948. Minneapolis: Milkwood Editions, 1993.

Justice. Minneapolis: Milkwood Editions, 1995.

White Crosses. New York: Washington Square Press, 1997.

Laura. New York: Pocket Books, 2000.

Welch, James

Winter in the Blood. New York: Harper & Row, 1974.

The Death of Jim Loney. New York: Harper & Row, 1979.

Fools Crow. New York: Viking, 1986.

The Indian Lawyer. New York: Norton, 1990.

Killing Custer: The Battle of Little Bighorn and the Fate of the Plains Indians. New York: Norton, 1994.

The Heartsong of Charging Elk. New York: Doubleday, 2000.

White, Edmund

Forgetting Elena. New York: Random House, 1973.

Nocturnes for the King of Naples. New York: St Martin's Press, 1978.

A Boy's Own Story. New York: Dutton, 1982.

Caracole. New York: Dutton, 1985.

The Beautiful Room Is Empty. New York: Knopf, 1988.

Skinned Alive: Stories. New York: Knopf, 1995.

Farewell Symphony. New York: Knopf, 1997.

The Married Man: A Love Story. New York: Knopf, 2000.

Wideman, John Edgar

A Glance Away. New York: Harcourt, Brace & World, 1967.

Hurry Home. New York: Harcourt, Brace, Jovanovich, 1970.

The Lynchers. New York: Harcourt, Brace, Jovanovich, 1973.

Damballah. New York: Avon, 1981.

Hiding Place. New York: Avon, 1981.

Sent for You Yesterday. New York: Avon, 1983.

The Homewood Trilogy. New York: Avon, 1985.

Reuben. New York: Henry Holt, 1987.

Fever: Twelve Stories. New York: Henry Holt, 1989.

Philadelphia Fire. New York: Henry Holt, 1990.

The Stories of John Edgar Wideman. New York: Pantheon, 1992.

All Stories Are True. New York: Random, 1993.

Fatheralong: A Meditation on Fathers and Sons, Race and Society. New York: Pantheon, 1994.

Identities: Three Novels by John Edgar Wideman. New York: Henry Holt, 1994.

The Cattle Killing. New York: Houghton Mifflin, 1996.

Two Cities. New York: Houghton Mifflin, 1998.

Wilcox, James

Modern Baptists. Garden City, NY: Dial Press, 1983.

North Gladiola. New York: Harper & Row, 1985.

Miss Undine's Living Room. New York: Harper & Row, 1987.

Sort of Rich. New York: Harper & Row, 1989.

Polite Sex. New York: HarperCollins, 1991.

Guest of a Sinner. New York: HarperCollins, 1993.

Plain and Normal. Boston: Little Brown, 1998.

Williams, Terry Tempest

Fancy Free. London: Evans, 1974.

Pieces of White Shell: A Journey to Navajoland. New York: Scribner's, 1984.

The Secret Languages of Snow. San Francisco: Sierra Club/Pantheon Books, 1984.

Between Cattails. New York: Scribner's, 1985.

Coyote's Canyon. Salt Lake City: Peregrine Smith Books, 1989.

Refuge: An Unnatural History of Family and Place. New York: Pantheon, 1991.

An Unspoken Hunger. New York: Pantheon, 1994.

Desert Quartet. New York: Pantheon, 1995.

Leap: A Traveller in the Garden of Delights. New York: Pantheon, 2000.

Wolfe, Tom,

The Kandy-Kolored Tangerine-Flake Streamline Baby. New York: Farrar, Straus, 1965.

The Electric Kool-Aid Acid Test. New York: Farrar, Straus, Giroux, 1968.

The Pump House Gang. New York: Farrar, Straus, 1968.

Bonfire of the Vanities. New York: Farrar, Straus, 1987.

A Man in Full. New York: Farrar, Straus, Giroux, 1998.

Ambush at Fort Bragg. New York: Bantam, 1998.

Wolff, Geoffrey

Bad Debts. New York: Simon & Schuster, 1969.

Sightseer. New York: Random House, 1974.

Black Sun: The Brief Transit and Violent Eclipse of Harry Crosby. New York: Random House, 1976.

Inklings. New York: Random House, 1977.

Duke of Deception. New York: Random House, 1979.

Providence. New York: Viking, 1986.

Final Club. New York: Knopf, 1990.

A Day at the Beach. New York: Knopf, 1992.

Age of Consent. New York: Knopf, 1995.

Wolff, Tobias

Ugly Rumours. London: Allen & Unwin, 1975.

In the Garden of the North American Martyrs. New York: Ecco Press, 1981.

The Barracks Thief. New York: Ecco Press, 1984.

Back in the World. Boston: Houghton Mifflin, 1985.

This Boy's Life. New York: Atlantic Monthly Press, 1989.

The Picador Book of Contemporary American Stories (ed. Tobias Wolff). London: Picador, 1993.

In Pharaoh's Army. New York: Knopf, 1994.

The Night in Question. New York: Knopf, 1996.

Writers' Harvest 3 (ed. Tobias Wolff). New York: Dell, 2000.

Zigman, Laura

Dating Big Bird. New York: Dial Press, 2000.

Secondary works

Alexander, M. *Flights from Realism: Themes and Strategies in Postmodernist British and American Fiction*. London: Edward Arnold, 1990.

Arnold E. T., and **Luce, D. C.** *Perspectives on Cormac McCarthy*. Jackson: University Press of Mississippi, 1999.

Baker, L. Jr, H. *Blues, Ideology and Afro-American Literature*. Chicago: University of Chicago Press, 1984.

Berman, N. D. *Playful Fictions and Fictional Players: Game, Sport and Survival in Contemporary American Fiction*. New York: Kennikat Press, 1981.

Bradbury, M. *The Modern American Novel*. 2nd edn. revised. Oxford: Oxford University Press, 1992.

—— and **Ro, S.** (eds.). *Contemporary American Fiction*. London: Edward Arnold, 1987.

Budick, E. *Fiction and the Historical Consciousness*. New Haven: Yale University Press, 1989.

Callinicos, A. *Against Postmodernism: A Marxist Critique*. New York: St Martin's Press, 1990.

Clayton, J. *The Pleasures of Babel: Contemporary American Literature and Theory*. Oxford: Oxford University Press, 1993.

Cook-Lynn, E. *Why I Can't Read Wallace Stegner and Other Essays: A Tribal Voice*. Madison: University of Wisconsin Press, 1996.

Cooper, A. *Philip Roth and the Jews*. Albany, NY: State University of New York Press, 1996.

Currie, M. *Metafiction*. London: Longman, 1995.

Davis, M. *City of Quartz: Excavating the Future in Los Angeles*. London: Verso, 1990.

Dunaway, D. K. (ed.). *Writing the Southwest*. Harmondsworth: Penguin, 1995.

During, S. (ed.). *The Cultural Studies Reader*. London: Routledge, 1993.

Fawcett, E., and **Thomas, T.** *The American Condition*. New York: Harper & Row, 1982.

Fitzgerald, F. *Cities on a Hill: A Journey through Contemporary American Cultures*. New York: Simon & Schuster, 1986.

Fowler, D. *Understanding E. L. Doctorow*. Columbia: University of South Carolina Press, 1992.

Friedman, M. J., and **Siegel, B.** (eds.). *Traditions, Voices, and Dreams: The American Novel since the 1960s*. Newark: University of Delaware Press, 1995.

Gass, W. *Habitations of the Word: Essays*. Ithaca, NY: Cornell University Press, 1985.

Gidley, M. (ed.). *Modern American Culture: An Introduction*. London: Longman, 1993.

Gilman, O. *Vietnam and the Southern Imagination*. Jackson: University Press of Mississippi, 1992.

Graff, G. *Beyond the Culture Wars: How Teaching the Conflicts can Revitalize American Education*. New York: Norton, 1992.

Greenblatt, S. J. *Learning to Curse: Essays in Early Modern Culture*. London: Routledge, 1990.

Hansen, E. T. *Mother Without Child: Contemporary Fiction and the Crisis of Motherhood*. Berkeley: University of California Press, 1997.

Harris, T. *Fiction and Folklore: The Novels of Toni Morrison*. Knoxville: University of Tennessee Press, 1991.

Heinze, D. *The Dilemma of Double Consciousness: Toni Morrison's Novels*. Athens: Georgia University Press, 1993.

Hendin, J. *Vulnerable People: A View of American Fiction since 1945*. Oxford: Oxford University Press, 1978.

Hilfer, T. *American Fiction since 1940*. London: Longman, 1992.

Jameson, F. *Postmodernism, or, The Cultural Logic of Late Capitalism*. London: Verso, 1991.

Jarvis, B. *Postmodern Cartographies: The Geographical Imagination in Contemporary American Culture*. London: Pluto Press, 1998.

Kaplan, A., and **Pease, D. E.** *Cultures of United States Imperialism*. Durham, NC: Duke University Press, 1993.

Keesey, D. *Don DeLillo*. New York: Twayne Publishers, 1993.

Kellner, D. *Jean Baudrillard: From Marxism to Postmodernism and Beyond*. Cambridge: Polity Press, 1989.

Kennedy, P. *The Rise and Fall of the Great Powers: Economic Change and Military Conflict from 1500 to 2000*. London: Unwin Hyman, 1988.

King, R. H., and **Taylor, H.** (eds.). *Dixie Debates: Perspectives on Southern Cultures*. London: Pluto Press, 1996.

Kowalewski, M. (ed.). *Reading the West*. Cambridge: Cambridge University Press, 1997.

Lasch, C. *Haven in a Heartless World: The Family Besieged*. New York: Basic Books, 1977.

Lentricchia, F. *Introducing Don DeLillo*. Durham, NC: Duke University Press, 1991.

—— (ed.). *New Essays on 'White Noise'*. Cambridge: Cambridge University Press, 1991.

Lerner, G. *The Majority Finds its Past: Placing Women in History*. Oxford: Oxford University Press, 1981.

Levine, P. *E. L. Doctorow*. London: Methuen, 1985.

Maltby, P. *Dissident Postmodernists: Barthelme, Coover, Pynchon*. Philadelphia: University of Pennsylvania Press, 1991.

Mbalia, D. D. *John Edgar Wideman: Reclaiming the African Personality*. Selinsgrove, Pa.: Susquehanna University Press, 1995.

McCaffery, L. *Alive and Writing*. Urbana: University of Illinois Press, 1987.

—— and **LeClair, T.** *Anything Can Happen: Interviews with Contemporary American Novelists.* Urbana: University of Illinois Press, 1983.

—— *The Metafictional Muse: The Works of Robert Coover, Donald Barthelme and William H. Gass.* Pittsburgh: University of Pittsburgh Press, 1982.

McInerney, J. (ed.). *Cowboys, Indians and Commuters: The Penguin Book of New American Voices.* Harmondsworth: Penguin, 1994.

Messenger, C. K. *Sport and the Spirit of Play.* New York: Columbia University Press, 1981.

Morris, C. *Models of Misrepresentation: On the Fiction of E. L. Doctorow.* Jackson: University Press of Mississippi, 1991.

Oates, J. C. *On Boxing.* London: Bloomsbury, 1987.

Parks, J. G. *E. L. Doctorow.* New York: Continuum, 1991.

Rich, A. *Blood, Bread and Poetry: Selected Prose 1979–1985.* London: Virago, 1987.

Roth, P. *Reading Myself and Others.* London: Jonathan Cape, 1975.

Sage, G. H. (ed.). *Sport and American Society: Selected Readings.* Reading, Mass./London: Addison Wesley, 1970.

Sage, L. *Women in the House of Fiction: Post-War Women Novelists.* Basingstoke: Macmillan, 1992.

Saltzman, A. *Designs of Darkness in Contemporary American Fiction.* Philadelphia: University of Pennsylvania Press, 1990.

Showalter, E. *Hystories: Hysterical Epidemics and Modern Cultures.* London: Picador, 1997.

Simmons, P. E. *Deep Surfaces: Mass Culture and History in Postmodern American Fiction.* Athens: University of Georgia Press, 1997.

Slotkin, R. *Gunfighter Nation: The Myth of the Frontier in Twentieth Century America.* New York: Atheneum, 1992.

Walsh, R. *Novel Arguments: Reading Innovative American Fiction.* Cambridge: Cambridge University Press, 1997.

Weinstein, A. *Nobody's Home: Speech, Self, and Place in American Fiction from Hawthorne to DeLillo.* Oxford: Oxford University Press, 1993.

Weston, R. D. *Barry Hannah: Postmodern Romantic.* Baton Rouge: Louisiana State University Press, 1998.

Wolff, T. (ed.). *The Picador Book of Contemporary American Short Stories.* London: Picador, 1993.

Young, E., and Caveney, G. *Shopping in Space: Essays on America's Blank Generation Fiction.* London: Serpent's Tail, 1992.

Zamora, L. *Contemporary American Women Writers: Gender, Class, Ethnicity.* London: Longman, 1998.

Index